Interpretive Readings

THE ORDEAL OF TWENTIETH-CENTURY AMERICA

Edited by **Jordan A. Schwarz**
Northern Illinois University

HOUGHTON MIFFLIN COMPANY   **Boston**

Atlanta   Dallas   Geneva, Illinois   Hopewell, New Jersey   Palo Alto   London

To my mother

Printed in the U.S.A.

Library of Congress Catalog Card Number: 73–9402

ISBN: 0–395–14519–8

Cover: *Untitled*, Robert Motherwell. Courtesy Museum of Fine Arts, Boston

CONTENTS

973.9
S411o

INTRODUCTION

In his acceptance speech for the 1952 Democratic nomination for President, Adlai Stevenson spoke of "The Ordeal of the Twentieth Century—the bloodiest, most turbulent era of the Christian age." Of course, not all of the twentieth century has been an ordeal; nor have all Americans shared its trials equally. Taken as a whole, however, the pain and problems of this century have made it unique in American history. It might be said that the agonies of nation building and civil war in the nineteenth century seem like mere adolescent adjustments when contrasted with the torment of our more mature America.

Twentieth century America is the most powerful nation in the world. Since our colonial beginnings we anticipated such national supremacy without truly knowing how to use it. We craved power to satisfy our competitive instincts and our certainty that we had erected the most ideal society in the history of mankind. Rightfully and righteously we boasted that only this nation gave individuals so much liberty, equality, and opportunity. No other nation enjoyed so much food, so many of the necessities of life or so much wealth that it could transform luxuries into necessities to suit its lifestyle.

No accusation of arrogance or smugness levelled against the United States can diminish its greatness. Still, in spite of our conceit and self-confidence, we remain aware of our inadequacies. Visitors from abroad are impressed with our capacity for self-criticism as well as with our self-promotion. "Reform," "improvement," and "development" are words fixed in our vocabularies.

Indeed, our ideals are our worst enemies. Too many exceptions to them intrude upon United States history, proving that this land of opportunity is not necessarily a land of fulfillment. The good life is disproportionately shared, some people hoarding too much of it, many people never achieving any of it despite their best efforts. Historical discussions of poverty are acceptable when the topic is emerging industrialism or the Great Depression, if only because poverty was so apparent then as to be undeniable. Racial discrimination and segregation now mock our assertions of individual freedom in America. We are learning that Social Security and universal public education are useless welfare institutions if our inability to stabilize economic growth depreciates the dollars needed to pay for those institutions. Sometimes we do not even recognize the irony of our national actions. How can we account for the fact that for the principle of self-determination we waged war against a nation, North Vietnam, which has incorporated the American Declaration of Independence into its constitution?

Twentieth-century America's greatest ordeal has been war. Every generation born in this century has lived through a foreign war; some of our elders have seen as many as four. American men have fought overseas for at least seventeen years of this century. About half of the twentieth century has been spent in readiness for war, and it seems safe to say that no living American will see a time when military production is not a vital part of our economy. Moreover, the expenses of each war haunt us while we are at peace: we pay for every war, literally and figuratively, for generations after the battles have ended. Wars create indebtedness to bond holders who finance the ventures and veterans who fight them. More than a century after the Civil War, the government still paid benefits in excess of a million dollars annually to dependents of Union soldiers. The cost of the Spanish-American War has already passed $5.3 billion, twelve times the original expense of that four-month conflict. The expense of World War I veterans' benefits finally began to decline nearly a half-century after the war ended. We will pay for World War II in the years following 2000 and for the Korean War long after that. The final cost of the Vietnamese War boggles the mind; it will be left to our grandchildren as a legacy.

Can we afford future twentieth-century wars? Many Americans insist that freedom has no price tag and that we must pay whatever is required. Perhaps; but other issues are at stake. Certainly every dollar spent for the economically unproductive project of war correspondingly depletes the resources of United States society. How do we quantify that depletion? What is its impact upon the quality of the American way of life?

The late President Dwight D. Eisenhower dealt with these questions when he tried to liquidate the Korean War. He told a meeting of the American Society of Newspaper Editors on April 16, 1953:

> Every gun that is made, every warship launched, every rocket fired signifies—in the final sense—a theft from those who hunger and are not fed, those who are cold and are not clothed.
>
> This world in arms is not spending money alone.
>
> It is spending the sweat of its laborers, the genius of its scientists, the hopes of its children.
>
> The cost of one heavy bomber is this: a modern brick school in more than thirty cities.
>
> It is: two electric power plants, each serving a town of 60,000 people.
>
> It is: two fine, fully equipped hospitals.

It is: some fifty miles of concrete highways.

We pay for a single fighter alone with a half million bushels of wheat.

We pay for a single destroyer with new homes that could have housed more than eight thousand people. . . .

This is not a way of life at all, in any true sense. Under the cloud of threatening war, it is humanity dangling from a cross of iron.

In 1969, historian James L. Clayton brought the cost sheets up to date in this manner:

> . . . The war in Vietnam (1960–1970) has cost ten times more than Medicare and medical assistance, sixteen times more than support for education, and thirty-three times more than was spent for housing and community development. We have spent ten times more money on Vietnam in ten years than we have spent in our entire history for public higher education or for police protection. Put another way, the war has cost us one-fifth of the value of current personal financial assets of all living Americans, a third again as much as all outstanding home mortgages, and six times the total U.S. money now in circulation.

Measured in these terms, it is no wonder that war is revolutionary in its impact upon belligerent societies. Such waste, expense and disruption should disturb any conservative who loves his nation enough to bear arms for causes its leaders deem worthy of combat. The patriot must remember that his freedom is diminished in a society at war. All wars require some civilian regimentation. That is what happened during the two world wars, even though we masked government coercion with the rhetoric of cooperation. Some people will point to the Korean and Indochinese conflicts as examples of war and freedom coexisting in our democratic society. Even so, despite their limited nature, in contrast to World War II's total nature, those wars taxed Americans through the less obvious ways of inflation and the re-allocation of priorities.

The impact of war upon twentieth-century American history is one focus of this book, but there are others. America's ordeal also includes her abortive quests for economic stability, racial justice, and an end to poverty. These struggles are made more difficult by the fact that collectively we are not an altruistic people. We tend to expect that the benefits of our society, justice included, be earned by aggrieved parties, rather than be bestowed upon them. Reform is successful only when spearheaded by the disadvantaged persons themselves. Poverty is not likely to be abolished by middle-class paternalism; the poor may have to demonstrate that their uplift has value for all Americans. The workingman won better wages and working conditions because he organized unions which demonstrated the collective power of workers, not necessarily the merit of their claims. That government was a disinterested party was a figment of middle-class imagination and rhetoric; workers and employers knew that government was an arbiter which they, as interested parties, could try to manipulate to their own advantage. Racial justice is more likely to be accomplished when blacks demand it of all whites and refuse to rely upon the good intentions of libertarians.

Thus, group conflict contributes to the ordeal. Modern America abounds with conflict which is not always confined to the familiar labor-capital, urban-rural or black-white dichotomies. We read almost daily about ethnic clashes, urban-suburban differences, cultural struggles, the generation gap, and the expanding battle between the sexes. In this century it seems as if we have institutionalized conflict. This book does not attempt to deal with all the turmoil of modern America. It highlights some of the events, foreign and domestic, which have shaped the twentieth century ordeal.

In composing this book of readings I have set certain guidelines of which the reader should be aware. I have chosen selections for the significance of what the authors have said. More importantly, I hope that many of the readings are provocative enough to inspire discussion and debate in the classroom. Inevitably they are not of even quality, but all of them, I trust, are eminently usable.

I believe that each author should have the opportunity to say what he wants in the way he wants. In most cases this has been possible, and an article or a chapter or a section of a book has been reproduced exactly as it was written. I sought not to omit passages or footnotes. Those were my rules, but unfortunately, for reasons of economy, I was compelled to make a few exceptions, and for that I apologize.

Finally, I want to acknowledge the comments and criticisms of some historians who improved the book: Leonard Dinnerstein of the University of Arizona, Meyer J. Nathan of Colorado State University, Arnold A. Offner of Boston University, and John S. Rosenberg of Bucknell University. My editors at Houghton Mifflin have been most patient and helpful. Mrs. Darla Woodward aided me with her splendid typing. Roosevelt, New Jersey, provided its own twentieth century ordeal and warm congeniality as background for the development of this book during a year's leave from DeKalb. Linda, Orrin, and Jessica Schwarz have inspired in so many ways; Linda Schwarz knows what this book is truly about.

J. A. S.
DeKalb, Illinois
December, 1972

Wide World

I
PROGRESSIVISM AND THE FIRST TWENTIETH-CENTURY WAR

Each generation survives at least one major crisis by which it gauges the rest of its experiences and then passes the legacy of that crisis on to the next generation. The Civil War and Reconstruction was such a momentous episode for Americans in the latter part of the nineteenth century; yet even the effect of that experience was diminished by the cataclysmic great depression of 1893–1894. As an upheaval the depression can be measured by the seismic shocks of the Pullman Strike of 1894, the march of unemployed petitioners in Coxey's Army, and the collapse of a Democratic majority in Congress which brought a Republican ascendancy for the next fifteen years.

In the years prior to World War I, the public behavior of most Americans was often governed by an awareness of the depression's portents. The depression of the nineties robbed Victorian America of its security and innocence. It served as a warning that this nation's destiny may not be, after all, in the hands of Providence. Young Americans, enjoying the "gay nineties" and confident that the twentieth century would be the American century, were jolted by the realization that the future's only certainty was its uncertainty. No warranty existed on the United States' greatness. Rather, that greatness had to be achieved through the conquering of America's own turmoil and in ruthless competition with other nations.

The leaders of the progressive era were the young men of the nineties. Rejecting their fathers' casual indirection, they sought a new age of predictability. With historical reflection they reasoned that American development prior to their time had been too haphazard and that the disaster of the previous decade suggested the need for cooperative planning and management in American society. Only weak men protested the loss of a pristine past; progressives schemed for a future with leadership and efficient organization. Little should hereafter be left to chance when planning can anticipate conditions.

The progressive era was a time of much philosophical discourse about public life in America, producing notable political treatises like Herbert

Croly's *The Promise of American Life,* Theodore Roosevelt's *The New Nationalism,* Woodrow Wilson's *The New Freedom,* and Walter Lippman's *Drift and Mastery* and *A Preface to Politics.* The era also marked the political coming-of-age of men like Herbert Hoover, Franklin Roosevelt, and others who preached the virtue of organization and order to combat the evils of social chaos. Deploring the polarization of the nineties, they erected the ideal of a stable community free from class, religious and ethnic conflict: a homogenous nation with harmonious interests that would be assured of prosperity and greatness.

The progressives prided themselves on being both idealists and realists. Power was the name of their game, and they were expert players. They shrewdly rejected the shibboleths of Jeffersonian decentralization, believing instead that centralization of power was required for the orderly growth of the nation, a city, or an industry. In an era of European imperialism, many of them thought that America's power also depended on overseas expansion. Also, they believed that individualism as an end in itself preserved disorder; only by joining together in associations could individuals assert the strength needed for America's internal stability, growth, and greatness.

But although they told themselves and others of their hard headedness, the progressives were romantics; and, as dreamers, they often deceived themselves. American society had more diversity than they could possibly cope with. They should have recognized that some ethnic groups had too much cultural integrity to be absorbed easily into a melting pot of stereotyped Americans. Moreover, despite their injunctions against class-consciousness, the progressives' approval of group organization probably enhanced unwanted group-awareness. Associations facilitated the ambitions of the "haves" and reminded the "have-nots" of what they could not achieve without organization. Few organizations represented the substrata of American society like blacks or workers in abject poverty. Contrary to progressive designs, the potential for group conflict increased.

Nevertheless, progressives like Theodore Roosevelt hoped they could, in the words of Samuel P. Hays, "legislate . . . conflict out of existence." They were wrong; in a society like ours, group conflict (not to be confused with class conflict) is a way of life. Robert Wiebe has pointed out that America did not need the conflict of classes alone to create instability; the diversity of economic function, geography, size, and cultural focus turned the national scene into a battleground of interests. Each social and economic group became more adept at pursuing its own parochial goals after it had assembled and clashed with other groups rivaling it for a bigger share of power and the dollar. Organization, rather than tranquilizing America, institutionalized the country's instability.

Even so, progressives rated organization as a blessing when the country faced preparation for World War I. Mobilization required much more managerial talent than Washington could afford in those days before big governmental bureaucracies. As this paucity of administration became increasingly evident, and the mobilization effort floundered in 1917, the federal government was compelled to call upon the business associations (which had been formed to duel each other) for the cooperative management of the war effort. Progressives happily scrapped chaotic competition as a peacetime luxury and set about organizing stability and defense of the nation. The war agencies submerged conflict under a welter of regulations and rhetoric of cooperation. Likewise, Washington, because it lacked the bureaucratic mechanisms needed for war mobilization, induced association expansion in unorganized industries. Thus, the institutionalized social conflict of the progressive years became the institutionalized stability of 1918. By centralizing organization and power in Washington, the war brought the progressives' goal of a predictable society closer to realization.

The progressive era and World War I saw a necessary expansion of participation in American government. This does not mean that the United States became a more democratic society or that the cause of social justice was advanced. In fact, greater participation tended to confer political power upon groups which already had social and economic power. The rhetoric of "the people vs. the interests" sounds hollow when it becomes clear that a neutral public interest was obscured in the political decision-making process. Plenty of idealism and altruism existed in the hearts of social workers and various do-gooders who promoted the welfare of the poor and the expansion of political participation. But these people represented the most unorganized constituency. It took another crisis like that of 1893–1894 before large numbers of unorganized Americans united to grasp a share of the stability pursued by the progressives.

Peter G. Filene

AN OBITUARY FOR
"THE PROGRESSIVE MOVEMENT"*

*"The more historians learn, the farther they move from consensus," writes
Peter G. Filene about the historiography of progressivism. In this fashion,
Filene pays tribute to history as an intellectual exercise and academic discipline whose growth is dependent upon extended research, renewed discussion, and improved methodology. For this and other reasons, his article is
an excellent starting point for a reexamination of America's twentieth-
century experience. It alerts the reader to the fact that American history is
in constant flux. While events remain constant, our understanding of them
changes.*

*Filene's purpose is to make students and scholars aware of the pro-
gressive movement's historical life as a non-movement. His argument is
open to an easy challenge. When he denies that there was a progressive
movement, does Filene quarrel over the definitions of "progressive" or
"movement"? He accepts the existence of a "progressivism" in America
during the first two decades of the twentieth century, but he denies the
authenticity of a definable movement. Does his argument erect a "straw-
man," a controversy generated for no other reason than controversy itself?
Obviously not. His analysis gives great substance for an elaborate debate. He justifiably questions whether the historian's need to synthesize
has distorted our perception of a complex reality. Do the generalizations*

*I am indebted to Frederick A. Bode and Donald G. Mathews, at the University of
North Carolina at Chapel Hill, for their valuable suggestions.

5

*gathered from contemporary and retrospective impressions have little sub-
stance? Although generalizations are necessary for communication, they
should not distort historical interpretations to the extent that diversity becomes homogeneity.*

*Of course progressivism existed. It is inconceivable that Americans of
that epoch had less faith in progress than they had in an American destiny. But is it apparent that too many versions of progress existed to be
defined as a movement?*

"What was the progressive movement?" This deceptively simple question, posed in different ways, holds prominent rank among the many controversies which have consumed historians' patient energies, spawned a flurry
of monographs and articles, and confused several generations of students.
Progressivism has become surrounded with an abundant variety of scholarly
debates: did it derive from agrarian or urban sources? was it a liberal renaissance or a liberal failure? was it liberal at all? was it nostalgic or forward-
looking? when did it end, and why? Into this already busy academic arena
Richard Hofstadter introduced his theory of a "status revolution" in 1955,
generating even more intensive argument and extensive publication. Yet
one wonders whether all this sound and fury does indeed signify something. If sustained research has produced less rather than more conclusive-
ness, one may suspect that the issue is enormously complex. Or one may
suspect that it is a false problem because historians are asking a false
question. This essay seeks to prove the latter suspicion—more precisely,
seeks to prove that "the progressive movement" never existed.

Before entering such an overgrown and treacherous field of historical
controversy, one should take a definition as guideline—a definition of
"movement." Significantly, historians have neglected the second half of
their concept. They have been so busy trying to define "progressive" that
they have overlooked the possibility that the word "movement" has equal
importance and ambiguity. According to most sociologists, a social movement is a collectivity acting with some continuity to promote or resist a
change in the society. On the one hand, it has more organization, more
sustained activity and more defined purpose than a fad, panic, riot or
other kind of mass behavior. On the other hand, it has a more diffuse following, more spontaneity and broader purpose than a cult, pressure group,
political party or other voluntary association. Like such associations, however, it consists of persons who share a knowing relationship to one another. The members of a social movement combine and act together in a
deliberate, self-conscious way, as contrasted to a noncollective or "aggrega-

tive" group (such as blondes or lower-income families) which has a common identity in the minds of social scientists or other observers rather than in the minds of members themselves.[1]

Having distinguished a social movement from other forms of collective behavior, one can then analyze its internal characteristics along four dimensions: program, the values which underline this program, membership and supporters. Of these four, the program or purpose is indispensable, for otherwise there would be no reason for persons to combine and to undertake action. Amid their many disagreements, historians of the progressive movement seem to disagree least on its goals. In fact, they maintain substantially the same definition as Benjamin De Witt offered in 1915: the exclusion of privileged interests from political and economic control, the expansion of democracy and the use of government to benefit the weak and oppressed members of American society.[2] More specifically, the standard list of progressive objectives includes: constraints on monopolies, trusts and big banking interests; regulation of railroad rates; lower tariffs; the direct primary; initiative, referendum and recall; direct election of U.S. Senators; women's suffrage; child- and female-labor laws; pure food and drug laws and conservation.

But as soon as some of these issues are examined in detail, the progressive profile begins to blur. For either the historians or their historical subjects have differed sharply as to whether a "real" progressive subscribed to one or another part of the program. The most familiar debate focused on federal policy toward trusts and has been immortalized in the slogans of "New Nationalism" versus "New Freedom." In 1911 Theodore Roosevelt bitterly rebuked those of his alleged fellow-progressives who wanted to split industrial giants into small competitive units. This kind of thinking, he claimed, represents "rural toryism," a nostalgic and impossible desire for an economic past. Roosevelt preferred to recognize big business as inevitable and to create a countervailing big government. But alas, he lamented, "real progressives are hampered by being obliged continually to pay lip loyalty to their colleagues, who, at bottom, are not progressive at all, but retrogressive."[3] Whether Roosevelt or the rural tories were the more

[1]Ralph M. Turner and Lewis M. Killian, *Collective Behavior* (Englewood Cliffs, N.J., 1957), pp. 308–9; Kurt Lang and Gladys Engel Lang, *Collective Dynamics* (New York, 1961), pp. 493, 496–97; Robert F. Berkhofer Jr., *A Behavioral Approach to Historical Analysis* (New York, 1969), pp. 76–79.

[2]Benjamin Parke De Witt, *The Progressive Movement: A Non-partisan Comprehensive Discussion of Current Tendencies in American Politics* (New York, 1915), pp. 4–5; Arthur S. Link, *Woodrow Wilson and the Progressive Era, 1910–1917* (New York, 1954), pp. 1–2, 59; George E. Mowry, *The Era of Theodore Roosevelt and the Birth of Modern America, 1900–1912* (New York, 1958), pp. 41–42, 81–82; Richard Hofstadter, *The Age of Reform: From Bryan to F.D.R.* (New York, 1955), pp. 5–6, 168, 227, 238, 240, 254, 257; Russel B. Nye, *Midwestern Progressive Politics: A Historical Study of Its Origins and Development, 1870–1958* (East Lansing, Mich., 1959), pp. 183–88; Irwin Yellowitz, *Labor and the Progressive Movement in New York State, 1897–1916* (Ithaca, N.Y., 1965), p. 83.

[3]Roosevelt to Alfred W. Cooley, Aug. 29, 1911, quoted in Mowry, *Era of Theodore Roosevelt*, p. 55.

"real" progressives depends, presumably, on which side of the argument one stands. In any case, subsequent historians have echoed the Bull Moose by typically describing the big-business issue as "one of the more basic fault lines" and as "uneasiness and inconsistency" in "the progressive mind"—although this singular split mentality suggests at least schizophrenia, if not two minds.[4]

If this were the only divisive issue within the progressive program, it would not raise serious doubts about the movement's identity. But it is just one of many. The Federal Reserve Act of 1913 created, according to Arthur Link, a conflict between "uncompromising" and "middle-of-the-road" progressives.[5] In another sector of the economy, legislation on behalf of workers split the movement into two factions, whom one historian distinguishes as the more conservative "political Progressives" and the more liberal "social Progressives." But even the latter group disagreed occasionally on the extent and the tactics of their general commitment to social welfare on behalf of labor.[6] A final example of progressive disunity concerns the struggle to achieve women's suffrage, a cause that has generally been attributed to the progressive movement. Yet progressive Presidents Roosevelt and Wilson entered late and grudgingly into the feminists' ranks; William Borah preached states rights in opposition to enfranchisement by federal action and Hiram Johnson never reconciled himself to the idea under any circumstances.[7] More general evidence emerges from a study of two Congressional votes in 1914 and 1915, both of which temporarily defeated the future 19th Amendment. Using a recent historian's list of 400 "progressives," one finds progressive Congressmen almost evenly split for and against women's suffrage.[8]

Thus, several central items in the progressive program divided rather than collected the members of that movement. This fact alone should raise questions and eyebrows, given the definition of a social movement as a "collectivity." Two other issues also deserve attention because their role in the progressive movement, significantly, has divided historians as

[4]*Ibid.* p. 55; Hofstadter, *Age of Reform*, p. 245. Recently some historians have claimed that Wilson actually shared Roosevelt's basic economic views, at least before 1913, and that the New Freedom-New Nationalism dichotomy is illusory. So far, however, this revisionist view has not been widely adopted. See James Weinstein, *The Corporate Ideal in the Liberal State: 1900–1918* (Boston, 1968), pp. 162–66; and Gabriel Kolko, *The Triumph of American Conservatism: A Reinterpretation of American History, 1900–1916* (New York, 1963), pp. 205–11.

[5]*Woodrow Wilson and the Progressive Era*, p. 55.

[6]Yellowitz, *Labor and the Progressive Movement in New York State*, pp. 2, 78, 112, and chaps, v–vi, *passim*.

[7]Eleanor Flexner, *Century of Struggle: The Woman's Rights Movement in the United States* (Cambridge, Mass., 1959), pp. 276–79, 307–10; Alan P. Grimes, *The Puritan Ethic and Woman Suffrage* (New York, 1967), pp. 101–3, 129–30; Claudius O. Johnson, *Borah of Idaho*, rev. ed. (Seattle, 1967), pp. 180–83.

[8]Counting votes paired, 19 of 46 progressives voted against the Amendment. Otis L. Graham Jr., *An Encore for Reform: The Old Progressives and the New Deal* (New York, 1967), pp. 213–17; *Congressional Record*, vol. 91, pt. 5, 63rd Cong., 2nd Sess., p. 5108, and vol. 52, pt. 2, 63rd Cong., 3rd Sess., pp. 1483–84.

much as the progressives themselves. Nativism offers a prime instance. Hofstadter, George Mowry, Oscar Handlin and William Leuchtenburg stress the progressives' more or less vehement repugnance toward the immigrants crowding into urban slums; Mowry even perceives a distinct strain of racism. But Eric Goldman and John Higham dispute this portrait. Although conceding that many progressives were troubled by the influx of foreigners and that a few favored restrictive laws, these two historians claim that progressive sentiment tended to look favorably upon the newcomers. Higham does find a swerve toward nativism among many progressives after 1910; yet Handlin uses the same date to mark increasing progressive cooperation with the immigrants. Still another scholar has at different times taken somewhat different positions. In 1954 Link claimed that immigration restriction was advocated by "many" reform leaders, while in 1959 he attributed it to the entire movement.[9]

The prohibition issue has fostered an equally bewildering disagreement. A few historians refer to prohibition of liquor simply as a progressive measure.[10] Most others, however, discern division within the movement, but they do not draw their dividing lines in the same ways. James H. Timberlake, for example, argues that the liquor question cut the progressive movement into two fairly homogeneous groups: the old-stock middle classes, who favored prohibition; and those identified with the lower classes, who opposed it. When the Senate overrode President Taft's veto of the Webb-Kenyon bill, for instance, nearly all of the midwestern progressives voted dry, whereas half of the wet votes came from the urban-industrial northeast. Studies of progressivism in California, Ohio and Washington confirm this class differentiation.[11] But Andrew Sinclair describes instead a rural (dry)—urban (wet) split within the progressive

[9]Mowry, *Era of Theodore Roosevelt*, pp. 92–94; Hofstadter, *Age of Reform*, pp. 179–81; Oscar Handlin, *The Uprooted: The Epic Story of the Great Migrations that Made the American People*, pp. 217–20, 224–25; William E. Leuchtenburg, *The Perils of Prosperity, 1914–1932* (Chicago, 1958), pp. 126–27; Eric Goldman, *Rendezvous with Destiny: A History of Modern American Reform* (New York, Vintage ed., 1958), p. 60; John Higham, *Strangers in the Land: Patterns of American Nativism, 1860–1925* (New Brunswick, N.J., 1955), pp. 116–23, 176–77; Link, *Woodrow Wilson and the Progressive Era*, p. 60; Link, "What Happened to the Progressive Movement in the 1920's?" *American Historical Review*, LXIV (July 1959), 847. An analyst of Iowa progressives infers from the larger percentage of foreign-born in his progressive than in his non-progressive sample that the progressive movement was not anti-immigrant: E. Daniel Potts, "The Progressive Profile in Iowa," *Mid-America*, XLVII (Oct. 1965), 261, note 19.

[10]Link, "What Happened to the Progressive Movement in the 1920's?" pp. 847–48; Leuchtenburg, *Perils of Prosperity*, pp. 126–27; George B. Tindall, "Business Progressivism: Southern Politics in the Twenties," *South Atlantic Quarterly*, XLII (Winter 1963), 93–94.

[11]James H. Timberlake, *Prohibition and the Progressive Movement, 1900–1920* (Cambridge, Mass., 1963), pp. 2–5, 152, 163; Spencer C. Olin Jr., *California's Prodigal Sons: Hiram Johnson and the Progressives, 1911–1917* (Berkeley and Los Angeles, 1968,) p. 54; Hoyt Landon Warner, *Progressivism in Ohio, 1897–1917* (Columbus, Ohio, 1964), pp. 153, 191, 473; Norman Clark, "The 'Hell-Soaked Institution' and the Washington Prohibition Initiative of 1914," *Pacific Northwest Quarterly*, LVI (Jan. 1965), 10–15.

movement.[12] Recent investigations by a political scientist and a sociologist propose a third typology, namely that prohibition was supported by those who were rural *and* old middle class.[13] Meanwhile, Hofstadter offers the most ambiguous analysis. On the one hand, he exculpates progressives from the taint of dryness, stating that "men of an urbane cast of mind, whether conservatives or Progressives in their politics, had been generally antagonistic, or at the very least suspicious, of the pre-war drive toward Prohibition." On the other hand, he acknowledges that most progressive Senators voted for the Webb-Kenyon bill in 1913 and that prohibition typified the moral absolutism of the progressive movement.[14]

In the flickering light of these myriad disagreements about progressive goals, both among progressives and their historians, the concept of a "movement" seems very much like a mirage. Not so, replies Hofstadter. "Historians have rightly refused to allow such complications to prevent them from speaking of the Progressive movement and the Progressive era," he contends. "For all its internal differences and counter-currents, there were in Progressivism certain general tendencies, certain widespread commitments of belief, which outweigh the particulars. It is these commitments and beliefs which make it possible to use the term 'Progressive' in the hope that the unity it conveys will not be misconstrued." Thus Hofstadter finds an integral movement by turning to the values underlying the specific goals. Optimism and activism—these, he says, are the ideological or temperamental traits distinguishing progressives.[15]

Discrepancies emerge quickly, however. As Hofstadter himself notes, threads of anxiety cut across the generally optimistic pattern of the progressive mind. Mowry describes the ambivalence even more emphatically: "the progressive was at once nostalgic, envious, fearful, and yet confident about the future," he writes. "Fear and confidence together" inspired progressives with a sense of defensive class-consciousness.[16] Of course, human attitudes are rarely all of a piece, and certainly not the attitudes of a large group of persons. Moreover, this mixture of ideological mood—this ambivalence—fits well into Mowry's and Hofstadter's description of progressives as status-threatened members of the middle class.

Nevertheless, even this more precise generalization about progressive values encounters difficulties, primarily because it is not precise enough. It generalizes to the point of excluding few Americans in the prewar era. As Henry F. May has remarked, the intellectual atmosphere before World War I consisted of a faith in moralism and progress—and almost everyone

[12]*Prohibition: The Era of Excess* (Boston, 1962), pp. 95–96.

[13]Grimes, *Puritan Ethic,* pp. 132–34; Joseph R. Gusfield, *Symbolic Crusade: Status Politics and the American Temperance Movement* (Urbana, Ill., 1963), pp. 7–8, 98–105, 108–9.

[14]Hofstadter, *Age of Reform,* pp. 287 and note, pp. 290, 16.

[15]Hofstadter, ed., *The Progressive Movement, 1900–1915* (Englewood Cliffs, N.J., 1963), pp. 4–5; similarly, Goldman, *Rendezvous with Destiny,* pp. 64–65; Graham, *Encore for Reform,* pp. 10–14; Henry F. May, *The End of American Innocence: A Study of the First Years of Our Own Time, 1912–1917* (New York, 1959), pp. 20–25.

[16]*Era of Theodore Roosevelt,* p. 103.

breathed this compound eagerly. In order to distinguish progressives from others, then, one must specify their values more strictly. Activism, Hofstadter's second progressive trait, at first seems to serve well. Unlike conservatives of their time, progressives believed that social progress could and should come at a faster rate via human intervention, particularly governmental intervention.[17] Yet this ideological criterion works paradoxes rather than wonders. It excludes not simply conservatives, but Woodrow Wilson and all those who subscribed in 1913 to his "New Freedom" philosophy of laissez faire and states rights. In order to salvage Wilson as a progressive, one must expand the definition of progressivism beyond optimism and activism to include a belief in popular democracy and opposition to economic privilege. Wilson's adherence to three of these four values in 1913 qualified him as a progressive, according to Arthur Link, but not as an "advanced progressive." In the latter faction of progressives, who demanded a more active federal government, Link includes socialists, New Nationalists, social workers and others.[18]

This expanded definition of progressive values performs the job required of any definition: distinguishing something from something else. But at the same time it recreates the very subdivisions within the "progressive movement" concept which Hofstadter had sought to overcome. Indeed, this internal fragmentation of the concept does not stop with "advanced" and unadvanced progressives. Robert H. Wiebe and other historians, for example, have discovered numerous businessmen who qualify as progressive by their support for federal economic regulation and civic improvement. But these same individuals diverged sharply in ideology. They doubted man's virtuousness, believed that progress comes slowly, trusted in leaders rather than the masses as agents of progress, and generally preferred to purify rather than extend democracy. In short, their progressive activism blended with a nonprogressive skepticism and elitism. Do these reform-minded businessmen—"corporate liberals," as James Weinstein calls them—deserve membership in the progressive movement? Wiebe claims that they do, despite the ideological exceptions. Weinstein and Gabriel Kolko go further, arguing that these businessmen formed a salient, if not dominant, thrust of influence and ideas within progressivism; they were not merely supporting actors but stars, even directors.[19] Regardless of their exact role in the cast of progressives, their

[17]May, *End of American Innocence*, pp. 9–21.

[18]*Wilson: The New Freedom* (Princeton, N. J., 1956), pp. 241–42.

[19]Robert H. Wiebe, *Businessmen and Reform: A Study of the Progressive Movement* (Cambridge, Mass., 1962), pp. 210–12; Weinstein, *The Corporate Ideal in the Liberal State*, esp. pp. ix–xv; Kolko, *Triumph of American Conservatism*. The enigmatic status of these businessmen also holds true for certain politicians. Massachusetts before 1900 instituted many of the democratizing and regulatory laws which progressives would later struggle to achieve elsewhere. In terms of practice, then, Bay State leaders like Henry Cabot Lodge belonged in the progressive movement; but in terms of political philosophy they did not qualify. See Richard M. Abrams, "A Paradox of Progressivism: Massachusetts on the Eve of Insurgency," *Political Science Quarterly*, LXXV (Sept. 1960), 379–99.

presence introduces still more disconcerting variety into the already varie-
gated historical concept.

The ideological identity of the progressive movement provokes confusion in one final way. "To the extent that they [the Wilsonian Democrats]
championed popular democracy and rebelled against a *status quo* that
favored the wealthy," Link has asserted, "they were progressives."[20] Yet
many progressives, self-styled or so-called or both, spoke in less than
wholeheartedly democratic tones. Louis D. Brandeis, for instance, called
upon his fellow lawyers to take "a position of interdependence between
the wealthy and the people, prepared to curb the excesses of either." Henry
L. Stimson nominated for the same mediating role his colleagues in the
Republican Party, whom he described as "the richer and more intelligent
citizens of the country." Numerous other progressives, drawing upon Mug-
wump ancestry or teachings, tinged their democratic creed with similar
paternalism. As defenders of the middle class, they shared none of the
essentially populist fervor expressed by William Jennings Bryan or Samuel
(Golden Rule) Jones,[21] They flinched from such unreserved democrats as
Robert La Follette, who once declared: "The people have never failed in
any great crisis in history."[22] Their misgivings toward immigrants, labor
unions and women's suffrage accentuate the boundaries within which many
progressives hedged their democratic faith.

Considering this mixed set of values which can be ascribed to the progressive movement, it is hardly surprising that old progressives later diverged drastically in their evaluation of the New Deal. Otis Graham has
studied 168 individuals who survived into the 1930s and whom contemporaries or historians have considered "progressive." (He confesses, incidentally, that "we cannot define what the word 'progressive' means with
precision. . . .") Of his sample, he finds five who were more radical than
the New Deal, 40 who supported it, and 60 who opposed it. The remainder
either retreated from political concern or left insufficient evidence for evaluation.[23] This scattered, almost random distribution reiterates indirectly the
fact that progressives espoused, at best, a heterogeneous ideology.

Analysis of a social movement begins with its goals and its values because without them there would be no movement. Progressivism lacked
unanimity of purpose either on a programmatic or on a philosophical level.
Nevertheless, these pervasive disagreements need not automatically preclude the use of a single concept, "the progressive movement," to embrace
them all. If the differences of opinion correlate with different socio-
economic groupings among the membership, then the incoherence would be
explained and rendered more coherent. If progressive opponents of
women's suffrage, for example, derived entirely from the South (which, by

[20]*Wilson: The New Freedom*, p. 241.
[21]Quoted in Hofstadter, *Age of Reform*, p. 264. See also Mowry, *Era of Theodore
Roosevelt*, chap. v, esp. pp. 89, 103–4.
[22]Quoted in Nye, *Midwestern Progressive Politics*, p. 186.
[23]*Encore for Reform*, pp. 187, 191–93.

the way, they did not), one could deny that "the progressive movement" vacillated on the issue. One could instead argue that their "southernness" caused some members of the movement to deviate from progressivism on this particular question. The exception would prove the rule. Multivariate analysis would thus find a collective pattern in a seemingly incoherent group of men and ideas.

Historians have indeed sought to extract such correlations. Russel B. Nye suggests a geographical criterion: "The reason for the Midwest's failure to produce a national leader," he writes, "lay in the fact that the movement itself was a distinctively Midwestern thing that developed regional politicians who were chiefly concerned with regional problems. Progressivism in its Eastern phase—as represented by Theodore Roosevelt and Woodrow Wilson—attained national power and dealt with national issues, but it was not the same thing."[24] Unfortunately, this regional dichotomy solves only the problem of leadership; by joining the ideologically incompatible Roosevelt and Wilson, it does nothing to explain how they belong in the same movement.

Mowry offers a more complex geographical categorization when he suggests that the Wilsonian "New Freedom" type of progressive came from regions of farms and small towns in the South and West. Men like Bryan, La Follette and Governor Albert Cummins of Iowa differed from Roosevelt by fearing strong federal government and preferring to destroy rather than regulate trusts.[25] Yet this analysis also collides with the facts. A biographical profile of several hundred Progressive Party leaders and their Republican opponents in Iowa in 1912 indicates no clear-cut geographical pattern. On the one hand, 70 per cent of the Cummins progressives came from rural or small-town areas. On the other hand, 54 per cent of the Roosevelt progressives came from the same types of places. The difference does tip slightly in favor of Mowry's thesis, but too slightly to sustain his argument.[26]

Attempts to establish a coherent pattern of multiple correlations between progressive factions and progressive ideas apparently lead to a dead end. In fact, even the less ambitious research simply to generalize about the movement's membership has produced baffling inconsistencies. The more that historians learn, the farther they move from consensus. In the

[24]*Midwestern Progressive Politics*, p. 184.
[25]*Era of Theodore Roosevelt*, pp. 54–55.
[26]Potts, "The Progressive Profile in Iowa," p. 262. The complete table, in absolute numbers rather than percentages, is as follows:

Progressives			
Roosevelt	Cummins	Standpats	
13	23	23	Rural
56	57	56	Towns 500 to 10,000
36	23	27	Cities over 10,000
12	2	15	Cities 30,000 to 50,000
11	10	5	Des Moines

1950s Mowry and Alfred D. Chandler drew the first systematic profiles of progressive leaders in California and the Progressive Party respectively. Their studies produced similar results: progressive leaders were over-whelmingly urban, middle-class, native-born, Protestant, young (often under 40 years of age), college-educated, self-employed in professions or modest-sized businesses, and rather new to politics. Almost none were farmers or laborers.[27] Subsequent composite biographies of progressives in Massachusetts, Washington, Iowa and Baltimore have found virtually identical traits.[28] On the basis of such data, Mowry and Hofstadter have devised their famous theory of "the status revolution": the progressive movement, they say, resulted from the attempts by the old urban middle class, whose status was threatened by the plutocrats above them and the workers and immigrants below, to restore their social position and to cure the injustices in American society.[29]

Recent research, however, has raised questions both about the reliability of these biographical data and about the validity of the "status revolution" theory. Samuel P. Hays, for example, has found that the municipal-reform movements in Des Moines and Pittsburgh were led by upper-class groups and opposed by both the lower and middle classes.[30] Progressive leaders in Ohio also deviated somewhat from the accepted profile. For one thing, more than 10 per cent of them were laborers; furthermore, the two outstanding figures, Samuel M. Jones of Toledo and Tom L. Johnson of Cleveland, were *nouveaux riches* businessmen who lacked a college education.[31] On a more impressionistic basis Joseph Huthmacher has claimed that members of the urban masses played a larger role in the progressive movement than has hitherto been recognized.[32]

Most challenging, however, is Otis Graham's statistical survey of 140 progressives surviving into the 1930s. Contrary to the urban character described by Chandler and Mowry, 50 per cent of these men and women were raised in small towns and 20 per cent on farms. Even more noteworthy is their diversity of class origins. Fewer than three out of five progressives

[27]Alfred D. Chandler Jr., "The Origins of Progressive Leadership," in Elting Morison, ed., *The Letters of Theodore Roosevelt* (Cambridge, Mass., 1954), Vol. VIII, Appendix III, pp. 1462–65; Mowry, *The California Progressives* (Berkeley, 1951), pp. 87–89.
[28]Richard B. Sherman, "The Status Revolution and Massachusetts Progressive Leadership," *Political Science Quarterly*, LXXVIII (Mar. 1965), 59–65; William T. Kerr Jr., "The Progressives of Washington, 1910–1912," *Pacific Northwest Quarterly*, LV (Jan. 1964), 16–27; Potts, "The Progressive Profile in Iowa," pp. 257–68; James B. Crooks, *Politics & Progress: The Rise of Urban Progressivism in Baltimore, 1895 to 1911* (Baton Rouge, La., 1968), chap. viii.
[29]Hofstadter, *Age of Reform*, pp. 135–66; Mowry, *Era of Theodore Roosevelt*, chap. v.
[30]"The Politics of Reform in Municipal Government in the Progressive Era," *Pacific Northwest Quarterly*, LV (Oct. 1964), 159–61.
[31]Warner, *Progressivism in Ohio*, pp. 22–23, 46 note 2.
[32]"Urban Liberalism and the Age of Reform," *Mississippi Valley Historical Review*, XLIX (Sept. 1962), 231–41. See also the analysis of North Dakota progressives in Michael Paul Rogin, *The Intellectuals and McCarthy: The Radical Specter* (Cambridge, Mass., 1967), pp. 116–20.

were born into the middle or upper-middle classes. Almost 20 per cent had "wealthy" parents, while 27 were born in lower or lower-middle economic ranks. By the time of adulthood almost all of them had climbed into or above the middle class, but the fact is that a significant proportion had not begun there.[33]

These various studies refine rather than refute the conventional portrait of the progressive movement. They relieve its uniformly middle-class WASP appearance. But other research has created greater reverberations, threatening to overturn the entire theory of a "status revolution." Composite biographies of progressive leaders in Massachusetts, Iowa, Washington, Wisconsin, and Toledo, Ohio, have generally confirmed the Chandler-Mowry-Hofstadter profile; but they have found almost identical traits in nonprogressives. That is, the progressives resembled their opponents in terms of class, occupation, education, age, religion, political experience and geographical origin. The sociological characteristics which had been presumed to be peculiarly "progressive" turn out to be common to all political leaders of the era. Hence one can no longer explain the progressive movement as the middle-class response to an upheaval in status because nonprogressives also shared that status.[34] Conversely, many businessmen in the towns and smaller cities of the South and Midwest suffered the anxieties of status decline, but they generally opposed change more often than they sponsored it. Prospering businessmen, not languishing ones, furnished both the ideas and the impetus for reform.[35] In short, any attempt to interpret the progressive movement in terms of status must confront the disconcerting fact that progressive leaders were indistinguishable from their nonprogressive contemporaries.[36]

If efforts to identify a coherent progressive program, ideology and membership shatter against the evidence of incoherence, there is still less hope for success in identifying a homogeneous progressive electorate. Historians working in the ante-computer era had to be content with impressionistic data. In general they claimed that progressivism drew polit-

[33]*Encore for Reform*, pp. 198, 201–3.

[34]Sherman, "The Status Revolution and Massachusetts Progressive Leadership"; Potts, "The Progressive Profile in Iowa"; Kerr, "The Progressives of Washington, 1910–1912"; David P. Thelen, "Social Tensions and the Origins of Progressivism," *Journal of American History*, LVI (Sept. 1969), 330–33; Jack Tager, "Progressives, Conservatives, and the Theory of the Status Revolution," *Mid-America*, XLVIII (July 1966), 162–75.

[35]Wiebe, *Businessmen and Reform*, p. 210; Sheldon Hackney, *Populism to Progressivism in Alabama* (Princeton, N.J., 1969), pp. 330-31.

[36]The significance of status anxiety, or status inconsistency—not only in the progressive case, but in general—is very uncertain. Social scientists are earnestly debating whether it bears a reliable relationship to political attitudes. See, e.g., K. Dennis Kelley and William J. Chambliss, "Status Consistency and Political Attitudes," *American Sociological Review*, XXXI (June 1966), 375–82; David R. Segal, "Status Inconsistency, Cross Pressures, and American Political Behavior," *ibid.*, XXXIV (June 1969), 352–59; Gerard Brandmeyer, "Status Consistency and Political Behavior: A Replication and Extension of Research," *Sociological Quarterly*, VI (Summer 1965), 241–56; and Gerhard E. Lenski, *Power and Privilege: A Theory of Social Stratification* (New York, 1966), pp. 86–88.

ical support from urban middle-class voters as well as farmers and organized labor.[37] So far only a few scholars have investigated this topic with
the sophisticated tools of behavioral social science. According to research in
the state of Washington, for example, the progressive electorate tended to
comprise the more prosperous and educated population, both in agricultural and in urban-industrial areas.[38] In South Dakota, prewar progressives
also found support among the rich, but not especially the urban, native-
born or Protestant rich.[39] In Wisconsin, on the other hand, Michael Rogin
has found that the poorer the county, the higher the progressive vote.[40]
His analysis of progressivism in California, South Dakota and North Dakota
uncovers still another electoral pattern: namely, a shift from middle-class
to lower-class support, and in California a shift as well from rural to urban.
Theodore Roosevelt's campaign as Progressive Party candidate in 1912,
however, did not conform to this latter pattern. According to Rogin, "the
electoral evidence questions whether the Progressive Party was typically
progressive."[41]

This intriguing, if not bewildering distinction between the legitimacies
of big-P and little-p progressivism neatly capsulates the problem. At least
since the time that Roosevelt claimed to represent the "real" progressives,
the identity of the progressive movement has been in doubt. The more
that historians have analyzed it, the more doubtful that identity. In each
of its aspects—goals, values, membership and supporters—the movement
displays a puzzling and irreducible incoherence. Definition thus becomes
a labored process. Arthur Link's effort deserves attention because, in its
very concern for precision, it dissolves "the progressive movement."

". . . the progressive movement," he writes, "never really existed as a
recognizable organization with common goals and a political machinery
geared to achieve them. [In short, it was not a group, or collectivity.] Generally speaking . . . , progressivism might be defined as the popular effort,
which began convulsively in the 1890's and waxed and waned afterward
to our own time, to insure the survival of democracy in the United States
by the enlargement of governmental power to control and offset the power
of private economic groups over the nation's institutions and life. [That
is, the movement endured through the New Deal and at least into the
Eisenhower years, when Link was writing.] Actually, of course, from the
1890's on there were many 'progressive' movements on many levels seeking sometimes contradictory objectives. [The single movement was really
multiple and sought not merely various, but inconsistent goals]." Yet "the
progressive movement before 1918. . . , despite its actual diversity and internal tensions . . . , did seem to have unity; that is, it seemed to share

[37]E.g., Link, "What Happened to the Progressive Movement in the 1920's? pp.
838–39.
[38]Kerr, "The Progressives of Washington, 1910–1912," pp. 21–27.
[39]Rogin, *Intellectuals and McCarthy*, pp. 144–46.
[40]*Ibid.*, p. 70.
[41]*Ibid.*, pp. 120, 148; and Michael Rogin, "Progressivism and the California Electorate," *Journal of American History*, LV (Sept. 1968), 301–3, 305, 308–10.

common ideals and objectives. This was true in part because much of the motivation even of the special-interest groups was altruistic (at least they succeeded in convincing themselves that they sought the welfare of society rather than their own interests primarily). . . ."[42]

Link's definition, climaxing in a statement which hovers between paradox and meaninglessness, suggests that historians of the progressive movement are struggling desperately to fit their concept onto data that stubbornly spill over the edges of that concept. Their plight derives largely from the fact that they are dealing with an aggregative group as if it were a collective group. That is, they move from the observation that many Americans in the early 20th century were "reformers" to the assertion that these Americans joined together in a "reform movement." But this logic is elliptical, slurring over the intermediate question of whether the reformers themselves felt a common identity and acted as a collective body. Certainly one would not assume that mystics or conservatives or conscientious objectors constitute "movements" in behalf of their beliefs. Yet students of the progressive movement have made precisely this assumption, only to find that the facts do not form a bridge leading from a progressive aggregate to a genuine progressive collectivity.

When historical evidence resists the historian so resolutely, one must question the categories being used. For those categories are constructs, artifices by which one tries to make sense of the inert and profuse evidence. When they create less rather than more sense, they should be abandoned. As Lee Benson has remarked about "Jacksonian Democracy": "If at this late date the concept remains unclarified, it seems reasonable to doubt that it is solidly based in reality."[43]

Benson rejected the category of "Jacksonian Democracy" and confronted the historical evidence without the distorting preconceptions which it entailed. He began inductively to make a new and better order out of the same data over which historians had quarreled for so long with increasingly contradictory conclusions. "The progressive movement" deserves the same treatment. Because it does not serve to organize the phenomena in coherent ways, it should be discarded. Modifications and qualifications are not sufficient, as Link's effort demonstrates, because they modify and qualify a "movement" that did not exist in historical reality, only in historians' minds.

Nor is a shift of terminology sufficient. George Tindall has tried, for example, to escape Link's dilemma by defining progressivism as "the spirit of the age rather than an organized movement. . . ."[44] The notion of a *Zeitgeist* performs the useful function of periodization, setting these decades apart from the "eras" before and after. But its usefulness stops at the general level of analysis. To speak of a "progressivism" or "the progressive

[42]"What Happened to the Progressive Movement in the 1920's?" pp. 836–37.
[43]*The Concept of Jacksonian Democracy: New York as a Test Case* (Princeton, N.J., 1961), p. 330.
[44]Tindall, "Business Progressivism: Southern Politics in the Twenties," p. 93.

era" is to wrap the entire period within an undifferentiated ideological embrace without saying anything about the diversity within the period. One thereby overwhelms the very distinctions which are crucial to an understanding of the conflicts and changes that took place.

Salvage efforts should be resolutely resisted. A diffuse progressive "era" may have occurred, but a progressive "movement" did not. "Progressives" there were, but of many types—intellectuals, businessmen, farmers, labor unionists, white-collar professionals, politicians; lower, middle and upper class; southerners, easterners, westerners; urban and rural. In explaining American responses to urbanization and industrialization, these socioeconomic differences are more important than any collective identity as "progressives." A cotton manufacturer and "unmistakably Progressive" governor like Braxton Comer of Alabama, for example, favored railroad regulation but opposed child-labor laws.[45] Urban machine politicians like Martin Lomasney of Boston and Edwin Vare of Philadelphia, who have usually been ranked as enemies of progressivism, supported the constitutional amendment for direct election of United States senators because this reform would reduce the power of rural state legislators. Significantly, Vare's rival, Boies Penrose, whose machine controlled politics on the state level, opposed the amendment.[46] Thus the conventional label of "progressive" not only oversimplifies the facts, but handicaps effective analysis of them. One might just as well combine Jane Addams, Frances Willard and Edward Bellamy as "reformers," or Andrew Carnegie and Samuel Gompers as "advocates of capitalism."

At this point in historical research, the evidence points away from convenient synthesis and toward multiplicity. The progressive era seems to be characterized by shifting coalitions around different issues, with the specific nature of these coalitions varying on federal, state and local levels, from region to region, and from the first to the second decades of the century.[47] It may be helpful to think of this period in the way that Bernard Bailyn has characterized the first half of the 18th century. The traditional patterns of social values and political interaction gave way under the force of American circumstances, but did not become transformed into a new pattern. Instead, political factionalism and ideological improvisation—what one might call opportunism—became more and more prevalent. Only in the face of British pressure did this fragmentation coalesce sufficiently to form something like a coherent social movement—namely, the Revolution.[48] In contrast to the 18th century, the diverse factions of the early 20th century never experienced the unifying crucible of a crisis.

[45]Hackney, *Populism to Progressivism in Alabama*, pp. 122, 243, 276–77.
[46]John D. Buenker, "The Urban Political Machine and the Seventeenth Amendment," *Journal of American History*, LVI (Sept. 1969), 305–22.
[47]See, e.g., Hackney, *Populism to Progressivism*, esp. chaps. xii–xiii; Richard M. Abrams, *Conservatism in a Progressive Era: Massachusetts Politics, 1900–1912* (Cambridge, Mass., 1964), pp. 235–38; Robert H. Wiebe, *The Search for Order, 1877–1920* (New York, 1967), chaps. vii–viii; John D. Buenker, "The Progressive Era: A Search for a Synthesis," *Mid-America*, LI (July 1969), 175–94.
[48]*The Origins of American Politics* (New York, 1968).

World War I, despite President Wilson's earnest "progressive" rhetoric, was too remote from the domestic concerns of so-called progressives. The war did not create a progressive movement; on the contrary, it served as yet another issue around which the factions formed new coalitions.

The present state of historical understanding seems to deny the likelihood of a synthesis as convenient and neat as "the progressive movement." In their commitment to making sense of the past, however, historians will continue to search for conceptual order. Perhaps, after further studies of specific occupations, geographical areas and issues, a new synthesis will appear. But if that is to occur, the "progressive" frame of reference, carrying with it so many confusing and erroneous connotations, must be put aside. It is time to tear off the familiar label and, thus liberated from its prejudice, see the history between 1890 and 1920 for what it was—ambiguous, inconsistent, moved by agents and forces more complex than a progressive movement.

Nancy J. Weiss
THE NEGRO AND THE NEW FREEDOM: FIGHTING WILSONIAN SEGREGATION

The progressive era emphasized the need to make representative government more representative. It was an age which discussed extensively innovations in the relationships between the governors and the governed. Many segments of American society complained that government was indifferent to their needs because its institutions were undemocratic and many groups feared their own political impotence. The middle class, farmers, workers, immigrants, and women called for new laws to protect their welfare. Some state governments experimented with new devices like the referendum, the initiative, and the recall in order to improve political responsiveness. Through some quirk of logic, an amendment to the Constitution reformed the United States Senate by changing its electors from the state legislators to the people-at-large. Of course, the legislatures were elected by the people; if the Senate had faults they lay as much with the people who chose the legislatures as with the legislatures themselves. Many states conceded the right of suffrage to women, and by 1918 a pre-

viously hostile Woodrow Wilson joined the advocates. In fact, whereas the Constitution had remained unchanged from 1870 to 1913, it was amended four times in the succeeding seven years. Government took on an aura of new responsiveness and flexibility in the progressive era.

However, as Nancy J. Weiss demonstrates in this article, the Negro did not participate in the expansion of democracy. Rather, he was a victim of "a New Freedom bringing a new bondage...." The progressive era was, for the black, one of proscription in our electoral and governing processes. The insurance of one man's rights seemed to require the curtailment of another man's. White Americans practiced racial discrimination as a matter of course. Blacks were too disorganized to protect themselves effectively, thereby assuring themselves of the scapegoat role.

The lesson Weiss draws is that the political system is a battlefield; the group which is not massed for maximum strength suffers because of its lack of organization. Articulate voices proclaiming injustices are theatrically impressive, but political power requires that available votes be given to responsive politicians.

If broadened opportunities, political democracy, and social justice describe Wilsonian Progressivism, the man on the furthest fringe of that movement was surely the American Negro. Woodrow Wilson's first administration inaugurated officially-sanctioned segregation in the federal departments and witnessed ill-concealed moves to cut into already meager Negro patronage.

White liberals and Negroes alike worried the same question: how could Progressivism find room for race discrimination? Or, how could one explain the introduction of official shackles on the black man at a time when America was legislating the liberation and protection of the individual? The President, liberal publicist Oswald Garrison Villard declared, "fails utterly to see that to discriminate in his democracy against anyone, is to bring his whole carefully reared edifice crashing to the ground."[1]

Yet, federal segregation was less a new departure than the logical culmination of a decisive Southern—and national—trend. Moreover, despite the anomaly of a New Freedom bringing a new bondage, Progressivism and racism were in many respects interdependent. The early years of the Progressive era coincided with widespread Negro disfranchisement and the birth of full-scale, state-level Jim Crow legislative discrimination. Accustomed by imperial design and judicial decision to thoughts of racial

Reprinted with permission from the *Political Science Quarterly*, Vol. 84 (March 1969), pp. 61–79.
[1]Oswald Garrison Villard, *Segregation in Baltimore and Washington* (n.p., 1913), 8; Villard, "The President and the Segregation at Washington," *North American Review*, CXCVIII (1913), 805.

superiority, white America linked Progressive democracy and equality to greater separation from Negroes.[2]

I

By the election of 1912 most Southern states had succeeded in purging their political systems of Negro voters and office-holders. Those Negroes retaining the franchise generally aligned themselves as a bloc with the party of emancipation. But 1912 marked a turning point in national Negro political participation. Angry at Theodore Roosevelt's "lily white" Progressivism and alienated by incumbent William Howard Taft's concessions to racism, Negroes were fair game for Democratic efforts to split the solidarity of the bloc vote.[3]

Democratic candidate Woodrow Wilson was a Southerner who concurred in his wife's outspoken belief in social separation of the races, a college president who barred Negroes from Princeton (and who later told darky stories in Cabinet meetings).[4] Prominent Negroes faced the issue squarely: "We do not believe that Woodrow Wilson admires Negroes," W. E. B. Du Bois wrote with considerable understatement. And yet, he told readers of the NAACP's magazine Crisis, Negroes might well expect such a "cultivated scholar" to treat them with "farsighted fairness."[5] Leaders of the race secured a much-publicized campaign pledge "to see justice done them in every matter, and not mere grudging justice, but justice executed with liberality and cordial good feeling." "Should I become President of the United States," Wilson promised in 1912, "[Negroes] may count upon me for absolute fair dealing and for everything by which I could assist in advancing the interests of their race in the United States."[6] Even Villard proclaimed himself "quite delighted" with the candidate's position.[7]

[2]C. Vann Woodward, The Strange Career of Jim Crow (rev. ed., New York, 1964), Chap. II, passim.

[3]W. E. B. Du Bois, Dusk of Dawn: An Essay Toward An Autobiography of a Race Concept (New York, 1940), 233–34; Henry Lee Moon, Balance of Power: The Negro Vote (Garden City, N.Y., 1948), 93–94; J. Milton Waldron and J. D. Harkless, The Political Situation in a Nut-Shell: Some Un-Colored Truths for Colored Voters (Washington, 1912), 11, 17, 20, 25; Arthur S. Link, "The Negro as a Factor in the Campaign of 1912," Journal of Negro History, XXXII (1947), 84, 93–96; John Hope Franklin, From Slavery to Freedom: A History of American Negroes (rev. ed., New York, 1956), 445; Crisis, Dec. 1912, p. 75; William F. Nowlin, The Negro in American National Politics (Boston, 1931), 90–91.

[4]Josephus Daniels, The Cabinet Diaries of Josephus Daniels, 1913–1921, ed. E. David Cronon (Lincoln, Nebr., 1963), 195, 204, 234, 321, 414, 493; Link, Wilson: The Road to the White House (Princeton, 1947), 3, 502.

[5]Crisis, Aug. 1912, p. 181.

[6]Quoted in Alexander Walters, My Life and Work (New York, 1917), 194–95. See also, Villard to Francis Jackson Garrison, Aug. 9, 1912, Villard to Wilson, Aug. 14, 1912, Wilson to Villard, Aug. 17, 23, 1912, all in the Oswald Garrison Villard Papers, Houghton Library, Harvard University; Link, "The Negro as a Factor," 88, 91–92; Elliott M. Rudwick, W. E. B. Du Bois: A Study in Minority Group Leadership (Philadelphia, 1960), 160.

[7]Link, Wilson: The Road to the White House, 503; Villard to Garrison, Aug. 14, 1912, Villard Papers.

Thus, the election of 1912 saw the curious spectacle of the champions of the Negro lining up, albeit hesitantly, behind a symbol of Southern Democracy. "We sincerely believe," the *Crisis* intoned,

> that even in the face of promises disconcertingly vague, and in the face of the solid caste-ridden South, it is better to elect Woodrow Wilson President of the United States and prove once for all if the Democratic party dares to be Democratic when it comes to black men.[8]

Although there is no way of measuring the Negro vote, observers speculated that roughly half a million black men would exercise the franchise in 1912. Du Bois has written that Wilson won the votes of nearly 100,000 Negroes in the North alone. While many Negroes voted for Roosevelt, Professor Arthur Link states that Wilson got "more [Negro votes], probably, than any other Democratic presidential candidate had ever received." In any event, it appears that influential Negro leaders and a significant part of the rank and file did break away from their traditional Republican affiliations.[9]

After Wilson took office Negroes quickly discovered that their support packed little bargaining power. By the summer of 1913 segregated toilets, lunchroom facilities, and working areas had been ordered in the Departments of the Treasury and the Post Office, among others. Job segregation was especially evident in cases where Negro men had previously supervised white women. Some construed the new policies as a backhanded way of phasing out all Negro civil service employes, and pointed to cases where Negroes were shifted into separate departmental divisions later slated for dissolution. For the first time photographs were required on all civil service applications. The impact was so great that Booker T. Washington could write of an August visit to the nation's capital: "I have never seen the colored people so discouraged and bitter as they are at the present time."[10]

Secretary of the Navy Josephus Daniels relates that the question of federal segregation was first introduced in high administration circles at a Cabinet meeting in April 1913, when Postmaster General A. G. Burleson brought up complaints over integration in the railway mail service. Burle-

[8]*Crisis*, Nov. 1912, p. 29.

[9]*Ibid.*, Aug. 1912, p. 180; Du Bois, *Dusk of Dawn*, 235; Link, "The Negro as a Factor," 98; August Meier, "The Negro and the Democratic Party, 1875–1915," *Phylon*, XVII (1956), 185.

[10]Copies of the segregation orders for the Treasury Department can be found in the Villard Papers. See, also, Boston *Guardian*, Nov. 15, 1913; John Palmer Gavit, "The Negro at Washington," New York *Evening Post*, Oct. 21, 1913; New York *Times*, Nov. 18, 1913; Villard, *Segregation in Baltimore and Washington*, 6; Laurence J. W. Hayes, The *Negro Federal Government Worker: A Study of His Classification Status in the District of Columbia* (Washington, 1941), 51; Paul P. Van Riper, *History of the United States Civil Service* (Evanston, 1958), 241; Henry Lincoln Johnson, *The Negro Under Wilson* (Washington, 1916), 1–3; Washington to Villard, Aug. 10, 1913, and Robert N. Wood to Wilson, Aug. 5, 1913, both in the Woodrow Wilson Papers, Manuscript Division, Library of Congress; Link, *Wilson: The New Freedom* (Princeton, 1956), 243ff.

son, a Southerner like Daniels, "was anxious to segregate white and negro employees in all Departments of the Government. . . . he believed segregation was best for the negro and best for the Service." Secretary of the Treasury William Gibbs McAdoo (another Southerner) especially seemed to agree with him. Then, Daniels recalls, the Cabinet discussed the general question of Negro appointments. "The President said he made no promises in particular to Negroes, except to do them justice, and he did not wish to see them have less positions than they now have; but he wished the matter adjusted in a way to make the least friction." Although no action was taken, the Cabinet certainly made no effort to halt the beginnings of deliberate segregation.[11]

Departmental segregation was a conspicuous reversal of a fifty year tradition of integrated civil service. With racism having infiltrated state and local systems, easily-delineated pressures pushed the Wilson administration toward federal discrimination. The administration, itself obviously Southern, paid considerable attention to senatorial influence from the James K. Vardamans, Benjamin R. Tillmans, and Hoke Smiths. Moreover, organizations like the National Democratic Fair Play Association worked as powerful lobbies for a racist outlook on the civil service. And the capital itself, as the New York *Evening Post's* Washington correspondent wrote, was "essentially a Southern city," where "the great majority of the white people . . . hold the Southern view of the negro . . . ." "The white men and women in the Government service," he continued, "have resented being compelled to associate with the negroes. *Never before has there been an Administration that dared to cater to this feeling, except in surreptitious ways* . . . . There has always been . . . a *wish* to do it, but not the *courage*."[12] Forces defending racial equality finally gave way to long-latent desires for discrimination.

While segregation orders were conceived and issued by subordinates, it is clear that Wilson made little or no effort to stop them. He summed up his own attitude in a letter to the editor of the *Congregationalist*:

> . . . I would say that I do approve of the segregation that is being attempted in several of the departments. . . . I certainly would not . . . have . . . if I had not thought it to their [Negroes'] advantage and likely to remove many of the difficulties which have surrounded the appointment and advancement of colored men and women.[13]

Federal appointment policy, on the other hand, initiated directly from the White House. Certain federal positions—like Register of the Treasury, Recorder of Deeds and Customs Collector for the District of Columbia, and Auditor of the Navy Department—as well as diplomatic assignments

[11]Daniels, *Cabinet Diaries*, 32–33.
[12]NDFPA to "Dear Madam," May 9, 1913, Wilson Papers; New York *Times*, May 4, 1913; Gavit to Villard, Oct. 1, 1913, Villard Papers. See, also Gavit, "The Negro at Washington."
[13]Wilson to H. A. Bridgman, Sept. 8, 1913, quoted in Ray Stannard Baker, *Woodrow Wilson, Life and Letters*, 8 Vols. (Garden City, N.Y., 1927–39), IV, 223.

to black nations, were traditionally held by Negroes. Given their support for the Democrats in 1912, Negro leaders expected increased patronage. When Wilson took office the *Negro Year Book* reported that Negroes held thirteen significant federal offices and filled eleven posts in the diplomatic and consular service. By the end of 1915 nine of the former (plus four officials not listed in the original account) and three of the latter had "retired from office and white men ... [had] been appointed to fill their places." Three years later just six diplomatic representatives and one judge were left.[14] Wilson made only two key Negro appointments: Minister to Liberia and Municipal Court Judge of the District of Columbia. Negroes were especially incensed when the black Register of the Treasury was replaced by an Indian. Wilson lamely noted the difficulty of pushing Negro nominations past a Vardaman-Tillman-Smith Senate, but failed to explain his predecessors' perseverance in pursuing the same end. Negro leaders underlined the irony of an administration preaching social separation of the races, but sending a white envoy to a black nation.[15]

Executive discrimination found considerable sympathy on Capitol Hill. During the first Wilson administration nearly two dozen anti-Negro measures were introduced in the House and Senate, "the greatest flood of bills proposing discriminatory legislation against Negroes" ever to come before the Congress. They ran the gamut from Jim Crow transportation regulations and armed forces enlistment to prohibition of miscegenation, civil service segregation, and repeal of the Fifteenth Amendment. Their sponsors were Southerners, and they made little or no progress, with only the miscegenation bill being reported by a committee.[16]

II

Incorporating a remarkable ethnic, social, and occupational diversity, the youthful National Association for the Advancement of Colored People seemed the logical forum for liberals of every cast who challenged the

[14]Alexander Walters (President, National Colored Democratic League) to Wilson, March 10, 1913, Wilson Papers; New York *Evening Post*, March 11, 1913; Monroe N. Work (ed.), *Negro Year Book and Annual Encyclopedia of the Negro* (Tuskegee, 1913), 99–100; *Negro Year Book: An Annual Encyclopedia of the Negro, 1916–1917* (Tuskegee, 1916), 36, *Negro Year Book: An Annual Encyclopedia of the Negro, 1918–1919* (Tuskegee, 1919), 208. Van Riper estimates a "decline of Negro federal employment from nearly six per cent of the total civil service in 1910 to about 4.9 per cent in 1918." *History of the United States Civil Service*, 242.

[15]*Crisis*, Sept. 1913, p. 215, March 1916, p. 215, Aug. 1916, p. 198. Lester A. Walton to Editor, New York *Times*, Aug. 14, 1913; New York *Times*, March 24, 1914; Villard, "The President and the Segregation at Washington," 801–02; Gavit, "The Negro at Washington"; New York *Evening Post*, Aug. 4, 1913; Washington to Villard, Aug. 8, 1913, Villard Papers.

[16]Franklin, 445; Hayes, 45; *Crisis*, June 1914, p. 77; U. S. Congress, House Committee on Reform in the Civil Service, *Segregation of Clerks and Employees in the Civil Service, Hearings ...*, 63d Cong., 2d Sess., 1914; U. S., *Congressional Record*, 63d Cong., 1st Sess.—64th Cong., 1st Sess., 1913–16, L–III, *passim; Crisis*, May 1914, p. 11.

thinking of those supporting segregation. As chairman of its executive committee, Oswald Garrison Villard, grandson of famed abolitionist William Lloyd Garrison, led off with a steady letter-writing campaign designed to clarify the administration's stand on the race issue. He urged the President to repudiate a disastrous policy, due, he hoped, "to the individual initiative of department heads without your knowledge and consent." 'But Wilson insisted that departmental segregation was "in the interest of the negroes . . . ." "My own feeling," he wrote, "is, by putting certain bureaus and sections of the service in the charge of negroes we are rendering them more safe in their possession of office and less likely to be discriminated against." This gave spokesmen for the Negro grounds for open attack. On August 15, 1913, the NAACP filed an official protest at the White House against the "drawing of caste lines." Negroes "desire a 'New Freedom,' too, Mr. President," they asserted. The organization called for public response to their appeal for social justice.[17]

Villard mobilized his liberal *Nation* and New York *Evening Post;* Boston *Guardian* editor William Monroe Trotter led off the Negro press reaction; and the NAACP's branches organized nationwide protest meetings.[18] The press, both Northern and Southern, white and Negro, answered the call. Responding to suggestions for a letter-writing marathon, countless citizens flooded the White House mailbags. Hundreds of letters bore the signatures of Negroes of every station. More notably, however, the NAACP's appeal brought forth vocal support from white clergymen, professors, social workers, philanthropists, Progressive politicians, and leaders of other minority groups like Jews and women. The "harsh and humiliating discrimination," they wrote, was "an insult and an outrage upon American citizenship," "violating the spirit of the Constitution and opposed to the teachings of Jesus Christ." From all corners there arose cries of dismay over the "unjust and disheartening" measures instituted "in plain derogation of the policy favored by our fundamental law."[19]

Beyond letters and editorials, white liberals exerted little, if any, more active pressure. Some appealed to their spokesmen in Congress to influence the President, and touched off critical communications from Capitol Hill to the White House. Congressman John J. Rogers of Massachusetts introduced resolutions urging investigation of treatment of Negro employes

[17]Villard to Wilson, July 21, 1913, Wilson to Villard, July 23, 1913, NAACP to Wilson, Aug. 15, 1913, all on Villard Papers; New York *Evening Post*, Nov. 17, 1913.

[18]NAACP, *Fourth Annual Report* (New York, 1914), 12, 15, 16, 48, 52–54, 59; New York *Times*, Dec. 19, 1913; Boston *Guardian*, Nov. 15, 1913; Boston *Post*, Dec. 1, 1913; Charles W. Puttkammer and Ruth Worthy, "William Monroe Trotter, 1872–1934," *Journal of Negro History*, XLIII (1958), 298–316.

[19]See, for example, letters in the Wilson Papers which the President received from the following: James Schouler, Sept. 8, 1913; Minneapolis Sunday Forum, Sept. 7, 1913; National Council of Congregational Churches of the United States, Nov. 14, 1913; Jacob H. Schiff, Aug. 20, 1913; Francis J. Garrison, Aug. 21, 1913; Alfred Hayes, Sept. 19, 1913; David I. Walsh, Oct. 26, 1914; Northeastern Federation of Women's Clubs, Aug. 15, 1913; Charles Fleischer, Nov. 3, 1913; Karl F. Geiser, Oct. 1913; Julius Rosenwald, Sept. 4, 1913; Alice P. Gannett, Aug. 20, 1913; Eugene N. Foss, Oct. 20, 1913.

in the Treasury and Post Office Departments, but both measures died on committee calendars without gaining so much as a hearing. Some whites debated arranging a peaceful protest at the White House by representatives of the segregated employes, but nothing ever materialized.[20] In short, white liberals spoke up vociferously for the Negro cause, but the issue never packed enough political leverage to evoke more effective tactics.

Negroes appealed to Wilson not only on grounds of humanitarianism, campaign pledges, constitutionalism, and plain American decency, but also on the basis of political expediency. The precarious Democratic strength established among members of their race in 1912 crumbled rapidly in the face of the President's policies, so that Negro Democratic politicians found themselves "in a political wilderness of dispair [sic]." The men who decried segregation were fighting for their very political lives. "We are constantly being called traiters [sic] and being threatened with bodily harm," the secretary of the National Colored Democratic League wrote to presidential secretary Joseph P. Tumulty. "We are publically [sic] and frequently charged with having sold the Race into slavery. . . ."[21]

But these men were talking about more than their own careers. What they saw was a fast-disappearing opportunity to capitalize on Negro disaffection from the Republican fold. They continually emphasized that Wilsonian discrimination would mean political suicide for any vestiges of Negro Democracy in 1916. And Wilson countered just as consistently by insisting that segregation was not a matter of politics, but of humanitarianism. Certainly the size of the Negro vote, and the political leverage it wielded, were small, so that the immediate political benefits of courting Negroes were limited. But the chances for constructive reconciliation and for a useful precedent were not insignificant.[22]

The future, and not only the political future, was very much on the minds of those who cried for a change in policy. What were the implications of the new caste system for future generations? There was no telling, protesters noted, what measures others might justify on the basis of the Wilsonian precedent. "Should the National Government adopt this seemingly simple provision," a prominent Negro professor wrote, "it would thereby sanction all of the discriminatory legislation on the statute books of the several states and would suggest and justify all such enactment in the future."[23] Hand in hand with this caution went a curiously am-

[20]See Sen. [Wesley] L. Jones (Wash.) to Wilson, Sept. 29, 1913, Wilson Papers; Villard to Rep. A. Mitchell Palmer (Pa.), Nov. 20, 1913, Sen. Henry F. Hollis (N.H.) to Villard, Sept. 6, 1913, both in Villard Papers; H. Res. 288 and 289, *Congressional Record*, 63d. Cong., 1st Sess., 1913, L, 5684; Villard to Archibald Grimke, Oct. 30, 1913, Villard Papers.

[21]Rufus L. Perry to Wilson, July 21, 1913, Peter J. Smith to Tumulty, June 1, 1913, both in Wilson Papers. See, also, A. B. Cosey to Tumulty, Aug. 22, 1913, Wilson Papers.

[22]Villard to Wilson, July 21, 1913, Villard Papers; New York *Evening Post*, Nov. 8, 1913.

[23]Kelly Miller, *Segregation: The Caste System and the Civil Service* (Washington [1914]), 11.

bivalent attitude toward the President himself. Carefully noting Wilson's sincerity and highmindedness, many tried to rationalize his program as the work of underlings unbeknownst to him. What they feared more than anything, however, was the future election of a less scrupulous, less principled chief executive who would tailor Wilsonian segregation policies to more disastrous, far-reaching ends, affecting not only Negroes but possibly other minority groups like Jews.[24]

With the public "campaign of making the White House just as uncomfortable as possible" gaining in momentum, Villard continued his own efforts at private persuasion. Finding Tumulty sympathetic to his arguments, he nevertheless had great difficulty in establishing any real understanding with the President on the race issue. While justifying departmental segregation, Wilson admitted that "in several instances the thing has been managed in a way which was not sufficiently thoughtful of their feelings . . . ," which provoked Villard to retort: "Believe me, it is not a question of handling segregation awkwardly or tactfully, or otherwise, it is a question of right and wrong." The interchange ended temporarily with the President pleading for time and tolerance:

> I hope . . . that by the slow pressure of argument and persuasion the situation may be changed and a great many things done eventually which now seem impossible. . . . I appeal to you most earnestly to aid at holding things at a just and cool equipoise until I can discover whether it is possible to work out anything or not.

Shifting focus from the White House to the departments proved no more rewarding. Villard informed Treasury Secretary McAdoo of a speech he intended to give concerning segregation instituted under McAdoo's jurisdiction. The ambivalence of the Secretary's reply summed up the sheer frustration encountered by those who tried to reverse the discriminatory policies. "There is no 'segregation issue' in the Treasury Department," McAdoo insisted. "It has always been a mischievous exaggeration." And yet, in the same letter he confessed,

> . . . I shall not be a party to the enforced and unwelcome juxtaposition of white and negro employees when it is unnecessary and avoidable without injustice to anybody, and when such enforcement would serve only to engender race animosities detrimental to the welfare of both races and injurious to the public service.[25]

From the Negro's point of view, departmental segregation was anything but a "mischievous exaggeration." In November 1913 a group of prominent Negroes representing the National Independent Political League and sponsored by Massachusetts congressmen went to the White

[24]New York *Evening Post*, Oct. 21, 1913; "The President and the Negro," *Nation*, Aug. 7, 1913, p. 114; Villard, "The President and the Segregation at Washington," 804; Villard, *Fighting Years: Memoirs of a Liberal Editor* (New York, 1939), 239.

[25]Villard to Garrison, July 31, Aug. 12, 1913; Wilson to Villard, Aug. 29, Sept. 22, 1913; Villard to Wilson, Sept. 18, 1913; Villard to McAdoo, Oct. 25, 1913; McAdoo to Villard, Oct. 27, 1913, all in Villard Papers.

House to deliver a petition of protest against discrimination in the government service. Wilson seemed impressed by the protest and surprised at the conditions they mentioned. He assured the delegation that "segregation had not been decided upon as an administration policy," and promised further investigation. The protests reputedly made some impact, so that in December the New York *Evening Post* could write, "it seems plain that the word has gone forth that the segregationists must take the back track. . . . it appears that a return to former conditions is underway all along the line."[26]

III

Despite token efforts, like removal of some signs on toilets, there seems to have been little concrete evidence of actual reversal of policies.[27] In November 1914 the delegation of Negro leaders called again at the White House to discuss the situation. Headed by Boston *Guardian* editor Trotter, the group detailed instances of continued segregation, charged certain officials with race prejudice, asked for investigation and redress by executive order, and predicted Negro opposition to the Democrats in 1916. Wilson, dismissing any political considerations, "said that the policy of segregation had been enforced for the comfort and best interests of both races in order to overcome friction." The President ended the interview abruptly, announcing that he was insulted by Trotter's approach, and warning that any future meetings would have to be conducted by another Negro spokesman. The so-called Trotter incident provoked a new flurry of editorials and correspondence; even those who found Trotter's conduct objectionable agreed on the positive results of reintroducing the segregation issue into public discussion. Whether Trotter actually did anything out of order is open to doubt; Tumulty told Villard that the Negro's speech was "one of the most eloquent he had ever heard," and the President later admitted privately to Tumulty that "he was very sorry he had lost his temper as he had made a great mistake."[28]

As the controversy over the Trotter interview died down another issue arose to take its place on Negro and white liberal editorial pages. President Wilson and his Cabinet had attended a private White House showing of "The Birth of a Nation," the controversial D. W. Griffith film based on Thomas Dixon's *The Clansman.* Featuring vicious distortions of Negro activities during the Reconstruction era, the movie was a potent weapon

---

[26]Boston *Guardian*, Nov. 15, 1913; New York *Evening Post*, Dec. 13, 1913. See, also, Villard, *Fighting Years*, 241; Villard in the Philadelphia *Public Ledger*, Jan. 2, 1914; NAACP to Wilson, Jan. 6, 1914, Wilson Papers; Garrison to Villard, Dec. 14, 26, 1913, Villard Papers.
[27]Gavit to Villard, Oct. 1, 1913, Villard Papers.
[28]New York *Times*, Nov. 13, 14, 1914; New York *Evening Post*, Nov. 12, 1914; "Friction," *Independent*, Nov. 23, 1914, p. 269; New York *Evening Post*, Nov. 13, 1914; Villard to Garrison, Nov. 18, 1914, Villard Papers; Villard to Garrison, Dec. 11, 1914, Villard Papers.

for inflaming white hatred of blacks. Indignant at this so-called "work of art," Negroes organized nationwide protests calling either for censorship of particularly offensive scenes or for total banning of the film. In only a smattering of communities were they at all successful. The movie's producers delighted in justifying its value by noting that it had been screened without objection before the President and his Cabinet. Wilson, driven into a corner by persistent inquiries, lamely directed Tumulty to explain that "the President was entirely unaware of the character of the play before it was presented, and has at no time expressed his approbation of it. Its exhibition at the White House was a courtesy extended to an old acquaintance."[29]

While "The Birth of a Nation" and federal segregation bred loud public protest, a private effort in behalf of the Negro was also taking shape. Largely unsuccessful at curbing Wilson's negative policies, white liberals and Negro leaders put forth a constructive suggestion of their own to grapple with the Negro's place in an expanding American democracy. The idea of a National Race Commission was first developed by R. H. Leavell, professor of economics at Texas A & M, and later taken up by Villard and the NAACP. The plan called for a presidentially-appointed, privately-financed, biracial, multi-sectional commission to investigate every phase of Negro life in the country, "with particular reference to his economic situation." Hopefully, the inquiry might ease racial tensions and provoke legislative recommendations from the White House. Moreover, the investigation would be in the best tradition of Progressive concern for social justice; it "would be of great service to the white South as well as to Negroes," for "a situation in which millions of people were living on the border line of destitution in the slums . . . ought to be intolerable in civilized communities. . . ."[30]

The Race Commission plan spoke the purest language of Progressivism. Its primary objective—"to promote realization of democracy in America" —could be attained "by providing adequate opportunity for self-realization by all individuals of all classes or all races in ways beneficial both to the individual and to society."[31] Those who drafted the proposal fully understood the American reform tradition of widening avenues of opportunity for the disadvantaged.

Villard took the plan to the White House in May 1913. He left the interview enthusiastic over Wilson's reaction; the President, he wrote to Pro-

[29]*Crisis*, May 1915, pp. 40–42, June 1915, pp. 69–71, 87–88; New York *Times*, March 7, April 18, 1915; Wilson to Tumulty, April 28, 1915, memorandum in Wilson Papers.

[30]Leavell to Villard, Feb. 20, April 4, July 7, 1912; Villard to Leavell, April 1, Aug. 15, 1912, Villard Papers; "A Proposal for a National Race Commission to be appointed by the President of the United States. Suggested by the National Association for the Advancement of Colored People," undated, Villard Papers; Leavell to Wilson, Feb. 20, 1912, Villard Papers; Villard, *Fighting Years*, 236.

[31]Leavell to Villard, Aug. 18, 1912; Leavell, Sketch of a (Tentative) Detailed Plan for Investigations Directed by the Proposed President's Commission of Race Facts and Race Relationships, both in Villard Papers.

fessor Leavell, was "wholly sympathetic," promising to consider the proposal in the light of "his relations with the Senate and Congress, and what
it will mean to him to antagonize the reactionary Southern politicians. As
to the necessity of some such inquiry he was quite clear . . . ."[32] Wilson
postponed subsequent interviews throughout the summer, insisting that
the Mexican crisis kept him too preoccupied for other considerations. Villard repeatedly sought authorization to proceed with the fund-raising;
"I am particularly urging this upon you now," he wrote in August, "because
of the intense dissatisfaction of the colored people at the treatment by
your Administration thus far."[33]

A few days later Wilson rejected the suggestion. With the balance of
his legislative program still awaiting congressional action, he shrank from
alienating powerful Southern congressional leaders. An investigation, he
maintained, inevitably implied an indictment. Recalling his earlier receptivity, he admitted, "I never realized before the complexity and difficulty
of this matter in respect of every step taken here."[34]

Strikingly, the President's stand on the Race Commission sparked absolutely no public protest. Villard had purposely avoided any publicity of
the negotiations, fearing that outside pressure might force Wilson's hand.
At the same time, departmental segregation and appointments more than
occupied the efforts of those championing the Negro cause. Indeed, the
Race Commission "lobby" consisted of only one man—Villard himself.
Various professionals and NAACP leaders made comments on the original
draft, but the organization itself remained officially silent.[35] The only re-
criminations after Wilson's refusal came in bitter letters from Villard.
"Frankly, I feel very sorry that you find yourself 'absolutely blocked by
the sentiment of senators,'" he wrote. "I believe that like your most immediate predecessors, the time will come when you will find it necessary
to go ahead and do what is right without considering their feelings. . . ."
But "[bowing] down to the god Expediency," Villard warned, ought not
to demand continued segregation and non-appointment of Negroes. Unless Wilson faced squarely the place of the Negro in his New Freedom, the
liberal editor predicted, "the feeling of bitterness among the colored people towards your Administration and the Democratic party shall steadily
increase."[36]

Villard was right. The election of 1916 justified warnings that segregation policies spelled the end of an unusual opportunity to convert Ne-

[32]Villard to Leavell, May 15, 1913, Villard to James H. Dillard, May 15, 1913, both
in Villard Papers. The plan had been broached to the then-candidate Wilson in 1912,
but he insisted that consideration of the commission be deferred until he actually
entered the White House. See Villard to Leavell, Aug. 15, 1912, Villard Papers.

[33]Villard to Wilson, Aug. 18, 1913, Villard Papers.

[34]Wilson to Villard, Aug. 21, 1913, Villard Papers.

[35]Albert Bushnell Hart to Villard, Jan. 16, 1913; Du Bois, Comments on the Fore-
going Plan; J. E. Spingarn, Suggestions in Regard to the Proposed Commission on the
Negro, Jan. 14, 1913, all in Villard Papers.

[36]Villard to Wilson, Aug. 27, 1913, Villard Papers.

groes to the Democratic party. Unfortunately, there are no satisfactory statistics to indicate just how many Negroes broke away to vote for Wilson in 1912, or how many deserted the Democrats in 1916. Beyond just holding their own, the Democrats seemed unable to absorb any significant portion of the Negro voters who had defected from Republicanism to support the Progressive ticket in 1912. General contemporary comment indicates that Negroes "returned en masse to the party of liberation."[37] In Negro Harlem, for instance, the Democratic vote slipped from 23.29 to 20.23 per cent, while the Republican share jumped from 17.67 to 77.99 per cent, undoubtedly including the 56.63 per cent who had voted for Roosevelt in 1912.[38] More important than the overall tallies, leaders of the race who stumped for the Democrats in 1912 faced the 1916 election with nothing but distaste for Wilson. Their continued allegiance, promising future Democratic dividends of large-scale Negro support, would have been especially valuable.

Surely, Negroes in general found in their press little reason to stick with the Democrats. The New York *Age*, expressing the philosophy of Booker T. Washington and a supporter of Taft in 1912, declared for Charles Evans Hughes, as did the Washington *Bee*.[39] The NAACP solicited explicit statements on the race question from both candidates. Tumulty responded for Wilson with a noncommittal "he stands by his original assurances. He can say with a clear conscience that he has tried to live up to them, though in some cases his endeavors have been defeated."[40] Hughes never answered the NAACP's letter, and left himself to be judged on the basis of a Nashville campaign pledge of "equal and exact justice to all. I stand for the maintenance of the rights of all American citizens, regardless of race or color."[41] At first Association leaders reluctantly found Hughes "practically the only candidate for whom Negroes can vote." The *Crisis* eventually urged Negroes to disown both major party candidates, suggesting formation of an all-Negro party and ultimately advising abstention or a vote for the Socialist candidate.[42]

[37]Moon, 97.

[38]At the time of the 1912 election Harlem Negroes had clustered in some two dozen blocks, indicated in detail in a map in Victor R. Daly, "The Housing Crisis in New York City," *Crisis*, Dec. 1920, p. 61. These votes are from fourteen election districts from the Twenty-first and Thirtieth Assembly Districts (selected from Assembly District slides in New York City's Municipal Reference Library) corresponding to the blocks most densely populated by Negroes. The returns are drawn from the "Official Canvass of the Votes Cast in the Counties of New York, Kings, Queens, and Richmond at the Election Held November 5, 1912," *City Record*, XL (Dec. 31, 1912), 2–119, and "Official Canvass of the Votes Cast in the Counties of New York, Bronx, Kings, Queens and Richmond at the Election Held November 7, 1916," *City Record*, XLIV (Dec. 30, 1916), 2–129.

[39]New York *Age*, Nov. 2, 1916; Washington *Bee*, Nov. 2, 1912, Nov. 1916, *passim*.

[40]NAACP to Wilson, Oct. 10, 1916, Wilson Papers; *Crisis*, Dec. 1916, pp. 84–85.

[41]*Crisis*, Nov. 1916, pp. 16–17, 33–34; Francis L. Broderick, *W. E. B. Du Bois: Negro Leader in a Time of Crisis* (Stanford, 1959), 94–95; NAACP to Hughes, Sept. 14, 1916, Villard Papers.

[42]*Crisis*, Oct. 1916, p. 268, Nov. 1916, p. 12.

In sum, in 1916 Negro leaders found their race courted by neither party. Despite years of agonizing controversy over their place in Progressivism, the political establishment was again trying its best to ignore the Negro question. Looking back on the election the *Crisis* summed up best of all the frustrating lack of progress toward enlisting those in power in the cause of a democracy not limited by the color line. By the peak of the Progressive era the President had proven "satisfactory as a reducer of the tariff, a promoter of currency reform, and as a man of Peace." "But," the editors wrote, "he was still the representative of the southern Negro-hating oligarchy, and acknowledged its leadership." By the same token, "Mr. Hughes was the author of several of the best decisions in favor of the Negro that the reluctant Supreme Court has ever handed down. At the same time, on specific Negro problems he was curiously dumb."[43]

IV

Why were Negroes and white liberals unsuccessful in extending the boundaries of a Progressivism limited "to whites only"? Wilson argued that his sentiments were on the side of the protesters, but that courting Southern senatorial support for his Progressive legislative package made it impossible for him to act in their behalf. Yet he straightforwardly advocated "separate but equal" as mutually beneficial to both races.

It is too easy, however, to attribute the stalemate to executive inhibitions alone. The key still seems to lie in the nature of the protest. Negro groups lacked a cohesive, tightly organized program. Gaining the right to vote, and fighting lynching, preoccupied much of their effort. This was the decade of landmark Supreme Court decisions striking down the Grandfather Clauses in state voting requirements and levelling an initial blow at residential segregation. For many, these struggles were much more important than gaining political positions. But Negroes disagreed over more than just priorities affecting their race alone. Looking at the national scene, many played down their grievances; "we believe," a North Carolina cleric told Wilson after Trotter's White House demands, "that he should not have approached you with a minor domestic protest when you are filled with graver responsibilities . . . ."[44]

These disavowals were well calculated to cripple the effectiveness of any organized protest. The Negroes who wrote to the President claiming that "Mr. Trotter does not represent the Negroes of the United States," or that "the more thoughtful" members of the race "don't approve of Mr. Trotter's insult to you," may honestly have been ashamed of his reported

[43]*Ibid.*, Dec. 1916, p. 59. See, also [NAACP], *Freeing America: Seventh Annual Report of the National Association for the Advancement of Colored People* (New York, 1917), unpaginated.

[44]Du Bois, *Dusk of Dawn*, 228; Work, *Negro Year Book*, 1916–1917, 51; Walton to Tumulty, March 25, 1913, E. D. W. Jones to Wilson, Nov. 13, 1914, both in Wilson Papers.

disrespect.[45] But they also testified to the exceptional fragmentation of Negro leadership. Theirs was largely the fading gasp of a Washingtonian theory of Negro conduct, reflecting the growing split in Negro philosophies of self-advancement.

In previous Republican administrations Booker T. Washington had been recognized as "the office broker for the race," or chief consultant on Negro patronage and policies. Publicly conciliatory toward the white South, the Tuskegee educator subordinated eventual attainment of political and civil rights to the more immediate goals of moral and economic progress through self-help and vocational training. The Wilson administration found Washington newly out of favor not only in official circles, but also among the ranks of leading Negroes.[46] New expectations and new spokesmen came to prominence with the Democrats. Seriously challenging the old, more accommodating outlook, fathers of the Niagara Movement, like Du Bois and Trotter, stressed immediate equality—social, economic, *and* political—and urged agitation to reach these goals. The inability of these men to agree among themselves contributed to a proliferation of loose factions and formal groups all in the same fight without meaningful coordination of efforts.

The protest movements petered out, too, because they eventually lost even their divided leadership. Villard, certainly their most influential white spokesman, became preoccupied with keeping the United States out of World War I. Washington died early in 1915, and Bishop Alexander Walters ("the new political leader of his race for the incoming Democratic administration at Washington") was dead before Wilson's second inaugural. Discredited (however unfairly) among Negroes and whites alike after the White House incident, Trotter quickly began to "slip . . . out of the main current of the protest movement." A foe of accommodation, he nonetheless divorced himself from the activist Du Boisian camp, and never took full advantage of cooperation with white liberals.[47] Du Bois, too, had already generated considerable friction with white NAACP leaders. In 1916 he decisively curbed his effectiveness when he told Negroes, in effect, to throw away their votes and abandon the regular political process, surely their best hope for any kind of influence on the status of the race in Wilsonian Progressivism.

Even if we accept this analysis of deficiencies in the protest movement, it is still important to ask whether we may not be overstating the case. In short, could Negroes have been expected to make much of a dent in Wilsonian segregation policies? The national apotheosis of Jim Crow militated strongly against any possible hope of success for the champions

[45]E. D. W. Jones to Wilson; I. W. L. Roundtree to Wilson, Nov. 13, 1914, Wilson Papers.

[46]Villard to Charles Dyer Norton, Sept. 20, 1910, Villard Papers; Du Bois, *Dusk of Dawn*, 71; Broderick, 114; Meier, *Negro Thought in America, 1880–1915; Racial Ideologies in the Age of Booker T. Washington* (Ann Arbor, 1963), *passim*.

[47]New York *Age*, Dec. 5, 1912; Puttkammer and Worthy, 309.

of the Negro cause. But the generation of the current Negro revolution may still wonder over the striking lack of militancy in the protests of the Progressive era. The afflicted exercised unusual restraint and self-discipline, engaging in thoroughly polite, deferential opposition. In the second decade of this century, hardly more than a generation removed from the demise of Reconstruction, Negroes were in considerable part an ex-slave population. Their educational level and political consciousness were still barely above a minimum. It is a commonly accepted principle of social science that a submerged group must reach a certain plateau before it can even begin to rebel, and most Negroes of the Wilson era were still struggling toward that level. The birth of the NAACP, fusing white liberal strength into the Niagara Movement, was barely three years past when Wilson took office. The transition in Negro thinking from a Washingtonian to a Du Boisian approach was an important one, and one whose earliest stages coincided with the birth of the New Freedom. Negro protest, symbolized and centralized chiefly in the NAACP, was a very new, highly improvised instrument in the Wilson era—an instrument which took nearly forty years to impress upon the nation the gravity and sincerity of its purpose.

Melvyn Dubofsky

THE RADICALISM OF THE DISPOSSESSED: WILLIAM HAYWOOD AND THE IWW

The Negroes Weiss writes about were frustrated pariahs anxious to participate in a social and political system which excluded them. In this article Melvyn Dubofsky reminds us that there are always those radicals who, unlike the Negro petitioners to President Wilson, would prefer to create their own system rather than submit to the iniquities of the existing one. The International Workers of the World, the Wobblies, for instance, were native American revolutionaries, romantic individuals who endeavored to overthrow the old exploiting order and erect an industrial utopia in its place. They developed the organization which Negroes lacked, but they refused to use the political processes to which Negroes sought entry. The Wobblies nearly completely rejected the American way

*of life; they were as alienated from our society as any group we are likely
to encounter in American history.*

*In recent years several books about the Wobblies have appeared, and
perhaps this interest is a sign of the growing alienation of elements of contemporary America. Beyond doubt, some readers are tempted to draw
parallels with modern radicals who reject the tenets of society and grapple with authority. The Wobblies refused to be absorbed by the bread-
and-butter unions in the American labor tradition or to accept a tranquil
socialist role. They were losers in a society which loathed them and felt
threatened by their ambitions. Yet the story of their conflict tells us a
great deal about the winning opposition and its repressive methods.*

. . . Haywood, St. John, and the ɪww created a derivative but distinctly
American radicalism. ɪww beliefs must be understood in terms of those to
whom the organization appealed and those whom it tried to organize.
After 1908 the ɪww concentrated upon workers who had been neglected
by the mainstream American labor movement. To "timber beasts," hobo
harvesters, itinerant construction hands, the exploited East and South European immigrants, racially excluded Negroes, Mexican, and Asian Americans the ɪww promised a new day. As Haywood told an inquisitive
reporter: "Here were millions and millions of people working desperately
and barely able to exist. All I needed was to stir those millions into a sense
of their wrongs."

Rexford G. Tugwell aptly described the kind of worker to whom the
ɪww carried its radical gospel. Writing about the Pacific Northwest logger,
Tugwell noted:

> His eyes are dull and reddened; his joints are stiff with the rheumatism al-
> most universal in the wettest climate in the world; his teeth are rotting; he
> is wracked with strange diseases and tortured by unrealized dreams that
> haunt his soul. . . . The blanket-stiff is a man without a home. . . . The void
> of his atrophied affections is filled with a resentful despair and bitterness
> against the society that self-righteously cast him out.

Wobbly recruits were Marx's *Lumpenproletariat,* individuals who felt
marginal, helpless, dependent, inferior. Impotent and alienated, they
harbored deep-seated grievances against the institutions of the ruling class:
police, government, and church. Although ɪww leaders did not come
from the ranks of these disinherited, they shared their alienation.

The disinherited joined the ɪww by the thousands because it offered, in

From "The Radicalism of the Dispossessed: William Haywood and the ɪww," by
Melvyn Dubofsky. Complete text originally published in *Dissent: Explorations in the
History of American Radicalism,* edited by Alfred F. Young, copyright © 1968 by
Northern Illinois University Press. Reprinted by permission of the publisher.

the words of Carleton Parker, "a ready-made dream of a new world where there is a new touch with sweetness and light and where for a while they can escape the torture of forever being indecently kicked about." To migratory workers the iww promised "the only social break in the harsh search for work that they have ever had: its headquarters the only competitor of the saloon in which they are welcome."

More important, the iww also promised its followers a way out of their "culture of poverty." It endowed them with class consciousness, organization, solidarity, hope for the future; that is, with a sense of identification with larger social groups that might destroy the psychological and social core of their marginality, dependence, and impotence. It tried to give them what revolutionaries the world over usually see as an absolute necessity: a sense of self-respect, importance, and power—a feeling that the disinherited were humanity's last best hope.

iww ideology visualized the downtrodden emerging from the abyss. They would seize industry for themselves; mere crumbs from their masters' tables were not enough. "We are many," proclaimed the iww's newspapers. "We are resourceful; we are animated by the most glorious vision of the ages; we cannot be conquered, and *we shall conquer the world for the working class.*" Simply put in the iww's favorite revolutionary hymn, the *Internationale*: "We have been *naught*—We shall be All!"

But Wobblies did not expect their revolution to make itself. It was inevitable, but they would help the course of history. "Our organization is not content with merely making the prophecy," insisted *Solidarity*, "but acts upon industrial and social conditions with a view to shaping them in accord with the general tendency." To help history, the Wobblies followed the pattern of all modern revolutionaries: they proposed a program, developed a doctrine concerning the transfer of power, and elaborated a system of organization. Unlike most other modern revolutionaries, however, with the exception of the anarcho-syndicalists whom they resembled, Wobblies rejected purely political tactics and organizations. The Wobblies believed they could best make history by obtaining power. Who held power ruled society!

The iww proposed to transfer power from the capitalists, who held it and used it for antisocial purposes, to the proletariat, who would exercise power for the benefit of humanity. Jack London in *The Iron Heel*, a novel referred to often and lovingly by Wobblies, expressed better than any iww editorial or pamphlet the organization's feelings about power. London's hero, Ernest Everhardt—a fictional Haywood—affirmed that "Power . . . is what we of the working class preach. We know and well we know by bitter experience, that no appeal for the right, for justice, for humanity can ever touch you. . . . So we have preached power." And he concluded, as coldly as London's capitalist, "Power will be the arbiter, as it has always been the arbiter. . . . We of the labor hosts have conned that word over till our minds are all a-tingle with it. Power. It is a kingly word."

The doctrine had Darwinian overtones. In its widely circulated organizing pamphlet for lumber workers the iww emphasized: "It is the law of nature that the strong rule and the weak are enslaved." George Speed, a veteran West Coast trade unionist and charter member of the iww, expressed the iww concept tersely: "Power is the thing that determines everything today . . . it stands to reason that the fellow that has got the big club swings it over the balance. That is life as it exists today." Thus workers had to develop their own sources of power; nobody could do it for them— neither Socialists, political action, nor legislation. "That is my contention," argued Speed. "They have to learn to do it themselves, and they are going to suffer until they do learn."

iww antipathy toward political action reflected the status of its members. Migratory workers moved too often to establish legal voting residences. Millions of unnaturalized immigrants lacking the franchise. So did Negroes, and women, and children, to whom the iww opened its doors. As Haywood informed the Commission on Industrial Relations: "The wage earner or producing classes are in the minority; second . . . they are not educated to the game of politics . . . their life is altogether industrial." Even immigrants and the native born who had the right to vote nourished a deep suspicion of government. The state, symbolized by the policeman's club and the magistrate's edict, hardly treated the poor kindly. Wobblies realized that the power of the state was used against them. Who knew better than an iww, who had been imprisoned for exercising his right of free speech or clubbed by a cop while peacefully picketing for higher wages? Wobblies never believed that stuffing pieces of paper, even socialist ones, into a ballot box would transform this repressive state into a humane one.

If the workers could not use political power to alter the rules of the game, what remained? Wobblies thought they had the answer. "Political power," said one, "is a reflex of economic power, and those who control economic power control the political power of the state." Another concluded: "Without economic power working-class political action is like a house without a foundation or a dream without substance."

iww leaders therefore taught their followers how to achieve economic power. "Get it through industrial organization." "Organize the workers to control the use of their labor power." "The secret of power is organization." "The only force that can break . . . tyrannical rule . . . is one big union of all the workers."

Through organization the iww could exert direct action, its essential means of bringing the new society into existence. By direct action it meant "any economic step taken by the workers. . . . It includes sabotage . . . passive resistance . . . and covers the ordinary strike, the intermittent strike, the silent strike, and the death blow to capitalism in the form of the social general strike." "Shall I tell you what direct action really means?" another iww manifesto asked. "The worker on the job shall tell the boss when and where he shall work, how long, and for what wages and under what conditions." Direct action, according to Haywood, would eventually reach the point where workers were strong enough to say: " 'Here, Mr. Stockholder, we won't work for you any longer. You have drawn dividends out of our hides long enough; we propose that you shall go to work now, and under the same opportunities that we have had.' "

Wobblies, in their emphasis on direct action, liked to compare themselves to ante bellum abolitionists, who had also defied the laws that sanctioned human bondage and who had publicly burned the American Constitution. "We are the modern abolitionists fighting against wage slavery," proclaimed general organizer James Thompson. Wobblies were willing to unsheath the Lord's terrible swift sword.

Although the IWW employed the vocabulary of violence, more often than not it utilized passive resistance and was itself the victim of violence that was instigated by law-enforcement officials, condoned by the law-abiding. The IWW, in fact, sought through organized activities to channel the frustrations and antisocial rage of the dispossessed into constructive courses. Even Haywood, whose career with the Western Federation had been associated with labor violence, told a reporter during the 1912 Lawrence textile strike: "I should never think of conducting a strike in the old way. . . . I, for one, have turned my back on violence. It wins nothing. When we strike now, we strike with our hands in our pockets. We have a new kind of violence—the havoc we raise with money by laying down our tools. Pure strength lies in the overwhelming power of numbers."

Wobblies also looked to nonviolent tactics in order to expose the brutality of their enemy and to win sympathy for their suffering. Passive resistance, editorialized *Solidarity*, "has a tremendous moral effect; it puts the enemy on record; it exposes the police and city authorities as a bunch of law breakers; it drives the masters to the last ditch of resistance. 'Passive resistance' by the workers results in laying bare the inner workings and purposes of the capitalist mind. It also reveals the self-control, the fortitude, the courage, the inherent sense of order, of the workers' mind. As such, 'passive resistance' is of immense educational value."

But IWW passive resistance should not be confused with pacifism. Nonviolence was only a means, never an end, and if passive resistance led only to beatings and deaths, the IWW threatened to respond in kind. Arturo Giovanitti, a sometime poet, sometime Wobbly, put the IWW's position bluntly: "The generally accepted notion seems to be that to kill is a great crime, but to be killed is the greatest." And Haywood cited Abraham Lincoln's alleged advice to citizens who suffered from hunger as a result of wartime food speculation: "Take your pick-axes and crowbars and go to the granaries and warehouses and help yourselves." That, said Haywood, "is a good I.W.W. doctrine."

In keeping with its commitment to nonviolence (at least when lacking the power to employ violence), the IWW even saw its revolution coming peaceably. It would come, according to Haywood, when "labor was organized and self-disciplined [so] it could stop every wheel in the United

States ... and sweep off your capitalists and State legislatures and politicians into the sea." The only violence involved, he added, would occur
after labor had drained the capitalists' pocketbooks.

The nonviolent overthrow of capitalism would result from a general
strike. Neither Haywood nor any other Wobbly, however, ever precisely
defined the general strike, but Haywood explained it as the stoppage of
all work and the destruction of the capitalists through a peaceful paralysis
of industry. Ben Williams insisted that it was no strike at all—simply "a
'general lockout of the employing class' leaving the workers in possession
of the machinery of distribution and production." Whatever the exact
definition of the general strike, Haywood wrote, whenever its day came
"control of industry will pass from the capitalists to the masses and capitalists will vanish from the face of the earth." This utopian day would
come peaceably if workers had their way, and violently if capitalists attempted to postpone it with "roar of shell and whine of machine-guns."

In Haywood's dream of his utopia, "there will be a new society sometime in which there will be no battle between capitalist and wage earner,
but ... every man will have free access to land and its resources. In that
day ... the machinery can be made the slave of the people instead of a
part of the people being made the slave of machinery." Another Wobbly's
utopia would have no room for poverty, jails, police, the army and
marines, Christians, churches, heaven and hell. Its cities would be clean
and beautiful, with wide streets, parks, flowers, and fine homes and its
workers "no longer stoop shouldered and consumptive looking." Prudery
would disappear, along with heaven and hell, and naked children would
frisk on the grass and bask in the sunshine. With economic freedom in
this utopia and an abundance of food, shelter, clothing, and leisure, and
education for everyone, "all hearts and minds [would be] turned towards
solving the mysteries of the Universe."

Wobblies never quite explained how this paradise would be governed; they agreed, however, that the state—as most Americans knew
it—would be nonexistent. "There will be no such thing as the State or
States," Haywood said. "The industries will take the place of what are now
existing States." "Whenever the workers are organized in the industry,
whenever they have a sufficient organization in the industry," added St.
John, "they will have all the government they need right there."

Somehow, each industrial union would possess and manage its own industry. Union members would elect superintendents, foremen, secretaries,
and managers. The separate industrial unions would then meet jointly to
plan for the welfare of society as a whole. This system, "in which each
worker will have a share in the ownership and a voice in the control of
industry, and in which each shall receive the full product of his labor,"
was variously called "the Cooperative Commonwealth," "the Workers'
Commonwealth," "the Industrial Commonwealth," "Industrial Democracy,"
and "Industrial Communism." Unsure of its proposed system, the IWW could
not label it definitively.

Like European syndicalists, the Wobblies aimed to abolish capitalism by nonpolitical means; and, like them, they also emphasized direct action. In the IWW's new society, as in that projected by European syndicalism, the political state would not exist; workers would administer industry directly through their industrial unions. The IWW even took over The French syndicalist concept of the militant minority. "Our task," said an IWW paper, "is to develop the conscious, intelligent minority to the point where they will be capable of carrying out the imperfectly expressed desires of the toiling millions." As a perceptive Socialist theorist noted, notwithstanding superficial variations caused by different economic and political conditions in different countries, "this living spirit of revolutionary purpose unifies French and British syndicalism and American Industrial Unionism (the IWW)."

Industrial unionism, Haywood once stated, was socialism "with its working clothes on." After 1913, however, when Haywood was recalled from the Socialist Party's highest council, IWW industrial unionists and American Socialists had little in common. When Socialists talked of capturing control of the government through the ballot box and of transforming the capitalist state into the "Cooperative Commonwealth," the IWW responded: "A wise tailor does not put stitches into rotten cloth."

Wobblies might obey the law, use the voting booth, and temporize on their revolutionism, but they could never—despite the intellectuals among them—entirely forego anti-intellectualism. To Socialists who prided themselves on their intellectual abilities, Haywood said: "Socialism is so plain, so clear, so simple that when a person becomes intellectual he doesn't understand socialism." IWW ideology always remained that of the poor, not of the educated; it was intended to motivate the disinherited, not to satisfy the learned. As an IWW member noted, reviewing John Graham Brooks' *American Syndicalism:* "It is not the Sorels . . . the Wallings, LaMontes and such figures who count for the most—it is the obscure Bill Jones on the firing line, with stink in his clothes, rebellion in his brain, hope in his heart, determination in his eye and direct action in his gnarled fist."

V

In the last analysis, the Wobblies and Haywood must be remembered more for what they did than for what they thought, more for what they fought for than what they learned. In 1914, the year he became the IWW's top official, Haywood succinctly explained the organization's role. "It has developed among the lowest strata of wage slaves in America a sense of their importance and capabilities such as never before existed. Assuming control and responsibility of their own affairs, the unorganized and unfortunate have been brought together, and have conducted some of the most unique strikes, fights for free speech and battles for constitutional rights." And that is just what the organization did both before and after Haywood took command of the IWW. From 1909 to 1917 it led workers who were neglected by other labor organizations in struggles that raised their self-esteem and improved their conditions of life.

By fighting for free speech in Spokane, Fresno, Missoula, Sioux City, and Minot (among other cities), the IWW proved to long-brutalized migratories that authority could be defeated through direct action and passive resistance. Taking to the streets in defense of their civil liberties, Wobblies courted arrest, and those arrested were quickly replaced on soap boxes by other free-speech speakers. Wobblies flooded the jails, paralyzed the courtrooms, and strained the purses of the cities they confronted. Most civic authorities, unable to cope with such passive resistance on a mass scale, succumbed to IWW demands; but some authorities, like San Diego's, dealt with the IWW "menace" by methods later made infamous in Mussolini's Italy and Hitler's Germany. The IWW also achieved reforms in private employment agencies that had traditionally exploited migratories, and improved working conditions in farming and forestry.

In industrial centers such as McKees Rocks (steel, in 1909), Lawrence (textiles, in 1912), Paterson (textiles, in 1913), and Akron (rubber, in 1913), the IWW showed mass-production workers the possibilities of industrial unionism. It also tempered ethnic divisions by organizing without regard to distinctions of national origin. Most important, the IWW taught previously unorganized mass-production workers how to wage their own struggles for improvement. IWW members learned industrial warfare and union tactics in the manner Marxist theorists and even John Dewey prescribed—by doing! If Wobbly strikers wanted higher wages, shorter hours, and better conditions, their organizers let them fight for them. If workers wanted agreements with their employers, IWW leaders let their followers negotiate them. The IWW organized, agitated, advised; but it was the workers themselves who led and decided. When authorities queried IWW strikers about their leaders, the men and women could respond in a single voice: "We are all leaders."

After the Wobblies' surprising strike victory at Lawrence in 1912, the revolution seemed near at hand. Commentators forgot about the rising tide of socialism and began to worry about the more dangerous threat of revolutionary industrial unionism. Such intellectuals as Max Eastman and the young John Reed saw in the IWW the agency that would accomplish the Nietzschean transvaluation of the values of existing society. And they saw William Haywood as the archetypal Nietzschean superman, as Jack London's Ernest Everhardt come to life. Haywood became the darling of New York's Greenwich Village rebels, enjoying the role of star proletarian performer in Mable Dodge Luhan's Fifth Avenue salon.

But the IWW's revolutionary threat disappeared as quickly as it had come; victory in Lawrence was followed by defeat in Paterson, Akron, and other Eastern cities. Economic adversity aggravated organizational ills. When the American economy declined in 1913 and 1914, IWW membership, never more than thirty thousand before 1916, fell to about fifteen thousand in 1915. By December, 1914, Haywood reported a bankrupt treasury and the IWW seemed on the verge of extinction. No longer did leading journals warn about the dangers of industrial unionism.

From 1909 to 1915, although the IWW had demonstrated to a segment of the American proletariat the virtues of organization, solidarity, and direct action, it could not keep them organized or united. It contended against forces that were simply too powerful to defeat. Employers, supported by local, state, and federal authorities, could vitiate IWW organizing efforts either through outright repression, or with the aid of progressive reforms, could offer workers immediate palliatives.

Throughout its history the IWW faced paradoxes the organization never resolved. If it offered only perpetual industrial warfare, how could it maintain its membership, let alone increase it? But if it won better contracts, and union recognition, and improved life for its members, what was to keep them from forswearing revolutionary goals and from following the established AFL pattern? If it declared a truce in the class war, how could it bring about the ultimate revolution? In the end, IWW leaders, including Haywood, subordinated reform opportunities to revolutionary necessities; the rank and file, when it could, took the reforms and neglected the revolution.

In adversity and decline, however, the IWW learned important lessons. In the summer of 1914 it began to concentrate upon the hardcore disinherited—the migrant workers who harvested the nation's wheat, picked its hops, cut its lumber, built its railroads, and mined its copper. To these men the IWW offered a purpose in life and a sense of identity and value; to the IWW they, in turn, gave allegiance and strength.

Migratories joined the IWW in increasing numbers as the organization demonstrated that it could improve their conditions of work. When Haywood took over the general headquarters in November, 1914, the IWW was almost broke. A year later, after its Agricultural Workers' Organization had begun an organizing campaign in the wheat belt, the IWW had a surplus in its treasury and thousands of new members on its roster, and it paid organizers to carry its word to lumber and construction workers and hardrock miners. The message Wobbly organizers carried in 1915 and 1916 emphasized organization, not revolution, and immediate gains, not utopian ideology. The new message was heard. Membership rose between 1915 and early 1917 to between sixty thousand and one hundred thousand. By 1916 the Wobblies could charter new industrial unions for lumber workers, hardrock miners, and construction hands.

As its membership and treasury increased, the IWW's tone seemed to alter. The 1916 convention was the first convention that fully asserted the authority of general headquarters; separate industrial unions were to be subject to closer supervision by Haywood's new, centralized Chicago office. Those who disagreed with the new emphasis or disliked Haywood's predominant influence left the IWW or were relegated to obscurity within the organization. After 1916 Elizabeth Gurley Flynn, Joseph Ettor, Arturo Giovanitti, and Carlo Tresca (among others)—leaders who had once shared the headlines and national publicity with Haywood—were pushed into the background. They were replaced by a new breed of Wobblies, those who propagandized less and organized more. Over this new iww, which flourished as never before, presided William D. Haywood.

Sitting behind his large roll-type desk at the new iww headquarters on Chicago's West Madison Street, Haywood never seemed happier than early in 1917. Ralph Chaplin, then the editor of *Solidarity*, later remembered that Haywood, his boss and close friend, appeared more self-assured, more firm of voice, and more youthful as he worked among busy clerks and secretaries. Haywood seemed "a revolutionary tycoon whose dream was coming true." His enthusiasm infected everyone at iww headquarters, which, in its effort "to build the new society within the shell of the old," became one of the liveliest places in Chicago. But Haywood's happiness and enthusiasm would prove shortlived; so, too, would the iww's success and growth. The factors that had brought the iww prosperity presaged its death, and Haywood's exile.

The European conflict contributed greatly to iww resurgence under Haywood, as war orders poured into the American market. Rising production brought rising profits and increasing labor scarcity. In a tight labor market the iww could not only organize successfully, it could also win material improvements for its members inasmuch as employers were loath to sacrifice wartime profits to anti-union principles. But when America intervened in April, 1917, employers discovered how they could have profits without the iww.

The iww had long preached antimilitarism and antipatriotism as basic principles, and the war did not make any changes in this, but the iww now concentrated upon organized, direct action, and on-the-job activities. It was too busy organizing harvest hands, lumber workers, and miners to lead antiwar campaigns. It was too busy fighting for higher wages and shorter hours to waste its time in an anti-conscription drive. The iww did nothing directly to interfere with the American war effort, but it did organize and strike in industries that were vital to that effort.

In the spring of 1917 iww strikes threatened the lumber industry, copper mining, and the wheat harvest. Stories were spread which received credence in the Justice and War Departments, that iww strikes were German-inspired and German-financed. Western employers pleaded with state and national authorities to suppress the iww in the interest of national security; they also took direct action of their own, organizing Citizens' Alliances and Vigilante Leagues, some of these with the sanction of the Justice Department. These vigilantes hunted out every worker who threatened war profits.

Everywhere the iww found itself beset by enemies. Local and state officials joined private businessmen in persecuting Wobblies. If their action proved ineffective, officials demanded federal intervention, and before long federal troops patrolled West Coast docks, Northwest woods and farmlands, and the mining towns of Arizona and Montana. Simultaneously, the Justice Department and Military Intelligence infiltrated agents into the IWW. Between Pinkertons, Thiel detectives, and federal agents, spies had the IWW under constant surveillance. Even the Labor Department, less anxious and more realistic about Western labor conflicts than the War and Justice Departments, did its part to curb the IWW. Labor Department agents, however, also tried to use the war crisis to improve working conditions, as well as to induce IWW laborers to join AFL affiliates. With Gompers' hearty approval and direct cooperation, the Labor Department attacked the IWW menace, promoting the AFL cause.

When these efforts failed to end the IWW's threat to Western industries, the federal government—pressured by private business, state governors, United States attorneys, and influential congressmen—took the final step. With presidential approval, the Justice Department proscribed the IWW. In a nationwide series of raids on September 5, 1917, the department's agents invaded every important IWW headquarters, seizing everything they could lay their hands on (including rubber bands, paper clips, and Ralph Chaplin's love letters). Sorting through tons of confiscated material, the Justice Department assembled the evidence to indict IWW leaders for sedition, espionage, and interference with the war effort.

By the end of 1917 almost every important IWW official, including Haywood, was in prison. In the interests of national security, industrial harmony, and business profits, the government put the IWW under lock and key. Due process followed, but what happened in the courtrooms in which Wobbly leaders were tried, convicted, and sentenced was only a legal charade. Whether in Chicago, Wichita, or Sacramento, the trial evidence was always the same, as were the results. In every case the IWW— as an organization, not its individual leaders or members—was placed on trial. In every case the IWW was judged not for what it had done but for what it said and wrote, although most of the "seditious" writings and speeches antedated America's overseas involvement and, to a great extent, 1914.

Some subordinates in the Justice Department realized that the government did not have a valid case against the IWW. They suggested that, in the interest of justice, trials be postponed until wartime hysteria subsided, but the Justice Department would not listen to such an argument. To its top officials, many drawn from Wall Street law offices, and often associates of leading businessmen, the IWW represented a real menace, both to America's war effort and to business profits. The trials went on and Wobbly leaders were sent to Leavenworth.

Thus ended the IWW's threat to the prevailing order. New and inexperienced Wobbly leaders took to fighting among themselves, becoming easy prey to the Pinkertons and military intelligence agents who continued to infiltrate the organization. And thus ended Haywood's role in the history of American radicalism. In 1917 he had led a dynamic organization that posed a growing threat to the established order. In 1918, after smashing the IWW, the United States government in effect said to Haywood and his fellow Wobblies what Leon Trotsky had said to Martov and the Russian Mensheviks after the Bolsheviks' November revolution: "You are miserable isolated individuals. You are bankrupt. You have played out your role. Go where you belong, to the dustheap of history."

VI

Most convicted Wobblies, accepting their punishment and what they thought of as martyrdom, went to Leavenworth, but Haywood refused to surrender. Plagued by a history of ulcers and diabetes, and perhaps by cirrhosis of the liver, and fearful of another prison term, he jumped bail and turned up in the Soviet Union in 1921. Neither his close friends nor inveterate critics knew why he declined martyrdom and chose political exile. Whatever the reason, that decision betrayed Haywood's bail backers, brought them financial loss (and in one case suicide), and turned most of his former IWW comrades against him.

Escape to Russia, however, did not save Haywood from history's dustheap. Not really a Bolshevik, he did not fit into Lenin's or Trotsky's schemes for a new and better world. Expecting to find the Wobblies' utopian workers' state—or nonpolitical anarcho-syndicalist society—he found instead a system busily constructing its own political and industrial bureaucracy. The IWW's anti-organizational approach proved as unacceptable to Russia's new rulers as it had to America's. For a time Haywood directed a labor project in the Kuznets district, but by 1923 his dream of building a Wobbly utopia in Russia had soured.

Tired, sick, the strength draining from his huge body, Haywood retired to a room in Moscow's Lux Hotel. He later married a Russian national, but almost nothing of substance can be discovered about this marriage. Haywood usually kept to his Moscow hotel at the time Alexander Trachtenberg, an American Communist leader, made his pilgrimages to Moscow in the 1920's. Later, Trachtenberg remembered Haywood as a desperately lonely man, alien to Moscow's new society, who found solace only in the bottle and in the companionship of old Wobblies who somehow drifted into his hotel room. They would join their former chief in drink and song, going through the *Little Red Song Book* from cover to cover interminably, until they collapsed in a drunken stupor.

Such was Haywood's Moscow exile; he played no part in the construction of Soviet society. Ailing and frequently hospitalized, he tried to keep abreast of labor developments at home, and he found time to complete his unsatisfactory and distorted autobiography. On May 28, 1928, he died unmourned in a Moscow hospital. Russian officials placed part of his ashes alongside those of John Reed beneath a plaque in the Kremlin wall, and the remaining ashes were shipped to Waldheim Cemetery in Chicago for burial beside the graves of the Haymarket Riot martyrs.

To President Theodore Roosevelt, Haywood was an undesirable citizen; to Frank P. Walsh, reform Democrat and chairman of Woodrow Wilson's

Commission on Industrial Relations, he was the "rugged intellectual, with his facility of phrasing, his marvelous memory and his singularly clear and apt method of illustration." To conservatives, Haywood was the voice of anarchy; to friends and admirers, he was the epitome of sweet, simple reason. To such labor foes as Samuel Gompers, he was an inept propagandizer and a smasher of trade unions; to his supporters, he was an effective administrator and a talented organizer. To Mary Gallagher, who directed the campaign to free Tom Mooney, he was a great leader in every way; to Ramsay MacDonald, he was a rough-hewn agitator, splendid with crowds but ineffectual as an administrator.

Scholars have done little to interpret Haywood's character other than allude to his rebellious spirit and frontier heritage. The essays of Charles Madison and Carl Hein tell us nothing that cannot be found in Haywood's autobiography; and in Patrick Renshaw's recent history of the iww his treatment of Haywood is notable for the number of errors he makes in only three pages. Haywood's grossly inaccurate autobiography is a masterpiece of precise history compared to Renshaw's summary. Perusing the comments of Haywood's contemporaries and the analyses of scholars gives us no understanding of his personality. Unfortunately there is little evidence to support any of the differing versions of Haywood's life.

The only comment one can make with certainty is that Haywood, like most Wobblies, was neither an original thinker nor a theoretician. Haywood, in short, was not plagued by the "hobgoblin of little minds": consistency; his life is a tale of inconsistency.

During his early years with the wfm he displayed outstanding ability as an administrator and organizer. Willing to work long hours and to drive himself furiously, Haywood mastered the intricacies of trade unionism. From 1914 to 1917, in a later and vastly different environment, he also proved to be an industrious union official. During those years, when the iww experienced its most rapid growth, Haywood gave the Wobblies their first taste of effective administration under a rationalized central office. Between these tours of duty as a union official he devoted himself to agitation and to freewheeling revolutionary oratory in which he impressed many observers with his anti-disciplinarian, anti-organizational, anarchistic personality.

The inconsistencies abound. In a life that was shadowed by violence, few radicals ever expressed the doctrine of passive resistance so forcefully or played so prominent a part in nonviolent labor demonstrations. A denigrator of effete intellectuals, Haywood nevertheless had intellectual pretensions of his own. He harangued strikers in the working-class vernacular, but he also read widely (and deeply), and wrote with considerable skill. It is impossible to pinpoint the time when he began to read serious fiction and nonfiction, but during his incarceration in 1917–18 he wrote movingly to Frank Walsh about the latest Mark Twain he had read. As a writer—he was temporary editor of the *Miners' Magazine*, a contributing editor to the *International Socialist Review,* and a regular commentator in the IWW press—Haywood developed from an immature and awkward stylist into a master of the caustic comment and the philippic phrase, if not an author of graceful and closely reasoned economic and social treatises. In his writings and speeches on economics, politics, sex, and religion he wielded one pen in the modern camp of harsh realism and the other in maudlin Victorian romanticism. Haywood appealed to immigrant workers in the East and to migrant workers in the West, as well as to such bohemian intellectuals as John Reed and Max Eastman.

In the last analysis, Haywood fits no pattern. Unlike the typical labor leader, who begins his career as a radical, finds success, and becomes more conservative, Haywood began his union career as a conservative, discovered success, and became a radical. A man of many talents—administrator, organizer, agitator, speaker, writer—he developed none of these to its utmost, which was perhaps his gravest failing. A labor leader who was at home both with wage workers and intellectuals (an unusual combination in the United States), he led a labor organization that was out of touch with most workers and he frustrated many intellectuals by his refusal to accept martyrdom in 1921. In Russia, he neither served American radicalism nor built the new utopia.

Haywood's life and the history of the Wobblies support an ambivalent conclusion about the results of dissent in America. Dissenting at the outset, Wobblies maintained that poor immigrants and dispossessed native Americans could be organized, given a sense of purpose, and taught to confront authority nonviolently. As they proceeded to do just this, American society accommodated the Wobbly-induced radicalism within the existing system. Rexford Tugwell, commenting upon the IWW's ability to organize casual workers, remarked in 1920: "No world re-generating philosophy comes out of them and they are not going to inherit the earth. When we are a bit more orderly they will disappear."

Tugwell was right. During World War I the federal government influenced Western employers to be more "orderly"; lumbermen established company unionism and the eight-hour day, and owners of copper mines improved working conditions and created grievance machinery. Many Wobblies watched American society vitiate their radicalism by accommodating to it, and ended up by joining that society. Ralph Chaplin is the best example of this process: he became a member of the Congregational church, an ardent patriot, and an even more ardent anti-Communist.

Wobblies who did not opt for reform capitalism lost the faith for other reasons. The IWW's anti-organizational credo, its utter abomination of existing institutions, and its refusal (or, perhaps, inability) to conceptualize an alternative of its own to the structural arrangements of American society (so much like the dilemma of the contemporary New Left) resulted in internal anarchy and recurrent secessions, divisions, and organizational collapses. Thus some Wobblies—Elizabeth Gurley Flynn, James P. Cannon, William Z. Foster are good examples—eventually located the disciplined organization they craved in the Communist Party.

Others kept the original faith, never losing their belief in a utopian society bereft of a coercive state. When their dissent moved from speech to action, from criticism to resistance, they felt the heavy hand of a repressive state. If America was capable of domesticating its radicals by offering them reforms, it could also smash them with a vengeance.

Never able to forget his 1915 utopian dream, yet unable to adjust to Communist discipline, Haywood's ashes were divided between the land of his miserable exile and America, among an earlier generation of martyred dissenters.

Robert D. Cuff

BUSINESS, THE STATE, AND WORLD WAR I: THE AMERICAN EXPERIENCE

The progressive era saw a continual redefinition of business-government relationships. Although earlier histories of this period argue that reform was initiated either in Washington by altruistic professionals, or by an alienated middle class, recent research suggests that regulatory changes were sought by businessmen as a means of advancing their group interests. Business in general remained hostile to governmental intervention in private enterprise, but many businessmen viewed the federal government as an instrument which could stabilize an unpredictable economic system. And, as Robert Cuff points out in the following article, some of those businessmen seized the occasion of World War I to extend Washington's involvement as an arbiter in the economy.

The exigencies of World War I prompted a variety of innovations in American public life. Washington subsidized expansion of the merchant marine; took over operation of the railroads; mediated minimum wage and maximum hour disputes between war workers and management; manipulated allocation of raw materials for industry; directly and indirectly controlled prices; and largely violated most precepts of the hallowed free enterprise system. Some businessmen inevitably chafed under this bureaucratic regimentation and tolerated it only because of patriotism or social pressure, or because they knew that the controls were ephemeral. Cuff, however, deals with those businessmen who sought and welcomed Washington's involvement in the hope that it would establish some precedents for ordering an inefficient and chaotic marketplace.

Many of the wartime government practices encouraged normally illegal business activities. The most obvious case is that of the anti-trust laws: in 1917 did businessmen intentionally abrogate the anti-trust rules? How did they attempt to set new rules which would govern trusts, pricing, and corporate cooperation in the post-war period? Was the War Industries Board of World War I the first "military-industrial complex" in our history?

Creation of a large emergency government was one of the most characteristic features of the war effort in the United States, as it was in every country. But while this bureaucratic explosion bulks large in history, it has received surprisingly little attention in American historiography. Students of the war years have not given this phenomenon nearly the attention it deserves. For the most part, we still derive our understanding of wartime administration from contemporary chronicles, or from works written in the 1940s when war planners looked to World War I for a usable past. Many of the histories of mobilization agencies remain to be written; and these individual stories have yet to be integrated into a general analysis of Wilsonian war government.[1]

Within these larger tasks, one of the most critical problems is to analyze the role played by dollar-a-year men in the federal establishment. It is true that businessmen were only one among several social groups to seek positions in the nation's war apparatus in 1917. Private careers and public offices intersected on a grand scale in these years; elite groups from a variety of private institutions involved themselves in governmental administration. Social scientists, social workers, labor leaders, churchmen, and more, flocked to Washington in an unprecedented application of social knowledge to public crisis. Still, none of these groups rivalled the businessmen in government in either numbers or power. After April 6, 1917, all volunteer mobilizers could associate themselves with the powers of a state energized by war, but only the businessmen among them could also tap the enormous power concentrated in large business corporations.

Reprinted from "Business, the State, and World War I: the American Experience," *War and Society in North America*, Robert D. Cuff and Granatstein.

[1]Frederic L. Paxson's *American Democracy and the World War*, 3 vols. (Boston, 1936–1948), still remains the most comprehensive treatment of the war years. Among the war agencies which still require scholarly analysis are the Food Administration, the War Finance Corporation, the War Trade Board, and the Council of National Defense. One of the best surveys to come out of the re-examination of the 1940s is Harold J. Tobin and Percy W. Bidwell, *Mobilizing Civilian America* (New York, 1940).

Only business administrators could possibly become extensions of both public bureaucratic power and private economic power. They had access to those who controlled the means of production as well as to those who directed the state. It was hoped that as brokers between the economy and society, business volunteers could merge private and public power on behalf of the national interest.

Historians have generally subsumed the recruitment and conduct of businessmen in government under the larger story of state expansion during the war. As a result, the image of the businessman in government has benefited from the general conception of the state as a neutral if not beneficent force in American development. This conception, so prevalent in the older Progressive historiography, has regarded state expansion as essentially the triumph of the people over predatory special interests. Recent research has, of course, seriously altered our conception of business, the state and social change, but the onslaught against the older version has not fully permeated discussion of the war years.[2] Revisionist studies of the Progressive era, for example, should alert us to the importance of unsnarling the complex relationship of business groups to public administration in wartime. For if there is one point which these newer studies make crystal clear, it is that state expansion cannot be regarded as springing solely from a desire to subordinate private power to public need.[3] More specifically, this work should raise serious questions about the role of a state which located businessmen in strategic positions in its bureaucratic structure. Could public and private interest be merged, even in wartime? Could businessmen in government transform themselves into neutral public officials? What was the public interest for a businessman in government?

In trying to answer these questions, one must first make clear the kind of businessmen in government who will be studied. A useful distinction can be made between those in central policy-making positions and those on the outer rings of the wartime organization: between agency chairmen and division heads, for instance, and business specialists who occupied positions in the administrative exterior. Now it is true, as so many general administrators discovered, that the narrow specialists dominated their specific preserves by virtue of a superior technical knowledge and closer trade connections, but the central administrators possessed the greatest influence over general questions of public policy. It was the central administrators and their advisors who ultimately set the course for their

[2]The close relationship between business interests and the state in social change is revealed most clearly for the nineteenth century in studies of economic growth. Robert A. Lively has analyzed much of this literature in "The American System: A Review Article," *Business History Review*, XXIX (March, 1955), 81–96.

[3]Among the studies which reflect on this fact, with varying degrees of success, are Gabriel Kolko, *Railroads and Regulation, 1877–1916* (Princeton, 1965) and *The Triumph of Conservatism* (New York, 1963); Robert H. Wiebe, *Businessmen and Reform: A Study of the Progressive Movement* (Cambridge, 1962); and James Weinstein, *The Corporate Ideal in the Liberal State* (Boston, 1968).

respective agencies. Among those who occupied such positions were Walter Gifford, AT&T executive and Director of the Council of National Defense; Howard Coffin, vice president of the Hudson Motor Company and chairman of the Aircraft Production Board; Herbert Hoover, engineer-entrepreneur and chairman of the Food Administration; Edward Hurley, machine-tool manufacturer and president of the United States Shipping Board; Eugene Meyer, Jr., Wall Street banker and a director of the War Finance Corporation; Bernard Baruch, Wall Street speculator and chairman of the War Industries Board; Robert Brookings, retired millionaire and chairman of the WIB's Price Fixing Committee; and Arch Shaw, business theorist, magazine publisher, and head of the WIB's Conservation Division.

These men came into their positions of central authority in diverse ways, and they exhibited very different styles on their march to high office. Of far more interest than such differences, however, are the qualities they held in common and the remarkable congeniality evident between their prewar habits and their wartime functions. Of the hundreds of businessmen in Washington, why did these particular men arrive in positions of high office? Accident alone does not explain the results.

Clearly, their special position in the prewar social structure, and the kind of values derived from it, prepared these administrative *generalists* for their functions during the process of mobilization. Some had already found themselves attracted to careers beyond the narrow grooves of business before 1917; and many others discovered this inner wish during the war itself. Taking up positions between economic and political, private and public institutions in the prewar years, they had already begun to identify with causes beyond a single business interest or beyond a single industry. They had begun to consider the needs of America's economic system as a whole. The further they had progressed in this direction in peacetime, the more valuable they became to the Wilson Administration in wartime. In this way not only could they offer a broad grasp of large administrative problems; they could also present themselves as men above special interests and dedicated to the public interest.

Howard Coffin, Bernard Baruch, and Edward Hurley exemplify the prewar transitional trend very well. As president of the Society of Automobile Engineers in 1910 Coffin saw that the fortunes of the Hudson Motor Company were inextricably intertwined with practices in the auto industry as a whole; after August 1914 Coffin made the question of the automobile industry part of the great problem of industrial conversion for war. Coffin launched an industrial preparedness campaign in 1915, determined to fashion the links between the business community and the military establishment and to design the administrative tools of advanced industrial planning. The same restlessness with private career was evident in Bernard Baruch, who found himself attracted to Democratic politics and industrial preparedness in the prewar years. Embarking upon his new role as presidential advisor, Baruch set about to bind business groups closer to the Wilson Administration for reasons of politics and defense, anxious all the while to have a major post in any prospective mobilization. Edward Hurley, like Baruch, found satisfaction in promoting the Wilson candidacy in 1912 and 1916. More fortunate than his colleague, though, Hurley gained a public post for his pains as vice chairman and then chairman of the Federal Trade Commission in 1915.[4]

These businessmen had confronted general questions of public policy before 1917, and they had already made personal attempts to overcome obstacles in the way of binding together military, business and government institutions. They appreciated the associational values so characteristic of advancing elites in the progressive era.[5] Their thought exhibited a marked integrative quality. They realized that the values and arrangements associated with an older *laissez faire* model no longer met the needs of an emerging corporate economy, and the European war experience after 1914 deepened their understanding of this order on a world scale. They insisted that America integrate her institutional blocs for order and stability, not alone for wartime, but for prosperity and power in the postwar world. Edward Hurley touched on this theme in a speech to the American Iron and Steel Institute in 1916: "Nowhere is cooperation among businessmen, and between them and government, more essential than in the development of our foreign trade," he explained. "The success of our European competitors is evidence enough of this."[6]

These men expected the state to provide guidance and assistance for business in creating the requisite institutional synthesis for war and for peace.[7] Take Arch Shaw, for example. Shaw lectured at the Harvard Business School on the importance of scientific principle in business enterprise, and he lectured to an even wider audience through his journal *System, The Magazine of Business.* Shaw was fascinated by the great changes that war brought to European business. It reaffirmed his belief in efficient method and applied intelligence, and he made his magazine a clearing house for information concerning the implications of war for

[4]George V. Thompson, "Intercompany Technical Standardization in the Early American Automobile Industry," *Journal of Economic History,* XIV (Winter, 1954), 1–20; Lloyd N. Scott, *Naval Consulting Board of the United States* (Washington, 1920), ch. II; Margaret Coit, *Mr. Baruch* (Cambridge, 1957) pp. 109–116, 131–147; Bernard M. Baruch, *My Own Story* (New York, 1957), pp. 176–182, 188, and *The Public Years* (New York, 1960), ch. I; Edward H. Hurley, *The Bridge to France* (Philadelphia, 1927), chs. 1 and 2.

[5]Robert Wiebe describes the outlook of these elites better than anyone else in *The Search For Order, 1877–1920* (New York, 1967), esp. chs. 5, 6 and 7.

[6]*Proceedings of the American Iron and Steel Institute, 1916,* p. 194. For a more extensive statement by Hurley of this theme see his *The Awakening of Business* (Garden City, 1917).

[7]There is a considerable contemporary literature on the virtues of business-government cooperation and the new corporate order. For one of the most intriguing statements see Charles P. Steinmetz, *America and the New Epoch* (New York, 1916).

American business. In January 1917, Shaw publicly called upon the Department of Commerce to shake off its lethargy and encourage American industry in the kind of rationalization which war had fostered among its European competitors. Two months later the Wilson Administration asked Shaw to come to Washington to implement his scheme as chief of an independent bureau in the Council of National Defense.[8]

For Shaw as for the rest, American entry into the war in April 1917 offered an unparalleled opportunity to forward the new industrial synthesis. Owing to the war emergency, public power became available to any private group or private individual who could attach a private strategy to the public cause. Such a development was of special significance to business ideologues and dreamers who could not personally wield the power of big business in private life. Possibly during the wartime emergency they could use the power of the state to mould business and the' nation to their private vision. Washington became a boomtown for organizational entrepreneurs, for men skilled in the bureaucratic technique, for men who sought alliances among the nation's leading institutions on behalf of a powerful, unified, economic system.

Once in Washington every major business advisor sought as much power as the political system would offer; and individuals and groups who obstructed this quest caught the collective scorn of these business statesmen. There were a number of prime offenders, among them businessmen antagonistic to the new corporate order, military departments which clung to older competitive instincts, politicians who objected to the gaping breach in the walls between private and public institutions, and civil servants who resented the wartime intruders. In the debate over the Food Administration, for example, many congressmen doggedly fought the kind of mandate which Herbert Hoover demanded as prospective head. At a very minimum, they preferred to entrust emergency authority to a commission rather than to Hoover alone. The Great Engineer complained later that apparently the American people had forgotten that ". . . a single executive head had been the basic concept of organization of our Government and our business world ever since the foundation of the Republic."[9] Personally, Hoover foresaw no danger in the absence of checks and balances in his administration.

The key descriptive words in the kind of social model these businessmen in government idealized were coordination, centralization, effi-

[8]Shaw outlined his proposal to the Department of Commerce in "In the Day of Prosperity," *System*, XXXI (January, 1917), 123–132. Shaw reprinted excerpts of opinion favourably disposed to his scheme in "Progress for 'A National Business Program'," *System*, XXXI (April, 1917), 444–447. "Plans for Handling War-Time Business," *System*, XXXI (May, 1917), 451–458, illustrates Shaw's use of *System* to transmit European experience to American businessmen. Shaw discusses his war experience in "Statement of Arch Shaw," Papers of Bernard M. Baruch, Princeton University.

[9]Herbert Hoover, *The Ordeal of Woodrow Wilson* (New York, 1958), p. 11.

ciency, and standardization. They displayed an engineering, managerial, manipulative mentality. "If I heard Coffin talking in his sleep," remarked a Washington official during the war, "I wouldn't take the trouble to go over and listen because I would know exactly what he would be saying. 'Standardize! Standardize! Standardize!' That's his motto, his slogan, his creed."[10] Moreover, the major dollar-a-year men demonstrated the same enthusiasm for substituting administrative process for political process as had their reform-minded colleagues during the progressive era.[11] Businessmen both in and out of government preferred to restrict their negotiations to a conference room rather than to open their differences to public debate.

The wartime tenure of the business synthesizers involved a continuous search for the kind of administrative centralization and coordinated public policy which would ease the way for an integrated system of private corporate planning. They were bent on creating through public power the kind of calculable environment in which their colleagues in industry would meet the demands now thrust upon them. They sought administrative centralization and concentrated power so as to secure their positions as champions and protectors of the country's industrial structure. Only insofar as they maintained control could they be sure that those hostile to or ignorant of industry's structural needs would not obstruct the proper process of integration. Obstruction from specific business groups placed them in a difficult and ambiguous position, of course, but it did not alter their rationale. At some points businessmen in government believed they had to act sternly to protect their colleagues in industry from bringing disaster upon themselves.

During the course of national mobilization the business statesmen became synonymous with the very concepts of business-government cooperation and businessmen in government. The myth-making process of wartime propaganda transformed these men into symbols of the corporate structure they aimed to strengthen and protect. As a consequence, their public actions and pronouncements were calculated to win approval not just for a particular functional program—like increased aircraft production or reduced steel consumption—but for the reputation and credibility of the corporate capitalist structure itself. These men, in other words, played for stakes far greater than the businessmen sent to Washington to lobby with them or the narrower specialists in their own organizations. They had to balance the short-run demands of interest-conscious groups with their estimation of the long-run interests and needs of the

---

[10]Quoted in Edwin Wildman, "Howard Coffin And The War In The Air," *Forum,* LIX (March, 1918), 260.

[11]Samuel P. Hays offers one of the best examples of this phenomenon in the prewar years in his "The Politics of Reform in Municipal Government in the Progressive Era," *Pacific Northwest Quarterly,* LV (October, 1964), 157–169. See also James Weinstein, "Organized Business and the City Commission and Manager Movements," *Journal of Southern History,* XXVIII (February, 1962), 162–182.

corporate economy as a whole, and the reputation of business leadership in it.[12]

These dollar-a-year men had to avoid public identification with special interests or with a clearly pro-business position. Confidence in their neutrality was a prerequisite for their credibility with the Wilson Administration, with Congress, with military leaders, and with the public at large. Their ability to shape public policy so as to fashion a stable, corporate capitalist system depended directly on how well they maintained the faith of key leadership groups in major public institutions. Public restraint and caution was an essential feature of their private strategy for power. They had far more freedom to act behind the scenes out of public view. Here, private conscience and institutional realities were the chief constraints. Here, behind the scenes, the administrators took their greatest risks.

The truly remarkable fact, however, is that businessmen in government managed to have it both ways. By a subtle combination of public caution and private daring they were able to serve both the short-run needs of specific interests and the long-run reputation of the business system and its corporate leadership. This is the great debt which the business system of the 1920s owed the dollar-a-year men of the Great War.

No single issue can illustrate all of the general comments made thus far about the business synthesizers of World War I, but the War Industries Board's experience with the antitrust problem helps to bring some of them into sharper focus. It illuminates the kinds of values which were important to men like Baruch and Eugene Meyer, Jr., Baruch's assistant at times during the war; it offers a practical example of their search for institutional coordination, as well as the kinds of obstacles they encountered; and it reveals very well how they succeeded in combining covert assistance to private groups with a renunciation of business pressure to launch a public campaign against traditional values and practices.

Almost every preparedness tactic which Bernard Baruch pursued from the summer of 1916 until he resigned from the WIB chairmanship in November 1918 ran contrary to the antitrust tradition. Throughout his wartime career Baruch strove to create an institutional and legal environment conducive to corporate planning. Especially was this the case in his early war work as head of the government's Committee on Raw Materials. He asked various big businessmen to establish volunteer committees among themselves and to design privately the distribution, price and production schedules for each major industry, nothing less than the cartel-

---

[12]For one example of the myth-making function of wartime propaganda see Robert D. Cuff, "Bernard Baruch: Symbol and Myth in Industrial Mobilization," *Business History Review*, XLIII (Summer, 1969), 115–133. My conception of the ideology of the business synthesizers leans heavily on the work of William Appleman Williams and on James Weinstein's recent book, *The Corporate Ideal in the Liberal State* (Boston, 1968).

ization of the American economy. Baruch readily admitted that his directives and suggestions contravened antitrust laws, but he argued that under such emergency conditions such laws no longer held. In the meantime he lobbied the Wilson Administration for an opinion "that such act or actions, when done for the benefit and in the interests of the Government, are not violations of that Act, and do not place these individuals . . . on those committees subject to penalty."[13]

John Ryan, president of the Anaconda Copper Company and Baruch's contact with that industry, presented the Raw Materials Commissioner with a typical problem in the summer of 1917. Several large producers had formed a cartel for buying in bulk and the Ordnance Department had asked it to make some purchases. In response to this request Ryan wrote Baruch as follows: "The members of the Sub-Committee on Copper do not feel that they should direct the making of a contract by one selling agency for the full amount of copper required by the Ordnance Department, or any other Department of our Government or any of the Allies, but it would undoubtedly facilitate matters and save an endless amount of work and confusion if this could be done." Ryan wanted relief from possible legal challenges for a procedure which he had every intention of pursuing, hoping Baruch would take all responsibility. "As the Sub-Committee on Copper is composed of men who are representing some of the largest producers in the country, they naturally want to be directed to consolidate this business rather than to consolidate it voluntarily, which might be considered open to question as a legal right and might be misconstrued."[14]

According to Ryan, Army and Navy officials had already indicated their approval and only awaited sanction from the proper civilian bodies. In effect, both Ryan and the military officials wanted someone else to assume all the political risks. However, Baruch's office had no intention of being used in this way, especially by the military services. Eugene Meyer, Jr., told Ryan that while no doubt existed about the superiority of the arrangements contemplated by the selling company, Baruch would not sanction them. If the military departments favoured the arrangements, he said, let them give the orders.[15]

Baruch had already endeavoured to breach the formal antitrust barrier but had had no success by July when Ryan made his inquiry. The issue was growing more embarrassing for Baruch, however, as his business clientele cried for action.[16] Editorial writers in the business press delighted in

[13]Raw Materials Committee to Chester C. Bolton, May 23, 1917, Records of the War Industries Board, File 21A–A4, Box 877, Federal Records Center, Suitland, Md.; hereafter cited as RG61.

[14]Ryan to Baruch, July 2, 1917, RG61, File 21A–A4, Box 463.

[15]Meyer, Jr., to Ryan, July 3, 1917, ibid.

[16]Walter S. Gifford to Attorney General Gregory, June 4, 1917, Records of the Council of National Defense, File 2-48, Box 86, Federal Records Center, Suitland, Md.; hereafter cited as RG62.

pointing out the inconsistency of the government's position and its refusal to accept the reality of its own system of supply. They needled the Administration constantly to promise openly an end to all prosecutions. Why not recognize forthrightly that the everyday operations of the cooperative committees contravened antitrust laws and admit the anomaly of the whole enterprise? The war proved the efficiency of bigness and cooperation in industry and this fact ought to be officially admitted.[17] "It has scarcely been realized how events have nullified the Sherman Law, and abrogated important parts of the Interstate Commerce Act," observed the *Wall Street Journal.* "Events, in fact, have shown the way to wise legislation, and it is surely not too much to hope that we have statesmen in Washington able to appreciate their significance."[18]

Baruch wanted to be one of those statesmen. He engaged Joseph Cotton, a prominent corporation lawyer, to do some "devilling" in Washington, as Cotton put it, and the lawyer talked with Justice Department officials in April, but without success.[19] Attorney General Gregory was in no mood to make life easier for the Administration's business advisors and their friends. The Justice Department had by no means been uniformly hostile to American big business in the pre-war years. Still, it irked Justice to see those specific interests which it had pursued use the emergency to enhance their positions. They were thus reluctant to close their eyes to antitrust violations throughout the war. Moreover, no regular federal department or agency took kindly to the idea of being pushed aside by obstreperous emergency boards like the WIB. In any case, argued Gregory, the whole question was not merely a legal one: it was "a question of national policy" and up to the President to decide.[20] It was probably in the summer of 1917 that Wilson decided to respond to Gregory's invitation, and it is clear from the outcome that he found business arguments persuasive in this as in so many areas of his wartime industrial policy.

"I had a conference with the President to see what he wanted done," Gregory later explained. "He remarked that if we attempted at that moment to vindicate the law, we would disorganize industry. We both agreed that we should let up on these people so that they would have no excuse for not contributing to their full capacities in the prosecution of the war."[21]

[17] See sample editorials from the *New York Times,* April 10, June 23, and June 28, 1917; and from *Iron Age:* "Antagonisms Lost in the War Crisis," 99 (February 22, 1917), 489, and "Federal Regulation of Steel," 101 (January 3, 1918), 98–99.

[18] *Wall Street Journal,* August 30, 1917. The *Journal* was particularly aggressive in calling upon Washington to face the implications of its industrial policy. See editorials of August 3, 7, 10, 13, 1917, September 28, 1917, and October 22, 1917.

[19] Cotton to John W. Davis, April 9, 1917, Joseph P. Cotton to Baruch, April 9, 1917, both in RG61, File 21A-A4, Box 784.

[20] Gregory to Gifford, June 6, 1917, RG62, File 2-A8, Box 86.

[21] "Memorandum of Conversations With Former Attorney General Gregory At Houston, Texas, March 14 and 15, 1927," in the Papers of Ray Stannard Baker, Manuscript Division, Library of Congress. Also see Gregory to Baker, August 29, 1931, *ibid.*

This conversation related specifically to the problem of antitrust suits then pending against the United States Steel Company and International Harvester, but its implications were of course far-reaching and indicative of the drift of official policy.

A much greater breakthrough in antitrust policy occurred in early August. Herbert Hoover had written Wilson that month inquiring about his powers under the Food Control Act. Specifically, he wanted to know if he had the right to enter agreements with industries to pool output and fix prices which would violate the Sherman Law if done by the trades themselves. Gregory replied in the affirmative ". . . because *governmental action* with respect to prices or methods of distribution is obviously not within the mischief at which the Sherman Law was aimed." According to Gregory the antitrust laws rested on the natural laws of trade which when given free rein prevented control of the market by private producers. But in times of chaos, like periods of war, these natural laws could no longer be depended upon to regulate the market. Then ". . . the only choice is between artificial control imposed by private interests and the artificial control imposed by public agencies. In these circumstances, therefore, such governmental action, so far from running counter to the purpose of the Sherman Law, is directly in line with it."[22] Such was the reasoning by which Gregory was forced to adjust to the economics of war. This pronouncement received no great publicity, yet it was really an extraordinary document in the wartime acceleration of combination and consolidation throughout American industry.

Surprisingly enough the WIB executive remained uneasy with it, and proved much more cautious than they need have been. The Board's legal advisors contributed most to a lingering unease. Concerned with the letter as well as the spirit of the law, the WIB's legal staff could not fully relax while the antitrust law remained on the statute books, and the jaundiced eye the Justice Department cast on business-government good fellowship augmented their concern. But the central difficulty from the lawyers' point of view was the anomalous legal position of the WIB. Unlike the Food Administration, which had been created by Congressional statute, the WIB was the product of administrative evolution and lacked a clear-cut, solid, legal base. It was not absolutely certain that the WIB could enter into collusive agreements with its clientele with the same impunity that the Attorney General's opinion offered Hoover's Food Administration. Both in hindsight and in the light of the WIB's actual practice such a question seems very much beside the point, but it consumed hours of debate among top WIB officials.[23]

Throughout the war, WIB leaders wondered whether or not they should

[22]Gregory to Woodrow Wilson, August 2, 1917, RG61, File 2D-A1, Box 203. Also see Department of Justice, *Annual Report of the Attorney General of the United States for the Year 1918* (Washington, 1918), p. 61.

[23]Baruch's chief legal aid, Albert Ritchie, expressed his doubts in Ritchie to Baruch, August 19, 1918, RG61, File 1-A5, Box 41.

launch a campaign to get Congress to abrogate the antitrust laws once and for all, or whether they should request legislation specifically to exempt them as Gregory's opinion had exempted the Food Administration. Discussion became especially intense during the summer of 1918 as a growing number of industries began to construct pooling agreements in response to coal and transportation shortages in the east coast areas. Albert C. Ritchie, the Board's major legal advisor, personally believed that such agreements among competitors would not violate the law if the government were a party to them, but he wanted a favourable word from Gregory just to make sure. Baruch wrote Gregory in June 1918 that ". . . if such a pooling agreement is authorized and would not violate the Sherman Law, I still think it should not actually be made, unless I am advised by you, as the official who enforces the Sherman Law, that the same will not violate the law."[24] Gregory was unsympathetic, twitting the Board for lack of information and suggesting rather peevishly that it could at least follow the form of regular executive departments in seeking opinions.[25]

The WIB withdrew at this point, deciding it was safer to remain without an open endorsement than to receive a negative opinion from Gregory. Only congressional legislation would guarantee the Board's legal right to enter such agreements unchallenged, but Ritchie raised a number of objections against actually lobbying for it. First, no assurance existed that Congress would pass such a law. Second, the European administrative experience had by no means proved that a system of government-sponsored regulation was superior to voluntary combinations. And finally, "As a practical matter, industries are able to work out the situation better than might be expected." Ritchie knew that industry made "more or less similar arrangements" and the Attorney General had not prosecuted, so why bring the issue to the public's attention and chance the likelihood of a bitter debate and ultimate defeat? Better to leave the situation alone and let industries combine at will and assume that wartime conditions would afford immunity.[26]

The agitation for legislation did not stop, but Ritchie's arguments convinced Baruch and he never broached either Wilson or Congress on the matter. As in so many policy areas, the Board practised privately and informally what it refused to proclaim publicly and formally. It wanted the advantages of industrial cooperation without having to assume legal responsibility for them. At the same time it felt a certain moral responsibility to stem legal challenges against its clientele.

Most officials acted as if the Attorney General's pronouncement *vis-à-vis* the Food Administration did in fact apply also to the WIB, something which Gregory himself finally admitted to be the case in his

---

[24]Baruch to Gregory, June 18, 1918, *ibid.* See also H. P. Ingels to Ritchie, June 11, 1918, and "Pooling Agreement" (n.d.), both in *ibid.*
[25]Gregory to Baruch, June 20, 1918, *ibid.*
[26]Ritchie to Baruch, August 19, 1918, *ibid.*

1918 report.[27] "Mr. Legge said that the Pulp and Paper Division should make this price directly with the mills without going to the price fixing committee," read the minutes of one meeting of the Pulp and Paper Division, "and that he had no fear of prosecution under the Anti-Trust Law, as agreements made through the Government were not subject to prosecution."[28] Pope Yeatman of the Non-Ferrous Metal Section encouraged agreements between producers and smelters in the zinc industry despite his inability to get an official opinion on the procedure from the Attorney General's office. And the zinc industry was appreciative of Yeatman's support. "By suggesting this," wrote one member of the industry, "you have made clear to your many friends that your conference plan is a real panacea for industrial difficulties. I bow to your good judgement."[29]

Defending such private agreements and the right to initiate them proved a delicate problem, especially when other government executive departments objected. The Board's executive, however, stood behind its staff and its business constituency, doing what it could to refute, modify or rationalize charges of monopoly, price fixing or unfair trade practices.

Consider the WIB's intervention on behalf of the cement industry, for example. In early spring the Attorney General's Department instituted an investigation at the request of government agencies and other dealers and concluded that combination among cement producers had stifled competition and raised prices. The Department was about to file suit when the WIB formally announced that an independent investigation it had conducted showed that the price rise had resulted simply from the wartime advance in the cost of labour and other materials. As G. Carroll Todd, Assistant to the Attorney General, observed, "Obviously a proceeding by this Department charging that cement manufacturers have combined to suppress price competition and thereby bring about unduly high prices would be seriously if not fatally embarrassed by an outstanding determination by another branch of the Government that competition in the cement industry has not been suppressed and that prices are no more than reasonable."[30]

The WIB stuck to its guns. It refused even to consider the charge of conspiracy in restraint of trade within the industry. "I have made no finding upon the subject of competition," wrote Baruch; "it is not my function to do so."[31] Eugene Meyer, Jr., explained the economic causes behind the general price rise to the Department, emphasizing particular conditions in the cement case.[32] Moreover, the WIB officially informed the Jus-

[27]*Annual Report . . . 1918,* p. 61.
[28]Minutes of Meeting of Section Heads, Pulp and Paper Division, Week October 26, 1918, to November 2, 1918, RG61, File 1-C2, Box 86.
[29]Victor Rakowsky to Yeatman, April 26, 1918, RG61, File 21A-A4, Box 1962; Yeatman to G. Carroll Todd (Assistant Attorney General), April 24, 1918, and G. Carroll Todd to Yeatman, April 27, 1918, both in *ibid.;* and Yeatman to Brookings, May 14, 1918, RG61, File 21A-A4, Box 1640.
[30]Todd to Eugene Meyer, Jr., February 13, 1918, RG61, File 21A-A4, Box 316.
[31]Baruch to Todd, March 14, 1918, *ibid.*
[32]Meyer, Jr., to Todd, *ibid.*

tice Department that in any price question it "uses a very broad business judgement in a great emergency without regarding too strictly Federal Trade Commission reports or other cost data."[33]

The Justice Department wanted the Board at least to reopen the case and reconsider its findings. If they were indeed correct then proceedings would naturally be halted. Until the matter was resolved among the government departments themselves, of course, Justice was paralyzed, as the WIB well knew. The WIB simply refused the challenge and let the matter drop. But in order to avoid liability for obstructing Department procedures, Baruch informed Gregory's Assistant that he could not see any reason why the Department could not take whatever action it wished.[34]

Feeling ran high within the Department to accept the WIB challenge. "I do not know how an appeal is taken from the price-fixing of the War Industries Board, but it certainly looks as if some effort should be made to overturn this curious result," one Justice attorney informed Todd. "If we have many more investigations where the Department of Justice reaches one conclusion, which is overruled without a hearing by some subordinate board or bureau, the whole morale of a Department investigation will be lost."[35] The only place to appeal was to the President himself. But the question never went that far. Todd believed that a suit against the industry "would probably be a waste of time and money."[36] Gregory agreed.

Gregory could do little else under the circumstances. Wilson could never have been expected to regard the issue as pressing, and he had already indicated his thinking in the matter of antitrust in any case. And for Justice to have challenged the WIB publicly would have chanced a political blow-up dangerous to the Administration's entire mobilization program. The WIB had Justice over a barrel and wanted to keep it that way. To be able to achieve such successes gave it considerable popularity among various business groups. Cooperation with the WIB offered a political environment which favoured corporate consolidation and a protective shield against embarrassing public investigations.

The greatest test to Baruch's leadership on the antitrust issue came with the end of the war. Enormous pressure was brought to bear on the WIB to end antitrust laws once and for all, to clear the road for economic consolidation in post-war America.[37] It was the kind of thinking which

[33]H. P. Ingels to Todd, March 4, 1918, RG61, File 1-A2, Box 29.

[34]Todd to Baruch, March 7, 1918, and Baruch to Todd, March 14, 1918, and Todd to Baruch, March 16, 1918, all in RG61, File 21A-A4, Box 316.

[35]Mark Hyman to Todd, May 17, 1918, General Records of the Department of Justice, File 60-10-0, National Archives, Washington, D.C.

[36]Todd to Mark Hyman, May 18, 1918, ibid.

[37]Robert F. Himmelberg describes the pressures on Baruch both from business specialists within the WIB and from business lobbies outside it in "The War Industries Board and the Anti-trust Question in November, 1918," Journal of American History, LII (June, 1965), pp. 59–74. I differ somewhat with Himmelberg on the motives and implications of Baruch's response to this issue.

had resulted in the Webb-Pomerene Act and would soon spawn the Edge Act—the one to permit commercial combination for international trade, the other to permit financial consolidation for expanding capital overseas.[38] A victory on the domestic scene could extend further the corporate vision for American economic power and trade expansion. Quite wisely, however, Baruch refused to depart from his general wartime strategy of doing what he could behind the scenes while steering clear of any public, political interventions which might undermine his reputation and the reputation of the concepts he and the WIB now symbolized.[39] Baruch had never been adverse to intervening on behalf of corporate groups in the federal decision-making process, but he had stayed away from public campaigns. The chief difference in November 1918 was that Baruch's room for private manoeuvering had suddenly narrowed. With the billows of patriotic rhetoric clearing away, a curious public could now see more clearly the kind of covert activity at which Baruch had been so adept in the past. Moreover, Baruch realized far better than many of the specialists and interest groups around him that no longer would the public tolerate the inroads which he and other synthesizers had made in traditional institutional relationships, as between business and government, or in traditional values like antitrust, under the press of wartime crisis. Rather than expose publicly the extent to which some business groups had indeed found their uses for the state, Baruch disbanded his agency as fast as discretion would allow and quit Washington for the glories of Versailles.[40]

One of the central goals of the business synthesizers throughout the war had been to prove what private corporate leadership could do in conjunction with a friendly state. What European countries might achieve through extensive state controls, so the argument ran, America would surpass by a process of private-public cooperation administered by businessmen in government. To suggest that a state-based officialdom may have proved equally necessary for the outcome raised some question about the viability and legitimacy of private corporate leadership in the postwar world. What was the lesson of the war for America in peacetime: greater state intervention, or greater freedom for private cooperation, or both? In the early weeks after the Armistice business leaders like Baruch wondered whether businessmen could really afford to sanction an

[38]Carl Parrini deals with these acts and the motives behind them in *Heir to Empire, United States Economic Diplomacy, 1916–1923* (Pittsburgh, 1969).

[39]Himmelberg, "Antitrust Question."

[40]Baruch indicated his fear of public inquiries to representatives of the steel industry on November 13, 1918. See "Special Meeting With Committee Representing The American Iron and Steel Institute . . ." in Baruch Papers. "You don't forget this now"; he said, "we talk about the government doing something when this war is over; there is going to be a critical examination of what has been done. Don't forget gentlemen, we have all got politics in front of us." On November 27, 1918, two days before he resigned, Baruch recommended that President Wilson terminate the WIB as of January 1, 1919. Baruch to Wilson, November 27, 1918, Papers of Woodrow Wilson, Manuscript Division, Library of Congress.

enlargement of the state in peacetime when businessmen would no longer be in government to supervise the expansion. Might that not lead to politically imposed controls rather than to the kinds of bargained compromises permitted under friendly business-government cooperation? The business synthesizers realized very well that the total absence of state administration could harm a corporate economy in peacetime, but they concluded that a powerful public bureaucracy dominated by politicians offered a far greater menace.[41]

One of the central tasks for business synthesizers in the 1920s was to redefine the relationships between business and government in an emerging corporate system so as to obtain the coordination and continuous management of wartime without the coercive power of an enlarged state bureaucracy. That such a goal was indeed possible lay at the heart of Herbert Hoover's search for the capitalist utopia, while the very ineffectiveness of his response to the depression after 1929 convinced many business leaders that indeed it was only a utopia after all.[42] By 1932, business groups were asking for, and political leaders were ready to accept, the kind of state intervention in peacetime which Baruch, for one, had refused to sponsor in November 1919. But by then, the ideology of a minority of progressive business synthesizers, expanded and deepened by a world war and depression, had become the conventional wisdom of New Deal liberalism.

[41]The following comment by Edward Hurley illustrates the embarrassment he and others felt over just how far they had strayed from private to state capitalism during the war. They were anxious not to give radicals any support for arguments on behalf of state controls in peacetime. "I have been a steadfast opponent of government ownership; it means inefficiency and waste, as a rule. It so happened that the Emergency Fleet Corporation, although a government agency, was organized and managed as if it were a private enterprise. We therefore had the mechanism of private enterprise, and yet governmental control. For this reason it became feasible to assume direct charge of yard-building and ship-building, for war purposes only," Edward Hurley, *The Bridge to France*, p. 77.

[42]For the best analysis of Hoover's quest for utopia in the 1920s see Barry Karl, "Presidential Planning and Social Science Research: Mr. Hoover's Experts," in Donald Fleming and Bernard Bailyn (eds.), *Perspectives in American History* (Cambridge, 1969), III, 347–409. See also Ellis W. Hawley, "Herbert Hoover and the Expansion of the Commerce Department: The Anti-Bureaucrat as Bureaucratic Empire-Builder," unpublished ms.

Wide World

II
REINTERPRETING
THE TWENTIES

In 1956 Henry F. May observed that most of the material written about the twenties was by journalists, literary critics, and social scientists, rather than by historians. The selections which are reprinted here were published after May's observation, and all were written by historians (although one of the authors is usually described as an expert in the field of industrial relations). This gap in time between the era and historical investigation of it is typical: many historians believe that an event does not become history until a few generations have passed. For instance, historians have not yet studied the years since 1945 with any appreciable intensity, leaving the field to journalists, economists, political scientists, and sociologists. Thus, recent history, always fair game for popular literature, awaits the professional historian's measured analysis and synthesis. In the interim, the perspective of the immediate past is apt to be governed by images rather than reality; moreover, those images lend themselves to analogues which influence our view of not only the past but current events as well.

The theme of this section is that familiar generalizations about the twenties are too narrow or simply wrong; yet, the fundamental value of journalistic observations is not disregarded. William E. Leuchtenburg noted in the late fifties that, "Every account of this period begins with Frederick Lewis Allen, *Only Yesterday* (1931), a social history in such lively style that academicians often underrate its soundness." His words remain true in the seventies. No student can fully appreciate the Jazz Age without reading Allen's book, written by a magazine editor a year after the epoch closed. Guided by his time's folklore (which had a substantial amount of validity) and his own intuitive insights, Allen shrewdly articulated what American society already believed about itself and had propagandized through the highly developed media of radio, advertising, and periodicals. Images of the twenties were reinforced and perpetuated by mass culture. An isolated fact reported as a generalization often be-

REINTERPRETING THE TWENTIES   67

came a general reality via the mass media: advertising depicted more Americans buying more cars and radios than ever. Actually, installment credit made it possible for consumers to substantiate that image. Rising wages also encouraged an aura of prosperity, and eventually exceptions no longer blurred the picture of America in the twenties as a bountiful society. The real picture belonged to historians, who did not publish studies contradicting that popular image until forty years later.

Still, the debacle which followed the twenties made it easier to doubt that image and stamp the decade as one of "wonderful nonsense." Americans in the thirties displayed two attitudes towards the experience of the twenties: nostalgia and bitterness. To some it was a period of enjoyable frivolity which they wished to relive but probably never expected to. They saw the twenties as an age of bathtub gin, ragtime, raccoon coats, flivvers, and flappers. To read F. Scott Fitzgerald's novels was to return to a time of hedonism, Coolidge Prosperity, and insouciance towards all politics. Other Americans condemned the social strife which attended the twenties' illusory pleasures. Sinclair Lewis's books *Babbitt* and *Main Street* recalled a hypocritical society with intolerant values, typified by the Harding scandals, the Ku Klux Klan's heyday in small towns and the Al Smith campaign of 1928. Ben Shahn's portrait of the *Passion of Sacco and Vanzetti* symbolized the clash of native and immigrant cultures, and the Scopes trial revealed the clash of urban and rural cultures.

Later, however, from the vantage point of the insecurity of the cold war, the twenties once more seemed almost enviable for the apparent innocence and gaiety which accompanied its pains.

But the cold war generation was contemptuous of the twenties' values, even as it admired the spirit of the time. The apparent freedom enjoyed during the twenties was seen as symptomatic of a society unwilling to respond to obligations to itself and the world. Its unwillingness to anticipate and protect itself against the Great Depression and World War II seemed its most unlovely aspects. With humorless scorn cold war critics assailed Americans of the twenties for turning their backs on the needs of agriculture and labor and for ignoring the few progressive politicians sensitive to growing disparities in American society. According to this angry retrospective, depression and war were natural consequences of the twenties' paper prosperity and isolationism. The lessons of 1919 became a fixation for Americans after 1945, who believed that the world had paid a terrible price for the frivolities which followed World War I.

Today, however, as the cold war seems to have concluded in a rapprochement with The People's Republic of China, we look back over a half-century with more sympathy and understanding. We appreciate better the fact that beneath the welter of great events and apparent aimlessness of national policy there is great significance in everyday social developments. We are more clinical in our observations of the twenties, but hardly more dispassionate. Of course the social and economic history of the twenties is not to be measured by the number of home runs hit by Babe Ruth, poker games played by Warren Harding, automobiles purchased, or by the price levels of securities. Beneath the headlines and aside from the legends is the real tale of a changing nation which was enthralled or enraged with the artifacts of its growth.

We are developing a new synthesis of the "roaring twenties." Historians are reaching beyond insipid discussions of the Volstead Act, McNary-Haugenism, the Dawes Plan, and the Muscle Shoals debate to include problems which have been overlooked: those of race in urban America; the working man; state governments' struggles to finance industrial development and health, education and welfare services; businessmen's involvement in international affairs versus politicians' apparent lack of interest. Similarly, historians have found that social workers were one group of reformers who did not hibernate through a long winter of reaction against reform and that during the politically placid twenties, startling new political realignments took place without needing the obvious turmoil of the thirties. Prohibition may have been the most widely discussed political issue of the twenties, but it remains to be proved that it was the most influential. Businessmen did not madly pursue *en masse* an avuncular laissez faire or rugged individualism. This ongoing reappraisal tells us much about the underside of the twenties and why succeeding generations preferred to ignore it.

Carl P. Parrini

WORLD COMMUNITY AND ITS
DISINTEGRATION: 1916–1929

Isolationism was an expression of nationalism and was not an attitude held exclusively by the United States. It sprang not from Americans' selfishness, egocentrism, or indifference, but from their awareness that nationalism prevailed in spite of Wilsonian internationalism and the League of Nations. Naturally we had geopolitical and economic interests which conflicted with those of other nations. Since Europe and Japan never forgot their primary interests, the United States saw no benefit in renouncing its needs in favor of international ideals not shared by other nations. Even Wilsonians, priding themselves in being realistic idealists, were quick to recall that President Wilson had preached an enlightened nationalism. America's representatives to the Paris Peace Conference in 1919 knew both the tyranny and necessity of nationalism. International cooperation was rare and not to be bought at the expense of our own national ambitions.

The United States, with as much power and wealth as it enjoyed following the Armistice of 1918, could not have been so myopic as popular legend insists. International participation was a commitment which Harding held in different degree from Wilson. The central issue was the extent and form of American participation in world politics.

In this summary-excerpt from his book, Heir to Empire, *Carl Parrini characterizes Republican economic foreign policy in the twenties as having the same goal as its Democratic predecessor—a stable international community in which United States leadership supplanted a war-weakened*

British pre-eminence. Parrini suggests that we examine the role which American economic nationalism played in international politics during the twenties.

From 1916 to 1923 the Europeans threw up every conceivable roadblock to the seemingly new American plan to manage the world's economy. In reality the American plan was to displace the faltering leader of the previous century, Great Britain. One by one American leaders tore down the obstacles to United States commercial leadership and the Europeans—with Britain in the lead—fell back to new positions, until in 1924 they surrendered.

The Allies agreed with the American contention that the European economy had to be reconstructed if the great damage wrought to the European social system by the war was to be repaired and Bolshevism successfully repelled. They were unwilling, however, to pay the financial cost of eliminating the economic and political dangers. In all essentials they wanted Germany and the United States to bear the financial burden.[1] Indeed, on May 22, 1919, Lloyd George went so far as to suggest to Wilson that the Succession States to the Austrian Empire be required to share in Austrian reparations obligations, explaining that they should not "get their freedom without paying for it."[2] If in the British view the Czechs and Hungarians were legitimately bound to pay for Austria's cocriminality with Germany in launching the war, so much more so were the Germans liable for the various costs of the war. Lord Cunliffe, former Governor of the Bank of England, a man educated to the facts of international economics and thus aware of the commercial disaster implied in his own proposal, argued that the Germans could sustain an overall reparations bill of $120 billion and an annual amortization of $5 billion. Lloyd George admitted that such a bill could never be paid, but insisted nevertheless that such an obligation should be written into the Treaty, with adjustment possible later.[3] By supporting Cunliffe in such an unworkable proposal Lloyd George undoubtedly hoped to score points for the British argument that reparations and inter-Allied war debts were intimately linked and to bring pressure to bear upon the United States for mutual cancellation of war debts. This would of course place the ultimate cost of financing the

Reprinted from Carl Parrini, *Heir to Empire,* University of Pittsburgh Press.

[1]Norman H. Davis to President Wilson, February 21, 1920, *Senate Document No. 86,* U.S. Senate, Committee on Judiciary, *Loans to Foreign Governments,* 67th Cong., 2d sess. (Washington, 1921), 77. Davis told the President that while "the allies have never bluntly so stated, their policy seems to be to make Germany indemnify them for having started the war and make us indemnify them for not having entered the war sooner."

[2]Seth P. Tillman, *Anglo-American Relations at the Paris Peace Conference of 1919* (Princeton, 1961), 258.

[3]*Ibid.,* 238–40.

war upon American taxpayers. German reparations obligations were to be reduced in relation to the amount of Allied debts the American Treasury might cancel.

But despite the ex post facto popularity of the view among European and American academics that as chief commercial victor in the war the United States should have been willing to cancel Allied war debts as a condition of Allied agreement to a practical reparations bill for Germany, United States leaders could not reasonably have been expected to accept any such proposal. President Wilson and the succeeding Harding Administration believed that German investments seized by the Allies in Southern, Eastern, and Central Europe and in the Turkish Empire, as well as the preferential trading agreements they had imposed on the weaker nations, were more than sufficient repayment for the costs of the war. Cancellation of war debts would simply provide additional spoils for the Allies, with American taxpayers footing the bill. American leaders were willing to cancel part of the war debts if the Allies would agree to a reasonable reparations bill for Germany, and if they would dismantle preferential trading agreements among themselves. But the British and the continental Allies were not ready to make concessions until their own preferential and closed door methods failed at the end of 1923.

It would have been impossible in 1918 and 1919 for British leaders to accept the relatively equitable American peace proposals. Public opinion in Britain during the war had been charged in the direction of a harsh peace, and so the British supported the successful French demand that Germany be denied her prewar commercial treaty rights for five years (as previously resolved at the Paris Economic Conference of 1916), while the Allies would continue to force Germany to give them unconditional most-favored-nation treatment. A Germany deprived of any sort of steady markets for five years would give to the Allies time in which to gain a lead on Germany in world markets. Even the threat of a Bolshevik Germany, which such commercial restrictions posed, failed to move British leaders to fix a definite payable reparations figure.[4]

The apparently more selfish view of Europe did not, as so many Americans assumed, reflect the innate superiority of the American plan. The differing British and American programs reflected the disparate and conflicting national interests of each society. Leaders of the European nations, with Britain in the vanguard, believed sincerely that they could begin to view the world as a community only after they had satisfied pressing demands of national interest which they defined as keys to their continued existence as viable states.

The leaders of Europe had of necessity to define conditions of stability in terms of their own experience. The Europeans lost material and human resources to such an extent that in the case of Britain, for example, the population was threatened with severely lowered living standards. Brit-

[4]Tillman, *Anglo-American Relations at the Peace Conference*, 242.

ain's means of creating national wealth, foreign investments, export markets, and access to vital industrial raw materials at low cost, and its ability to perform international services in the fields of insurance, shipping, and finance were considerably diminished. At the same time the ability of the United States to expand its wealth had grown immensely—to a considerable extent at the expense of Great Britain. The British believed fervently that before they could cooperate with the United States in rebuilding a world market with a system of trade, payments, and investment encouraging growth and expansion—in other words, a world similar to the one that had existed for most of the century prior to 1914—they had first to rebuild their own system of expanding national wealth. Together with France in Europe and the self-governing dominions around the world, they hoped to accomplish this by means of preferential trading agreements and tariff assimilation. Indeed, such policies reflected a hard-headed assessment of national interest. But so too did the more objectively generous American program reflect national interest.

The difference among the great powers over priorities to be observed in building a world community of interest were compounded by the fact that for the first time in a century the fundamental system of values shared by the nations of Europe and North America were dangerously challenged by the Bolshevik Revolution and, to an alarming extent, by the Nationalist revolutionary movements of the Arab East, North Africa, and China. Unlike the participants in the liberal and democratic revolutions of the nineteenth century, who wanted merely to extend to themselves full rights in a system based on parliamentary democracy and free enterprise, and who believed the system itself to be equitable, the leaders of the revolts growing out of World War I sought to destroy the existing system.[5]

To a very large extent the outbreak of the Bolshevik Revolution, causing the first breach in the international system evolved up to 1914, was the result of the interplay of two factors to which World War I gave rise: (1) economically, the outbreak of war destroyed the delicate network of commercial ties which constituted the world market, diminishing the amount of real wealth available to each contestant for purposes of waging war and sustaining the civil population; (2) politically, the consequence of this economic breakdown and the eroded living standards it implied resulted in a loss of faith in and respect for traditional hierarchies of political authority. To a greater or lesser degree all the European combatants suffered civil disaffection. But in Russia the ideological impact was so great that it tended to throw up political power to any element capable of seizing it. Lenin recognized this reality and took advantage of it to seize power in Russia. He also urged revolutionary leaders in other countries, imperfectly enjoying the fruits of the existing international division of labor, to follow Russia's example.[6]

[5]Edward Hallett Carr, *Conditions of Peace* (New York, 1942), 11–12.
[6]*Ibid.*, 11–12.

But it was the war which gave the Bolsheviks an audience for their appeal; in the absence of the destruction of capital, natural resources, and human life flowing from the war, few people, even in the weakest national segments of the pre-1914 international economy, would have had probable cause for protesting the way in which the world market distributed income and concomitant privileges. President Wilson showed that he understood this when he argued at the Peace Conference that the "poison of Bolshevism" was a "protest against the way in which the world had worked," the antidote to which was in Wilson's view a "new world order."[7]

But while the world would benefit from the American version of a "new world order," the United States as the managing element in the recreated world market would benefit most. The United States was to be the "engine" of the world economy,[8] which would haul the world to prosperity. The United States was the only nation emerging from World War I with a surplus of capital available to develop at long term the world's resources and to finance the world's day-to-day merchandise trade. Before any new resources could be developed the products of previous investment had to be marketed. The links between Europe and Latin America, among other prewar commercial ties, had to be reopened. But in order for Europe to buy from and sell to Latin America on anything like its prewar scale, Europe had to be reconstructed—both vanquished and victor nations concurrently. Simple reconstruction of the victors would not suffice, because markets would continue to be too narrow.

During the period 1918 to 1922 American bankers made an effort to

---

[7]Tillman, *Anglo-American Relations at the Peace Conference*, 61.

[8]This phrase is Dean Acheson's. He was arguing his view of what America's role should be in the post World War II period. Acheson wrote: "the system has been destroyed which expanded the power of Western Europe and permitted industrial development in societies in which individual liberty survived. One to replace it will be devised, managed, and largely (but not wholly) financed by the United States; otherwise it is likely to be provided by the Soviet Union, under circumstances destructive of our own power and of an international environment in which independent and diverse nations may exist and flourish." *Power and Diplomacy* (New York, 1963), 19–20. America's leaders during the 1920's shared with Acheson the goal of constructing an American-led world community to replace the British-led community which World War I had destroyed. But Acheson and his successors are much more ready to use force than were Harding, Hoover, and Hughes to protect such an American-led community against challenge. Acheson argues that the measured use of force (which is a dangerous euphemism implying that any amount of force necessary to suppress a challenge is legitimate) is requisite to protecting the system. Acheson has of course deceived himself and the American public by arguing that the force is to be used against the Soviet Union. But in reality the Acheson view of the world (shared by Dean Rusk) sets the United States up in the business of revolution suppression. The ease with which revolutions of all kinds can be defined as Soviet (or Chinese) threats under this view of the world is well demonstrated in American policy toward the Dominican Republic and Vietnam. To suppress a revolution is *not* the first step toward building a community. On the contrary, it is the first step toward waste of resources which could be used to build a true community. In this connection American leaders of the 1920's had a healthy skepticism about the easy use of force, even for limited objectives. We could learn a good deal from them.

finance the orderly marketing of primary products in Latin America. The system of branch banks the Morgan and Rockefeller interests established in Latin America during these years were largely designed to funnel short-term capital on deposit in the United States banking system into financing Latin American merchandise trade. But by 1922 these efforts suffered dismal failure; many of the American branch banks sank into insolvency and suffered considerable losses. This proved to American bankers, and to some extent American manufacturers and political leaders, that without the reintegration of Germany into a world economy, markets would continue to be too narrow to absorb even existing production, much less encourage the investment of American capital in the development of additional resources.

Since American leaders thought of a recreated world market as the only long-run basis for social stability and economic expansion, they concentrated their efforts on forging weapons with which to force the Allies to dismantle preferential trading agreements affecting areas which had changed hands as a result of the war and the peace treaty and to allow Germany to reenter the world economy without excessive reparations obligations. The United States created tools to attain the former objective when it enacted into law the Webb-Pomerene Act in 1918, the Edge Act in 1919, and the Fordney-McCumber Tariff in 1922. The American weapon to obtain a workable place for Germany in the world economy consisted of its ability to refuse to lighten the burden of the war debts the Allies owed the United States, until they in turn eased Germany's burden.

The American effort was successful. By the fall of 1922 Britain found itself unable to sustain its own program without extensive United States investment in Europe and the underdeveloped countries. New negotiations began on the subject of German reparations, with Britain showing a strong willingness to compromise on the issue. The same was true on the issue of closed door administration of the mandates. By the time of the Lausanne Conference of 1922 the British acknowledged that the closed door had failed; and so they accepted the open door in the Near East.[9] Shortly thereafter, during 1923, British and American banking officials began to cooperate closely in matters of international finance, a move symbolized on a grand scale by discussion of a joint loan by Anglo-American bankers to the German government to stabilize that country's currency. On the more

[9]Hughes to Harding, November 25, 1922, Charles Evans Hughes Manuscripts, Manuscript Division, Library of Congress, Letters 1921–1925. In reporting to Harding on the results of the Lausanne Conference and saying in effect that the British had come round to accept the American demand for the open door in the Middle East, Hughes told Harding: "Curzon stated, after some discussion, that as long ago as the Tripartite agreement, the British began to abandon any moves toward zones, concessions and special privileges and were now prepared to support at the conference open door policy in the Near East. He disclosed that the Italians and the French were not in accord as to this. Not withstanding press reports to the contrary, it is his belief that the French will abandon Cilicia, but that both the Italians and the French desire selected Prizes." The words are Hughes' paraphrase of Child.

mundane scale British banking leaders agreed that the pound and the dollar could both be used profitably in the day-to-day finance of world trade.

In 1922 and 1923 the United States leaders also made some concessions in order to obtain British and French adherence to the projected world community. For example, they expressed some willingness to discuss the extent to which British and other Allied war debts to the United States might be scaled down. Treasury Secretary Andrew Mellon agreed with his predecessor, David F. Houston, who argued that cancellation, "does not involve mutual sacrifices on the part of the nations concerned. It simply involves a contribution mainly by the United States." He agreed too that any adjustment of war debts would have to "take into account advantages obtained by such debtor countries under the treaty of peace." Such advantages of course included seized German investments, "discriminatory advantages and exclusive concessions."[10]

But under neither Harding nor Wilson was the United States unreasonable. With the active assistance of Mellon and over the confused opposition of such a future New Deal statesman as Congressman Cordell Hull (Dem., Tenn.), the Harding and Coolidge Administrations reduced the war debts on the basis of ability to pay. This kind of distinction meant, of course, that Britain as the great victor in terms of commercial spoils, and the wealthiest in terms of per capita income, would have to pay a much higher percentage of its original war debt than Italy with its much lower per capita income and its impoverished southern regions. Indeed, Mellon defended the extent to which the United States had reduced the debt against Congressional attacks urging a more intensive collection on two essential grounds: 1) the Allies should not have to pay that portion of their debts which they had actually spent in fighting World War I; 2) it was in the national interest of the United States to "think of the financial reorganization of Europe along the same general lines as the reorganization of some large industrial corporation heavily involved after some severe depression. We have become, whether we like it or not, the most important creditor of Europe. In this capacity we are like the general creditors of the embarrassed corporation. Our money is in and we want it out, but it is impossible to get more than the debtor can pay. If we insist on too difficult terms, we receive nothing. We must then settle upon such terms as will give our debtor reasonable opportunity to live and prosper."[11]

Rightly or wrongly, Mellon believed that the United States had fixed a level of payments that Europe could sustain and that would not interfere with the reintegration of the world economy and the development of world markets upon which the ultimate prosperity of the world depended.[12]

[10]U.S. World War Foreign Debts Commission, *Combined Annual Reports of the World War Foreign Debts Commission: With Additional Information Regarding Foreign Debts Due the United States* (Washington, 1927), 69–70, 74.

[11]Speech to the Union League of Philadelphia, March 24, 1926 in *ibid.*, 299–300.

[12]*Ibid.*, 301–02.

Once it was clear in 1923 that the European Allies were willing to allow Germany to reenter world markets on a relatively equal basis, American political leaders were willing to encourage American bankers to float, jointly with British bankers, a $200 million loan to a new German Central Bank. But American participation was conditioned on the agreement that these Dawes loans would take priority over reparations payments. Two problems remained. Some means had to be found to enable Germany to make fixed reparations payments, and some means had to be found or created to allow Germany to sell its exports in world markets. American leaders thought the Dawes Plan would create a mechanism to deal with reparations and, at the same time, create conditions for the long-run expansion of markets for German exports.

American leaders also regarded the Tariff Act of 1922 as a contribution to a reintegrated world economy and a world community of interest. During the debates and hearings in Congress on the Fordney-McCumber Bill the various special-interest groups had about arrived at a consensus that reciprocity, the exchange of mutual tariff-cutting concessions, was the best way for each interest and the collective majority to expand foreign markets for American goods. But such reciprocal negotiations led inevitably to special bargains and discrimination among nations. They encouraged preferential arrangements which would have tended to prevent the reformation of a true world market based on nondiscrimination. Without an integrated world market, world trade would expand at a relatively sluggish rate. The Administration had to muzzle the influence of special interests in the writing of the tariff. It did so; the Tariff Commission, together with the State and Commerce Departments, wrote the basic clauses of the Tariff Act of 1922 in such a way as to offer to foreign nations access to the huge American market on condition that they accept the unconditional most-favored-nation clause as the underlying basis of the network of world commercial agreements.

Once the United States and its former co-belligerents compromised on such basic issues as war debts, Germany's reparations bill, the open door, and an American tariff facilitating the unconditional most-favored-nation clause as the governing principle in the framing of commercial treaties, the United States was willing to open its formerly locked gates to American capital investment abroad. In that connection too, American leaders believed that they made a significant contribution to a world community of interest. Under Herbert Hoover's direction the United States attempted to frame a foreign investment policy which would (1) guide foreign investments into ventures expanding the production of real goods and services, therefore benefiting both the investors and the capital receiving nation and (2) prevent wasteful investment which might impoverish both foreign investors and the peoples of the investment-receiving countries.

Without a doubt American foreign economic policy from 1916 to 1929 was a continuum. Wilson and his Republican successors desired an economic community of interest which the United States would manage, with the Western Europeans and Japan acting as associates with full rights in the system. That was, in all essentials, what the United States in fact created from 1916 to 1929.

George B. Tindall
BUSINESS PROGRESSIVISM:
SOUTHERN POLITICS IN THE TWENTIES

George B. Tindall asserts that if we accept the likelihood of five different tendencies in "the progressive spirit," then, because two of them existed in the twenties, one cannot believe that progressivism lay moribund or dormant during that decade. State and local concern for industrial development and the concomitant upgrading of public services, he argues, is evidence that the progressive concept of an active government persisted through the business-minded twenties. He characterizes this progressivism as "moderate"; i.e., it lacked an altruistic fervor to change working and living conditions or to create a more equitable economic and social system. Moderate progressivism emphasized construction of roads, schools, and hospitals rather than improvement of social justice: prison and child welfare reform were exceptions and hardly softened this brick, concrete, and steel progressivism. Civic-minded Southerners, the focus of Tindall's research, intended to attract investment in their states' retarded industries by spending their comparatively meager revenues on public services.

How was the South's business progressivism in the twenties different from the business conservatism of Republican Washington? Why was there business progressivism but so little farm, labor, or welfare progressivism? Do Americans measure progress by selectively used concrete and steel? Did business progressivism flourish outside the South? Was it confined to the states with the least industrial development?

Tindall's focus is upon the South and its development problems, but those problems were not at all peculiarly regional or limited to the twenties. And, just as we need to know more about the process of apportioning expenditures, so we need to know more about the cultivation of revenue. A political study of taxation might reveal that the revenue-sharing controversy of the seventies germinated in the teens or twenties.

"Fundamentalism, Ku Kluxry, revivals, lynchings, hog wallow politics—these are the things that always occur to a northerner when he thinks of the south." Thus spake Mencken in 1924. In this and a hundred other catalogues of Southern grotesqueries on which he wielded his meat-ax in the clever twenties, the blessed sage of Baltimore contributed mightily to a neo-abolitionist image of the savage South. And Mencken was mightily assisted by great multitudes of southerners who swarmed into the Ku Klux and fundamentalist movements, to a degree that the peculiar forces of nativism and repression seemed to have, if not their native seat, at least their major centers of influence and power in the South of the twenties. The hypnotic power of certain arresting events—the Democratic convention of 1924, the Scopes trial, the election of 1928—have given Ku Kluxry and fundamentalism the appearance of dominating Southern politics to such a degree that more permanently significant developments have been overshadowed. Southern politicians, it is true, for the most part tried to avoid offending those forces—yet few were owned by them. Neither movement ever perfected the machinery to dominate any southern state to the extent that the Klan briefly dominated Indiana; neither movement was responsible for any extensive program of legislation; neither had much durability—at least as a major political force.

Any serious attempt to understand Southern politics in the twenties must begin with recognition that the progressive urge of previous decades did not disappear but was transformed through an emphasis upon certain of its tendencies to the neglect of others, that in its new form progressivism pervaded Southern politics of the twenties. Outrageous as the statement may seem at first, both Austin Peay, who signed the Tennessee anti-evolution act, and Bibb Graves, the Alabama Klan candidate in 1926, were authentic progressive governors of the twenties. In order to demonstrate this, it is not necessary to fall back upon the interpretation advanced by Richard Hofstadter and others, that the peculiar forces represented by fundamentalism and the Klan constituted a degradation of the progressive drive for moral reform. The relationship doubtless was there, but other, and more positive, continuities of progressivism may be traced into the twenties.

A growing interest in this approach among historians was pointed up

From George B. Tindall, "Business Progressivism: Southern Politics in the Twenties." Reprinted by permission of the Publisher. Copyright 1963, Duke University Press, Durham, North Carolina.

three years ago in an article by Arthur S. Link in the *American Historical Review,* "What Happened to the Progressive Movement in the 1920's?" In contrast to the traditional textbook hypothesis that progressivism was submerged under a tide of revulsion against idealism and reform, Mr. Link has indicated a number of continuities and suggested other areas for exploration. This article pursues one avenue of continuity: progressivism in Southern state government.

We need first a working definition of "progressivism." Although we speak of a progressive "movement," actually we have reference to the spirit of the age rather than an organized movement—much as when we speak of Jacksonian democracy. A dictionary definition of anything so amorphous is impossible, but certain salient tendencies of the progressive spirit can be readily identified. One was democracy: reforms such as the party primary to bring government closer to the people. Second, efficiency: good government meant not only democracy but reorganization to eliminate waste. Third, corporate regulation: governmental action against corporate abuses and the threat of monopoly. Fourth, social justice: involving a variety of reforms from labor legislation to prohibition. Fifth and finally, the public service concept of government: the extension of governmental responsibilities into a wide range of direct services to the people—good roads, education, public health and welfare, rural credits, conservation, among others.

Two of these themes were highlighted and extended in the twenties: efficiency and public services. The other three were dimmed or partially eclipsed: democracy, corporate regulation, and social justice.

The transition from a militant democratic and anticorporation progressivism in the early twentieth century, as described by Vann Woodward, to the progressivism of expansion and efficiency in the twenties was already apparent in the Wilson era. Several factors served paradoxically to make progressivism more pervasive and at the same time to temper its militancy. It fell out that Wilsonian progressivism was associated in nearly every one of its major measures with the name of one or more southerners, from the Underwood-Simmons tariff to the Smith-Hughes Act for aid to education. Powerful forces wedded even reluctant southerners to the Wilsonian leadership: the need for a party record of achievement, the spirit of party regularity, the use of the patronage, the existence of progressive factions in the southern states. The entire effect was to "Wilsonize" the Southern Democratic party much as it had been "Bryanized" before, to make progressivism the fashion, but with the result of thinning down somewhat its reform urge by reliance upon a relatively conservative leadership in the Congress.

The anticorporation drive was further diluted by the cold, pure springs of prohibition. Building upon the general moral disrepute of saloons, the prohibitionists were able somehow to equate the "liquor traffic" with rural and progressive suspicion of the trusts and "special interests." When reform pressures built up, an easy outlet was through the advocacy of prohibition. For the churches, prohibition could easily become "a surrogate for the Social Gospel."

> In a peculiarly satisfying way, [Dewey Grantham has written,] the growing agitation over the liquor question absorbed the yearnings for reform and fulfillment of a people whose God had become Progress but whose basic ideas remained fundamentally conservative. No other proposal expressed the ambivalent desires of the South so well, nor did any other so effectively combine the varied reform elements that were struggling to assert themselves.

The militant tone of progressivism was weakened not alone by the adherence of belated Wilsonians and prohibitionists. To quote Grantham again, "the force of progressivism was blunted by the widespread faith in industrial progress." The middle-class leaders who gave progressivism its predominant tone had fought largely against "monopoly" and railroad practices that they thought inhibited economic development. They were not hostile to the factory and corporation as such, and faced with the need for outside capital, with the complexity and difficulty of corporate regulation, they gradually turned their attention in the direction of prohibition, good government, and public services. In their zeal for efficiency and expansion, in fact, the progressives manifested the principal features of business development itself.

By the twenties, the long-heralded industrial New South had entered what might today be called its "take-off" period. It was the period during which Southern textiles finally took the lead from those in New England; hydroelectric power sparked industrial revolution in the Southeast, and petroleum in the Southwest; a period during which industry and urbanization rapidly altered the face of the land. The urban transformation inspired Gerald Johnson to write that in a hundred towns from the Potomac to the Rio Grande "There is no God but Advertising, and Atlanta is his prophet." It was a period of triumph for the "Atlanta spirit," the spirit of progress. "Conservatism," Maristan Chapman wrote in 1922, "has become a term of reproach." But now the term "progress" appeared in a subtly different context. It was more closely associated with the urban middle class, with chambers of commerce and Rotary Clubs. It carried the meaning of efficiency and development rather than of reform. In Asheville, Thomas Wolfe wrote his mother in 1923, they "shout 'Progress, Progress, Progress'—when what they mean is more Ford automobiles, more Rotary Clubs, more Baptist Ladies Social unions." "Greater Asheville" meant "100,000 by 1930." The "progressive" community now was the community that had good governments, great churches, improved schools, industry and business, real estate booms. The reform urge, the social justice movement, never strong in the South, had been muted; the drive to regulate corporations had all but disappeared. The old agrarian battle cries against big business and Wall Street subsided with the passing of the Farmers' Union from the Southern scene and the rise of "business" methods in agriculture. Progressivism in the age of normalcy had become almost synonymous with the Atlanta spirit. Lyle H. Lanier, one of the original Vanderbilt Agrarians, wrote in 1930: "A steady barrage of propaganda issues through newspapers, magazines, radios, billboards, and other agencies . . . , to the effect that progress must be maintained. It requires little sagacity to discover that progress usually turns out to mean business. . . ."

If, however, militant progressivism had been diluted by the need for capital, by chasing after the elusive goal of prohibition, and to some degree even by the Wilsonian policies, one thing is certain: that by 1920 new responsibilities of the state had become a familiar part of the political landscape. Progressivism had conquered the old dictum that that government is best which governs least, whatever political rhetoric might be heard to the contrary, and had left the more extreme doctrines of limited government as dead as Yancey and Rhett. Out of two decades of progressive ferment and reform the great fundamental residue of the progressive era in Southern government was the firm establishment and general acceptance of the public service function of government. It is in this respect that Southern progressivism marked the great departure from the era that went before, and in which the twenties were a decade of fruition and harvest.

The outlook of what we may now call the business progressivism of the twenties was summarized in a perceptive article by H. C. Nixon in 1931 in the *Annals of the American Academy of Political and Social Science:*

> The business class political philosophy of the new South is broad enough to include programs of highway improvement, educational expansion, and health regulation. But it does not embrace any comprehensive challenge to laissez faire ideas in the sphere of relationship between capital and labor, and the section is lagging in social support of such matters as effective child labor regulation and compensation legislation. [On the theme of efficiency, Nixon found] an influence toward change in the meaning and spirit of government as against the rather political and theoretical concepts of the country lawyer. . . . Business methods in government tend to get the right of way over the ideas of checks and balances, and governmental functions tend to expand in response to social or business needs. . . . Government tends to become an agent of industrial prosperity, with urban elements modifying the agrarian content of politics. Even professional politicians, attaining power to exploit government, do so in the name of "progress."

These trends were manifested in a number of business-progressive governors in the twenties—a relatively colorless group on the whole, respectable and circumspect in demeanor, conservatively "constructive" in their approach to public problems, storming no citadels of intrenched "privilege," but carrying forward the new public functions that had gained acceptance in the progressive era, especially good roads and schools. Good government was for them almost a fetish. Sometimes this attitude took the rhetorical form of political cries for economy, but upon closer examination economy usually meant the elimination of waste rather than the reduction of services, and expenditures climbed rapidly. Not always did they use economy even as a rhetorical device. "Economy," "reduce taxes," "abolish useless offices and reduce salaries," Governor Thomas E. Kilby of Alabama warned as he left office in 1923, "These cries may be popular, but . . . they contain a positive and serious menace to the welfare of Alabama and particularly to her educational and health interests and to the unfortunate and helpless wards of the State. Not only do they threaten those interests but they threaten our agricultural and industrial interests as well." That same year the *Southern Textile Bulletin* of Charlotte ran an editorial headed "Expenditures Produce Prosperity." "The man who is educated," it argued, "starts new enterprises or engages in new lines of business that pay taxes." Good roads opened new markets for farmers and improved economic conditions. Strange doctrine, in retrospect, for the most conservative organ of the textile industry to be advocating, in effect, that the state should spend its way into prosperity!

North Carolina was at the forefront of the movement, and it was more in the twenties than in the so-called progressive era that the state established its reputation as "the Wisconsin of the South," the leading progressive state of the region. It was during this period that it developed under President Harry Woodburn Chase the leading state university in the South, embarked upon the most ambitious highway program in the South, and developed extensive programs in education, public health, and welfare. In the war and postwar years the state had a succession of governors— Thomas W. Bickett, Cameron Morrison, and Angus W. McLean—who carried forward a consistent tradition of moderate progressivism reaching from Charles B. Aycock at the turn of the century. In the active expansion of public services North Carolina set the pace for other southern states and ranked high in the nation at large. Several fiscal indexes will establish the point. Between 1913 and 1930, taxes in North Carolina increased by 554 per cent, a rate of increase exceeded only by Delaware. Expenditures by the state increased 847 per cent between 1915 and 1925. This rate of increase was greater than in any other state, substantially more than double the national average. In total expenditure North Carolina ranked tenth among all the states in 1925, fourth in total state debt, second in per capita state debt. The total state bonded debt increased from $13,300,000 in 1920 to $178,265,000 in 1930.

The great era of expansion came after 1920, but it had its beginnings in the administration of Governor Bickett, 1917–1921. That period saw, among other things, the creation of a state public welfare system in 1917, the state guarantee of a six-month school term in 1919, and increasing expenditures for salaries, public health, and state institutions. In 1919–1920 Bickett sponsored a reorganization of the tax system that involved allocation of the general property tax to local and county uses, extension of the income tax to incomes from property, and a revaluation of property that doubled the assessments from 1919 to 1921. Increases in income taxes brought receipts from that source in 1926 almost twelve times those in

1920, constituting nearly half the state revenues. Inheritance, license, privilege, franchise, automobile, and gasoline levies all were increased during the twenties.

It was Cameron Morrison, however, who in the face of postwar depression led the great expansion. With revivalistic zeal, in his 1921 inaugural address he called upon the forces of "progressive democracy" to "war for righteousness with the reactionary and unprogressive forces of our State." In the face of his crusade for highways and schools, the reactionary forces faltered, and the legislature in 1921 approved a $50,000,000 bond issue for state highways, nearly six and three-quarter million for state educational and charitable institutions, and five million for school buildings. Before the end of Morrison's administration a total of $65,000,000 in bonds had been voted for highways, $33,718,700 appropriated for benevolent and educational institutions, public school expenditures more than doubled, and public school property tripled.

Under the direction of Frank Page, chairman of the highway commission after his return from wartime road engineering in France, administration of the highway program was kept reasonably free from political manipulation and graft. Within seven years the State Highway Commission spent $153,546,677; developed a state system of 7,551 miles, 3,738 of which were hard-surfaced; and reclaimed "lost provinces" behind the mountains and the coastal swamps. North Carolina's act of faith was recompensed by increased revenues from gasoline and automobile taxes, enough to cover the cost. The state ended the decade second only to Texas in the South and eleventh in the nation in the total mileage of surfaced roads.

The contribution of Morrison's successor, McLean, successful banker and lawyer of Lumberton, was foreshadowed in his inaugural promise to give the state "an administration characterized by efficiency, economy, and rational progress." McLean carried forward, even expanded, the programs set in motion by Morrison, but emphasized efficiency, inaugurated an executive budget system, and through other measures sought to insure fiscal regularity in the growing activities of the state.

If North Carolina was most consistent in the support of progressive governors and programs, other states moved significantly in the same direction. A transitional figure in Alabama was Thomas E. Kilby, a wealthy Anniston manufacturer. Indorsed by the Anti-Saloon League in 1918, he was swept into office on a wave of enthusiasm for the Eighteenth Amendment. His victory revitalized Alabama progressivism, and Kilby proceeded methodically and doggedly to the redemption of elaborate campaign pledges. Presented originally as a potential "business governor," he directed the establishment of a state budget system, and reorganization of the tax system. State services were extended and reforms enacted in many directions, including the administrative reform of the school system after a systematic survey and the highest appropriations for public education to that time; the establishment of a state child welfare department; a reorganization of the prison system, including construction of a new penitentiary; sizable increases in appropriations for public health; a workmen's compensation law; and a $25,000,000 bond issue for roads.

After a fallow period under Governor William W. "Plain Bill" Brandon, who promised no increases in taxes but carried ahead programs started by Kilby, Alabama progressives entered another period of rapid development under Bibb Graves. Elected in 1926, he presided over another great forward surge in the last years of prosperity: another $25,000,000 road bond issue, the creation of a State Bridge Corporation, expansion of public schools and state colleges, added support to hospitals and charitable institutions, the achievement of national leadership in the percentage of rural population covered by full-time health service, increased support to the child welfare departments, and further development of the port of Mobile. Additional revenues were secured by levies upon public utilities, coal and iron operators, and tobacco, and by doubling the franchise tax of all corporations. Grover C. Hall, editor of the Montgomery *Advertiser*, later summed it up with the comment that "Bibb Graves makes a good governor, but an expensive one."

A striking contrast to the dynamic "little Colonel," "Bibb the Builder," was Austin Peay, governor of Tennessee from 1923 to 1927. A small town lawyer from Clarksville who had served in the legislature, the epitome of colorlessness, he announced for governor in 1922, leaving to others "any pleasure of fine periods in the campaign," and confining himself "to bare facts and statistics, with which my mind is accustomed to deal." After the fashion of business-progressive rhetoric, he called for a "clean, honest and courageous Legislature, working under sane direction to repeal laws and reduce government in Tennessee," Carried to victory in the Democratic primary, he defeated Alfred Taylor, last Republican governor of the state, in the general election. Alf Taylor cracked jokes and told stories about his dog, "Old Limber." Peay stuck to his statistics and his paradoxical exposition of the state's need for tax reform, reduced expenditures, highways, and schools.

Swept into office with a comfortable majority, Peay summoned expert assistance at his own expense to develop a reorganization bill that regrouped sixty-four scattered agencies under eight commissioners directly responsible to the governor. The resulting efficiency, it was claimed, saved the state over a million dollars in two years. The state tax system was overhauled, with reductions in land taxes but a new privilege tax on corporate earnings, a gasoline tax for highways, and a tobacco tax for an eight-month school term in rural schools. Despite his appeal for the reduction of government, Peay directed an expansion of the road system and public schools that cost far more than the savings from his reorganization plan. By 1929 Tennessee had developed 5,000 miles of surfaced roads in its state system, in contrast to about 500 in 1920, and all but thirteen of its ninety-five counties had an eight-month school term in contrast to fewer than one-third with more than five months in 1920.

The reluctant progressive may be typified by the young Harry Flood Byrd, governor of Virginia, 1926–1930, whose strong points were efficiency and the promotion of industry. An F.F.V., newspaper publisher, apple-grower, a self-made businessman, heir to the old "machine," in one reveal-ing address he compared government to business: the governor as president of the corporation, the legislature as board of directors, the taxpayers as stockholders, the dividends paid in public services. "The administra-tion of government," he said, "should be efficiently conducted along the lines of well organized business enterprises, but the benefits of govern-ment cannot be measured by the yardstick of the dollar. The cost . . . has enormously increased . . . and the need of improved efficiency be-comes daily more important." However, once made efficient, a state gov-ernment should not extend beyond the discharge of functions "public necessities have imposed it"; "undue extension" of government activities should be avoided.

True to his philosophy, Byrd, like Peay, carried through an extensive re-organization. A total of more than one hundred bureaus, boards, and commissions were integrated into fourteen departments and a short bal-lot inaugurated. These reforms, Byrd wrote, were "progressive and mod-ern, and yet they were approved by popular vote in one of the oldest and most conservative of the states." Tax reform included the segregation of land taxes to local uses and the reduction of taxes on capital investments, and Governor Byrd personally embarked on a campaign to attract indus-tries to the state. But even Byrd, whose watchword was economy above all, was carried along by the highway campaign of the twenties. Op-ponent of a state bond issue in 1923, which was defeated by a popular majority, he turned in his campaign to support of a pay-as-you-go system and championed generous tax increases that made possible annual state expenditures of fourteen million dollars on highways, and nearly 5,000 miles of surfaced roads in the state system by 1929.

In other states business-progressive governors and programs enjoyed greater or lesser success. The slogan of Arkansas' Governor John E. Mar-tineau, "Better Roads and Better Schools," could stand almost as a motto for the decade, although in Arkansas failure to rationalize state government and the development of roads through a proliferation of unco-ordinated local districts led the state finally to assume heavy debts that bankrupted it in the Depression. In some states progressive governors were unable to get the support of legislatures for their programs: Pat Neff and Dan Moody in Texas, for example, and Lamartine G. Hardman in Georgia. In Ken-tucky suspicious voters decisively rejected in 1924 a bond issue of $75,000,000 which was to be spent chiefly for highways and schools. In others there was no strong central figure in the development of policies, but everywhere efficiency and expansion were central themes in state politics. South Carolina politics, a state historian wrote, experienced an era of "vacuity," but the state started the decade with the lowest public school expenditure per pupil in the country and ended it with the highest rate of increase. It climaxed the decade with a $65,000,000 highway bond issue in 1929. In Florida the land boom provided resources for the expansion of services.

State after state took up administrative and tax reforms, and despite much pious talk about economy, state and local governments were undertaking ambitious programs on every hand. Every southern state adopted some kind of budget system between 1918 and 1928 and several went through general reorganizations while similar programs were advanced or partially adopted in all. The expansion of state services, battening on industrial prosperity and optimism, moved along at an accelerated pace.

The rate of increase in both state revenues and debt in the South far exceeded that for the rest of the nation. The search for revenue led to a variety of new taxes. Gasoline taxes, non-existent before 1919, produced some $129,000,000 for southern states in 1929, about one-third of their revenues. Motor vehicle registrations produced receipts of $54,299,442 in 1933. By 1929 eight southern states in a total of twenty-one had adopted the income tax, and revenues from that source rose 137 per cent between 1923 and 1928. Of nine states having a sales tax in 1932, five were southeastern; nine of thirteen having cigarette and tobacco taxes. The revenues of local government meanwhile were increased by the rise in property assessments and by the tendency to apply property taxes to local purposes.

There can be no question that the South more than any other region was straining its resources for the support and expansion of public services. In both the ratio of tax collections to aggregate private income and in per capita state indebtedness, the region ranked ahead of all others by 1930. And yet the old story of relative poverty remained. In spite of enormous increases the South still lagged behind in actual revenues. In actual per capita collections in 1930, nine southern states were at the bottom of the list and eleven in the lowest quartile. Florida, the highest, ranked only eighteenth in the nation. In 1932 the general revenues of state and local governments in the thirteen southern states amounted to $33.26 per capita, less than half the $69.63 per capita for the non-South.

In the development of state government, a student of Tennessee finances has claimed, three main stages may be identified down to 1929. The first, until 1904, was the "debt" period, during which debt service outranked other expenditures; this was followed by a period of increasing expenditures for schools until about 1921; while expenditures for schools continued to rise after that, the twenties were overwhelmingly dominated by highways. This was characteristic of other states. "Good roads," Francis B. Simkins wrote, "became the third god in the trinity of Southern progress"—after industry and education. In all the southern states by 1930 highways and education far outdistanced other state functions. In none was expenditures for the two functions less than 60 per cent of state expenditures, and in only three, less than 70. Some idea of the priorities of business progressivism, however, may be derived from the fact that in all but the same three states, the state expenditures for highways were greater than those for education.

The story of the good-roads movement still awaits its historian. As yet there is scarcely any monographic literature tracing its development. It is a diffuse story, of conventions and associations, bicyclists and motorists, the promotion of name highways by aggregations of local promoters, of "heroic caravans in dusters and goggles," and finally broad-gauged planning of integrated programs with the federal highways act of 1916 and 1921 and the development of state systems. In any case, it is clear from the results that the movement had won general support by the twenties. Expenditures for the construction of state-administered highway systems increased by 157 per cent in the South during the twenties (1920–1929) and 123 per cent outside the South.

For education as for roads, the twenties were a period of emergence from the phase of crusading into an era of efficiency and expansion. School busses increasingly moved across improved highways to new consolidated schools. The foundations in the field, led by the great central directorate of the General Education Board, still did a tremendous job of promoting schools. But gradually state and local governments were taking over the programs the foundations had inaugurated: agents for rural secondary and Negro schools; surveys and studies of educational needs; special administrative divisions for the systematic collection of information, school-house planning and construction, the promotion of libraries, developing standards of teacher training and certification. And, if the average cost per pupil in every southern state was still in 1930 well below the national average, eight southern states since 1920 had exceeded the national rate of increase in cost per pupil. Nine had exceeded the national rate of increase in length of school term, although none reached the national average length of school term, with the exception of Oklahoma.

Concentration upon schools and highways, however, should not obscure the fact that the state and local governments were moving ahead in other public services, if on a more restricted scale. Beginning with North Carolina in 1917, every southern state except Mississippi had established by 1927 some kind of state system of public welfare. By 1930 welfare expenditures amounted to 3.8 per cent of total governmental costs in the Southeast and 4.2 per cent in the Southwest.

A much more rapid growth was the development of public health programs under the impact of successive crusades for the conquest of tuberculosis, hookworm, malaria, pellagra, and syphilis. The result was a rapid development of county health departments to carry the word and the cures to the people on a continuing basis. In eleven southeastern states county health departments increased from 94 in 1920 to 166 in 1925 to 347 in 1930, the latter constituting nearly 63 per cent of the departments in the nation.

A rough measure of the full scope of governmental expansion might be derived from reference to the state handbooks prepared for the legislatures. The North Carolina manuals indicate that state administrative departments, boards, and commissions increased from twelve in 1913 to twenty in 1921 to sixty in 1929, and state educational, charitable, and correctional institutions from eighteen to twenty-one to thirty-two. New functions represented by the new agencies in the twenties included conservation, promotion of industry, new budgetary and fiscal programs, child welfare, the licensing of various professions, a state bureau of investigation, and new penal and correctional institutions.

What happened to Southern governments in the twenties was not unrelated to what happened in other fields. It was a period of emergence, in which numerous forces began to reach fruition. If what W. J. Cash called the savage ideal of intolerance and repression seemed to have achieved a new ferocity in the Klan and the fundamentalists, it may be suggested that it was the ferocity of those who found themselves in a losing battle against broadening horizons. If it was the period of the Klan and fundamentalism, it was also the period of economic emergence, the interracial movement, the renaissance in literature, the rise of universities which inspired critical analysis of Southern problems. In the very same column quoted at the beginning of this essay, Mencken noted that ". . . Odums hatch out day by day all over the late Confederacy. The very heat of the fundamentalist and Ku Klux Klan fury is hurrying them out of the egg."

Meanwhile, the Atlanta spirit had caught up the governments of the South, as well as its businessmen, in a zeal for the New South Triumphant. The business-progressive philosophy, to be sure, had its limitations. Race relations were assumed to be a settled problem. The larger economic problems of the underprivileged, farm tenants and factory workers, were not its problems; their remedy would come, if at all, through economic expansion. In turn, business progressivism created new problems: the political influence of the new agencies, the highway departments, the road contractors, the trucking lobbies, the teachers' associations; and soon, in the Depression, the debts came due with severe repercussions on the extended state and local governments. Expansion of state activities itself required a pressure and strain to accomplish what was a matter of course in wealthier states. But the continuing development of public services in the twenties was at least a partial confirmation of the old maxim that yesterday's radicalism is today's moderation. Deep forces flowed through the period, forces that originated before the twenties and issued into later decades. The business-progressive philosophy had deep roots in both the progressive movement and the "New South" creed of economic development. It was severely shaken by the Depression and the New Deal, but the progressivism of expansion and efficiency became by and large the norm of Southern statecraft in the decades that followed.

Gilbert Osofsky

HARLEM TRAGEDY: AN EMERGING SLUM

Although thousands of Negroes abandoned the rural South for northern cities in search of a better life prior to World War I, the period during the war and immediately following it is better known in black history as "the Great Migration." According to the 1930 census, 26.3 per cent of blacks born in the Southeast had left their native states. We can surmise that a majority of these nearly 2 million people went to northern cities.

The impact of this flight upon both the emigrant and the city is described in the following selection on New York City's Harlem. "The most profound change that Harlem experienced in the 1920's," Osofsky asserts, "was its emergence as a slum." From a preferred multi-ethnic community in the early 1900's Harlem became a depressed preserve inhabited mostly in blacks. Other groups moved out along "the tenement trail" while blacks replaced them in greater numbers. Whites and some blacks exploited the occupational and physical immobility of most blacks, and Harlem, asserts Osofsky, became a slum.

Were the blacks victims of racism or economics, or both? How analogous are the urban problems of the twenties to those of our own time?

*I sit on my stoop on Seventh
Avenue and gaze at the sunkissed
folks strolling up and down and
think that surely Mississippi is
here in New York, in Harlem, yes,
right on Seventh Avenue.*

—*The Messenger,* 1923

*I have been in places where cattle
and dogs sleep with masters, but
never before have I been in such a
filthy house.*

—Judge William Blau's description of a Harlem tenement, 1922

I

The creation of a Negro community within one large and solid geographic area was unique in city history. New York had never been what realtors call an "open city"—a city in which Negroes lived wherever they chose— but the former Negro sections were traditionally only a few blocks in length, often spread across the island and generally interspersed with residences of white working-class families. Harlem, however, was a Negro world unto itself. A scattered handful of "marooned white families . . . stubbornly remained" in the Negro section, a United States census-taker recorded, but the mid-belly of Harlem was predominantly Negro by 1920.[1]

And the ghetto rapidly expanded. Between the First World War and the Great Depression, Harlem underwent radical changes. When the twenties came to an end Negroes lived as far south as One Hundred and Tenth Street—the northern boundary of Central Park; practically all the older residents had moved away; the Russian-Jewish and Italian sections of Harlem, founded a short generation earlier, were rapidly being depopulated; and Negro Harlem, within the space of ten years, became the most "incredible slum" in the entire city. In 1920 James Weldon Johnson was able to predict a glowing future for this Negro community: "Have you ever stopped to think what the future Harlem will be?" he wrote. "It will be the greatest Negro city in the world. . . . And what a fine part of New York City [the Negro] has come into possession of!"[2] By the late 1920's and early 1930's, however, Harlem's former "high-class" homes offered, in the words of a housing expert, "the best laboratory for slum clearance . . . in the entire city." "Harlem conditions," a *New York Times* reporter concluded, are "simply deplorable."[3]

II

The Harlem slum of the twenties was the product of a few major urban developments. One of the most important was the deluge of Negro migration to New York City then. The Negro press, now largely dependent on the migrant community for support, changed its former critical attitude of

"Harlem Tragedy: An Emerging Slum" from *Harlem: The Making of a Ghetto* by Gilbert Osofsky. Copyright © 1963, 1965, 1966 by Gilbert Osofsky. Reprinted by permission of Harper & Row, Publishers, Inc.

[1]The Mayor's Commission on Conditions in Harlem, "The Negro in Harlem: A Report on Social and Economic Conditions Responsible for the Outbreak of March 19, 1935" (unpublished manuscript in La Guardia Papers, Municipal Archives), p. 53. This important study, prepared under the direction of E. Franklin Frazier, will hereafter be cited as "The Negro in Harlem."

[2]"The Future Harlem," *The New York Age*, January 10, 1920.

[3]John E. Nail to James Weldon Johnson, March 12, 1934, Johnson Collection, Yale University; "Harlem Conditions Called Deplorable," *The New York Times*, September 6, 1927.

migration to one openly advocating urban settlement. (The exodus was so large, a Negro minister preached, that it must have been "inspired by Almighty God.")[4] If one is looking for a dramatic turning point in the history of the urbanization of the Negro—"a race changing from farm life to city life"—it was certainly the decade of the twenties. Between 1910 and 1920 the Negro population of the city increased 66 per cent (91,709 to 152,467); from 1920 to 1930, it expanded 115 per cent (152,467 to 327,706). In the latter year less than 25 per cent of New York City's Negro population (79,264) was born in New York State. There were more Negroes in the city in 1930 than the combined Negro populations of Birmingham, Memphis and St. Louis. Similar population increases occurred in urban areas throughout the country.[5]

Negro migration in the twenties drew on areas of the South that had previously sent few people to New York City. The seaboard states of the Upper South—especially Virginia and the Carolinas—continued to be the main sources of New York's migrant Negro population, but people from Georgia and Florida and other Deep South states formerly underrepresented also came in greater numbers: "Harlem became the symbol of liberty and the Promised Land to Negroes everywhere," the Reverend Dr. Powell wrote. "There was hardly a member of Abyssinian Church who could not count on one or more relatives among the new arrivals."[6] In 1930, some 55,000 foreign-born Negroes added to the growing diversity of the city's Negro population.

The following chart presents an exact description of the geographical origins of Negro migrants to New York City in 1930. I have selected states with 900 or more residents in the city:[7]

Negro In-Migration, New York City, 1930

Born in:		Born in:	
Virginia	44,471	Alabama	3,205
South Carolina	33,765	Massachusetts	2,329
North Carolina	26,120	Louisiana	2,182
Georgia	19,546	Ohio	1,721
Florida	8,249	Tennessee	1,651
Maryland	6,656	Texas	1,592
Pennsylvania	6,226	Kentucky	1,216
New Jersey	5,275	Mississippi	969
District of Columbia	3,358	Foreign-born	54,754

[4]"Let Them Come," "The New Exodus," *The New York Age*, March 3, 1923, October 16, 1920, September 14, 1929.

[5]Bureau of the Census, *Fifteenth Census, 1930: Population* (Washington, D.C., 1933), II, 216–218; Walter Laidlaw, *Population of the City of New York, 1890–1930* (New York, 1932), p. 51.

[6]Reverend Dr. Adam Clayton Powell, Sr., *Against the Tide: An Autobiography* (New York, 1938), pp. 70–71.

[7]Bureau of the Census, *Fifteenth Census, 1930:* Population (Washington, D.C., 1933), II, 216–218. Note the difference in Chicago's migrant population. In order of greatest numbers Chicago Negroes came from Mississippi, Tennessee, Georgia, Alabama and Louisiana.

The rapid settlement of a heterogeneous Negro population coincided with another important population change—the migration of whites from all sections of Manhattan to other boroughs. For the first time since Dutch settlement Manhattan's population *declined* in the 1920's as first- and second-generation immigrants moved to nicer residential areas in the Bronx, Brooklyn and Queens. Many of the homes they left behind had deteriorated significantly. By 1930 a majority of New York City's foreign-born and second-generation residents lived outside Manhattan.[8] As whites moved out of Manhattan, Negroes moved in. The population of that borough declined 18 per cent in the 1920's as its Negro population increased 106 per cent. By 1930 Negroes represented 12 per cent of Manhattan's population—although they composed only 4.7 per cent of the population of the entire city.[9]

Harlem was the New York neighborhood most radically revamped by the population movements of the 1920's, although the Lower East Side also changed rapidly. Harlem underwent a revolution—what one contemporary accurately called a "stupendous upheaval." Between 1920 and 1930, 118,792 white people left the neighborhood and 87,417 Negroes arrived.[10] Second-generation Italians and Jews were responding to the same conditions of prosperity that promoted mobility in all the immigrant neighborhoods of Manhattan—they were not *only* moving away because Negroes settled near them. Conditions of life which satisfied immigrant parents were often unacceptable to children: "The tenements which housed their parents," immigration expert Edward Corsi wrote in 1930, "are being left behind by the children. . . ." "East Harlem used to have a great deal larger population," a survey of the Mayor's Committee on City Planning during the Great Depression concluded. "Like others of the older residential districts, it has suffered by the exodus of families to newer surroundings. . . ."[11]

The city's newest migrants moved into the Harlem flats vacated by Italians and Jews. Puerto Ricans came to live in East Harlem, created community organizations, and laid the foundations for "El Barrio" of today. By 1930 some 45,000 Puerto Ricans resided in New York City and most were heavily concentrated in East Harlem.[12] Negroes moved north along St. Nicholas Avenue—"On the Heights," they called it—and south into the heart of "Little Russia," the former Jewish section. "Just Opened

[8]James Ford, *et al.*, *Slums and Housing: With Special Reference to New York City* (Cambridge, Mass., 1936), II, 311–315.

[9]*Ibid.*, p. 317; Bureau of the Census, *Negroes in the United States, 1920–1932* (Washington, D.C., 1935), p. 55.

[10]Winfred B. Nathan, *Health Conditions in North Harlem, 1923–1927* (New York, 1932), pp. 13–14.

[11]*Harlem Magazine*, XIX (June 1930), 8; Mayor's Commission on City Planning, *East Harlem Community Study* (typescript in New York Public Library, 1937), p. 16.

[12]*Slums and Housing*, p. 370; Antonio T. Rivera to La Guardia, June 24, 1935, La Guardia Papers; "Harlem Puerto Ricans Unite to Prove Faith," *The New York Times*, July 2, August 9, 16, 1926; *Opportunity*, IV (October 1926), 330.

for Colored" signs were common in the neighborhood. Mount Olivet Baptist Church occupied, and still occupies, the once exclusive Temple Israel of Harlem. Prince Hall Masons bought a building that "was formerly a home for aged Jews." Graham Court, a magnificent block-length apartment house on One Hundred and Sixteenth Street, with eight separate elevators and apartments of seven to ten rooms, was opened to Negroes in 1928.[13] By 1930, 164,566 Negroes, about 72 per cent of Manhattan's Negro population, lived in Harlem.[14] The Negro ghetto remained and expanded as the other ethnic ghettos disintegrated. The economic and residential mobility permitted white people in the city was, and would continue to be, largely denied Negroes. Most Negroes were "jammed together" in Harlem—even those who could afford to live elsewhere—with little possibility of escape.[15] "One notable difference appears between the immigrant and Negro populations," an important federal study of Negro housing concluded. "In the case of the former, there is the possibility of escape, with improvement in economic status, in the second generation, to more desirable sections of the city. In the case of Negroes, who remain a distinguishable group, the factor of race and certain definite racial attitudes favorable to segregation, interpose difficulties to ... breaking physical restrictions in residence areas."[16] A rather ponderous paragraph, but a significant truth.

III

The settlement of West Indian Negroes in Harlem in the 1920's added another complicating dimension to the racial problems of this community —one that fostered discord rather than harmony among the city's Negroes. There were ten times as many foreign-born Negroes in New York City as in any other American urban area. In 1930, 54,754 foreign Negroes lived in the city—39,833 of whom resided in Manhattan. Miami, the next largest American city in terms of immigrant Negroes, was settled by only 5,512 people; Boston ranked third with 3,287 West Indians. About 25 per

[13]*The New York Age*, August 27, 1927, March 31, 1928, January 11, 1930; *The New York Times*, October 19, 1924.

[14]*Slums and Housing*, p. 314.

[15]The attempt of Negroes to move into Washington Heights, Yonkers and Westchester was opposed in these sections as it had been in Harlem earlier. The Neighborhood Protective Association of Washington Heights urged landlords to sign racially restrictive covenants. Mortgage pressures from financial institutions closed down a Negro housing development in Yonkers. As a result of population pressure, however, another large ghetto was created in the Bedford-Stuyvesant section of Brooklyn in the 1920's. Of the 68,921 Negroes in Brooklyn in 1930, 47,616 lived in what is now called Bedford-Stuyvesant. "Negro Community Near Yonkers Abandoned," *The New York Age*, July 3, 1926, March 24, August 4, 1928, April 19, 26, 1930; *Slums and Housing*, p. 314. For a sketch of Brooklyn's Negro community see Ralph Foster Weld, *Brooklyn Is America* (New York, 1950), pp. 153–173.

[16]The President's Conference on Home Building and Home Ownership, *Report of the Committee on Negro Housing* (Washington, D.C., 1931), p. 5.

cent of Harlem's population in the twenties was foreign-born. Harlem was America's largest Negro melting pot.[17]

In the era of immigration restriction, West Indian Negroes came to America through what a contemporary called the "side door." The immigration laws of the 1920's seriously restricted the migration of Europeans and totally excluded Orientals but had little effect on peoples of the Caribbean. At first there were no restrictions on West Indian Negroes. After 1924, they could enter the country under quotas set aside for their mother countries. Since these quotas were never filled there was, in reality, a free flow of people from the islands to the United States in the 1920's.[18]

Although American Negroes tended to lump all the migrants together in a uniform image—"There is a general assumption," one migrant wrote, "that there is everything in common among West Indians"—it is important to recognize that Harlem's Negro immigrants represented a diverse group of peoples from dozens of different islands in the Caribbean.[19] Most Negro immigrants felt a strong attachment to their homeland. They demonstrated an "exaggerated" nationalism in America—a buffer against the strangeness of the new culture and the hostility they experienced—which was typical of white immigrant groups. It was common, for example, to find former British subjects at the office of the British consul protesting some difficulty they experienced in America.[20] Nationalistic organizations kept close check on American foreign policy in the Caribbean and often gave banquets for and listened to addresses by West Indian dignitaries. West Indian Negroes from all countries had the lowest rate of naturalization of all immigrant groups. The people white Americans and American Negroes called "West Indians" were really individuals from Jamaica, Trinidad, Barbados, Martinique, St. Vincent, St. Lucia, Dominica, British Guiana, St. Kitts, Nevis, Montserrat, Antigua, Virgin Islands, Bermuda, the Bahamas, and so on. Although the majority spoke English, some considered French their first tongue; others Spanish; a few Dutch. The fraternal and benevolent associations they founded were not inclusive organizations for all Negro immigrants, but exclusive ones—*landsmannschaften*— for people from specific islands. Danish settlers kept pictures of the King of Denmark in their homes; former British subjects held coronation pag-

---

[17]Bureau of the Census, *Fifteenth Census, 1930: Population* (Washington, D.C., 1933), II, 70; Ira De Augustine Reid, *The Negro Immigrant* (New York, 1938), pp. 248–249; Barrington Dunbar, "Factors in the Cultural Background of the American Southern Negro and the British West Indian Negro that Condition their Adjustment in Harlem" (M.A. thesis, Columbia University, 1935), *foreword*, p. 4.

[18]Reid, *The Negro Immigrant*, pp. 31–35; Reid, "Negro Immigration to the United States," *Social Forces*, XVI (March 1938), 411–417; W. A. Domingo, "Restricted West Indian Immigration and the American Negro," *Opportunity*, II (October 1924), 298–299.

[19]W. A. Domingo, "Gift of the Black Tropics," in Alain Locke, ed., *The New Negro: An Interpretation* (New York, 1925), p. 343.

[20]*The New York Age*, July 9, 1924, February 4, 1928; Harry Robinson, "The Negro Immigrant in New York" (WPA research paper, Schomburg Collection), p. 9.

eants and balls ("Boxes, 12s. 6d.—Loges, 8s. 4d.") and flew the Union
Jack in Harlem; Frenchmen had annual Bastille Day dances.[21]

Negro immigrants differed from each other in origin, yet in a broader
sense they shared general experiences, desires and mores which set them
apart *as a group* from their American brethren. Most came from societies in
which class distinctions played a more important role in one's life than
the color line—although the latter was certainly significant. Unaccus-
tomed to common American racial slurs, they often refused to accept
them without protest. The Pullman Company, for example, hesitated to
employ West Indian Negroes, it was said, "because of their refusal to
accept insults from passengers quietly."[22] Out of this heightened class
consciousness came a small group of political and economic radicals in Harlem—"foreign-born agitators," local Negroes called them.[23] Many of Harlem's street-corner orators in the 1920's, though not all, were West Indian
migrants. Hubert H. Harrison, a Virgin Islander, was among the most
prominent. Harrison was a socialist, an expert in African history, a militant critic of American society and a proud defender of the "Negro's
racial heritage." He conducted formal lectures in what he called the "Harlem School of Social Science," and others from street corners—his "outdoor
university." A Harlem church, the Hubert H. Harrison Memorial Church,
honors his memory. Others presented talks on "Socialism vs. Capitalism,"
organized tenants' leagues, published Marxist journals and tried to make
Harlemites labor-conscious. Richard B. Moore, Frank R. Crosswaith and
the Reverend Ethelred Brown—all Negro immigrants—were prominent
local candidates for Board of Aldermen, Assembly and Congress on Socialist and Communist tickets—they usually polled an exceedingly small vote.
Some organized rent strikes, "rent parades," lobbied for social legislation at
City Hall and Albany and distributed radical literature in Harlem. "There
is no West Indian slave, no American slave," the short-lived radical magazine *Challenge* commented. "You are all slaves, base, ignoble slaves."[24]

This concern with "class" led to the emergence of a broader tradition
in America. What is striking about the Negro immigrant is the way his
response to American conditions, such as his exaggerated sense of nationalism, was similar to the typical reactions of most European immigrants.
The Negro immigrant "did not suffer from the local anesthesia of custom"[25] and he tried to create a meaningful economic position for himself
within American society. Menial labor was, among the most first-generation

[21]Garrie Ward Moore, "A Study of a Group of West Indian Negroes in New York
City" (M.A. thesis, Columbia University, 1923), pp. 19–20; Reid, *The Negro Immigrant*, pp. 126–128; *The New York Age*, February 28, 1931, July 29, 1933.
[22]"The Negro in New York" (unpublished WPA manuscript, Schomburg Collection), pp. 25–27; Gardner N. Jones, "The Pilgrimage to Freedom" (WPA research
paper, Schomburg Collection), p. 25.
[23]Reid, *The Negro Immigrant*, p. 159.
[24]*Ibid.*, p. 123; "Communists in Harlem," *The New York Age*, September 21, 1929,
October 2, 9, 1926, December 24, 1927, January 21, May 12, December 8, 1928,
September 21, 1929.
[25]Domingo, "Gift of the Black Tropics," p. 347.

Negro immigrants, considered a sign of social degradation and looked upon with "disgust." Most were forced to accept such jobs initially, but were strongly motivated by their traditions to improve themselves. As a group, West Indians became noted for their ambition, thrift and business acumen. They were called "pushy," "the Jews of the race," "crafty," "clannish."[26] Negro journalist George S. Schuyler "admired their enterprise in business, their pushfulness."[27] "The West Indians [are] legendary in Harlem for their frugalness and thrift," one student noted. When a West Indian "got ten cents above a beggar," a common local saying ran, "he opened a business." Contemporary surveys of Negro business in Harlem and Columbus Hill demonstrate that a disproportionate number of small stores—the traditional "Race Enterprise"—were owned by Negro immigrants. Dr. P. M. H. Savory, one of the leading spokesmen of New York's foreign-born Negro community from the 1920's to his death in June 1965, owned and published the *Amsterdam News*. Many others achieved economic success within the racial barrier.[28]

Another significant distinction between the foreign-born Negro and the American was their attitude toward family life. Slavery initially destroyed the entire concept of family for American Negroes and the slave heritage, bulwarked by economic conditions, continued into the twentieth century to make family instability a common factor in Negro life. This had not been true for most West Indians, and they arrived in America with the orthodox respect for family ties that was traditional of rural people. The West Indian family was patriarchal in structure—contrasted with the typically matriarchal American Negro home. The father, as key worker and wage earner in the islands, ruled the household with a solid hand. It was beneath his dignity to help with domestic chores. (This led American Negroes to brand West Indian men "cruel.")[29]   Children were supposed to obey their parents rigidly—American Negroes considered them strait-laced; have long and formal courtships; and receive parental approval before marriage. Illicit sexual relations were considered the worst form of moral evil.[30] These traditions began to change in the second generation, but throughout the 1920's family solidarity was a pervasive force among New York's Negro immigrants.[31]

These differences in style of life were also evident in another important institution—the church. The majority of Harlemites were Baptists and

[26]Robinson, "Negro Immigrant in New York," pp. 21–22; Moore, "West Indian Negroes in New York City," p. 26.

[27]"The Reminiscences of George S. Schuyler" (Oral History Research Office, Columbia University, 1960), p. 73.

[28]Robinson, "Negro Immigrant in New York," p. 9; "The Negro in New York," p. 25; Moore, "West Indian Negroes in New York City," p. 25; Reid, *The Negro Immigrant*, p. 133; *The Messenger*, VII (September 1925), 326, 337–338; *The New York Age*, February 22, 1930; Baltimore *Afro-American*, January 9, 1932.

[29]Moore, "West Indian Negroes in New York City," p. 5.

[30]Dunbar, "Negro Adjustment in Harlem," pp. 14–25.

[31]Reid, *The Negro Immigrant, passim.*

Methodists; the immigrants were predominantly Episcopalian and Catholic.[32] The beautiful St. Martin's Episcopal Church was founded in Harlem in 1928 to minister to the needs of West Indian migrants. Services in immigrant churches were generally staid and quiet; Sunday a day of prayer, rest and visiting—as it had been on the islands. Observers were impressed with the differences between the emotionalism of a typical Harlem religious service and the moderation and restraint shown in churches of the foreign-born. Negro immigrants also objected to the general frivolity and "fast ways" that were part of a typical Sunday in Harlem.[33]

All these factors combined to make Harlem in the 1920's a battleground of intraracial antagonism. American Negro nativism spilled over to taint Harlemites' reactions to the West Indian. The Negro immigrant was ridiculed; his tropical clothing was mocked; children tossed stones at the people who looked so different; foreigners were taunted with such epithets as "monkey-chaser," "ring-tale," "king Mon," "cockney." "When a monkey-chaser dies/Don't need no undertaker/Just throw him in de Harlem River/He'll float back to Jamaica," was a verse from a Harlem ditty of the twenties. West Indians came to Harlem, ran another common saying, "to teach, open a church, or start trouble." "Bitter resentment grew on both sides." Each group called the other "aggressive." "We have . . . in Harlem," NAACP director Walter White wrote, "this strange mixture of reactions not only to prejudice from without but to equally potent prejudices from within." "If you West Indians don't like how we do things in this country," an American Negro said tersely, "you should go back where you came from. . . ."[34]

The obvious hostility of American Negroes forced Negro immigrants to unite in defense organizations larger than their individual national groups. The West Indian Committee on America, the Foreign-Born Citizens' Alliance and the West Indian Reform Association were founded in the twenties to soften these intraracial tensions and promote "cordial relations between West Indians and colored Americans." Radio programs were devoted to discussions of "Intra-Race Relations in Harlem," and immigrants were urged to become naturalized citizens. American Negroes, in turn, were asked to tone down their "considerable prejudice against West Indians." A semblance of co-operation was achieved as mass meetings were held in Harlem churches. The hatreds of the 1920's did not die,

[32]*Ibid.*, p. 125; Greater New York Federation of Churches, *Negro Churches in Manhattan* (New York, 1930).
[33]Reid, *The Negro Immigrant*, p. 174; Moore, "West Indian Negroes in New York City," pp. 20–25; Dunbar, "Negro Adjustment in Harlem," chap. IV, pp. 22–23.
[34]Roi Ottley, *'New World A-Coming': Inside Black America* (New York, 1943), pp. 47–48; Gardner Jones, "The Pilgrimage to Freedom" (WPA research paper, Schomburg Collection), p. 25; Beverly Smith, "Harlem—Negro City," *New York Herald Tribune*, February 14, 1930; Reid, *The Negro Immigrant*, p. 115; *The New York Age*, July 19, 1924, March 17, 1934; Dunbar, "Negro Adjustment in Harlem," chap. III, p. 4; Walter White, "The Paradox of Color," in Alain Locke, ed., *The New Negro: An Interpretation* (New York, 1925), p. 367.

however, until West Indian Negroes stopped migrating to New York. During the Depression more immigrants left New York than entered and intraracial tensions slowly eased. Young Harlemites today, even third-generation descendants of Negro immigrants, are often unaware of these old divisions. The unique type of intraracial hostility so prominent in the twenties has never reappeared. While it lasted, however, it served to weaken a Negro community in great need of unity. A divided Harlem confronted major social problems that desperately called for the co-operation of all.[35]

IV

The most profound change that Harlem experienced in the 1920's was its emergence as a slum. Largely within the space of a single decade Harlem was transformed from a potentially ideal community to a neighborhood with manifold social and economic problems called "deplorable," "unspeakable," "incredible." "The State would not allow cows to live in some of these apartments used by colored people . . . in Harlem," the chairman of a city housing reform committee said in 1927. The Harlem slum of today was created in the 1920's.[36]

The most important factor which led to the rapid deterioration of Harlem housing was the high cost of living in the community. Rents, traditionally high in Harlem, reached astounding proportions in the 1920's— they skyrocketed in response to the unprecedented demand created by heavy Negro migration and settlement within a restricted geographical area. "Crowded in a black ghetto," a sociologist wrote, "the Negro tenant is forced to pay exorbitant rentals because he cannot escape." In 1919 the average Harlemite paid somewhat above $21 or $22 a month for rent; by 1927 rentals had *doubled* and the "mean average market rent for Negro tenants in a typical block" was $41.77. In 1927 Harlem Negroes paid $8 more than the typical New Yorker for three-room apartments; $10 more for four rooms; and $7 more for five rooms, an Urban League survey noted.[37] Another report concluded that the typical white working-class family in New York City in the late twenties paid $6.67 per room, per month, while Harlem Negroes were charged $9.50.[38]

Realty values which had declined significantly prior to World War I *appreciated* in Harlem in the twenties.[39] Harlem experienced a slum boom.

[35]*The New York Age,* March 3, 24, April 21, 1928; Domingo, "The Gift of the Black Tropics," p. 344–345; Reid, *The Negro Immigrant,* p. 235.

[36]"Harlem Slums," *The Crisis,* XLVIII (December 1941), 378–381; *The New York Age,* January 22, 1927.

[37]New York Urban League, "Twenty-four Hundred Negro Families in Harlem: An Interpretation of the Living Conditions of Small Wage Earners" (typescript, Schomburg Collection, 1927), pp. 16–18.

[38]*Report of the Committee on Negro Housing,* p. 64.

[39]"Appreciation" of prices "came [when owners] remained calm. . . ." T. J. Woofter, *et al., Negro Problems in Cities* (New York, 1928), p. 75. *The New York Times* printed dozens of articles on Harlem's new business prosperity.

"The volume of business done in the section . . . during the last year is
. . . unprecedented," *Harlem Magazine* announced in 1920. "Renting conditions have been very satisfactory to the owners and the demand for
space . . . is getting keener every year [due] to the steady increase in the
negro population," a *New York Times* reporter wrote in 1923. There was,
in the language of a Harlem businessman, an "unprecedented demand for
Harlem real estate."[40] For landlords—Negro and white (Negro tenants
continually complained that Negro landlords fleeced them with equal facility as whites)—Harlem became a profitable slum.[41]

High rents and poor salaries necessarily led to congested and unsanitary
conditions. The average Negro Harlemite in the 1920's, as in the 1890's,
held some menial or unskilled position which paid low wages—work
which was customarily "regarded as Negro jobs." There were generally two
types of businesses in New York in terms of Negro hiring policy, E. Franklin Frazier wrote: "Those that employ Negroes in menial positions and
those that employ no Negroes at all." Macy's, for example, hired Negroes
as elevator operators, escalator attendants and cafeteria workers; Gimbels
used none. "We have felt it inadvisable to [hire] colored people," a Metropolitan Life Insurance Company executive explained in 1930, "not because of any prejudice on the part of the company, but because . . . there
would be very serious objection on the part of our white employees. . . ."[42]
Throughout the city the vast majority of Negro men worked as longshore-
men, elevator operators, porters, janitors, teamsters, chauffeurs, waiters
and general laborers of all kinds. Negro women continued to work as do-
mestics ("scrub women"), although in the 1920's an increasing number
were employed as factory operatives in the garment industry and in laun-
dries. Less than 20 per cent of Harlem's businesses were owned by Negroes.[43] The average Harlem family, according to President Hoover's
Conference on Home Building and Home Ownership, earned $1,300 a year
in the twenties; the typical white family in the city, $1,570. A variety of so-
cial investigations noted that working-class whites expended approximately
20 per cent of their income for rent, considered the proper amount by
economists; Harlemites, 33 per cent and more.[44] An Urban League study

[40]"Harlem Real Estate Increasing in Value," *Harlem Magazine*, VIII (February
1920), 18b; "Unprecedented Demand for Harlem Real Estate," *ibid.*, X (November
1920), 6; "Revival of Speculative Activity on Harlem's Main Thoroughfare," *The New
York Times*, January 18, 1920, July 24, 1921, June 10, 1923, February 13, 1927.

[41]"Of all the gouging landlords in Harlem, the colored landlords and agents are
the worst, according to the records of the Seventh District Municipal Court." "Race
Landlord is Hardest on His Tenants," *The New York Age*, November 20, 1920,
June 16, September 22, 1923, May 29, 1926.

[42]"The Negro in Harlem," pp. 27–32; *The New York Age*, April 26, 1930.

[43]Bureau of the Census, *Fourteenth Census, 1920*: Population (Washington, D.C.,
1923), IV, 366–367, 1157–1179; *Fifteenth Census, 1930; Occupations* (Washington,
D.C., 1933), 1130–1134; Helen B. Sayre, "Negro Women in Industry," *Opportunity*,
II (August 1924), 242–244.

[44]*Report of the Committee on Negro Housing*, p. 64; *Negro Problems in Cities*,
p. 122.

of 2,160 Harlem families demonstrated that almost half (48 per cent) spent 40 or more per cent of their earnings on rent. A 1928 sample of tenement families found that Harlemites paid 45 per cent of their wages for housing. Similar conclusions were reached in a variety of local community studies.[45] Whatever the exact figure, few Negroes looked to the first of the month with expectancy.

Added to the combination of "high rents and low wages"[46] was the fact that Harlem's apartment houses and brownstones were originally built for people with a radically different family structure from that of the new residents. Seventy-five per cent of Harlem's tenements had been constructed before 1900.[47] The Negro community of the twenties, like all working-class peoples in times of great migration, continued to be most heavily populated by young adults—men and women between the ages of 15 and 44. Family life had not yet begun for many Negro Harlemites—as it had for older Americans and earlier immigrants who lived in the community previously. In 1930, 66.5 per cent of Harlem Negroes were between the ages of 15 and 44, contrasted with 56.5 per cent for the general population of Manhattan and 54.4 per cent for New York City at large. Harlemites who were married had few children. In 1930, 17.5 per cent of Harlem's population was under 14; the corresponding figure for New York City was 24.5 per cent. The number of Harlemites under the age of 15 declined 14 per cent between 1920 and 1930, as whites left the neighborhood. There was a corresponding decrease of 19 per cent for those over 45 years of age.[48]

What all these statistics mean is simply that apartments of five, six, and seven rooms were suitable for older white residents with larger families and larger incomes—they obviously did not meet the needs of the Negro community in the 1920's. "The houses in the section of Harlem inhabited by the Negro were not only built for another race," E. Franklin Frazier noted, "but what is more important, for a group of different economic level, and consisting of families and households of an entirely different composition from those which now occupy these dwellings." "Unfortunately," Eugene Kinckle Jones of the Urban League stated, "the houses built before the [Negroes'] arrival were not designed to meet the needs . . . of Negroes." "The class of houses we are occupying today are not suited to our economic needs," John E. Nail said in 1921. Negro Harlemites desperately needed small apartments at low rentals: "One of the community's greatest needs

[45]"Twenty-four Hundred Negro Families in Harlem," p. 19; Sidney Axelrad, *Tenements and Tenants: A Study of 1104 Tenement Families* (New York, 1932), p. 15; New York Building and Land Utilization Committee, *Harlem Family Income Survey* (New York, 1935), p. 3; James H. Hubert, "Harlem—Its Social Problems," *Hospital Social Service*, XXI (January 1930), 44.
[46]*Report of the Committee on Negro Housing*, p. vii.
[47]William Wilson to La Guardia, October 6, 1944, La Guardia Papers.
[48]*Health Conditions in North Harlem*, pp. 16–17; *Fifteenth Census, 1930: Population* (Washington, D.C., 1933), II, 733–734; "The Negro in Harlem," p. 20.

[is] small apartments for small families with a reasonable rent limit. . . ."[49] Few realtors were philanthropic enough to invest their capital in new construction; older homes, properly subdivided, produced sufficient income. Only a handful of new houses were built in Harlem in the 1920's.[50]

A variety of makeshift solutions were found to make ends meet: "What you gonna do when the rent comes 'round," had been an old Negro song. The most common solution was to rent an apartment larger than one's needs and means and make up the difference by renting rooms to lodgers —"commercializing" one's home. In the twenties, approximately one white Manhattan family in nine (11.2 per cent) took in roomers, contrasted with one in four (26 per cent) for Negroes. Most lodgers were strangers people let into their homes because of economic necessity. It was difficult to separate "the respectable" from "the fast." "The most depraved Negroes lived side by side with those who were striving to live respectable lives," a contemporary complained. Urban reformers blamed many of Harlem's social problems on this "lodger evil."[51]

Every conceivable space within a home was utilized to maximum efficiency: "Sometimes even the bathtub is used to sleep on, two individuals taking turns!" Negro educator Roscoe Conkling Bruce wrote. Boarding-houses were established which rented beds by the week, day, night or hour. A large number of brownstones were converted to rooming houses: "Private residences at one time characteristic of this part of the city have been converted into tenements. . . ." One landlord transformed apartments in nine houses into one-room flats, a state commission investigating New York housing reported. Space which formerly grossed $40 a month now brought in $100 to $125. People were said to be living in "coal bins and cellars." In an extreme case, one social investigator discovered seven children sleeping on pallets on the floor of a two-room apartment. More common was the "Repeating" or "Hot Bed System"—as soon as one person awoke and left, his bed was taken over by another.[52]

An additional Harlem method devised to meet the housing crisis of the twenties was the "Rent Party." Tickets of admission were usually printed

[49]". . . The greatest need is the construction of model tenements. These should consist of one, two, three and four room apartments." "Modern Housing Needs," *The New York Age,* February 12, 1921, January 20, 1923, January 26, 1926, January 29, 1927; "The Negro in Harlem," p. 53; Eugene Kinckle Jones, "Negro Migration in New York State," *Opportunity,* IV (January 1926), 9.

[50]Victor R. Daly, "The Housing Crisis in New York City," *The Crisis,* XXXI (December 1920), 61–62.

[51]National Urban League, *Housing Conditions Among Negroes, New York City* (New York, 1915), *passim; Ford, et al., Slums and Housing,* p. 338.

[52]"Very often it is found that there are two shifts." William Wilson to La Guardia, October 6, 1944, La Guardia Papers; *The New York Age,* March 12, 1921, February 26, 1927; "Along Rainbow Row," *The New York Times,* August 15, 1921, January 27, 1922; "Twenty-four Hundred Negro Families in Harlem," *passim;* Roscoe Conkling Bruce, "The Dunbar Apartment House: An Adventure in Community Building," *The Southern Workman,* LX (October 1931), 418.

and sold for a modest price (25¢). All who wanted to come were invited to a party. Here is an example:[53]

> If you're looking for a good time,
>   don't look no more,
> Just ring my bell and I'll answer
>   the door.
> Southern Barbecue
> Given by Charley Johnson and Joe
>   Hotboy, and How hot!

Chitterlings, pigs' feet, coleslaw and potato salad were sold. Money was raised in this way to pay the rent: "The rent party," *The New York Age* editorialized in 1926, "has become a recognized means of meeting the demands of extortionate landlords. . . ." The white world saw rent parties as picturesque affairs—in reality they were a product of economic exploitation and they often degenerated into rowdy, bawdy, and violent evenings.[54]

A significant part of the deterioration of the neighborhood was caused by the migrants themselves. Some needed rudimentary training in the simplest processes of good health and sanitation (Booker T. Washington, it will be remembered, preached the "gospel of the toothbrush.")[55] E. Franklin Frazier called many Negro Harlemites "ignorant and unsophisticated peasant people without experience [in] urban living. . . ." They often permitted homes and buildings to remain in a state of uncleanliness and disrepair. Landlords complained that apartments were looted and fixtures stolen, that courtyards and hallways were found laden with refuse. Clothes and bedding were hung out of windows; trash sometimes thrown down air shafts; dogs walked on rooftops; profanities shouted across streets; "ragtime" played throughout the night. "Ragtime is a sufficient infliction of itself," one wag complained, "but when it keeps up all night, it becomes unbearable." "Since the so-called 'Negro invasion,'" a colored woman noted, "the streets, the property and the character of everything have undergone a change, and if you are honest, you will frankly acknowledge it has not been for the . . . improvement of the locality. . . . Are we responsible for at least some of the race prejudice which has developed since the entry of Negroes in Harlem?" Negro journals criticized "boister-

---

[53]*New York Herald Tribune,* February 12, 13, 1930.

[54]"I promoted a weekly party, to get money to pay rent." "Boisterous rent parties, flooded with moonshine, are a quick and sure resource." "The Reminiscences of Benjamin McLaurin" (Oral History Research Office, Columbia University, 1960), p. 155; *The New York Age,* August 11, 1923, June 21, December 11, 1926; Clyde Vernon Kiser, *Sea Island to City* (New York, 1932), pp. 44–45.

[55]Booker T. Washington, *Up from Slavery: An Autobiography* (New York 1959), pp. 122–123. Note the following statement of a recent study: "There are many cases in which migratory workers do not understand or properly use ordinary living facilities, such as toilets, showers, bedding, kitchen appliances, and garbage cans. The result has been unnecessary damage to property and needless expense for repairs." 87th Cong., 1st Sess., *Senate Report 1098* (1961), p. 8.

ous" men who laughed "hysterically" and hung around streete corners, and those who used "foul language on the streets." An editorial in the *Age*, one of many, attacked "Careless Harlem Tenants": "A great deal might be said about the necessity for training some of the tenants in the matter of common decency," it suggested. The absence of a sense of social and community responsibility, characteristic of urban life, obviously affected Negro Harlemites.[56]

All these factors combined to lead to the rapid decline of Harlem. The higher the rents, sociologists said, the greater the congestion: "Crowding is more prevalent in high-rent cities than in cities in which rent per room is more reasonable." In 1925, Manhattan's population density was 223 people per acre—in the Negro districts it was 336. Philadelphia, the second most congested Negro city in the country, had 111 Negroes to an acre of land; Chicago ranked third with 67. There were two streets in Harlem that were perhaps the most congested blocks in the entire world.[57]

People were packed together to the point of "indecency."[58] Some landlords, after opening houses to Negro tenants, lost interest in caring for their property and permitted it to run down—halls were left dark and dirty, broken pipes were permitted to rot, steam heat was cut off as heating apparatus wore out, dumb-waiters broke down and were boarded up, homes became vermin-infested. Tenants in one rat-infested building started what they called "a crusade against rats." They argued that the rats in their house were "better fed" and "better housed" than the people. Some common tenant complaints in the 1920's read: "No improvement in ten years"; "Rats, rat holes, and roaches"; "Very very cold"; "Not fit to live in"; "Air shaft smells"; "Ceilings in two rooms have fallen"; "My apartment is overrun with rats"; and so on.[59] There were more disputes between tenants and landlords in Harlem's local district court—the Seventh District Court—than in any municipal court in the five boroughs. Traditionally, municipal courts were known as "poor-men's courts"; Harlemites called the Seventh District Court the "rent court." Occasionally, socially conscious judges of this court made personal inspections of local tenements that were subjects of litigation. Without exception what they saw horrified them: "Conditions in negro tenements in Harlem are deplorable"; "Found few fit for human habitation"; "Negro tenants are being grossly imposed upon by their landlords"; "On the whole I found a need for great reformation"; were some of their comments. One municipal of-

[56]*The New York Age*, August 1, 1912, June 5, 1920, September 16, 1922, July 14, 1928; National Urban League, *Housing Conditions Among Negroes,* pp. 9–10; "The Negro in Harlem," p. 113; Eslanda Goode Robeson, *Paul Robeson: Negro* (London, 1930), p. 46.

[57]Woofter, *et al., Negro Problems in Cities,* pp. 79, 84; "The Negro in Harlem," p. 53; Ernest W. Burgess, "Residential Segregation in American Cities," *The Annals,* CXL (November 1928), 105–115; Ford, *et al., Slums and Housing,* p. 749.

[58]Owen R. Lovejoy, *The Negro Children of New York* (New York, 1932), p. 15.

[59]*The New York Age*, October 28, 1922, January 17, 1925; *Housing Conditions Among Negroes, passim;* "Twenty-four Hundred Negro Families in Harlem," *passim*.

ficial accurately called the majority of Harlem's houses "diseased proper-
ties."[60]

V

And the disease did not confine itself to houses. To touch most areas of
Harlem life in the 1920's is to touch tragedy. This was especially true of the
health of the community. Theoretically, a section of the city inhabited
by relatively young people should have ranked below the general population in mortality and sickness rates. Just the reverse was true. Undertaking was a most profitable Harlem business.[61]

From 1923 to 1927 an Atlanta University professor made an intensive
study of Harlem health. His findings were shocking. During these years
Harlem's death rate, for all causes, was 42 per cent in excess of that of the
entire city. Twice as many Harlem mothers died in childbirth as did
mothers in other districts, and almost twice as many Harlem children
"passed" as did infants in the rest of New York. Infant mortality in Harlem, 1923–1927, was 111 per thousand live births; for the city, 64.5. Families wept at the processions of "so many little white caskets." Similar
statistics are recorded for deaths from tuberculosis (two and a half to three
times the city rate), pneumonia, heart disease, cancer and stillbirths.[62] An
astounding number of Harlemites had venereal diseases. Negro children
commonly suffered from rickets—a disease of malnutrition. More women
than ever reported themselves "widows" to census-takers. Negro deaths
by violence increased 60 per cent between 1900 and 1925.[63] With the single exception of the Lower West Side Health District, which included the

[60]"I do not think I need to say that our problem of Harlem is one of the most serious
we have to face." Langdon W. Post (Chairman of New York City Housing Authority)
to La Guardia, April 30, 1936, La Guardia Papers. "The Negro Families of the West
Harlem section have undoubtedly the most serious housing problem in the City."
Ford, *et al.*, *Slums and Housing*, p. 326. *The New York Times*, September 16, 1920,
October 17, 23, 1921, April 22, 1922, January 17, June 13, 1925; *The New York Age*,
February 28, August 8, 1925, January 9, 1926; "Preliminary Report on the Subject of
Housing (1935)," La Guardia Papers.

[61]"High Cost of Dying," *The New York Age*, February 25, 1928.

[62]*Health Conditions in North Harlem, passim; The Negro Children of New York*,
p. 22; "Fighting the Ravages of the White Plague Among New York's Negro Population," *Opportunity*, I (January 1923), 23–24; Dr. Louis R. Wright, "Cancer as It
Affects Negroes," *ibid.*, VI (June 1928), 169–170, 187; Louis I. Dublin, "The Effect
of Health Education on Negro Mortality," *Proceedings of the National Conference
on Social Work, 1924* (Chicago, 1924), 274–279. Hereafter cited as PNCSW.

[63]". . . Syphilitic infection is one of the most fruitful causes of stillbirths, miscarriages,
and early death of infants." New York Association for Improving the Condition of the
Poor, *Health Work for Mothers and Children in a Colored Community* (New York,
1924), p. 3; "The Negro's Health Progress During the Last Twenty-five Years,"
Weekly Bulletin of the Department of Health, XV (June 12, 1926), 93–96; *Fifteenth
Census, 1930: Population* (Washington, D.C., 1933), II, 959; E. K. Jones, "The Negro's
Struggle for Health," *PNCSW, 1923* (Chicago, 1923), 68–72.

Health center districts, 1930	Infant mortality per 1,000 live births	TB mortality per 100,000 population	Pulmonary TB new case rate per 100,000 population	Other infectious diseases, rate per 100,000 population	Venereal disease new case rate per 100,000 population	General mortality rate per 1,000 population
Manhattan						
Central Harlem	98	251	487	987	2,826	15.3
Lower East Side	62	116	302	1,160	892	14.0
Kips Bay–Lenox Hill	73	75	184	937	629	12.7
East Harlem	75	137	311	1,326	913	12.0
Lower West Side	83	156	391	1,201	1,318	16.7
Riverside	64	75	196	827	778	12.3
Washington Heights	52	72	203	937	668	10.5
Total	73	122	294	1,049	1,455	13.3

old San Juan Hill neighborhood, Harlem was the most disease-ridden community in Manhattan.[64]

Whatever the causes of Harlem's health problems—and medical investigators continue to search for all the answers—a good deal can be laid at the door of slum environment. Urban reformers consistently showed a high correlation between poverty and congestion on the one hand and disease and death on the other. Mortality rates for infants whose mothers worked away from home, for example—and twice as many Negro women as white women in the city did—was higher than for children whose mothers remained at home; working-class families in old-law tenements (pre-1901) died at a higher-rate than those in newer houses; poverty led to the consumption of the cheapest foods, and this in turn fostered diseases of poor diet; working mothers died more readily in childbirth than unemployed women; and so on.[65] Added to all these considerations, however, was a deep strain of peasant ignorance and superstition embedded in the minds of thousands of migrants—foreign-born as well as native—who settled in Harlem. Quackery abounded in the community in the 1920's.[66]

Harlem had the reputation of a "wide-open city." Whatever you wanted, and in whatever quantity, so the impression went, could be bought there. This was certainly true for the variety of "spiritualists," "herb doctors," "African medicine men," "Indian doctors," "dispensers of snake oils," "layers-on-of-hands," "faith healers," "palmists," and phrenologists who performed a twentieth-century brand of necromancy there: "Harlem sick people are flocking to all sorts of Quacksters," an *Age* reporter noted. One man, "Professor Ajapa," sold a "herb juice" guaranteed "to cure consumption, rheumatism, and other troubles that several doctors have failed in." Powders could be purchased to keep one's wife home at night, make women fertile and men sexually appealing. "Black Herman the Magician" and "Sister P. Harreld" held séances and sold "blessed handkerchiefs," "potent powders," love charms, lodestones, amulets and "piles of roots." "Ignorance, cherished superstitions and false knowledge often govern Negroes in illness and hamper recoveries," a colored physician with the Board of Health wrote in 1926. Nine wood lice gathered in a little bag and tied around a baby's neck, some believed, would end teething. An

[64]Adapted from Godea J. Drolet and Louis Werner, "Vital Statistics in the Development of Neighborhood Health Centers in New York City," *Journal of Preventive Medicine*, VI (January 1932), 69.

[65]In 1920, 30.3 per cent of white women in the city worked, and 57.9 per cent of colored women were employed. *Fourteenth Census, 1920: Population* (Washington, D.C., 1923), IV, 367. Robert Morse Woodbury, *Causal Factors in Infant Mortality* (Washington, D.C., 1925); L. T. Wright, "Factors Controlling Negro Health," *The Crisis*, XLII (September 1935), 264–265, 280, 284; Mildred Jane Watson, "Infant Mortality in New York City, White and Colored, 1929–1936" (M.A. thesis, Columbia University, 1938); Charles Herbert Garvin, "White Plague and Black Folk," *Opportunity*, VIII (August 1930), 232–235.

[66]For "voodoo" and "devil worship" among West Indians see Reid, *The Negro Immigrant*, pp. 48–49, 136–138.

egg fried brown on both sides and placed on a woman's abdomen would hasten labor. If a mother in the course of childbirth kicked a Bible from her bed to the floor, either she or her child would die. People had faith in the medicinal qualities of dried cobwebs, rabbit brains, "dirt-dauber tea," and something called "cockroach rum." In spite of efforts of physicians, health agencies and the Negro press to bring modern-day medical information to the community, quackery "continued to thrive with impunity in Harlem." It aggravated an already tragic situation.[67]

Accompanying the proliferation of healers, and rooted in the same rural consciousness which made quackery possible,[68] was the host of storefront churches founded in Harlem in the twenties. These were places that healed one's soul: "Jesus is the Doctor, Services on Sunday," read a sign which hung over one door. An investigator found 140 Negro churches in a 150-block area of Harlem in 1926. "Harlem is perhaps overchurched," W. E. B. DuBois said modestly. Only about a third—fifty-four—of Harlem's churches were housed in regular church buildings—and these included some of the most magnificent and costly church edifices in New York City. The rest held services in stores and homes and appealed to Harlem's least educated people. "Jack-leg preachers," "cotton-field preachers," as their critics called them, hung out their poorly printed signboards and "preached Jesus" to all who wanted to listen. One self-appointed pastor held meetings in the front room of his home and rented chairs from the local undertaker to seat his small congregation. In Harlem in the twenties ·one could receive the word of the Lord through such nondenominational sects as: "The Metaphysical Church of the Divine Investigation," "The Temple of the Gospel of the Kingdom," "The Church of the Temple of Love," "Holy Church of the Living God," "Temple of Luxor," "Holy Tabernacle of God," "Royal Fraternity Association," "Knights of the Rose and Cross," "Sons of God," "Sons of Christ," "Sons of Jehovah," "Sanctified Sons of the Holy Ghost," and the "Live-Ever-Die-Never" church. People not only had their

[67] "... Many [are] bringing with them their simple faith in roots, herbs, home remedies, [and are] imposed upon by unscrupulous venders of worthless ... remedies," Dr. Peter Marshall Murray, "Harlem's Health," *Hospital Social Service*, XXII (October 1930), 309–313; C. V. Roman, "The Negro's Psychology and His Health," *PNCSW*, *1924* (Chicago, 1924), 270–274; *Opportunity*, IV (July 1926), 206–207; *The Crisis*, XLII (August 1935), 243; *The New York Age*, September 23, 1922, February 17, July 21, August 11, 25, 1923, January 6, April 5, 1924, February 21, March 14, 1925, January 18, July 23, 1927.

[68] Note the striking similarities between the medical and healing superstitions of urban Negroes in the twentieth century and those of slaves in the early nineteenth century. The following is a description of slave superstition by an ex-slave: "There is much superstition among the slaves. Many of them believe in what they call 'conjuration,' tricking, and witchcraft; and some of them pretend to understand the art, and say that by it they can prevent their masters from exercising their will over their slaves. Such are often applied to by others, to give them power to prevent their masters from flogging them. The remedy is most generally some kind of bitter root; they are directed to chew it and spit toward their masters. ... At other times they prepare certain kinds of powders, to sprinkle their masters' dwellings." *Narrative of the Life and Adventures of Henry Bibb, An American Slave, Written by Himself* (New York, 1849), pp. 25–31.

worries removed in these places, a Negro clergyman wrote, but "their meager worldly goods as well."[69]

The ministers of these churches preached a fundamentalism which centered around the scheming ways of Satan, who was everywhere, and the terror and joy of divine retribution, with an emphasis on terror. One congregation expelled members who attended the theater or movies. "The devil runs every theater," its pastor said. "He collects a tax on the souls of men and robs them of their seat in heaven." Services were fervent, loud and boisterous as members felt the spirit of the Lord and shouted and begged for His forgiveness. Tambourines sometimes kept up a rhythmic beat in the background and heightened the emotionalism to a state of frenzy. Neighbors of one storefront church sued the congregation for "conducting a public nuisance." The "weird sounds" which emanated from the building, they complained, seemed like a "jazz orchestra."[70]

> Are you ready-ee? Hah!
> For that great day, hah!
> When the moon shall drape her face in mourning, hah!
> And the sun drip down in blood, hah!
> When the stars, hah!
> Shall burst forth from their diamond sockets, hah!
> And the mountains shall skip like lambs, hah!
> Havoc will be there, my friends, hah!
> With her jaws wide open, hah!
> And the sinner-man, hah!
> And cry, Oh rocks! Hah!
> Hide me! Hah!
> Hide me from the face of an angry God, hah!
> Hide me, Ohhhhhh! . . .
> Can't hide, sinner, you can't hide.[71]

Contemporaries were uniformly critical of these evangelists—there were many Harlem "Prophets"—and most of these preachers were probably charlatans in some form. There was at least one exception, however. A new denomination, the Church of Christ, Apostolic Faith, was founded on the streets of Harlem by the Reverend Mr. R. C. Lawson in 1919. The Reverend Mr. Lawson, of New Iberia, Louisiana, "the only real Apostolic–Holy Ghost–Bible Preacher," presented what he called "Full Gospel" on street corners of Harlem's worst blocks. He decried the lack of emotionalism in the more established urban churches—copying "the white man's style," he said—and offered recent migrants a touch of fire and

[69]Beverly Smith, "Harlem—Negro City," *New York Herald Tribune*, February 11, 1930: Ira De Augustine Reid, "Let Us Prey!" *Opportunity* IV (September 1926), 274–278; Reverend James H. Robinson, *Road Without Turning: An Autobiography* (New York, 1950), 231.

[70]*The New York Age*, February 19, 1927; *The New York Times*, September 24, 1919.

[71]Zora Neale Hurston, *Dust Tracks on a Road* (Philadelphia, 1942), pp. 279–280.

brimstone and personal Christianity characteristic of religion in the rural South:

> I have found it, I have found it,
> the meaning of life, life in God,
> life flowing through me by the
> Holy Spirit, life abundant, peace,
> joy, life in its fullness.

Lawson started preaching on One Hundred and Thirty-third Street, east of Lenox Avenue. This area "was to Harlem what the Bowery is to the lower East Side," a Negro journalist recorded. From the streets, the Reverend Mr. Lawson moved into a small building and held services for those "fast drifting to a life of eternal darkness" every day and every night of the week. His Refuge Church of Christ became the founding church of the new denomination, and the Reverend Mr. Lawson its first bishop. By 1930 the Apostolic Church had some forty branches throughout the country and ran an orphanage, elementary school and "Bible Supply House"; it continues to prosper today. Annual conventions met in Refuge Church, "the most honored in the sisterhood of the Apostolic Church," and local leaders praised and publicized its good works for Harlem Negroes: "This church has had one of the most remarkable growths of any religious organizations in the country."[72]

Harlem was also a "wide-open city" in terms of vice and gambling.[73] The annual reports of the anti-vice Committee of Fourteen, founded in 1905, showed Harlem as the leading or near-leading prostitution center of Manhattan throughout the twenties. The Committee hired a Negro doctor, Ernest R. Alexander, to do a secret study of Harlem vice in 1928. His report emphasized the "openness of vice conditions in this district." Dr. Alexander personally found sixty-one houses of prostitution in the neighborhood—more than the combined totals of four other investigators hired at the same time to survey other districts. "There is a larger amount and more open immorality in Harlem than this community has known in years," Negro alderman George W. Harris noted in 1922. "It is a house of assignation ... this black city," Eric D. Walrond wrote bitterly in the Negro journal *The Messenger*.[74]

> Her dark brown face
> Is like a withered flower
> On a broken stem.
> Those kind come cheap in Harlem,
> So they say.[75]

---

[72]*The New York Age*, January 15, 1927, February 9, 1929, August 23, 1930, August 8, September 19, 1931, July 23, 1932, August 26, 1933, September 1, 1934.
[73]"A Wide Open Harlem," *ibid.*, September 2, 1922.
[74]Committee of Fourteen, *Annual Reports*, 1914–1930; *The Crisis*, XXXVI (November 1929), 417–418; *The Messenger*, VI (January 1924), 14.
[75]Langston Hughes, "Young Prostitute," *The Crisis*, XXVI (August 1923), 162.

The Committee of Fourteen also disclosed that more than 90 per cent of these "daughters of joy" institutions were owned and managed by whites. Other evidence verifies this.[76]

Gambling also prevailed in the neighborhood: "Bootleggers, gamblers, and other panderers to vice have found it profitable to ply their vicious trades in this section." The poorest of the poor sought instant riches through the numbers racket. No sum was too small to bet—starting with pennies. "One can bet with plenty of takers on anything from a horse race to a mule race," the *Age* editorialized. Many Harlemites "would rather gamble than eat," it concluded. People selected numbers to coincide with birthdays, dreams, hymns or chapters and verses of Scripture in expectation that they would coincide with the clearing-house figures of the day. The odds were thousands to one against success, yet the smallest hope for a richer life was better than none and Negroes continued to play "policy" avidly. "The chief pastime of Harlem seems to be playing the numbers," George S. Schuyler wrote in 1925.[77]

"Buffet flats," "hooch joints," "barrel houses," and cabarets supplied Harlemites with illegal liquor, and occasionally other things, in the Prohibition era. Drugstores, cigar stores, sweetshops and delicatessens were used as "fronts" for speakeasies. "Harlem can boast of more drugstores than any similar area in the world," one Negro commented. "A plethora of delicatessen stores may be found in the Negro sections of New York, most of which are simply disguised bootlegging stores," a Harlemite concluded in 1924. "And so many confectioners! One never dreamed the Negroes were so much in need of sugar." "Speakeasies downtown are usually carefully camouflaged," a *New York Tribune* reporter noted. "In Harlem they can be spotted a hundred yards off."[78]

Poverty and family instability also led to a high incidence of juvenile delinquency. A community with fewer young teenagers should have shown a proportionally lower juvenile crime rate; as with Negro health, just the reverse was true. "The records of the Children's Court of New York for every year from 1914 to 1927 show a steady increase in the percentage of all crimes committed by Negro boys and girls," Owen R. Lovejoy of the Children's Aid Society reported. In 1914 Negro children represented 2.8

[76]"Gambling is popular in Harlem, but the big shots of the racket are white." Fiorello La Guardia, "Harlem: Homelike and Hopeful" (unpublished manuscript, La Guardia Papers), p. 9; "A Summary of Vice Conditions in Harlem," Committee of Fourteen, *Annual Report for 1928* (New York, 1929), 31–34; *The New York Times,* February 13, 1922; *The New York Age,* February 28, 1925, May 18, 1929. Although whites seemed to control most of Harlem vice, Virgin Islander Casper Holstein— well-known as a philanthropist and café owner—was reputed to be a head of the numbers racket.

[77]"Harlem—The Bettor," *The New York Age,* March 7, 1925, November 6, 20, 1926, June 4, 1927, June 23, 1928; *The New York Times,* June 12, 1922, March 11, 1927; "New York: Utopia Deferred," *The Messenger,* VII (October, November 1925), 344–349, 370.

[78]*The New York Age,* September 16, 1922, April 21, 1923; *New York Herald Tribune,* February 13, 1930; *The Messenger,* VI (August 1924) 247, 262.

per cent of all cases before the juvenile court of New York City; in 1930 this figure rose to 11.7 per cent.[79]

Working mothers had little time to care for their children. Youngsters "with keys tied around their necks on a ribbon" wandered around the streets until families came home at night. A substantial portion were products of broken homes—families without a male head. One Harlem school principal testified that 699 of his 1,600 pupils came from families whose fathers were not living at home. Nor did the majority of Harlem school-children ever have time to accustom themselves to the regularity of school life; many families were rootless. Three-fourths of all the Negro pupils registered in one Harlem school, for example, transferred to some other before the end of one school year; some schools actually experienced a 100 per cent turnover. Pupils from the South were seriously deficient in educational training: "They are at times 14 to 15 years of age and have not the schooling of boys of eight," a Harlem principal wrote. "We cannot give a boy back seven years of wasted life. . . ." The typical Harlem school of the twenties had double and sometimes triple sessions. The "usual class size" was forty to fifty and conditions were generally "immensely over-crowded": "The school plant as a whole is old, shabby, and far from modern." In some schools 25 per cent and more of the children were over-age or considered retarded.

Negro children in Harlem often led disrupted and harsh lives from the earliest years of their existence: "Testimony has been given before us as to the moral conditions among children, even of tender age," a municipal agency investigating Harlem schools recorded, "which is not to be adequately described by the word 'horrifying.'" These conditions were obviously reflected in high rates of juvenile crime but more subtly, and worst of all, in a loss of respect for oneself and for life in general. Harlem youngsters developed "a sense of subordination, of insecurity, of lack of self-confidence and self-respect, the inability . . . to stand on their own feet and face the world with open eyes and feel that [they have] as good a right as anyone else."[80]

This then was the horror of slum life—the Harlem tragedy of the 1920's. "Court and police precinct records show," a municipal agency maintained, "that in arrests, convictions, misdemeanants, felons, female police problems and juvenile delinquencies, these areas are in the lead. . . ." It was no wonder that narcotics addiction became a serious problem then and that Harlem became "the center of the retail dope traffic of New York"; nor

[79]Lovejoy, *The Negro Children of New York*, p. 37; *New York Herald Tribune*, February 12, 1930; Joint Committee on Negro Child Study in New York City, *A Study of Delinquent and Neglected Negro Children Before the New York City Children's Court* (New York, 1927).

[80]Jacob Theobald, "Some Facts About P.S. 89, Manhattan," *The New York Age*, January 17, 1920; "Report of Subcommittee on Education," La Guardia Papers: "The Problem of Education and Recreation," *ibid.;* "The Negro in Harlem," p. 73; Lovejoy, *The Negro Children of New York*, p. 22; *The New York Age*, March 12, 1921.

that local violence and hatred for the police were continually reported in the press.[81] The majority of Harlemites even during normal times lived "close to the subsistence level." Many were "under care" of charitable agencies in the period of relatively full employment. Those who needed money quickly and had no other recourse were forced to turn to loan sharks, Negro and white, who charged 30 to 40 per cent interest: Harlem "has been infested by a lot of loan sharks," a municipal magistrate who dealt with such cases stated. In one form or another the sorrow and economic deprivation of the Depression had come to Harlem in the twenties: "The reason why the Depression didn't have the impact on the Negroes that it had on the whites," George S. Schuyler said, "was that the Negroes had been in the Depression all the time."[82]

Irving Bernstein
THE WORKER IN AN UNBALANCED SOCIETY

Irving Bernstein knows that statistics often reveal the true nature of social developments, and he has a great gift for integrating figures into an interesting narrative. In writing the history of American workers in the twenties he was confronted with a lack of first-hand material: individual workers did not leave manuscript collections or other information about the life and concerns of laborers; few journalists reported on the ordinary workers' living or working conditions, because such material did not make "good copy." But, fortunately, sociologists, economists, and statisticians had probed factories, neighborhoods, and the censuses, as well as occasional government inquiries into the labor market. Bernstein

[81]"Results of the Crime and Delinquency Study," La Guardia Papers; *The New York Age*, January 6, February 17, June 23, 1923, June 12, 1926, December 3, 1927, July 28, 1928, January 4, 1930. A white Harlem policeman, at a later date, wrote the following: "Every one of [us] is made to feel like a soldier in an army of occupation. He is engulfed by an atmosphere of antagonism." *The Crisis*, LII (January 1945), 16–17.

[82]Lovejoy, *The Negro Children of New York*, p. 15; "The Negro in Harlem," p. 110; *The New York Age*, February 9, 1929; "The Reminiscences of George S. Schuyler" (Oral History Research Office, Columbia University, 1960), p. 232.

uses sources to tell the story of an aspect of America that is rarely glimpsed in standard histories of the Jazz Age.

American workers in the twenties were, generally speaking, a most unheroic proletariat. The abortive struggles of 1919–1920 had enervated their will to fight management. Their wages were running ahead of rising prices yet lagging far behind the escalating standard of living enjoyed by businessmen. The few workers who were organized and dared to strike (in an age when unions were weak and threatened by intimidating employers) were likely to lose their positions to immigrant or Negro scabs. They were also often displaced by machinery, farmers whose crops had failed, or needy women and children. They constantly feared business upheaval which could cast them into the streets without recourse to relief.

In other passages of The Lean Years, *Bernstein relates the numerous obstacles in the way of strong labor organization: the courts' nineteenth-century interpretations of the law; repression by employers using private armies; welfare capitalism which built a facade of industrial justice; and the doctrinaire laziness of the American Federation of Labor with its Babbitt-minded leadership. Millions of workers awaited unionization in the turbulent decade of the thirties.*

The symbol of the twenties is gold. This was the age of the gold standard, a time when people with money slept with confidence: their banknotes were redeemable in the precious metal. Small boys received gold watches on ceremonial occasions, and little girls were given gold pieces as birthday gifts. The noted Philadelphia banking family, the Stotesburys, equipped their bathroom with gold fixtures ("You don't have to polish them you know"). Writing in gloomy 1932, the economist Frederick C. Mills spoke of the economy of the twenties as having "the aspects of a golden age." The historians Charles and Mary Beard titled the introductory chapter on the twenties of *America in Midpassage* "The Golden Glow." To a contemporary reader the title seemed just right.

Yet hindsight finds the image unfitting. The twenties were, indeed, golden, but only for a privileged segment of the American population. For the great mass of people whose welfare is the concern of this study— workers and their families—the appropriate metallic symbol may be nickel or copper or perhaps even tin, but certainly not gold. Although on the surface American workers appeared to share in the material advantages of the time, the serious maladjustments within the economic system fell upon them with disproportionate weight. This interplay between illusion and reality is a key to the period. In fact, this was a society in imbalance and workers enjoyed few of its benefits.

From Irving Bernstein, *The Lean Years*. Reprinted by permission of Houghton Mifflin Company.

I

In the twenties two population changes occurred that were to prove profoundly significant to labor: the shift from farm to city speeded up and immigration from abroad slowed down. The American farmer's venerable propensity to move to town reached a climax. During the ten years from 1920 to 1929, according to the Department of Agriculture, 19,436,000 people made the trek; in every year except 1920 and 1921 over 2 million left the land, though many returned. The farm population, despite a higher fertility rate, declined by 3.7 per cent between 1920 and 1930 (31.6 to 30.4 million), while the nonfarm population rose by 24.6 per cent (74.1 to 92.3 million). Not only did these displaced husbandmen go to town; they appear to have gone to the big towns. Communities with over 100,000 grew by 32.4 per cent from 1920 to 1930, while those with 2500 to 5000 increased by only 7.6 per cent. Never before had the United States experienced such an immense flow from farm to city.

This was, in the words of the National Resources Committee, "a migration of hope," folks moving to improve their lot. They had to reckon with the economic paradox of the time, rural depression in the midst of relative urban prosperity. Agricultural prices had collapsed in 1921 and simply failed to recover. For many farmers city employment at almost any wage represented a rise in income. Another factor was the marked increase in agricultural productivity. This was the era in which the internal combustion engine revolutionized American agriculture by displacing the horse, the mule, and, most important, the farmer, his wife, and his children. Between 1920 and 1930, the number of trucks on farms rose from 139,000 to 900,000 and tractors from 246,000 to 920,000. In contrast with a sale of only 3000 combines in 1920, the implement factories disposed of 20,000 in 1929. Finally, there was the eternal lure of the city—the opportunities, satisfactions, and glamour of urban living as compared with the drudgery and isolation of life on the land. As the boys sang at American Legion conventions: "How ya gonna keep 'em down on the farm after they've seen Paree?"

The impact of this movement upon labor can hardly be exaggerated. Employers, despite the drop in immigration from abroad, had at their disposal a great pool of workmen, particularly the unskilled and semiskilled. This large labor supply, inured to the low level of farm income, relieved an upward pressure on wage rates that might have occurred. Workers drawn from a rural background were accustomed to intermittency and so did not insist on regularity of employment. Although they adapted readily to machinery, they were without skills in the industrial sense. The fact that the price of skilled labor was high and of unskilled low induced management to substitute machines for craftsmen. The displaced farmers carried into industry the agricultural tradition of mobility, especially geographic and to a lesser extent occupational. They brought with them, as well, the conservative outlook and individualistic accent of the rural mind. Since they were predominantly of older stocks, their entry into the urban labor force had an Americanizing influence, reversing the tendency to ethnic diversity produced by the wave of immigration that preceded World War I. There was, however, one divisive element in this trend to homogeneity: the Negro's emergence on a large scale in the urban working class.

The unskilled rural Negro of the South won his foothold in northern industry during the war, particularly in the metalworking, auto, and meat industries. By 1923, for example, Ford had 5000 colored employees. In the early twenties the demand for this class of labor was brisk, but slacked off after 1924, when industry in the North achieved a labor supply equilibrium. Some 1,200,000 Negroes migrated from South to North between 1915 and 1928. At this time the Negro took a long stride in the direction of integration with the dominant urban industrial society in America. Folklorists at the end of the twenties, for example, found a Negro cook in Houston singing:

Niggers gittin' mo' like white folks,
Mo' like white folks every day.
Niggers learnin' Greek and Latin,
Niggers wearin' silk and satin—
Niggers gittin' mo' like white folk every day.

To the employer the agricultural influx was a blessing. The resulting surplus of labor gave him little cause to fear turnover; money wage rates were stable; and unionism was in the doldrums. To the labor movement the migration was a short-term disaster. In the economic and political context of the twenties this accretion to the urban labor force was unorganizable. For the economy as a whole the movement was, of course, both inevitable and desirable, but it carried a danger. With a larger number of people now wholly dependent upon wages and salaries, President Hoover's Committee on Social Trends noted, "any considerable and sustained interruption in their money income exposes them to hardships which they were in a better position to mitigate when they were members of an agricultural or rural community."[1]

As important to labor as the flight of the farmer to the city was the fundamental change in immigration policy, almost shutting a door that had remained wide open for three centuries. The turn came in 1917 with the passage of a law over President Wilson's veto requiring aliens over sixteen seeking admission to demonstrate the capacity to read "the English lan-

[1]The basic data appear in Historical Statistics, 29, 31; National Resources Committee, The Problems of a Changing Population (Washington: 1938), 88; Harry Jerome, Mechanization in Industry (New York: National Bureau of Economic Research, 1934), 122–25; Edward E. Lewis, The Mobility of the Negro (New York: Columbia University Press, 1931), 131–32; National Urban League, Negro Membership in American Labor Unions (New York: National Urban League, 1930), 8; John A. and Alan Lomax, comps., American Ballads and Folk Songs (New York: Macmillan, 1934), xxx; Recent Social Trends, vol. 2, p. 806.

gauge, or some other language or dialect." The purpose was to discriminate against immigrants from southern and eastern Europe, who were presumed to be less literate than those from the northwestern part of the continent. The end of the war in 1918 promised a flood of immigrants from the Mediterranean and Eastern nations despite the literacy test. Hence restrictionists pushed through an emergency statute in 1921 that limited the annual inflow from any country to 3 per cent of its nationals resident in the United States in 1910. This national origins principle was made permanent in 1924 in a law that reduced the rate to 2 per cent and employed the census of 1890 as the base. The restriction was to take effect in stages, reaching full impact in fiscal 1931. The objectives were dual: to cut the total volume sharply and to establish a national origins distribution in favor of the British Isles, Germany, and Scandinavia. Under the final quotas Germany, for example, was permitted 50,000 immigrants annually as contrasted with only 4000 for Italy.

The legislation achieved the aims of its sponsors. The average annual number of immigrants entering the United States fell from 1,034,940 in the prewar years 1910–14 to 304,182 in 1925–29, a drop of 70.6 per cent. In the case of Germany the average annual inflow actually rose from 32,237 in 1910–14 to 47,506 in 1925–29. For Italy, by contrast, the average fell from 220,967 in 1910–14 to 13,498 in 1925–29.

Immigration restriction had a significant impact upon labor in the twenties and a greater one in the following decade. The earlier tendency toward ethnic, social, and cultural heterogeneity was reversed. The AFL's failure in the great steel strike of 1919 was symbolized by a poster got out by United States Steel, displaying an impassioned Uncle Sam ordering:

Go back to work!
Ritornate al lavoro!
Wracajcie do pracy!
Griz kite prie darbo!
Idite natragna posao!
Chodte nazad do roboty!
Menjenek vissza a munkaba!

During the twenties most of the corporation's foreign-born employees learned to speak English, and the proportion of native-born rose. "With the doors almost closed," an International Labor Office report declared, "education is expected gradually to destroy the obstacles which language and illiteracy have hitherto raised . . . and so to produce in time a homogeneous working population seeking the same objectives and the same standard of well-being."

During the twenties declining immigration joined a falling birth rate to slow population growth, with the obvious implication for the labor force. As significant as the gross change was its selective character; the entry of unskilled labor from abroad was virtually halted, while the inflow of skilled workmen, for whom there was a considerable demand, was little

impaired. The old American custom of employing the most recent immigrants to do the heaviest and dirtiest work had produced constant upward occupational mobility. Now it would be harder for the worker to
rise and, by the same token, easier for him to develop class consciousness.
Further, as Sumner H. Slichter pointed out, restriction required management to reverse its policy "to adapt jobs to men rather than men to
jobs." Hence employers sought to use labor more efficiently. A key solution, of course, was mechanization, helping to explain the high rate of
technological advance during the decade.[2]

Immigration restriction, by making unskilled labor more scarce, tended
to shore up wage rates. Equally important was the effect upon wage
differentials. Low rates for untrained immigrants were in large part responsible for the very wide spread between unskilled and skilled rates. Restriction would tend in time to narrow this differential.

II

Both the flight of the farmer and the curtailment of immigration spurred
the mechanization of industry. A dominant characteristic of the American economy in the twenties was the speeding up of the rate of technological change. "In the big plants visited," a British mission reported, "no man
is allowed to do work which can be done by a machine." During this
decade people in other parts of the world exhibited a consuming curiosity about American factories in much the same way that Americans were
curious about Admiral Byrd's discoveries in the Antarctic. The foreign
observers who toured United States industry in large numbers were invariably impressed with the eagerness of management to replace workers
with machines, to scrap old machines for new ones. The British group,
manifesting mixed admiration and disquiet over so large a dose of Progress, found something to cheer about: "It was a relief to get away from
the rattle of the conveyor . . . into the comparative quietude of these tool
rooms, where one could hear the honest impact of hammer on chisel,
the scraping of a file, and watch the fashioning of tools. . . ."

The main reason for the quickening pace of technological change was
that machinery was cheaper than labor. "I think," a foreign observer declared, "the use of specialized machines is mainly the result of a great
scarcity of skilled labor." Turning the coin over from labor supply to labor's price, an employer wrote in 1927:

> In spite of the fact that wages in our factory have more than doubled in the
> past fifteen years, our manufacturing costs are actually lower now than they
> were at the beginning of that period. High wages, forcibly thrust upon us by

[2]Preston William Slosson, *The Great Crusade and After, 1914–1928* (New York:
Macmillan, 1930), 299–301; *Historical Statistics,* 33; "The U.S. Steel Corporation:
III," *Fortune,* 13 (May 1936), 136; H. B. Butler, *Industrial Relations in the United
States* Geneva: International Labor Office, 1927, 14; Sumner H. Slichter, "The
Current Labor Policies of American Industries," *QJE,* 43 (May 1929), 393.

the war, and always opposed by those in charge of our business, have lowered our manufacturing costs, by making us apply machinery and power to tasks formerly done by hand.

The conditions for mechanization were almost ideal: wages were high in relation to the price of machinery, immigration was limited, and the capital market was abundant and easy. These factors created—as the current phrase had it—the Machine Age. Eugene O'Neill wrote a play about it, *Dynamo,* as did Elmer Rice with *The Adding Machine.* The term "robot," exported from Czechoslovakia, became part of the American language.[3]

The march of machinery in the twenties affected almost every segment of the economy, and a few dramatic illustrations suggest its impact. In 1927 the introduction of continuous strip-sheet rolling opened a new era in sheet-steel and tin-plate production; a continuous mill had the capacity of forty to fifty hand mills. The Danner machine for glass tubing, first offered in 1917, completely replaced the hand process by 1925. The Ross carrier for handling lumber came into general use. The first successful machine to produce a complete cigar was patented in 1917; by 1930, 47 per cent of the 6.5 billion cigars turned out were made by machine. Mechanical coal-loading devices were widely accepted, while mine locomotives displaced the horse and the mule for haulage. Heavy construction was revolutionized by the power shovel, the belt and bucket conveyor, pneumatic tools, the concrete mixer, the dump truck, and the highway finishing machine. The street-railway industry converted to the one-man trolley. Several communication devices won general acceptance: the automatic switchboard and dial telephone, the teletype, and the market-quotation ticker. The motion picture industry entered a new phase with production of the first "talkie" in 1926. More important in the aggregate than these spectacular innovations, however, were the countless small changes which produced, for example, extraordinary increases in output in blast furnaces, in pulp and paper manufacture, in the automobile and rubber tire industries, and in beet sugar mills. Between 1919 and 1929, horsepower per wage earner in manufacturing shot up 50 per cent, in mines and quarries 60 per cent, and in steam railroads 74 per cent.[4]

Advancing technology was the principal cause of the extraordinary increase in productivity that occurred during the twenties. Between 1919 and 1929, output per man-hour rose 72 per cent in manufacturing, 33 per cent in railroads, and 41 per cent in mining. Put somewhat differently

[3]*The Daily Mail Trade Union Mission to the United States* (London: Daily Mail, [1927], 81, 84. See also Parliament of the Commonwealth of Australia, *Report of the Industrial Delegation* ... (Canberra: 1927), 16–17, and André Siegfried, *America Comes of Age* (New York: Harcourt, Brace, 1927), 149; Edward Bliss Reed, ed., *The Commonwealth Fund Fellows and Their Impressions of America* (New York: Commonwealth Fund, 1932), 90. The American employer is quoted in D. D. Lescohier, *What Is the Effect and Extent of Technical Changes on Employment Security?* (American Management Association, Personnel Series No. 1, 1930), 12.

[4]Jerome, *Mechanization, passim.*

by David Weintraub, unit labor requirements (the number of man-hours required per unit of output) declined between 1920 and 1929 by 30 per cent in manufacturing, 20 per cent in railroads, 21 per cent in mining, and 14 per cent in telephone communications. Mills estimated that the physical volume of production for agriculture, raw materials, manufacturing, and construction climbed 34 per cent from 1922 to 1929, an average annual increment of 4.1 per cent. It was his impression that services, if they had been measurable, would have shown an even faster rate of growth. In fact, Americans generally were inclined to explain their economic society largely in terms of its mounting fruitfulness. When W. Wareing, an official of the British Amalgamated Engineering Union, asked John W. Lieb, vice-president of the Edison Company of New York, the secret of high wages, the reply came back promptly: "Productivity."

Rising output was the central force in the steady growth of national income during the twenties. Measured in current prices, which fluctuated narrowly, Simon Kuznets found that national income moved from $60.7 billion in 1922 to $87.2 billion in 1929, a gain of 43.7 per cent, or an average increment of 6.2 per cent per year. The share going to wages and salaries mounted from $36.4 billion to $51.5 billion, an increase of 41.5 per cent. The wage and salary proportion remained unusually constant at about 59 per cent of national income. The share of dividends rose more sharply from $3 billion in 1922 to $6.3 billion in 1929, up 110 per cent. This resulted in a relative increase in dividends from 5 per cent to 7.2 per cent of national income. Wage earners, in other words, did not enjoy as great a rise in income as did those in the higher brackets. A noted study by the Brookings Institution confirms this with respect to the wage and salary share, concluding that "since the war salaries have expanded much more rapidly than wages."[5]

III

The labor force that shared this national income entered a new phase in the twenties, a slowing rate of growth accompanied by a shift from manual to nonmanual employment. Immigration restriction joined with a falling birth rate to retard population advance. In contrast to a gain of 24 per cent in the first decade of the century, between 1920 and 1930 the number of people ten years old and over rose only 19 per cent.

More dramatic than slowing over-all growth was the marked movement from blue-collar to white-collar work, from physically productive to over-

[5]*Historical Statistics*, 71–72; David Weintraub, "Unemployment and Increasing Productivity," in National Resources Committee, *Technological Trends and National Policy* (Washington: 1937), 77; Frederick C. Mills, *Economic Tendencies in the United States* (New York: National Bureau of Economic Research, 1932), 243–51; *Daily Mail*, 21; Simon Kuznets, *National Income and Its Composition, 1919–1938* (New York: National Bureau of Economic Research, 1941), vol. 1, pp. 216–17; Maurice Leven, Harold G. Moulton, and Clark Warburton, *America's Capacity to Consume* (Washington: Brookings, 1934), 28.

head employment. The total number of gainful workers advanced from 41.6 to 48.8 million between 1920 and 1930, a gain of 17.4 per cent. Despite this, the extractive industries—agriculture, forestry and fisheries, and mining—suffered a loss of 3.4 per cent, from 12.2 to 11.9 million persons. Similarly, the manufacturing labor force remained almost stationary, rising only 0.9 per cent from 10,890,000 in 1920 to 10,990,000 in 1930. By contrast, the predominantly white-collar and service industries rose sharply. Trade, finance and real estate, education, the other professions, domestic and personal service, and government employment climbed 45.7 per cent from 11.5 to 16.7 million.

The same pattern emerges when the analysis is transferred from industry to occupation. Between 1920 and 1930, the number of manual workers in the labor force (farmers, farm laborers, skilled workers and foremen, semiskilled workers, and laborers) rose only 7.9 per cent from 28.5 to 30.7 million. Nonmanual workers (professionals, wholesale and retail dealers, other proprietors, and clerks and kindred workers) advanced 38.1 per cent from 10.5 to 14.5 million. During the twenties, that is, the American worker on an increasing scale took off his overalls and put on a white shirt and necktie.

Or, put on an elegant frock, silk stockings, and high-heeled shoes, for women entered the labor force at an accelerated pace at this time. The number of females fifteen and over gainfully occupied rose 27.4 per cent between 1920 and 1930, from 8.3 to 10.6 million. By the latter date, in fact, almost one of every four persons in the labor force was a woman. In Middletown the Lynds found that 89 per cent of the high school girls expected to work after graduation, only 3 per cent indicating they definitely would not. This female employment came as a jolt to foreigners, especially the British.

> It was a remarkable sight to see rows of bobbed, gum-chewing, spruce females seated on each side of a rapidly moving conveyor and so busily engaged with their work that not one of them had time to cast a passing glance upon the group of stalwart Britishers, who had considerable difficulty in following the movements of their nimble fingers.

Even more impressive was the 28.9 per cent increase between 1920 and 1930 in the number of employed married women, a rise from 1.9 to 3.1 million. In Middletown the old rule that a girl quit her job with marriage broke down under economic necessity in the twenties. A jobless husband or a need to support a child's education forced working-class mothers into the factories, shops, and offices. The female influx was another bar to organization. Even women who intended to work permanently carried over a vestigial attitude of impermanency that made them hesitant to take out union cards.

The decade of the twenties by contrast witnessed a decline in the employment of children. While in 1910 about one fourth of the boys aged ten to fifteen and one eighth of the girls of the same ages were employed, by 1930 the proportion of boys dropped to 6 per cent and of girls to 3 per cent. The Lynds found an almost total absence of child labor in Middletown. This great social advance was accompanied by a sharp rise in school attendance. The total increase at all levels of education exceeded 6 million between 1919 and 1928. The percentage of those between 14 and 17 enrolled in high school rose from 32 per cent in 1920 to 51 per cent in 1930. "If education is oftentimes taken for granted by the business class," wrote the Lynds, ". . . it evokes the fervor of a religion, a means of salvation, among a large section of the working class." There were many reasons for the decline in child labor: laws in most states fixing a minimum age for employment and compelling school attendance, the pressure of reform groups and organized labor, advancing mechanization, an adequate adult labor supply, and rising personnel standards in industry.

At the other end of the age scale, older workers struggled with diminishing success to hold on to their positions in the labor force. An advancing economic society placed a premium on speed and nimbleness over experience and judgment. Management came generally to accept the view that senior employees were not as productive as younger workers and that they imposed added liabilities upon those firms that provided insurance, medical, and pension plans. As a typical Middletown employer expressed it: "I think there's less opportunity for older men in industry than there used to be. The principal change I've seen in the plant here has been the speeding up of machines and the eliminating of the human factor by machinery." This opinion crystallized in the widespread adoption of age limits for hiring. Studies of Dayton, Ohio, and the states of Maryland and California revealed that a large proportion of employers fixed these limits at ages ranging from thirty-five to fifty, particularly in utilities and transportation, where pension plans were common. The inevitable consequence was a higher incidence of unemployment among older workers; once let go, they found it extremely difficult to find new jobs. This problem so concerned the Couzens Committee, investigating unemployment for the Senate in 1929, that it urged industry, the states, and the federal government to consider a system of old age pensions.[6]

The organization of the labor market was haphazard in the extreme. Since the United States Employment Service was ineffective and collective bargaining governed hiring in only a handful of industries, the typical employer picked at will. The only restraint upon his power to hire was tightness in the labor market, and this simply did not exist during the decade except for a few months in 1923. The person seeking work in most cases

[6]*Historical Statistics*, 64–65; *Daily Mail*, 83; Lynds, *Middletown*, 1–2, 13, 33, 187; *Recent Social Trends*, vol. 1, pp. 305, 713, 730–31, vol. 2, pp. 777–79, 810–11; National Resources Committee, *Technological Trends*, 194–97; Ewan Clague and W. J. Couper, "The Readjustment of Workers Displaced by Plant Shutdowns," *QJE*, 45 (Feb. 1931), 326; Isador Lubin, *The Absorption of the Unemployed by American Industry* (Washington: Brookings, 1929), 18; "Age Limits in Industry in Maryland and California," *MLR*, 32 (Feb. 1931), 39; *Hearings before Committee on Education and Labor, Senate*, 70 Cong., 2 sess. (1928–29), xv.

was both powerless and incapable of exercising a rational choice if alternatives were available. In Middletown, for example, "most of the city's boys and girls 'stumble on' or 'fall into' the particular jobs that become literally their life work." The fetish workmen made of education was in part, at least, a yearning for rationality in an unreasoning world.

The worker was seldom afforded the opportunity to rise in the social scale. He lacked the qualifications for the professions and the capital for business. His main hope for upward mobility was within the hierarchy of the firm that employed him. Even here, however, the opportunities were limited. In twenty-one months in 1923–24, plants employing 4240 workers in Middletown had only ten vacancies for foremen—one chance in 424. A businessman, the Lynds found, looked forward to the steady improvement of his lot. But, "once established in a particular job, the limitations fixing the possible range of advancement seem to be narrower for an industrial worker." His position, of course, was more dismal if he happened to be a member of a minority group. In greater or lesser degree, the Irish, the Italians, the Jews, the Mexicans, and the Negroes suffered in the labor market. To dwell only upon the last, the ones who probably enjoyed the doubtful distinction of sustaining the most severe discrimination: Negroes were the last to be hired and the first to be fired, were seldom allowed to do skilled work and almost never given supervisory jobs, were assigned the older, dirtier, and less pleasant work places, were paid less for the same work, and were often denied membership in labor unions. A Negro song of protest went this way:

Trouble, trouble, had it all mah day.

. . .

Can't pawn no diamonds,
Can't pawn no clo'
An' boss man told me,
Can't use me no mo'.

Rather get me a job, like white folks do.
Rather get me a job, like white folks do.
Trampin' 'round all day,
Say, "Nigger, nothin' fo' you."[7]

This complaint could have been voiced as well by white members of the labor force, since the prosperity of the twenties was accompanied by heavy unemployment. Foreign observers reported more men than jobs in each locality they visited. The absence of government statistics, disgraceful in itself, makes it impossible to report the actual volume of joblessness. Evidence that severe unemployment existed, however, is beyond dispute.

[7] Lynds, *Middletown*, 48, 68; Herman Feldman, *Racial Factors in American Industry* (New York: Harper, 1931), ch. 2; John Greenway, *American Folksongs of Protest* (Philadelphia: University of Pennsylvania Press, 1953), 113.

The noted Brookings Institution study, *America's Capacity to Produce,* estimated that the economy in 1929 operated at only 80 per cent of its practical capacity. Weintraub calculated that the jobless constituted 13 per cent of the labor force in 1924 and 1925, 11 per cent in 1926, 12 per cent in 1927, 13 per cent in 1928, and 10 per cent in 1929. Woodlief Thomas made minimum unemployment estimates for nonagricultural industries of 7.7 per cent in 1924, 5.7 per cent in 1925, 5.2 per cent in 1926, and 6.3 per cent in 1927.

Studies of particular localities and firms reinforce this conclusion. The University of Pennsylvania's Wharton School of Finance survey of Philadelphia in April 1929 revealed that 10.4 per cent of the wage earners were idle, the great majority because of inability to find work. A study in November of the same year in Buffalo showed 10 per cent of the labor force totally unemployed and an additional 6.5 per cent on part time. Half of the men and almost two thirds of the women had been out of work more than ten weeks. In Middletown in the summer of 1924 a firm that considered 1000 workmen its "normal force" actually employed 250. In the first nine months of that year only 38 per cent of the heads of the working-class families studied worked steadily. When out-of-town firms offered to run ads for machinists in 1924, Middletown employers persuaded the local papers not to carry them in order to preserve the town's pool of skilled workmen. United States Rubber closed its New Haven plant in April 1929, throwing 729 out of work, and its Hartford plant in September 1929, making another 1105 jobless. A study of their experience in finding work revealed that average lost time in New Haven was 4.38 months and in Hartford 4.33 months. Both groups suffered disastrous losses in earnings even when they were fortunate enough to find new jobs. A similar survey of displaced cutters in the Chicago men's clothing industry in the twenties told much the same story.

So severe, in fact, was unemployment during the decade that social workers, burdened with the misery that followed in its wake, became alarmed. The International Conference of Settlements, meeting at Amsterdam in 1928, heard the Belgian economist Henri de Man claim that industrialism produced both more goods and more permanently unemployed. The National Federation of Settlements, convening in Boston that same year, found that unemployment was the prime enemy of the American family. Nor were all employers as callous as those in Middletown. It was on December 17, 1928, that President Daniel Willard of the Baltimore & Ohio made his famous statement before the Couzens Committee:

It is a dangerous thing to have a large number of unemployed men and women—dangerous to society as a whole—dangerous to the individuals who constitute society. When men who are willing and able to work and want to work are unable to obtain work, we need not be surprised if they steal before they starve. Certainly I do not approve of stealing, but if I had to make a choice between stealing and starving, I would surely not choose to starve —and in that respect I do not think I am unlike the average individual.

The least onerous form of unemployment—seasonal—worsened during the twenties. Mild government pressure to regularize production in those trades noted for intermittency—construction, garments, maritime, and entertainment—had no noticeable effect. In addition, the great new automotive industry and its suppliers contributed heavily to seasonality. "Because of the ease with which labour can be obtained and discarded," an Australian observed, "there is little necessity for the employer to stabilize his rate of production over the year."

Far more serious was technological unemployment, the price paid for progress. A paradox of the American economy in the twenties was that its glittering technical achievement gave birth to a dismal social failure. At the top of the boom in 1929 Wesley Mitchell wrote that technological unemployment "is a matter of the gravest concern in view of the millions of families affected or threatened ... and in view of their slender resources." Weintraub estimated that between 1920 and 1929 in manufacturing, railways, and coal mining, machines displaced 3,272,000 men, of whom 2,269,000 were reabsorbed and 1,003,000 remained unemployed. There were, naturally, sharp variations in employment impact among industries. This is evident from Jerome's figures on labor time saved by particular machines: talkies saved 50 per cent, cigar machines 50 to 60 per cent, the Banbury mixer 50 per cent, the highway finishing machine 40 to 60 per cent, and various coal loaders 25 to 50 per cent. One of the coal devices was invented by a man named Joy. Union miners in Kentucky had a song about his contraption which they called "Joy Days."

Here is to Old Joy, a wonderful machine,
That loads more coal than any we've seen.

. . .

Ten men cut off with nothing to do,
Their places needed for another Joy crew.

. . .

We will pick out a spot with plenty of room
Where Joy can rest till the day of doom.

We will call it a holiday to dig him a nice grave,
Then march in a body to lay him away.

We will lay him away as it should be done,
And pay all expenses from our burial fund.

Monuments we will buy, inscribed nice and neat,
And place one each at his head and feet:

"Here lies Old Joy, a man we couldn't use,
For the damned old hellion wouldn't pay any dues."[8]

[8]Hugh Grant Adam, *An Australian Looks at America* (London: Allen and Unwin, 1928), 23, 80; "British Report on Industrial Conditions in the United States," *MLR*, 24

Mr. Joy's coal loaders and the other mechanical marvels of the time did more than displace men; they radically and continuously changed the content of jobs in American industry. Whether the net effect was to raise or lower the general level of skill is a nice question to which there is no ready answer. In the expanding New York commercial printing industry, for example, the substitution of machine-fed for hand-fed presses increased the demand for skilled operators and reduced demand for less skilled hand-feeders. Jerome found that mechanization had a differential impact in various segments of the industrial process: in material handling it displaced the unskilled; in systematizing the flow of production it reduced the skilled; in displacing manual by machine processing it usually diluted skills; in improving already mechanized operations it cut down on the semiskilled; in stimulating machine construction and repair it increased the demand for the skilled. A workman taking a job in the twenties had little way of knowing whether his skills would improve or decline; he could be reasonably certain, however, that a machine would soon change the content of his job.

The labor surplus during the decade was the principal reason for the low turnover rate, which fell to one half the prewar level. A contributory, though secondary, factor was the personnel management movement, one of whose main objectives was to stabilize the labor force within the firm. Excepting a few months in early 1923, turnover was unusually low. A study of manufacturing industries by the Metropolitan Life Insurance Company revealed that the median monthly rate of accessions fluctuated narrowly between 3.3 and 5.2 per cent and of separations between 3.1 and 4.0 per cent in the years 1924–29. Industry made few hires, and workers seldom quit. This was, in W. S. Woytinsky's words, "a period of increasing labor market rigidity."[9]

The issue of unemployment, serious though it was, excited little general interest. It received no more than passing attention in the 1928 presidential campaign. In Middletown, despite severe joblessness, "unemployment as a 'problem' virtually does not exist." The business people granted that steady work was a desirable objective but considered it quite utopian. Clinch Calkins found three widely held ideas at the

---

(June 1927), 1199; Edwin G. Nourse and Associates, *America's Capacity to Produce* (Washington: Brookings, 1934), 416; Weintraub, "Unemployment," 70; *Recent Economic Changes*, vol. 2, pp. 469–78, 876; "Unemployment Survey of Philadelphia," *MLR*, 30 (Feb. 1930), 227; Fred C. Croxton and Frederick E. Croxton, "Unemployment in Buffalo, N.Y., in 1929 . . . ," *MLR*, 30 (Feb. 1930), 236; Lynds, *Middletown*, 56–59; Clague and Couper, "Readjustment of Workers," 309–46; Robert J. Myers, "Occupational Readjustment of Displaced Skilled Workmen," *JPE*, 37 (Aug. 1929), 473–89; Clinch Calkins, *Some Folks Won't Work* (New York: Harcourt, Brace, 1930), 18–20; Senate Hearings, 84; *Recent Social Trends*, vol. 1, p. 309, vol, 2, p. 808; Jerome, *Mechanization*, 367–82; George Korson, *Coal Dust on the Fiddle* (Philadelphia: University of Pennsylvania Press, 1943), 141–42.

[9]Elizabeth Faulkner Baker, *Displacement of Men by Machines* (New York: Columbia University Press, 1933), 28 ff.; Jerome, *Mechanization*, 393 ff.; W. S. Woytinsky, *Three Aspects of Labor Dynamics* (Washington: Social Science Research Council, 1942), 29–33; Slichter, "Current Labor Policies," 429–31.

time: that unemployment existed only in bad times, that the only ones who suffered were those too thriftless to save, and that a man who really wanted work would find it. The fact that all were false in no way limited their currency.

The pervasiveness of the problem, however, compelled some squaring off with reality. The stirrings among social workers have already been noted. A handful of firms—notably Dennison Manufacturing, Hills Brothers, Procter & Gamble, Columbia Conserve, Packard, and Leeds & Northrup—sought to level out seasonality. The Amalgamated Clothing Workers and the International Ladies' Garment Workers set up unemployment insurance or guaranteed employment schemes in a few markets. Mr. Justice Brandeis and industrial engineer Morris Llewellyn Cooke tried to persuade President Frank Aydelotte of Swarthmore to establish an unemployment study unit at the college under the direction of Paul Douglas, a project that had barely got under way when the market crashed. Finally, the Senate Couzens Committee held hearings on unemployment in late 1928 and early 1929 and proposed this modest program: adequate statistics, reorganization of the United States Employment Service, encouragement of private unemployment insurance schemes, planning public works with an eye to stabilizing employment, and study of both the effects of industrial concentration on employment and the feasibility of a system of old age pensions. Virtually no one listened.[10]

IV

Labor's burden in this period of prosperity was not limited to unemployment; workers faced as well an unequal distribution of income. There were in 1929, the Brookings Institution found, 27,474,000 families of two or more persons. Nearly 6 million families, over 21 per cent, received less than $1000 per year; about 12 million, more than 42 per cent (including those below $1000), had incomes under $1500; nearly 20 million, 71 per cent (including those under $1500), took in less than $2500. The combined incomes of 0.1 per cent of the families at the top of the scale were as great as those of the 42 per cent at the bottom. The number who received over $1 million per year rose from 65 in 1919 to 513 in 1929. The distorted distribution of savings was even more striking. The 21,546,000 families at the low end, 78.4 per cent, had no aggregate savings at all, while the 24,000 families at the high end, 0.9 per cent, provided 34 per cent of total savings. The authors of *America's Capacity to Consume* went further:

[10]Lynds, *Middletown*, 63; Calkins, *Some Folks*, 20–21; on the abortive Swarthmore project there is an extensive correspondence between Brandeis and Cooke and Douglas and Cooke, dealing mainly with raising money and convincing Douglas to leave the University of Chicago, Cooke Papers; Senate *Hearings*, vii–xv.

It appears ... that ... income was being distributed with increasing in-equality, particularly in the later years of the period. While the proportion of high incomes was increasing ... there is evidence that the income of those at the very top was increasing still more rapidly. That is to say, in the late twenties a larger percentage of the total income was received by the portion of the population having very high incomes than had been the case a decade earlier.

Inequality in distribution exerted a constant pressure upon those at the bottom of the scale to supplement the head of family's job earnings. A study of federal workers in five cities in 1928 with salaries not in excess of $2500 showed that 15 to 33 per cent of the husbands took outside work, 15 to 32 per cent of the wives got jobs, and many children contributed to family income. Only 2 to 10 per cent of the families lived within the hus-band's government salary.

Even in the relatively prosperous year 1929 a majority of workers' fam-ilies failed to enjoy an "American standard of living." This conclusion can-not be substantiated precisely, because the government made no survey of workers' budgets between 1919 and the mid-thirties, another illustra-tion of the sorry state of labor statistics. The most careful contemporary student of the problem, Paul Douglas, made estimates for larger cities that can be keyed in roughly with the family income distribution published in *America's Capacity to Consume*. Though Douglas' work, *Wages and the Family*, appeared in 1925 it is not inapplicable to 1929, because retail prices fluctuated fairly narrowly.

Douglas set out four standards of living: poverty, minimum subsistence, minimum health and decency, and minimum comfort ("the American standard"). At the poverty level the family would have an inadequate diet, overcrowding, and no resources for unexpected expenses. This would cost a family of five $1000 to $1100. In 1929 there were 5,899,000 families of two or more with incomes of less than $1000. The minimum subsistence level was sufficient to meet physical needs with nothing left over for emer-gencies or pleasures. To reach it a family of five needed $1100 to $1400. There were 11,653,000 families of two or more who received less than $1500. The minimum health and decency level supplied adequate food, housing, and clothing as well as a modest balance for recreation. It cost $1500 to $1800. There were 16,354,000 families with incomes under $2000. Since "the American standard" required an income of $2000 to $2400, it seems safe to conclude that the majority of wage earners' families failed to reach this level.

Income inequality and the relatively low standard of living of Ameri-can workers, however, did not arouse social protest. There were two principal reasons for this silence. The first, doubtless the more important, was that the material well-being of the employed sector of the labor force was improving. Lincoln Steffens wrote in 1929: "Big business in America is producing what the Socialists held up as their goal: food, shelter and clothing for all." Douglas estimated that the average annual earnings of employed workers in all industries, including agriculture, advanced from $1288 in 1923 to $1405 in 1928, a gain of 9.1 per cent. Their real annual earnings improved slightly more, 10.9 per cent. The movement of wages, money and real, actually understates the impact of the rising standard of life because it fails to account for either the diversity of items on which income was spent or the benefits available free. In the twenties consumption broadened markedly to encompass goods and services that made life easier and more diverting—automobiles, telephones, radios, movies, washing machines, vacuum cleaners, and electric iceboxes, as well as improved medicine, hospitalization, and life insurance. The growth of installment buying made the consumer durables available to many with small cash resources. To a limited extent workers were able to share in this advance; ownership of a Model T, even if shared with the finance company, was more than entertaining: it inclined one to accept things as they were. In addition, all segments of the population benefited from the sharp improvement in free social services, most notably education, but including also public libraries, playgrounds and parks, and public health facilities.

The other reason for the failure of social protest to emerge was that the standard of living of American workmen, regardless of its deficiencies, was among the highest in the world, a consideration of no mean importance to urban masses who were largely immigrants themselves or the children of immigrants. Foreign observers visiting this country were, on the whole, impressed with the differential in living standards between the United States and their own nations. "Taken all in all," André Siegfried remarked, "the American worker is in a unique position."[11]

[11]Leven, et al., America's Capacity, 54–56, 93, 103–4; "Cost of Living of Federal Employees in Five Cities," MLR, 29 (Aug. 1929), 315; Paul H. Douglas, Wages and the Family (Chicago: University of Chicago Press, 1925), 5–6; Steffens to Jo Davidson, Feb. 18, 1929, in Letters of Lincoln Steffens, Ella Winter and Granville Hicks, eds. (New York: Harcourt, Brace, 1938), vol. 2, p. 830; Paul H. Douglas, Real Wages in the United States, 1890–1926 (Boston: Houghton Mifflin, 1930), 391; Paul H. Douglas and Florence Tye Jennison, The Movement of Money and Real Earnings in the United States, 1926–28 (Chicago: University of Chicago Press, 1930), 27. Wages in 1929 differed little from 1928 figures. Annual earnings in manufacturing rose to $1341 in 1929 from $1325 in 1928. Since the cost of living also advanced, by one point, real wages rose by a fraction of 1 per cent. Paul H. Douglas and Charles J. Coe, "Earnings," American Journal of Sociology, 35 (May, 1930), 935–39; Recent Economic Changes, vol. 1, pp. 60–67, 325; Recent Social Trends, vol. 2, pp. 827, 858–89, 915–26; Siegfried, America Comes of Age, 159. See also Daily Mail, 23. Some of the British made the admission more cautiously, while an Australian stated flatly that real wages were higher in his country. Report of the Delegation Appointed to Study Industrial Conditions in ... the United States, Cmd. 2833 (Mar. 1927), 33; Adam, An Australian, 46.

III
ONCE MORE
DEPRESSION AND WAR

It often has been observed that World War I plunged the world into an age of constant crisis from which it has yet to emerge. As a premier power, the United States has been the nation least immune to the ills afflicting twentieth-century mankind. We enjoyed a time of comparative serenity during the twenties, but the thirties began with domestic turmoil and exited amidst international strife; since then, the nation has known no freedom from fear and is still searching for economic and international security.

There is a small irony accompanying the tale of America in the Great Depression: the generation which confronted the panic was better equipped intellectually to deal with an economic crisis than any preceding generation had been. Despite the media rhetoric which proclaimed an undeterred prosperity in the foreseeable future, many national leaders during the twenties suspected that economic growth was ephemeral. Moreover, they saw laissez faire as an impossibility and believed that the federal government should organize the industrial structure against an imminent collapse, or at least make plans to mitigate the impact of a decline. Few men were so involved in this problem as Herbert Hoover. As Secretary of Commerce in 1921, Hoover organized a conference to study the causes and consequences of unemployment. Throughout the twenties he built in his department a bureaucracy devoted to the scientific investigation of economic behavior and to the organization of powerful influences which insured the economic system's maintenance or, in case of a decline, its quick revival. Hoover was among the engineers and businessmen who, in 1917, had eagerly accepted governmental war stewardships in the hopes of coordinating an individualistic system when community cooperation was needed most. Hoover and his friends viewed the wartime experience of cooperation as an enormous success and were certain that it could be applied to peacetime organization. Educated to study economic behavior scientifically, bolstered by Washington's plans to accelerate normal expenditures for public works, prepared by business groups for "spontaneous cooperation" with the federal government, and themselves ready to provide relief in case of emergency, American enterprisers stood ready to conquer any crisis which challenged their leadership.

But Hoover and the other "dollar-a-year men" had erected a myth of cooperation which proved to be deceptive. Hoover's own presidency witnessed the testing—and failure—of voluntary cooperation by American business. True, industry largely refrained from laying off workers or cutting their wages while Hoover bought time for recovery. But by 1932, about 10 million jobless people testified to industry's unsustained faith in cooperation. Financiers gave lip-service to pooling their own resources but privately hankered for federal dollars to sustain the flow of investment; they finally won Hoover's endorsement of the Reconstruction Finance Corporation in late 1931. Voluntary welfare agencies, along with state and local governments, struggled to give relief to the unemployed until a dearth of contributors and tax revenues collapsed their increasingly-needed efforts.

The New Deal applied the cooperation theme more realistically. In 1933, General Hugh S. Johnson, an Army man who had served on the War Industries Board and as a management consultant during the twenties, built the National Recovery Administration along the general lines of the WIB. With a variety of intimidating devices, the NRA cajoled cooperation from businessmen. "While we agree fully that Industry must voluntarily accept and ask for coordination, and that any appearance of dictation must be avoided," Johnson wrote in 1935, "the power of discipline must exist. At least we found it so in the war experiment." (Johnson nevertheless persisted in using the "spontaneous cooperation" rhetoric as if it explained the NRA's coercive operation.) Although the NRA was dead by 1935, and Johnson became a bitterly anti-New Deal newspaper columnist, the ideal of voluntary cooperation continued to attract subscribers. It was endorsed by agriculture in the Agricultural Adjustment Act and the Soil Conservation Administration, by labor unions in the collective bargaining provisions of the Wagner Act, and by white Southerners in the Tennessee Valley Authority. In most instances Washington did not extract cooperation from conflicting interests but conferred its power upon the most numerous and powerful factions within an economic sector. In this manner, "cooperation" benefited the strong and organized at the expense of the weak and unorganized.

Economic recovery and job relief were not hallmarks of the New Deal, but several long-overdue financial reforms and a conservative welfare system remain its most durable monuments. Bankers received their keenly-anticipated deposit insurance, and Wall Street welcomed—and quickly circumvented—supervisory reform. An excessively cautious and limited social security bill won congressional approval in 1935. Three years later, Washington placed a floor under wages and a ceiling over hours for workers in industry. The TVA provided a unique experiment in regional development. Unfortunately, Negro sharecroppers and tenant farmers were victimized by the New Deal's reforms: the principle of local control bolstered racism everywhere. Still, it is a tribute to the New Deal's political acumen that so many of its programs became fixtures in American life.

Even so, the America we know today owes more to the domestic exigencies imposed by World War II than to the broker state planning of the New Deal. Although the epic battles in North Africa, Europe, and the Pacific are given more attention in history textbooks than the vital social and economic developments on the homefront, the mobilization and demobilization decisions of 1940–1945 shaped the social trends of the succeeding quarter-century. Twentieth-century America came of age during World War II.

For many Americans who were not affected by the death of a friend or relative, the war years were the best times they had ever known. Individually and collectively Americans enjoyed their dream of full production, although it was made bitter-sweet by the austerity of consumer rationing. Changes on the American scene were swift and far reaching: the industrially disadvantaged South and West reaped a large percentage of government contracts; many states like California and Washington in the West and Georgia and Texas in the South became enamored of prosperous defense industries. Such a large number of impoverished farmers found employment in the cities that they required new health, housing, and educational facilities. Government tax rolls expanded rapidly, and individuals who had never had enough money to put into savings accounts found themselves obliged by consumer scarcities to save their surplus income. As in all war economies, incomes were in an inflationary race with prices; only government price controls permitted most Americans to win the race.

During World War II military production was the country's number one priority, and stability was its necessary condition. In such a climate of imperative accord, organized labor and agriculture thrived. Collective bargaining under federal supervision insured higher wages for labor. Parity at 110 per cent boosted rural income far beyond a Populist's wildest dream. American technology for war produced enough spin-offs to keep the wheels of industry humming for many years after V-J Day. Federal investment in the magnesium and aluminum and other industries made them key areas for expansion in the postwar period.

But this expansion brought other attendant perils. Social services were neglected, and an institutionalized inflationary spiral made it difficult for state and local governments to make up for lost time. The housing shortage of World War II was passed on to the present generation. Racial strife erupted as the quest for good jobs pitted blacks against poor whites, who usually won. A nation which abhorred the presence of military uniforms in a civilian society learned to cultivate its armed services. World War II was the most significant watershed in American history since the Civil War. It restored the nation's prosperity and assured the federal government of a strong role in the economy. Washington's involvement in most phases of American life no longer remained the issue it had been in the Hoover years. Although they debated its nature and extent, most Americans welcomed an enlarged federal function.

William E. Leuchtenburg
THE NEW DEAL AND THE ANALOGUE OF WAR

"In tracing the genealogy of the New Deal, historians have paid little attention to the mobilization of World War I," admonishes William E. Leuchtenburg in the following essay. In his book, The Perils of Prosperity, 1914–1932, *Leuchtenburg makes the same point while focussing upon the war experience. Here he centers his attention upon the depression and how Americans utilized the experience, symbols, and organization of war to deal with the crisis confounding them in the thirties. Many of the younger war administrators had gone on to successful political or business careers which brought them to prominence during the depression. The war congressmen who held leadership posts fifteen years later could not forget their earlier brush with crisis leadership in 1917–1918.*

But it was easier to recall experiences than to apply them. For that matter, were those experiences of wartime mobilization really applicable to a peacetime depression? Leuchtenburg thoughtfully analyzes the varied ways in which Americans applied their wartime involvement and suggests that the war analogue "proved either treacherous or inadequate." From an observation that "There was scarcely a New Deal act or agency that

The writer is indebted to David Brody, Clarke Chambers, Bernard Cohen, Paul Conkin, Robert Cross, Bertram Gross, Charles Hirschfeld, Richard Hofstadter, Robert Holt, Henry Kaiser, Val Lorwin, Warren Miller, Carl Resek, James Shideler, and Rexford Tugwell for helpful comments on an earlier draft of this essay. The essay was originally presented as a paper at the meetings of the American Historical Association in New York in December, 1960, and was substantially revised when the writer was a Fellow at the Center for Advanced Study in the Behavioral Sciences, Stanford, California, 1961–62.

did not owe something to the experience of World War I," he raises grave questions involving the nature of our institutions and the beliefs underlying them. For instance, we return to the central issue of war's incompatibility with democracy: in a society which esteems the individualistic behavior of free enterprise, is it possible to elicit self-discipline for a national cooperative effort without resorting to government coercion? Does the American economy require the exigencies of war or its surrogates to achieve prosperity? Are we a society in which individuals are at war with each other and can find community harmony only when confronted with external threats?

The metaphors a nation employs reveal much about how it perceives reality. The unconscious choice of symbols bares the bedrock of its beliefs. Moreover, the words people use are not neutral artifacts; they shape ideas and behavior. Just as the psychoanalyst listens for slips of the tongue or strange incongruities of ideas to help him understand the patient, or the literary critic studies the symbols in a poem or novel, so the historian finds it rewarding to explore the imagery a particular period has used, consciously or unconsciously, to interpret its experience.

In the months and years that followed the stock market crash of 1929, America searched for some way to make comprehensible what was happening. Sometimes people thought of the Great Depression as a breakdown of a system, sometimes as the product of the machinations of evil or stupid men, sometimes as the visitation of a plague like the Black Death. But from the very first, many conceived the depression to be a calamity like war or, more specifically, like the menace of a foreign enemy who had to be defeated in combat. Occasionally, the analogue of war was a general one, more often it referred specifically to World War I. When President Hoover summoned the leading industrialists to meet in Washington, one financial journal commented: "'Order up the Moors!' was Marshal Foch's reply at the first battle of the Marne. . . . 'Order up the business reserves,' directed President Hoover as pessimistic reports flowed in from all quarters, following the stock market crash."

For the rest of his years in office, Hoover resorted constantly to the imagery of war to describe the depression. In one of his addresses, he claimed that the country had just won its "battle of Chateau-Thierry" and must "reform [its] forces for the battle of Soissons." "Again and again he used military terms in describing the struggle in which he was engaged," recalled one of his aides. "He was the commanding officer at general head-

⁹"The New Deal and the Analogue of War," by William E. Leuchtenburg, was originally published in *Change and Continuity in Twentieth-Century America*, edited by John Braeman, Robert H. Bremner, and Everett Walters, and is Copyright © 1964 by the Ohio State University Press. All rights reserved.

quarters, so visualized himself." Hoover's advisers perceived the crisis in the same terms. In June, 1931, after the President unfolded his reparations plan, Secretary of State Henry Stimson confided to his diary: "We have all been saying to each other the situation is quite like war."

In addition to employing the metaphor of war to explain the meaning of the depression, the 1930's drew on the experience of the economic mobilization of World War I for instrumentalities to combat hard times. These are two discrete themes. Some who resorted to the analogue of war had no interest in the precedent of the wartime mobilization, and a few who turned to the example of the mobilization did not employ the imagery of war. Hence, it would be possible to examine these strands separately. But so closely did most Americans associate the metaphor of war with the specific legacy of the war mobilization that it has seemed more fruitful to discuss both these themes in a single context.

In the New Deal years, the two strands were inseparable. As early as his "forgotten man" speech in the 1932 campaign, Franklin Roosevelt manipulated the analogue of war to his advantage. In that same address, he referred to the specific operations of the war mobilization, a heritage he was to acknowledge on many occasions after his election to the presidency. But the legacy of the war was to prove a mixed blessing. Useful as a justification for New Deal actions, it also served to limit and divert the reformers in ways that had not been anticipated.

In tracing the genealogy of the New Deal, historians have paid little attention to the mobilization of World War I. Instead they have centered their interest on two movements: populism and progressivism. Both were important antecedents—a reasonably straight line may be drawn from the Populist sub-treasury plan to the Commodity Credit Corporation, from the Pujo committee to the Securities and Exchange Commission. Yet in concentrating on populism and progressivism, writers have given too little attention to the influence of the wartime mobilization, which may have been as great as the example of the Progressive era and certainly was more important than populism.

Much of the experience of the Progressive era proved irrelevant to the task facing Roosevelt in 1933. Very little in the Populist and Progressive periods offered a precedent for massive federal intervention in the economy. Many of the reforms of the prewar generation were modest ventures in regulation or attempts to liberate business enterprise rather than ambitious national programs of economic action. Moreover, in these years, reformers thought the state and the city more important arenas than the national capital.

World War I marked a bold new departure. It occasioned the abandonment of laissez faire precepts and raised the federal government to director, even dictator, of the economy. The War Industries Board mobilized production; the War Trade Board licensed imports and exports; the Capital Issues Committee regulated investment; the War Finance Corporation lent funds to munitions industries; the Railroad Administration unified the nation's railways; the Fuel Administration fixed the price of coal and imposed "coal holidays" on eastern industry; and the Food Administration controlled the production and consumption of food. The Lever Food and Fuel Control Act of 1917 gave the President sweeping powers: to take over factories and operate them, to fix a maximum price for wheat, and to license businesses in necessaries. By a generous interpretation of its powers, the War Industries Board supervised pricing, compelled corporations to accept government priorities, and forced companies to obey federal edicts on how to dispose of their products. "This is a crisis," a War Industries Board representative scolded steel-industry leaders, "and commercialism, gentlemen, must be absolutely sidetracked." Actions of this character, as well as the proliferation of public corporations ranging from the United States Housing Corporation to the Spruce Production Corporation, proved important precedents for New Deal enterprises fifteen years later. . . .

. . . Through war priorities, as Bernard Baruch later explained, the economy could be "made to move in response to a national purpose rather than in response to the wills of those who had money to buy." The nationalistic demands of war denied, if only for a time, the claims of the profit system. ". . . When production and distribution became really a matter of life and death, immediate and dramatic, every warring nation, after a few months of appalling waste, threw laissez-faire out of the window," noted Stuart Chase. "Wars must be won, and it was painfully obvious that laissez-faire was no help in winning them." The individualistic, competitive economy of the prewar years had to submit to the discipline of conscious government direction. Not business profit but the national interest was to determine how resources were to be allocated. The old system of competition, Rexford Tugwell wrote jubilantly, "melted away in the fierce new heat of nationalistic vision."

When the stock market crash of 1929 precipitated the Great Depression of the 1930's, progressives turned instinctively to the war mobilization as a design for recovery. The War Industries Board, Stuart Chase pointed out, had, like the Soviet *Gosplan*, demonstrated that "super-management" could replace "industrial anarchy." George Soule contended that the war had shown that planning was neither beyond human capacity nor alien to American values. "Many of those who now advocate economic planning have been doing so, in one way or another, ever since the experiences of 1917–18, and mainly as result of the possibilities which those experiences suggested for better performance in times of peace." The same "deliberate collective effort" which had made possible a tremendous expansion of production could be turned to peacetime ends, he argued. "If that military and industrial army had been mobilized, not to kill, burn and shatter, but to substitute garden cities for slums, to restore soil fertility and reforest our waste regions, to carry out flood control, to increase the necessities of life available for those in the lower income groups, we could have achieved in a short time a large number of really desirable objectives," Soule claimed.

Such men as Gerard Swope of General Electric, a veteran of the war mobilization, and Otto T. Mallery, the leading advocate of public works in the World War I era, recommended floating large federal bond issues like Liberty Bonds to finance a massive public-works program. Swope wrote President Hoover: "If we were faced with war, the President would immediately call a special session of Congress to declare war and to raise armies. This unemployment situation in many ways is more serious even than war. Therefore it is suggested that an extra session of Congress be called and the President request it to issue a billion dollars of bonds, bearing a low interest rate, and that then a campaign be organized to sell these bonds, much as the Liberty Bond campaigns were organized when we entered the war thirteen years ago." The Wisconsin economist Richard T. Ely went a step farther. He proposed the creation of a peacetime army which, when a depression struck, could be expanded by recruiting from the ranks of the unemployed. Under the direction of an economic general staff, the army, Ely urged, "should go to work to relieve distress with all the vigor and resources of brain and brawn that we employed in the World War."

By the middle of 1931, both businessmen and politicians were calling on President Hoover to adopt the procedures of the War Industries Board to pull the country out of the depression. When William McAdoo, who had headed the wartime Railroad Administration, proposed a Peace Industries Board in June, 1931, he found ready support. The War Industries Board, one correspondent wrote McAdoo, "accomplished wonders during the war, and there is no question but that a board established now to coordinate things in our national industries will also do wonders. This historical precedent is a great asset and ought to guide us in our national planning for the benefit of all." A month later, Charles Beard urged the creation of a National Economic Council with a Board of Strategy and Planning which would follow the pattern of "the War Industries Board and other federal agencies created during the titanic effort to mobilize men and materials for the World War." The following month, Representative Chester Bolton of Ohio advanced a similar proposal. "If we could have another body like the old War Industries Board," he wrote the head of Hoover's voluntary relief agency, "I believe the situation today could be greatly bettered." In September, 1931, Gerard Swope came forth with the most influential of all the pre-New Deal proposals: the "Swope Plan" to stabilize employment and prices through a constellation of trade associations under a national economic council. Early in 1932, a group of more than a hundred businessmen requested Hoover to declare a two-year truce on destructive competition and urged him "to consider a return to war-time experience by bringing into existence A National Economic Truce Board."

The cornucopia of proposals included suggestions with widely differing ideological implications. Some called on the war example to support radical recommendations for national planning; others used the war precedent simply as a stratagem to free business of the encumbrance of the trust laws. Most of them had in common a demand for greater initiative by the

federal government, and many of them—especially the public-works proposals—called for a sharp increase in government spending.

Such proposals ran far ahead of anything President Hoover and his followers would countenance. Most businessmen seemed chary of taking the
War Industries Board as a model for peacetime. The President himself
gave little indication of a readiness to have the federal government assume a larger role. To be sure, he signed an Employment Stabilization Bill
in 1931, and gave a major share of credit for the measure to Mallery. But
he deplored recommendations for lavish federal spending. Ventures of this
sort, the President protested, would unbalance the budget and destroy
business confidence in public credit.

These doctrines received small credence from men who recalled the
war expenditures. "If it is permissible for government to expend billions in
wartime in the organization of production, it is no less legitimate for government in a great emergency of peacetime to do what it is also impossible
for private individuals to accomplish," reasoned the distinguished economist Edwin R. A. Seligman. The popular economic writer William Trufant
Foster scolded:

> If any one still doubts that our economic troubles are mainly mental, let him
> consider what would happen if the United States declared war today. Every-
> body knows what would happen. Congress would immediately stop this inter-
> minable talk and appropriate three billion dollars—five billion—ten billion
> —any necessary amount. . . .
> Some day we shall realize that if money is available for a blood-and-bullets
> war, just as much money is available for a food-and-famine war. We shall see
> that if it is fitting to use collective action on a large scale to kill men abroad,
> it is fitting to use collective action on an equally large scale to save men at
> home.

Although Hoover rejected the demand that he draw on the war legacy
to mount a program of public works, he could not resist for long the clamor
for government initiative to expand relief to the jobless. By the summer
of 1931, the number of unemployed totaled eight million. William Allen
White wrote: "Hundreds of thousands of men, women and children are
going to suffer terribly this winter in spite of all that the natural laws of
economic change can do, however soon change may start, however rapidly it may move. Yet the situation is not hopeless, for if we can recreate
the dynamic altruism outside of government which moved us during the
war, we can harness forces that will bring relief and make us a better and
nobler people." If Hoover could arouse the "latent altruism" of the people, White believed, great sums could be raised for relief "as we raised the
Liberty Loan, Red Cross and Y drive funds during the war."

On August 19, 1931, President Hoover named Walter S. Gifford, president
of the American Telephone and Telegraph Company, to head the President's Organization on Unemployment Relief. A week later Newton Baker,
a member of the Advisory Committee of the POUR, noted that Gifford
seemed to be planning to organize the country along the lines of the

Council of National Defense, and added: "I am going a step farther and suggest that as far as possible men with military experience in the World War be used. They have had lessons in effective and disciplined action which will be valuable." That fall, the Gifford committee launched a "mobilization" to win support for local fund-raising drives. National advertisements proclaimed: "Between October 19 and November 25 America will feel the thrill of a great spiritual experience." A few weeks later, when Senator Edward Costigan of Colorado questioned the advisability of employing such techniques, Gifford responded: "We certainly did it in the war. I do not know that I like it, but, as I say, it is more or less the established practice. . . ."

President Hoover made much more forceful use of the war precedent to meet the financial crisis of the autumn of 1931. In December, 1931, Hoover asked Congress to create a Reconstruction Finance Corporation frankly modeled on the War Finance Corporation. The proposal appeared to originate at about the same time in the minds of several different men: Hoover, Federal Reserve Governor Eugene Meyer, who had been managing director of the WFC, Louis Wehle, who had been the WFC's general counsel, and Senator Joseph Robinson of Arkansas. All drew their inspiration from the WFC. "The RFC was a revival of the War Finance Corporation, that's all, but with expanded powers," Meyer recalled. Observers were astonished by the speed with which Congress approved the RFC bill. "It puts us financially on a war basis," noted the *New Republic*. When the RFC began operations, it employed many of the WFC's old staff, followed its pattern and that of the wartime Treasury in financing, and even took over, with slight modifications, the old WFC forms for loans applications.

The RFC, declared one periodical, was to be the "spearhead of the economic A.E.F." But Hoover and his aides insisted that the intervention of the RFC be held to a minimum. Hoover's reluctance to use the RFC as an agency in a new kind of mobilization suggested that the war analogy meant different things to different men and that it could be turned to conservative purposes as readily as to those envisaged by the progressives. While the progressives thought of the war as a paradigm for national planning, Hoover remembered it as a time when the government had encouraged a maximum of voluntary action and a minimum of disturbance of the profit system. He wished the crucial decisions to be made, as they had been in wartime, by corporation leaders. He employed the metaphor of war to serve a conservative function: that of draining internal antagonisms onto a common national enemy. In his address to the Republican national convention in 1932, the permanent chairman, Bertrand Snell, declared in defense of Hoover: "He solidified labor and capital against the enemy."

New York's Governor Franklin D. Roosevelt sought to reap political advantage from these different perceptions of the war experience. In his campaign for the Democratic presidential nomination in 1932, Roosevelt contrasted Hoover's performance with the achievements of the war mobilization. In his "forgotten man" address in Albany on April 7, 1932, Roosevelt declared that American success in the war had been due to leadership which was not satisfied with "the timorous and futile gesture" of sending a small army and navy overseas, but which "conceived of a whole Nation mobilized for war, economic, industrial, social and military resources gathered into a vast unit." The United States in 1932, Roosevelt asserted, faced "a more grave emergency than in 1917," and in meeting that emergency the Hoover administration had neglected "the infantry of our economic army." "These unhappy times," the Governor observed, "call for the building of plans that rest upon the forgotten, the unorganized but the indispensable units of economic power, for plans like those of 1917 that build from the bottom up and not from the top down, that put their faith once more in the forgotten man at the bottom of the economic pyramid." Less than two weeks later, at the Jefferson Day Dinner at St. Paul on April 18, Roosevelt repeated that the nation faced an emergency "more grave than that of war" and once more derided Hoover's efforts to meet the crisis. He added pointedly:

> Compare this panic-stricken policy of delay and improvisation with that devised to meet the emergency of war fifteen years ago.
> We met specific situations with considered, relevant measures of constructive value. There were the War Industries Board, the Food and Fuel Administration, the War Trade Board, the Shipping Board and many others.

The 1932 election brought the Democrats to power for the first time since Wilson's war administration. It was "only natural," as Swisher has observed, "that some of the World-War leaders should return to federal office and that others should become unofficial advisers of the administration. They, like the President, thought in terms of the dramatic concentration of power in the federal government which they had helped to bring about for the defeat of a foreign enemy. It is not surprising that modes of procedure were carried over from one period to the other." In the interregnum between Roosevelt's election in November 1932, and his inauguration in March, 1933, war recollections became even more compelling. The whole political system seemed doomed to self-asphyxiation. The discords of party, the deadlock in Congress, the maxims of the classical economists, the taboos of the Constitution all seemed to inhibit action at a time when action was desperately needed. In contrast, the war was remembered as a time of movement and accomplishment.

During the interregnum, the country debated a series of new proposals for utilizing the war experience to vanquish the depression. Daniel Roper, who would soon be Roosevelt's Secretary of Commerce, suggested a few days after the election that the new President "appoint one 'super' secretary with the other secretaries assistant to him and organize under this 'super' secretary the plan of the National Council of Defense composed of, say 21 men working without compensation as they did in War times." Many believed the crisis could be met only by vesting in the President the same arbitrary war powers that Woodrow Wilson had been given.

The depression, declared Alfred E. Smith on February 7, 1933, was "doing more damage at home to our own people than the great war of 1917 and 1918 ever did." "And what does a democracy do in a war?" Smith asked. "It becomes a tyrant, a despot, a real monarch. In the World War we took our Constitution, wrapped it up and laid it on the shelf and left it there until it was over." Four days later, Republican Governor Alf Landon of Kansas inquired: "Why not give the President the same powers in this bitter peacetime battle as we would give to him in time of war?" . . .

There was scarcely a New Deal act or agency that did not owe something to the experience of World War I. The Tennessee Valley Authority—the most ambitious New Deal experiment in regional planning—grew out of the creation of a government-operated nitrate and electric-power project at Muscle Shoals during and after the war. In his message asking for creation of the TVA, President Roosevelt concluded: "In short, this power development of war days leads logically to national planning. . . . " When the TVA bill was introduced in April, 1933, it seemed appropriate to refer it to the House Military Affairs Committee. Although war considerations played an inconsequential part in the birth of the Authority, the TVA Act of 1933 stipulated that in case of war or national emergency, any or all of the property entrusted to the Authority should be available to the government for manufacturing explosives or for other war purposes. The original World War I nitrate plant, which was turned over to the TVA, was to be held as a standby which might be needed in a future war. When foes of the TVA challenged it in the courts, Chief Justice Charles Evans Hughes found constitutional authority for the construction of the Wilson Dam by resting his ruling, in part, on the war power. The TVA was only one of a number of resources operations—from soil conservation to public power development —that employed the war rhetoric or drew from the World War I experience.

The public-housing movement of the thirties had first come of age during the war. In World War I, Congress authorized the Emergency Fleet Corporation and the United States Housing Corporation to provide housing for war workers. The war established the principle of federal intervention in housing, and it trained architects like Robert Kohn, who served as chief of production of the housing division of the U.S. Shipping Board. After the armistice, Kohn observed: ". . . The war has put housing 'on the map' in this country." In 1933, President Roosevelt named Kohn to head the New Deal's first public-housing venture.

Imaginative wartime experiments with garden-city ideas paved the way for the greenbelt towns of the thirties, while the rural resettlement and subsistence homestead projects of the New Deal reaped the harvest of seeds planted by Elwood Mead and Franklin K. Lane in the war years. Roy Lubove has pointed out:

In such residential communities as Yorkship Village (New Jersey), Union Park Gardens (Delaware) and the Black Rock and Crane Tracts (Bridgeport, Connecticut), the Emergency Fleet Corporation and the United States

Housing Corporation offered American architects and planners their first opportunity to apply garden city principles in comprehensive fashion: curvilinear street systems and street sizes adapted to function; park and play facilities; row-house design; the skillful spacing of mass and volume for maximum aesthetic effect and maximum sunlight and ventilation. The memory of the federal war-housing program persisted over the next two decades, a reminder of the potentialities of non-speculative, large-scale site planning for working-class housing.

The New Deal's program of farm price supports owed something to the wartime Food Administration and even more to a decade of proselytization by George Peek, a hard-bitten farm-belt agitator who had served as "a sort of generalissimo of industry" under the War Industries Board. Peek's war experience with the ways government could benefit industry had led him to argue that the government should give the same measure of aid to the distressed farmer. Frustrated in the twenties by Republican presidents in his campaign to win support for McNary-Haugenism, Peek pinned his hopes on the election of Franklin Roosevelt in 1932. "It looks to me as though in the campaign for Roosevelt for President we are in the last line of trenches and if he is not elected that agriculture is doomed to peasantry," Peek wrote. Roosevelt's victory touched off a serious debate over how to curb farm surpluses which, after months of wrangling, ended in the passage of the Agricultural Adjustment Act in the spring of 1933. To head the new Agricultural Adjustment Administration, Roosevelt named George Peek. "To him, with his war experience, this whole thing clicks into shape," Peek's wife noted, "and some of the fine men of the country are coming to his call as they did in 1917, and with the same high purpose." . . .

While the CCC, the AAA, the TVA, housing, economy, and banking legislation all shared in the war legacy, it was the National Recovery Administration that was the keystone of the early New Deal, and the NRA rested squarely on the War Industries Board example. The National Industrial Recovery bill, modeled on WIB procedures, wove together a series of schemes for government-business co-ordination of the kind that had prevailed in the war. One of the most influential recovery designs, sponsored by Meyer Jacobstein, a Rochester (New York) banker, and H. G. Moulton, president of the Brookings Institution, recommended the creation of "a National Board for Industrial Recovery, with powers similar to those so effectively utilized during the World War by the War Industries Board." When the President commissioned Raymond Moley to frame legislation for industrial recovery, Moley asked General Hugh Johnson, who in World War I had functioned as a liaison between the Army and the War Industries Board, to take over for him. "Nobody can do it better than you," Moley coaxed. "You're familiar with the only comparable thing that's ever been done—the work of the War Industries Board." The recovery bill, drafted by Johnson and others, won Senate approval by only the narrowest of margins; conservatives foresaw that the measure would enhance the power of the state and progressives believed the proposal would encourage cartel-ization. Franklin Roosevelt was more sanguine. When the President signed the recovery act of June 16, he commented: "Many good men voted this new charter with misgivings. I do not share these doubts. I had part in the great cooperation of 1917 and 1918 and it is my faith that we can count on our industry once more to join in our general purpose to lift this new threat. . . ."

Before labor would agree to the industrial-recovery program, it insisted on the same degree of government recognition of the right to organize as it had enjoyed in World War I. In December, 1932, shortly after he learned that Frances Perkins would be the new Secretary of Labor, Sidney Hill-man sent her a memorandum which urged the government to pursue the kinds of policies the War Labor Board had initiated. In framing the recov-ery bill, W. Jett Lauck, who had been secretary of the War Labor Board, served as spokesman for John L. Lewis's United Mine Workers. Lauck, who sponsored a plan for "a national board composed of labor modeled after the War Labor Board," played a prominent part in shaping the la-bor provisions of the legislation. When the national industrial-recovery bill emerged from the drafting room, it incorporated the pivotal section 7 (a) which granted labor's demand for recognition of the right of collec-tive bargaining. The essential provisions of 7 (a), noted Edwin Witte, were "but restatements" of principles first recognized by the National War Labor Board.

Franklin Roosevelt had not only had a prominent part in framing World War I labor policies, but had, as Gerald Nash has pointed out, "sketched out the blueprint for the War Labor Policies Board which was modeled on his directive." To staff the National Labor Board of 1933, the President named men he had first encountered in developing war labor programs. William Leiserson, executive secretary of the board, had been Roosevelt's personal adviser on labor affairs in 1918. In formulating labor policy— from interpreting 7 (a) through the adoption and administration of the Wagner Act—Roosevelt and his lieutenants drew heavily on war prece-dents. The war agencies had established the basic principles of the New Deal labor program: that workers had the right to unionize, that they must not be discharged for union activity, and that presidential boards could restrain employers from denying such rights. More than this, they had evolved the procedure of plant elections to determine bargaining representatives which was to be the crucial instrumentality employed by Roosevelt's labor boards.

To head the NRA Roosevelt named the fiery General Johnson, who could boast pertinent experience not only with the War Industries Board but in organizing the draft. In mid-July, Johnson launched a national campaign dramatized by the symbol of the Blue Eagle. "In war, in the gloom of night attack, soldiers wear a bright badge on their shoulders to be sure that comrades do not fire on comrades," explained the President. "On that principle, those who cooperate in this program must know each other at a glance. That is why we have provided a badge of honor for this purpose. . . ."

Cabinet members greeted with skepticism Johnson's proposal for a mass movement to enlist the nation behind the NRA. Homer Cummings pointed out that the country was not at war, and it might be difficult to get everyone to sign a pledge. Johnson replied that he felt it could be put over, for the depression was more real than the war had been to most Americans. "Almost every individual has either suffered terribly, or knows of friends and relatives who have; so there is waiting here to be appealed to what I regard as the most fertile psychology that you could imagine. . . . I think this has anything that happened during the War backed off the board."

To enforce the Blue Eagle, Johnson enlisted the housewives of the country. "It is women in homes—and not soldiers in uniform—who will this time save our country," he proclaimed. "They will go over the top to as great a victory as the Argonne. It is zero hour for housewives. Their battle cry is 'Buy now under the Blue Eagle!' " By kindling the spirit of the Liberty Loan drives and the draft registration of World War I, Johnson kept alive the intense spirit of the Hundred Days through another season. "There is a unity in this country," declared Franklin Roosevelt, "which I have not seen and you have not seen since April, 1917. . . ."

The Recovery Administration conceived of the depression as, in part, a crisis in character. The New Dealers hoped that businessmen would place the public weal above their private interests, just as the copper magnates had responded to Baruch's appeal in 1917 by supplying metal to the army and navy at less than half the market price. In 1933, businessmen were asked to accept as a patriotic duty the assignment to raise wages and agree to a "truce" on price-cutting. The recovery drive, it was argued, would succeed only if it aroused the same kind of "spiritual" fervor that World War I had awakened. Morris Cooke wrote:

> Conversations with a good many different kinds of people convince me that there is needed to expedite industrial recovery a talk by the President in which he would read into our 57 varieties of effort an ethical and moral quality and call on us individually and collectively to put our shoulders to the wheel just as if we were at war. . . .
>
> Everywhere I get the impression of our people wanting to be told that the main purpose of the Recovery Administration is not exclusively the rehabilitation of our material wellbeing but a reaffirmation of the spiritual values in life.

To man the New Deal agencies, Roosevelt turned to the veterans of the war mobilization. Top NRA officials included Johnson's chief of staff, John Hancock, who had managed the War Industries Board's naval industrial program; Charles F. Horner, the genius of the Liberty Loan drive; Leo Wolman, who had headed the section on production statistics of the War Industries Board; and Major General Clarence Charles Williams, who had been Chief of Ordnance in charge of the vast war purchasing. Many other New Dealers had had their first taste of government service during the war. The first Administrator for Public Works, Colonel Donald H. Sawyer, had built cantonments; Felix Frankfurter had chaired the War Labor Policies Board; Captain Leon Henderson of Ordnance had served with the War Industries Board; and Senator Joseph Guffey had worked in the War Industries Board on the conservation of oil. For many, the summer of 1933 seemed like old times. "Washington is a hectic place," wrote Isador Lubin in August. "The hotels are filled, and the restaurants remind me very much of war times. One cannot go into the Cosmos Club without meeting half a dozen persons whom he knew during the war." . . .

The war example saw service too as a way to refute opponents of the President's economic policies. When critics objected that the country could not "afford" New Deal reforms, Roosevelt's supporters responded with the now familiar retort that if the country could spend as it had in war, it could spend in this new emergency. "When people complain to me of the amount of money that the government has been borrowing," commented Thomas Lamont of the House of Morgan, "I always answer it by saying: 'Well, if the country was willing to spend thirty billion dollars in a year's time to try to lick the Germans, I don't see why people should complain about spending five or six billion dollars to keep people from starving.'" By 1936, when Roosevelt returned to Forbes Field in Pittsburgh, where, four years before, he had promised to slash Hoover's reckless spending, the President concluded that the argument now offered the best reply to critics who accused him of a profligate disregard of campaign promises. "National defense and the future of America were involved in 1917. National defense and the future of America were also involved in 1933," Roosevelt asserted. "Don't you believe that the saving of America has been cheap at that price?"

Roosevelt's argument would have been more compelling if he had spent at anywhere near the rate that both he and his conservative foes implied he had. For a time in the winter of 1933–34, the Administration gave a fillip to the economy when it embarked on lavish spending through the Civil Works Administration, but early in 1934, the President, alarmed by mounting deficits, decreed the death of the CWA. Distressed by Roosevelt's verdict, Senator Robert LaFollette, Jr., of Wisconsin inquired: "In 1917, Mr. President, what Senator would have dared to rise on the floor of the Senate and suggest that we could not fight the war against Germany and her allies because it would unbalance the Budget?" *The Nation* voiced a similar protest: "The country is confronted with a vastly greater crisis than it had to meet in the World War but has not yet extended itself financially as it did at that time." Progressives warned that unless the President began to spend at a wartime pace the country might take years to pull out of the depression. The progressive Cassandras proved correct. The New Deal mobilization of 1933–34, from which so much had been expected, brought disappointing economic returns.

The crux of the difficulty lay in the fact that the metaphor of war was, in more than one way, inapt. As a model for economic action, World War I was unsatisfactory, for the problems confronting Roosevelt in 1933 were quite unlike those Woodrow Wilson had been called on to meet in 1917. As the Harvard economist Edwin Gay wrote: "War stimulates the full expansion of productive energy, but the deep depression cripples every economic process and discourages even the most sanguine business leaders." Some who recalled the war experience hoped that it could provide a prototype for the same kind of impressive increases in output that had been achieved in 1917–18. But the aims of the New Deal mobilization were not the same as those of the war; General Johnson even called for "an armistice on increasing producing capacity." Frank Freidel has pointed out:

> Unlike wartime measures, the new agencies were to reduce output in most areas rather than raise it, and encourage price increases rather than restrain them. Thus, waging a war on the depression was in some ways the reverse of waging one on a foreign foe.

John M. Clark has made a similar point. The war, Clark noted, provided precedents for emergency controls, deficit spending, and expanded powers for the Federal Reserve System, but the problems of war and of depression "were radically different; in fact, they were in some respects opposite to one another." The question of determining priorities in a war economy, Clark observed, was not at all the same as that of reinvigorating sick industries. Clark concluded:

> All the machinery for allocating limited supplies of essential resources among conflicting uses, which played so large a part in the wartime controls, had no application to the depression. Where the actuating motives of private industry fail and the result is partial paralysis, the problem is essentially opposite to that of war.

These misgivings were not simply the result of hindsight. In the midst of the Hundred Days, the economist Paul Douglas warned that the country did not face the wartime task of rationing scarce resources but the quite different problem of stimulating production. "Industry must get some business before it can proceed to ration it out," Douglas gibed. He was disconcerted by the New Deal's obsession with the menace of overproduction when the critical question was how to increase purchasing power. Douglas noted: "Certainly those who are arguing from the analogy of the War Industries Board miss the point. That body had behind it the gigantic purchasing power of the government, and with this weapon it was able to instill some order in the industrial system. But unless the government creates such purchasing power in the present emergency, the regulatory body will be operating in a void."

The war analogy proved mischievous in an even more significant respect. The Tugwells thought of the war as a time when the intellectuals had exercised unprecedented power over the economy, and when the feasibility of a planned society had been brilliantly demonstrated. Yet, although the intellectuals did wield power, agencies like the War Industries Board had, after all, been run chiefly by business executives. If they learned anything from the war, it was not the virtues of collectivism but the potentialities of trade associations, the usefulness of the state in economic warfare with the traders of other nations, and the good-housekeeping practices of eliminating duplication and waste. The immediate consequence of the war was not a New Jerusalem of the planners but the Whiggery of Herbert Hoover as Secretary of Commerce. While the war mobilization did establish meaningful precedents for New Deal reforms, it was hardly the "war socialism" some theorists thought it to be. Perhaps the outstanding characteristic of the war organization of industry was that it showed how to achieve massive government intervention without making any permanent alteration in the power of corporations.

The confusion over the meaning of the war experience helped conceal the ambiguities of the so-called "First New Deal." The architects of the early New Deal appeared to be in fundamental agreement, since they united in rejecting the New Freedom ideal of a competitive society in favor of business-government co-ordination in the 1917 style. In fact, they differed sharply. Tugwell hoped that the co-ordination authorized by the NRA would enable the Recovery Administration to become an agency for centralized government direction of the economy, a possibility insured in part by the NRA's licensing power. Most of the other "First New Dealers," however, meant by business-government co-ordination an economy in which businessmen would make the crucial decisions. As administrator of the NRA, General Johnson gave small scope to the government direction Tugwell had envisaged. He never used the licensing power, but relied instead on negotiation with business and on the force of social pressure. Like Moley and Richberg and the President, Johnson placed his faith not in a planned economy but in voluntary business co-operation with government.

The New Deal administrators shared, too, the conviction of the war bureaucrats that progress would be achieved not through worker or farmer rebellions, but through government programs, conceived and executed by agency officials. A month after the armistice, Wesley Mitchell had voiced the need for "intelligent experimenting and detailed planning rather than for agitation or class struggle." The war approach which the New Dealers adopted rejected both mass action and socialist planning, and assumed a community of interest of the managers of business corporations and the directors of government agencies. Roosevelt's lieutenants believed that the great danger to such an experiment lay not in the opposition of the conservatives, who were discredited, but in the menace of antiplutocratic movements. Yet in damping the fires of popular dissent, they also snuffed out support they would need to keep the reform spirit alive.

The New Dealers, distrustful of the policies of group conflict, sought to effect a truce like that of 1917 when class and sectional animosities abated. Perhaps no other approach could have accomplished so much in the spring of 1933, yet it was a tactic which had obvious perils for the cause of reform. By presenting the depression not as the collapse of a system but as a personalized foreign enemy, Roosevelt as much as Hoover sought to mend the social fabric. In doing so, Roosevelt, like his predecessor, deflected blame away from business leaders whom many thought responsible for hard times, and diverted attention from the fact that the depression was not the consequence of an assault by a foreign foe but evidence of internal breakdown.

Even more important, the New Dealers, in the interest of national solidarity, tried to suppress anti-business expressions of discontent. President Roosevelt warned the AF of L convention in 1933: "The whole of the country has a common enemy; industry, agriculture, capital, labor are all engaged in fighting it. Just as in 1917 we are seeking to pull in harness; just as in 1917, horses that kick over the traces will have to be put in a corral." General Johnson left no doubt of the intent of the President's words: "Labor does not need to strike under the Roosevelt plan. . . . The plain stark truth is that you cannot tolerate strikes. Public opinion . . . will break down and destroy every subversive influence." Far from operating a "labor government," as conservatives charged, the New Dealers in 1933 deeply resented strikes as acts of "aggression" which sabotaged the drive for recovery. Frances Perkins recalls that Johnson believed that "during the period when NRA was attempting to revive industry no stoppage of work could be tolerated under any circumstances. It was like a stoppage of work in war time. Anything had to be done to prevent that."

An administrator who spurned direct government sanctions but who was determined to have his way soon found that he was either resorting to bluster or encouraging vigilantism. Such had been the pattern in World War I. On one occasion, the War Industries Board's price-fixing committee had warned a producer to co-operate, or become "such an object of contempt and scorn in your home town that you will not dare to show your face there." Ray Lyman Wilbur, chief of the conservation division of the Food Administration, recalled: "Indiana I found the best organized state for food conservation that I had yet seen. The people were approaching rapidly the stage where violations of wheatless days, etc., were looked upon as unpatriotic enough to require that inquiries as to the loyalty of the guilty citizen, baker or hotel-keeper be made."

If the New Dealers never ran to such excesses of vigilantism, they were not beyond employing this kind of social coercion, and they matched the war administrators in the technique of bluster. "I have no patience with people who follow a course which in war time would class them as slackers," declared Attorney-General Homer Cummings of the alleged hoarders of gold. "If I have to make an example of some people, I'll do it cheerfully." When Frances Perkins hit out at the effort of the steel industry to dodge the intent of section 7 (a) by setting up company unions, she denounced these unions as "war bridegrooms," the popular epithet for matrimonial draft-dodging during the war. When the economist Oliver W. M. Sprague resigned in protest at the Administration's gold-buying policy, Hugh Johnson accused him of "deserting with a shot in the flank of the army in which he had enlisted." During the Blue Eagle drive, Donald

Richberg insisted that in a time of crisis there could be "no honorable excuse for the slacker who wastes these precious moments with doubting and debate—who palsies the national purpose with legalistic arguments."

Such statements infuriated the conservatives. Senator Carter Glass of Virginia found particularly galling Richberg's denunciation of NRA opponents as "slackers who deserved to have white feathers pinned on them by the women of the country." Glass wrote of Richberg's war record: "He never heard a percussion cap pop; he did not know the smell of gun powder; he did not even reach a training camp to learn the difference between 'Forward March' and 'Parade Rest.' When asked by a responsible newspaperman to give his war record in justification of his vituperative assault on other people, he could do no better than allege he had helped sell some Liberty bonds." Glass's resentment was shared by other conservative critics. "The man who lives well within his income," protested Lewis Douglas, "has come to be regarded as unpatriotic and as a slacker in the fight against the depression."

If the rhetoric of coercion disturbed the conservatives, it troubled some of the New Dealers even more. In the summer of 1933, a group of AAA officials protested:

> General Johnson, in picturing the results of his campaign, has frequently used the analogy of the war-time 'gasless Sundays.' Then, General Johnson recalls, if a man drove a car on Sunday, his neighbors pushed the car into the ditch. Popular opinion at that time was so inflamed that it expressed itself by violence.
>
> General Johnson's analogy is profoundly significant and disturbing. If his program is adopted, professional drive organizations will soon reappear in full force. Agitators may take advantage of the possible resulting hysteria to set group against group, such as farmers against wage earners, and thus defeat the real progress toward cooperation already made by the Roosevelt Administration.

Some even thought they detected in Johnson's administration of the NRA the glimmerings of a corporate state. If such was Johnson's purpose—and the grounds for such a supposition are unsubstantial—the General received no encouragement from the President. Roosevelt moved quickly to squelch signs of militarism. When Harry Woodring, Assistant Secretary of War, wrote early in 1934 that the Army stood prepared to organize the CCC, veterans of World War I, and reliefers into a corps of "economic storm troops," the White House reprimanded him. In late 1934, the authoritarian-minded Johnson was let go. That same year, Henry Wallace, seeking to pursue a "middle course," wrote: "There is something wooden and inhuman about the government interfering in a definite, precise way with the details of our private and business lives. It suggests a time of war with generals and captains telling every individual exactly what he must do each day and hour."

Most of all, the Brandeisian faction of the New Dealers objected to the crisis spirit. Felix Frankfurter wrote Louis Brandeis: "Much too much of 'slacker' talk & old coercions." For the Brandeisians, the "enemy" was not "depression" but "business." They welcomed the breakup of the nation in 1934 and 1935 from the national interest into class and group interests. The early New Dealers had emphasized the war spirit of cooperation, coordination, and exhortation, because they feared that the bonds that held society together might be snapped. By 1935, it was clear that the crisis had been weathered, and the mood of war seemed inappropriate. Brandeisians felt free to assault business interests, other New Dealers lost faith in their ability to convert businessmen, and business groups increasingly viewed Roosevelt as their enemy. As in wartime, the first enthusiasm as the troops paraded to the front had given way to the realization that the army was not invincible, the casualty lists would be long, and the prospect of early victory was no longer promising. Yet the danger of annihilation had been averted too, and as the sense of urgency lessened, the spirit of national solidarity slackened. "The enemies who began to emerge in the eyes or the imagination of men," Paul Conkin has observed of the end of the "wartime effort" in 1935, "were not such as could demand the hostility of all Americans, for these enemies were not natural, or providential, or foreign, but human and native. A class and group consciousness was forming."

. . . Precisely as the Keynesians had foreseen, defense and war demands sparked an economic boom. In the summer of 1940, Keynes noted that the United States had failed to achieve recovery, because the volume of investment had been "hopelessly inadequate." The "dreadful experience" of war might teach the United States what it had failed to learn in peacetime. He predicted: "Your war preparation, so far from requiring a sacrifice, will be the stimulus, which neither the victory nor the defeat of the New Deal could give you, to greater individual consumption and a higher standard of life." Keynes observed sadly: "It is, it seems, politically impossible for a capitalistic democracy to organize expenditure on the scale necessary to make the grand experiment which would prove my case—except in war conditions."

Keynes's remark was to the point. The "grand experiment" of the New Deal had achieved much. But it had not created, or indeed in any serious sense even attempted to create, a new model for American society. The New Dealers resorted to the analogue of war, because in America the sense of community is weak, the distrust of the state strong. Up to a point, the metaphor of war and the precedent of World War I proved invaluable. They helped provide a feeling of national solidarity which made possible the New Deal's greatest achievement: its success in "nation saving," in mending the social fabric. The heritage of World War I justified the New Deal's claim to represent an overarching national interest to which business and other parochial interests must conform. The war proved that, at a time of crisis, the power of private individuals with money to turn the nation's resources to their own benefit could be limited by the prior claim of providing a "social minimum." Since the war mobilization had brought to fruition much of progressivism, it offered a useful example for the New

Dealers, and since the wartime control of industry went much further than earlier efforts in recognizing the place of the twentieth-century state, it was especially pertinent for some of the problems the New Deal confronted.

Yet in other respects the war analogue proved either treacherous or inadequate. The very need to employ imagery which was so often inappropriate revealed both an impoverished tradition of reform and the reluctance of the nation to come to terms with the leviathan state. Only in war or in a crisis likened to war was it possible to put aside inhibiting doctrines, create a sense of national homogeneity, and permit the government to act in the national interest. But once the war ended, or the sense of crisis dissipated, traditional doctrines once again prevailed. The country had yet to find a way to organize collective action save in war or its surrogate. Nor had it faced up to the real problems of the relation of order to liberty which the power of the twentieth-century state creates.

World War II rescued the New Deal from some of its dilemmas and obscured others. In the war years, many of the New Deal programs were set aside—the wpa, Roosevelt said, had earned an "honorable discharge." The New Dealers turned their talents to "manning the production line." The aaa helped increase farm production instead of restricting crops; the new industrial agencies sought to speed factory output rather than curtail it. Perhaps the greatest irony of the New Deal is the most familiar. Only in war was recovery achieved. Only in war did the country finally rescue that one-third of a nation ill-housed, ill-clad and ill-nourished. Only in war was the "army of the unemployed" disbanded.

Paul W. Schroeder

THE AXIS ALLIANCE AND JAPANESE-AMERICAN RELATIONS, 1941

Is American foreign policy too often designed to uphold abstract principles which have little relationship to real situations? Do national interests become what we wish them to be rather than what they actually are? Do American policy-makers moralize about evils like aggression in order to desist from conciliatory diplomacy which could be characterized as appeasement? While principles are vital to the conduct of foreign affairs, does a nation's unwillingness to compromise them, even in its own national interest, leave the country with the ineluctability of war? These are some general questions suggested by Paul Schroeder's analysis of events which precipitated our involvement in World War II.

Schroeder is more immediately concerned, however, with America's involvement in war in the Pacific. Did American policy in 1941 court war for the sake of curbing aggression in the Orient rather than bringing succor to China? Schroeder dismisses the latter possibility while raising the issue of a true American interest in Asia. Did we really seek to save Asia from a Japanese-imposed East Asia Co-prosperity Sphere? Or, rather, did we consider our own interests first by hoping to preserve an Open Door in Asia?

America has been a Pacific power throughout the century and, as such, has interests in Asia which it finds necessary to protect. It is noteworthy that the Spanish-American War began in the Philippines and gave the United States Asian possessions which we relinquished very reluctantly. As long ago as Theodore Roosevelt's presidency (1901–1909), Americans in government service perceived that both the United States and Japan sought to expand their interests in the Orient and were thus set on a collision course. We need to know more about why the Japanese undertook a course of aggression and why Americans were determined to resist it.

In judging American policy toward Japan in 1941, it might be well to separate what is still controversial from what is not. There is no longer any real doubt that the war came about over China. Even an administration stalwart like Henry L. Stimson and a sympathetic critic like Herbert Feis concur in this.[1] Nor is it necessary to speculate any longer as to what could have induced Japan to launch such an incredible attack upon the United States and Great Britain as occurred at Pearl Harbor and in the South Pacific. One need not, as Winston Churchill did in wartime, characterize it as "an irrational act" incompatible "with prudence or even with sanity."[2] The Japanese were realistic about their position throughout; they

Reprinted from Paul W. Schroeder: *The Axis Alliance and Japanese-American Relations, 1941.* © 1958 by the American Historical Association. Used by permission of Cornell University Press.
[1]"If at any time the United States had been willing to concede Japan a free hand in China, there would have been no war in the Pacific" (Stimson and Bundy, *On Active Service*, 256). "Our full induction into this last World War followed our refusal to let China fend for itself. We had rejected all proposals which would have allowed Japan to remain in China and Manchuria. . . . Japan had struck—rather than accept frustration" (Herbert Feis, *The China Tangle* [Princeton: Princeton University Press, 1953], 3).

[2]Speech to U.S. Congress, Washington, Dec. 26, 1941, *War Speeches of Churchill*, II, 150.

did not suddenly go insane. The attack was an act of desperation, not madness. Japan fought only when she had her back to the wall as a result of America's diplomatic and economic offensive.

The main point still at issue is whether the United States was wise in maintaining a "hard" program of diplomatic and economic pressure on Japan from July 1941 on. Along with this issue go two subsidiary questions: the first, whether it was wise to make the liberation of China the central aim of American policy and the immediate evacuation of Japanese troops a requirement for agreement; the second, whether it was wise to decline Premier Konoye's invitation to a meeting of leaders in the Pacific. On all these points, the policy which the United States carried out still has distinguished defenders. The paramount issue between Japan and the United States, they contend, always was the China problem. In her China policy, Japan showed that she was determined to secure domination over a large area of East Asia by force. Apart from the legitimate American commercial interests which would be ruined or excluded by this Japanese action, the United States, for reasons of her own security and of world peace, had sufficient stake in Far Eastern questions to oppose such aggression. Finally, after ten years of Japanese expansion, it was only sensible and prudent for the United States to demand that it come to an end and that Japan retreat. In order to meet the Japanese threat, the United States had a perfect right to use the economic power she possessed in order to compel the Japanese to evacuate their conquered territory. If Japan chose to make this a cause for war, the United States could not be held responsible.

A similar defense is offered on the decision to turn down Konoye's Leaders' Conference. Historians may concede, as do Langer and Gleason, that Konoye was probably sincere in wanting peace and that he "envisaged making additional concessions to Washington, including concessions on the crucial issue of the withdrawal of Japanese troops from China." But, they point out, Konoye could never have carried the Army with him on any such concession.[3] If the United States was right in requiring Japan to abandon the Co-Prosperity Sphere, then her leaders were equally right in declining to meet with a Japanese Premier who, however conciliatory he might have been personally, was bound by his own promises and the exigencies of Japanese politics to maintain this national aim. In addition, there was the serious possibility that much could be lost from such a meeting—the confidence of China, the cohesiveness of the coalition with Great Britain and Russia. In short, there was not enough prospect of gain to merit taking the chance.

This is a point of view which must be taken seriously. Any judgment on the wisdom or folly of the American policy, in fact, must be made with caution—there are no grounds for dogmatic certainty. The opinion here to be developed, nonetheless, is that the American policy from the end of

[3]Langer and Gleason, *Undeclared War*, 706–707.

July to December was a grave mistake. It should not be necessary to add that this does not make it treason. There is a "back door to war" theory, espoused in various forms by Charles A. Beard, George Morgenstern, Charles C. Tansill, and, most recently, Rear Admiral Robert A. Theobald, which holds that the President chose the Far East as a rear entrance to the war in Europe and to that end deliberately goaded the Japanese into an attack.[4] This theory is quite different and quite incredible. It is as impossible to accept as the idea that Japan attacked the United States in a spirit of overconfidence or that Hitler pushed the Japanese into war. Roosevelt's fault, if any, was not that of deliberately provoking the Japanese to attack, but of allowing Hull and others to talk him out of impulses and ideas which, had he pursued them, might have averted the conflict. Moreover, the mistake (assuming that it was a mistake) of a too hard and rigid policy with Japan was, as has been pointed out, a mistake shared by the whole nation, with causes that were deeply organic. Behind it was not sinister design or warlike intent, but a sincere and uncompromising adherence to moral principles and liberal doctrines.

This is going ahead too fast, however; one needs first of all to define the mistake with which American policy is charged. Briefly, it was this. In the attempt to gain everything at once, the United States lost her opportunity to secure immediately her essential requirements in the Far East and to continue to work toward her long-range goals. She succeeded instead only in making inevitable an unnecessary and avoidable war—an outcome which constitutes the ultimate failure of diplomacy. Until July 1941, as already demonstrated, the United States consistently sought to attain two limited objectives in the Far East, those of splitting the Axis and of stopping Japan's advance southward. Both aims were in accordance with America's broad strategic interests; both were reasonable, attainable goals. Through a combination of favorable circumstance and forceful American action, the United States reached the position where the achievement of these two goals was within sight. At this very moment, on the verge of a major diplomatic victory, the United States abandoned her original goals and concentrated on a third, the liberation of China. This last aim was not in accord with American strategic interests, was not a limited objective, and, most important, was completely incapable of being achieved by peaceful means and doubtful of attainment even by war. Through her single-minded pursuit of this unattainable goal, the United States forfeited the diplomatic victory which she had already virtually won. The unrelenting application of extreme economic pressure on Japan, instead of compelling the evacuation of China, rendered war inevitable, drove Japan back into the arms of Germany for better or for worse, and precipitated the wholesale plunge by Japan into the South Seas. As it ulti-

[4]Charles A. Beard, *President Roosevelt and the Coming of the War, 1941* (New Haven: Yale University Press, 1948); George E. Morgenstern, *Pearl Harbor: The Story of the Secret War* (New York: Devin-Adair, 1947); Charles C. Tansill, *Back Door to War* (Chicago: Regnery, 1952); Rear Admiral Robert A. Theobald, *The Final Secret of Pearl Harbor* (New York: Devin-Adair, 1954).

mately turned out, the United States succeeded in liberating China only at great cost and when it was too late to do the cause of the Nationalist Chinese much real good.

This is not, of course, a new viewpoint. It is in the main simply that of Ambassador Grew, who has held and defended it since 1941. The arguments he advances seem cogent and sensible in the light of present knowledge. Briefly summarized, they are the following: First is his insistence on the necessity of distinguishing between long-range and immediate goals in foreign policy and on the folly of demanding the immediate realization of both.[5] Second is his contention that governments are brought to abandon aggressive policies not by sudden conversion through moral lectures, but by the gradual recognition that the policy of aggression will not succeed. According to Grew, enough awareness of failure existed in the government of Japan in late 1941 to enable it to make a beginning in the process of reversal of policy—but not nearly enough to force Japan to a wholesale surrender of her conquests and aims.[6] Third was his conviction that what was needed on both sides was time—time in which the United States could grow stronger and in which the tide of war in Europe could be turned definitely against Germany, time in which the sense of failure could grow in Japan and in which moderates could gain better control of the situation. A victory in Europe, Grew observed, would either automatically solve the problem of Japan or make that problem, if necessary, much easier to solve by force.[7] Fourth was his belief that Japan would fight if backed to the wall (a view vindicated by events)[8] and that a war at this time with Japan could not possibly serve the interests of the United States. Even if one considered war as the only final answer to Japanese militarism, still, Grew would answer, the United States stood to gain nothing by seeking a decision in 1941. The time factor was entirely in America's favor. Japan could not hope to gain as much from a limited relaxation of the embargo as the United States could from time gained for mobilization; Roosevelt and the military strategists were in fact anxious to gain time by a *modus vivendi.*[9]

There is one real weakness in Grew's argument upon which his critics have always seized. This is his contention that Konoye, faced after July 26 with the two clear alternatives of war or a genuine peace move, which would of necessity include a settlement with China, had chosen the

[5] Grew, *Turbulent Era,* II, 1255.
[6] *Ibid.,* 1290.
[7] *Ibid.,* 1268–1269, 1286.
[8] The opposite belief, that Japan would give way, not only was inconsonant with the best available political and military intelligence, but was also a bad estimate of Japanese national psychology and of expansionist psychology in general. F. C. Jones rightly criticizes it as "the folly of supposing that the rulers of a powerful nation, having committed themselves to an expansionist policy, will abandon or reverse that policy when confronted by the threat of war. So long as they see, or think they see, any possibility of success, they would elect to fight rather than face the humiliation and probable internal revolt which submission to the demands of their opponents would entail" (*Japan's New Order,* 461).
[9] Grew, *Turbulent Era,* II, 1276–1277.

latter course and could have carried through a policy of peace had he been given the time. "We believed," he writes, "that Prince Konoye was in a position to carry the country with him in a program of peace" and to make commitments to the United States which would "eventually, if not immediately" meet the conditions of Hull's Four Points.[10] The answer of critics is that, even if one credits Konoye's sincerity and takes his assurances at face value, there is still no reason to believe that he could have carried even his own cabinet, much less the whole nation, with him on any program approximating that of Hull. In particular, as events show, he could not have persuaded the Army to evacuate China.[11]

The objection is well taken; Grew was undoubtedly over-optimistic about Konoye's capacity to carry through a peaceful policy. This one objection, however, does not ruin Grew's case. He countered it later with the argument that a settlement with Japan which allowed Japanese garrisons to remain in China on a temporary basis would not have been a bad idea. Although far from an ideal solution, it would have been better, for China as well, than the policy the United States actually followed. It would have brought China what was all-important—a cessation of fighting—without involving the United States, as many contended, in either a sacrifice of principle or a betrayal of China. The United States, Grew points out, had never committed herself to guaranteeing China's integrity. Further, it would not have been necessary to agree to anything other than temporary garrisons in North China which, in more favorable times, the United States could work to have removed. The great mistake was to allow American policy to be guided by a sentimental attitude toward China which in the long run could do neither the United States nor China any good. As Grew puts it:

> Japan's advance to the south, including her occupation of portions of China, constituted for us a real danger, and it was definitely in our national interest that it be stopped, by peaceful means if possible, by force of arms if necessary. American aid to China should have been regarded, as we believe it was regarded by our Government, as an indirect means to this end, and not from a sentimental viewpoint. The President's letter of January 21, 1941, shows that he then sensed the important issues in the Far East, and that he did not include China, purely for China's sake, among them.... The failure of the Washington Administration to seize the opportunity presented in August and September, 1941, to halt the southward advance by peaceful means, together with the paramount importance attached to the China question during the conversations in Washington, gives rise to the belief that not our Government but millions of quite understandably sympathetic but almost totally uninformed American citizens had assumed control of our Far Eastern policy.[12]

There remains the obvious objection that Grew's solution, however plausible it may now seem, was politically impracticable in 1941. No

[10]*Ibid.*, 1263–1264.
[11]Feis, *Road to Pearl Harbor*, 275–277; Jones, *Japan's New Order*, 457–458.
[12]Grew, *Turbulent Era*, 1367–1368.

American government could then have treated China as expendable, just as no Japanese government could have written off the China Affair as a dead loss. This is in good measure true and goes a long way to explain, if not to justify, the hard American policy. Yet it is not entirely certain that no solution could have been found which would both have averted war and have been accepted by the American people, had a determined effort been made to find one. As F. C. Jones points out, the United States and Japan were not faced in July 1941 with an absolute dilemma of peace or war, of complete settlement or open conflict. Hull believed that they were, of course; but his all-or-nothing attitude constituted one of his major shortcomings as a diplomat. Between the two extremes existed the possibility of a *modus vivendi*, an agreement settling some issues and leaving others in abeyance. Had Roosevelt and Konoye met, Jones argues, they might have been able to agree on a relaxation of the embargo in exchange for satisfactory assurances on the Tripartite Pact and southward expansion, with the China issue laid aside. The United States would not have had to cease aid, nor Japan to remove her troops. The final settlement of the Far Eastern question, Jones concludes,

> would then have depended upon the issue of the struggle in Europe. If Germany prevailed, then the United States would be in no position to oppose Japanese ambitions in Asia; if Germany were defeated, Japan would be in no position to persist in those ambitions in the face of the United States, the USSR, and the British Commonwealth.[13]

Such an agreement, limited and temporary in nature, would have involved no sacrifice of principle for either nation, yet would have removed the immediate danger of war. As a temporary expedient and as an alternative to otherwise inevitable and useless conflict, it could have been sold by determined effort to the public on both sides. Nor would it have been impossible, in the writer's opinion, to have accompanied or followed such an agreement with a simple truce or standstill in the China conflict through American mediation.

This appraisal, to be sure, is one based on realism. Grew's criticism of Hull's policy and the alternative he offers to it are both characterized by fundamental attention to what is practical and expedient at a given time and to limited objectives within the scope of the national interest. In general, the writer agrees with this point of view, believing that, as William A. Orton points out, it is foolish and disastrous to treat nations as morally responsible persons, "because their nature falls far short of personality," and that, as George F. Kennan contends, the right role for moral considerations in foreign affairs is not to determine policy, but rather to soften and ameliorate actions necessarily based on the realities of world politics.[14]

13Jones, *Japan's New Order,* 459.
14William A. Orton, *The Liberal Tradition* (New Haven: Yale University Press, 1944), 239; George F. Kennan, *American Diplomacy, 1900–1950* (Chicago: University of Chicago Press, 1951), 95–103.

160   PAUL W. SCHROEDER

From this realistic standpoint, the policy of the State Department would seem to be open to other criticisms besides those of Grew. The criticisms, which may be briefly mentioned here, are those of inconsistency, blindness to reality, and futility. A notable example of the first would be the inconsistency of a strong no-compromise stand against Japan with the policy of broad accommodation to America's allies, especially Russia, both before and after the American entrance into the war.[15] The inconsistency may perhaps best be seen by comparing the American stand in 1941 on such questions as free trade, the Open Door in China, the territorial and administrative integrity of China, the maintenance of the prewar *status quo* in the Far East, and the sanctity of international agreements with the position taken on the same questions at the Yalta Conference in 1945.[16]

The blindness to reality may be seen in the apparent inability of American policy makers to take seriously into account the gravity of Japan's economic plight or the real exigencies of her military and strategic posi-

[15]One notes with interest, for example, a pre-Pearl Harbor statement by Senator Lister Hill of Alabama, a strong proponent of a radical anti-Japanese policy, as to America's attitude toward the Soviet Union: "It is not the business of this government to ask or to receive any assurance from Stalin about what he will do with regard to Finland after the war. . . . It is the business of this government to look out for and defend the vital interests of the United States" (*New York Times*, Nov. 5, 1941). If in the above quotation one reads "Tojo" for "Stalin" and "China" for "Finland," the result is a statement of the extreme isolationist position on the Far East which Hill and other supporters of the administration found so detestable.

[16]The writer has no desire to enter here into the controversy over the merits of the Yalta decisions, but only to draw a certain parallel. The standard defense for the Yalta policy on the Far East has been the contention that the United States conceded to Soviet Russia only what the U.S.S.R. could and would have seized without American leave, that the only alternative to agreement would have been war with Russia, and that securing Russian entrance into the Far Eastern war was considered militarily necessary (George F. Lensen, "Yalta and the Far East," in John L. Snell, Forrest C. Pogue, Charles F. Delzell, and George F. Lensen, *The Meaning of Yalta: Big Three Diplomacy and the New Balance of Power* [Baton Rouge: Louisiana State University Press, 1956], 163–164). The argument may be quite sound, but surely it would serve equally well— indeed, much better, *mutatis mutandis*—to justify a policy of conciliation toward Japan in 1941. Applied to Japan, the argument would then read as follows: The United States would have conceded to Japan only the temporary possession of a part of what Japan had already seized without American leave; the only alternative to agreement would have been war with Japan; and preventing Japanese entrance into the European war was considered militarily necessary. The great difference between the two situations would seem to be that the concessions envisioned by Japan in 1941 were temporary and reversible; those gained by Russia in 1945 were not. The very necessity of pursuing the Yalta policy in 1945 casts doubt on the wisdom of the hard-and-fast stand of 1941. Felix Morley has put the parallel neatly: "To assert that the sudden and complete reversal of the long-established Far Eastern policy was justified was also to say, by implication, that the policy reversed was fundamentally faulty, that to fight a war with Japan in behalf of Chinese nationalism had been a dreadful mistake" (*The Foreign Policy of the United States* [New York: Alfred A. Knopf, 1951], 87–88). One may, as Morley does, reject both the above premise and the conclusion, or one may accept both; but it is difficult to see how one may affirm the premise and deny the conclusion. For those who believe that a vital moral difference existed between the two cases, the problem would seem to be how to show that it is morally unjustifiable to violate principle in order to keep a potential enemy out of a war, yet morally justifiable to sacrifice principle in order to get a potential ally into it. The dilemma appears insoluble.

tion, particularly as these factors would affect the United States over the long run.[17] Equally unrealistic and more fateful was the lack of appreciation on the part of many influential people and of wide sections of the public of the almost certain consequences to be expected from the pressure exerted on Japan—namely, American involvement in a war her military strategists considered highly undesirable. The attitude has been well termed by Robert Osgood, "this blind indifference toward the military and political consequences of a morally-inspired position."[18]

The charge of futility, finally, could be laid to the practice of insisting on a literal subscription to principles which, however noble, had no chance of general acceptance or practical application. The best example is the persistent demand that the Japanese pledge themselves to carrying out nineteenth-century principles of free trade and equal access to raw materials in a twentieth-century world where economic nationalism and autarchy, trade barriers and restrictions were everywhere the order of the day, and not the least in the United States under the New Deal. Not one of America's major allies would have subscribed wholeheartedly to Hull's free-trade formula; what good it could have done to pin the Japanese down to it is hard to determine.[19]

But these are all criticisms based on a realistic point of view, and to judge the American policy solely from this point of view is to judge it unfairly and by a standard inappropriate to it. The policy of the United States was avowedly not one of realism, but of principle. If then it is to be understood on its own grounds and judged by its own standards, the main question will be whether the policy was morally right—that is, in accord with principles of peace and international justice. Here, according to its defenders, the American policy stands vindicated. For any other policy, any settlement with Japan at the expense of China, would have meant a betrayal not only of China, but also of vital principles and of America's moral task in the world.

This, as we know, was the position of Hull and his co-workers. It has been stated more recently by Basil Rauch, who writes:

[17]In his very interesting book, *America's Strategy in World Politics* (New York: Harcourt, Brace, 1942), Nicholas Spykman displays some of the insights which seem to have been lacking in the American policy of the time. He points out, for example, that Japan's economic and geographic position was essentially the same as that of Great Britain; that her position vis-à-vis the United States was also roughly equivalent to England's; that therefore it made little sense for America to aid Great Britain in maintaining a European balance of power, while at the same time trying to force Japan to give up all her buffer states in Asia; that the Japanese war potential could not compare to that of a revivified and unified China; and that one day (a striking prediction in 1942!) the United States would have to undertake to protect Japan from Soviet Russia and China (pp. 135–137, 469–470). Spykman saw then what is today so painfully evident—that without a Japanese foothold on the Asiatic mainland no real balance of power is possible in Asia.

[18]Robert E. Osgood, *Ideals and Self-Interest in America's Foreign Relations* (Chicago: University of Chicago Press, 1953), 361.

[19]A memorandum by the Chief of the State Department Division of Commercial Policy and Agreements (Hawkins) to Ballantine, Washington, Nov. 10, 1941, offers interesting comments on the extent and nature of the trade discriminations then being practiced against Japan by nations throughout the world, including the United States (*Foreign Relations, 1941*, IV, 576–577).

> No one but an absolute pacifist would argue that the danger of war is a greater evil than violation of principle. . . . The isolationist believes that appeasement of Japan without China's consent violated no principle worth a risk of war. The internationalist must believe that the principle did justify a risk of war.[20]

This is not an argument to be dismissed lightly. The contention that the United States had a duty to fulfill in 1941, and that this duty consisted in holding to justice and morality in a world given to international lawlessness and barbarism and in standing on principle against an unprincipled and ruthless aggressor, commands respect. It is not answered by dismissing it as unrealistic or by proscribing all moral considerations in foreign policy. An answer may be found, however, in a closer definition of America's moral duty in 1941. According to Hull, and apparently also Rauch, the task was primarily one of upholding principle. This is not the only possible definition. It may well be contended that the moral duty was rather one of doing the most practical good possible in a chaotic world situation and, further, that this was the main task President Roosevelt and the administration had in mind at least till the end of July 1941.

If the moral task of the United States in the Far East was to uphold a principle of absolute moral value, the principle of non-appeasement of aggressors, then the American policy was entirely successful in fulfilling it. The American diplomats proved that the United States was capable of holding to its position in disregard and even in defiance of national interests narrowly conceived. If, however, the task was one of doing concrete good and giving practical help where needed, especially to China, then the American policy falls fatally short. For it can easily be seen not only that the policy followed did not in practice help China, but also that it could not have been expected to. Although it was a pro-China and even a China-first policy in principle, it was not in practical fact designed to give China the kind of help needed.

What China required above all by late 1941 was clearly an end to the fighting, a chance to recoup her strength. Her chaotic financial condition, a disastrous inflation, civil strife with the Communists, severe hunger and privation, and falling morale all enfeebled and endangered her further resistance. Chiang Kai-shek, who knew this, could hope only for an end to the war through the massive intervention of American forces and the consequent liberation of China. It was in this hope that he pleaded so strongly for a hard American policy toward Japan. Chiang's hopes, however, were wholly unrealistic. For though the United States was willing to risk war for China's sake, and finally did incur it over the China issue, the Washington government never intended in case of war to throw America's full weight against Japan in order to liberate China. The American strategy always was to concentrate on Europe first, fighting a defensive naval war in the Far East and aiding China, as before, in order to keep the

[20]Rauch, *Roosevelt*, 472.

Japanese bogged down. The possibility was faced and accepted that the Chinese might have to go on fighting for some years before eventual liberation through the defeat of Japan. The vehement Chinese protests over this policy were unavailing, and the bitter disillusionment suffered by the Chinese only helped to bring on in 1942 the virtual collapse of the Chinese war effort during the latter years of the war.[21]

As a realistic appraisal of America's military capabilities and of her world-wide strategic interests, the Europe-first policy has a great deal to recommend it. But the combination of this realistic strategy with a moralistic diplomacy led to the noteworthy paradox of a war incurred for the sake of China which could not then be fought for the sake of China and whose practical value for China at the time was, to say the least, dubious. The plain fact is that the United States in 1941 was not capable of forcing Japan out of China by means short of war and was neither willing nor, under existing circumstances, able to throw the Japanese out by war. The American government could conceivably have told the Chinese this and tried to work out the best possible program of help for China under these limitations. Instead, it yielded to Chinese importunities and followed a policy almost sure to eventuate in war, knowing that if the Japanese did attack, China and her deliverance would have to take a back seat. It is difficult to conceive of such a policy as a program of practical aid to China.

The main, though not the only, reason why this policy was followed is clearly the overwhelming importance of principle in American diplomacy, particularly the principle of nonappeasement of aggressors. Once most leaders in the administration and wide sections of the public became convinced that it was America's prime moral duty to stand hard and fast against aggressors, whatever the consequences, and once this conviction became decisive in the formulation of policy, the end result was almost inevitable: a policy designed to uphold principle and to punish the aggressor, but not to save the victim.[22]

It is this conviction as to America's moral duty, however sincere and understandable, which the writer believes constitutes a fundamental misreading of America's moral task. The policy it gave rise to was bad not simply because it was moralistic but because it was obsessed with the

[21]Levi, *Modern China's Foreign Policy*, 229–237. On the danger of internal collapse in China as early as 1940, see U.S. Department of State, *Foreign Relations of the United States: 1940*, vol. IV, *The Far East* (Washington: Government Printing Office, 1955), 672–677.

[22]It is Secretary of War Henry L. Stimson who gives evidence on how strong was the role of avenging justice in the prevailing picture of America's moral duty. He displays a striking anxiety to acquit the administration of the charge of being "soft" on Japan and to prove that the administration was always fully aware of the Japanese crimes and morally aroused by them. The nation's leaders, he insists in one place, were "as well aware as their critics of the wickedness of the Japanese." Avenging justice, too, plays an important role in the defense he makes of the postwar Nuremberg and Tokyo war crimes trials. These trials, he claims, fulfilled a vital moral task. The main trouble with the Kellogg Pact and the policy of nonrecognition and moral sanctions, according to Stimson, was that they named the international lawbreakers but failed to capture and

wrong kind of morality—with that abstract "Let justice be done though the heavens fall" kind which so often, when relentlessly pursued, does more harm than good. It would be interesting to investigate the role which this conception of America's moral task played in the formulation of the American war aims in the Far East, with their twin goals of unconditional surrender and the destruction of Japan as a major power, especially after the desire to vindicate American principles and to punish the aggressor was intensified a hundredfold by the attack on Pearl Harbor.[23] To pursue the later implications of this kind of morality in foreign policy, with its attendant legalistic and vindictive overtones, would, however, be a task for another volume.

In contrast, the different kind of policy which Grew advocated and toward which Roosevelt so long inclined need not really be considered immoral or unprincipled, however much it undoubtedly would have been denounced as such. A limited *modus vivendi* agreement would not have required the United States in any way to sanction Japanese aggression or to abandon her stand on Chinese integrity and independence. It would have constituted only a recognition that the American government was not then in a position to enforce its principles, reserving for America full freedom of action at some later, more favorable time. Nor would it have meant the abandonment and betrayal of China. Rather it would have involved the frank recognition that the kind of help the Chinese wanted was impossible for the United States to give at that time. It would in no way have precluded giving China the best kind of help then possible— in the author's opinion, the offer of American mediation for a truce in the war and the grant of fuller economic aid to try to help the Chinese recover—and promising China greater assistance once the crucial European situation was settled. Only that kind of morality which sees every sort of dealing with an aggressor, every instance of accommodation or conciliation, as appeasement and therefore criminal would find the policy immoral.[24]

---

punish them. The United States, along with other nations in the prewar world, had neglected "a duty to catch the criminal. ... Our offense was thus that of the man who passed by on the other side." Now, this is a curious revision of the parable of the Good Samaritan, to which the Secretary here alludes. According to the Stimson version, the Good Samaritan should not have stopped to bind up the victim's wounds, put him on his beast of burden, and arrange for his care. Had he been cognizant of his real moral duty, he would rather have mounted his steed and rode off in hot pursuit of the robbers, to bring them to justice. This is only an illustration, but an apt one, of the prevailing concept of America's moral duty, with its emphasis on meting out justice rather than doing good (Stimson and Bundy, *On Active Service*, 262, 384).

[23]Admiral William D. Leahy (*I Was There* [New York: McGraw-Hill, 1950,] 81) expresses his view of America's war aims in dubious Latin but with admirable forthrightness: "*Delenda est Japanico.*" He was, of course, not the only American leader to want to emulate Cato.

[24]See the introductory remarks on the possibilities of appeasement, under certain circumstances, as a useful diplomatic tool, along with an excellent case study in the wrong use of it, in J. W. Wheeler-Bennett, *Munich: Prologue to Tragedy* (London: Macmillan, 1948), 3–8.

What the practical results of such a policy, if attempted, would have been is of course a matter for conjecture. It would be rash to claim that it would have saved China, either from her wartime collapse or from the final victory of communism. It may well be that already in 1941 the situation in China was out of control. Nor can one assert with confidence that, had this policy enabled her to keep out of war with Japan, the United States would have been able to bring greater forces to bear in Europe much earlier, thus shortening the war and saving more of Europe from communism. Since the major part of the American armed forces were always concentrated in Europe and since in any case a certain proportion would have had to stand guard in the Pacific, it is possible that the avoidance of war with Japan, however desirable in itself, would not have made a decisive difference in the duration of the European conflict. The writer does, however, permit himself the modest conclusions that the kind of policy advocated by Grew presented real possibilities of success entirely closed to the policy actually followed and that it was by no means so immoral and unprincipled that it could not have been pursued by the United States with decency and honor.

Richard Polenberg
THE WANING OF THE NEW DEAL IN WORLD WAR II

World War II hurt the New Deal no more than World War I had scrubbed the New Freedom. Both reform programs had run their courses by the time hostilities erupted in Europe. Ironically, however, both wars actually enlarged the imaginations of American liberals as to Washington's potential for effecting reform and reconstruction in American society. In fact, World War II accomplished the economic recovery which had eluded the New Deal. This success spurred liberals to rethink old problems. They already had entrusted to Washington the burden of protecting civil liberties and ensuring the welfare of Americans. During the reconversion debate of 1943–1946, liberals drew heavily from the experience of the war to perfect their plans for economic stabilization. Deficit spending, mammoth government activity, and price controls no longer seemed the bêtes noires they had been before the war.

If the outlines for the management of prosperity seemed clearer, the details remained nebulous, and the political dangers were just as evident. If war production had restored abundance in America, did continued prosperity require an economy geared to defense mobilization? Could the United States avert great swings in the business cycle, as the Keynesians claimed, through public investment and managed inflation? And what political impact would war-influenced social developments have upon the nation?

Speaking to a gathering of reformers in 1944, Archibald MacLeish voiced the widely-held belief that war had dealt the liberal cause a deadly blow. "Liberals meet in Washington these days," he said, "if they meet at all, to discuss the tragic outlook for all liberal proposals, the collapse of all liberal leadership and the inevitable defeat of all liberal aims." All through the war years reformers noted signs of a conservative resurgence and looked on helplessly as Congress jettisoned New Deal programs and businessmen displaced New Dealers in positions of power. When in December 1943 President Roosevelt declared that "Dr. New Deal" had outlived his usefulness and should give way to "Dr. Win-the-War," liberal morale hit rock bottom. Nor was it much restored by speculating about what the future might hold. As MacLeish observed, "It is no longer feared, it is assumed, that the country is headed back to normalcy, that Harding is just around the corner, that the twenties will repeat themselves."[1]

To some extent the notion that World War II crippled the New Deal depended on the assumption that it had been healthy when the war began. The reform program had in reality limped along for some time. A series of events in 1937 and 1938—particularly the Supreme Court packing plan and a devastating recession—had produced widespread dissatisfaction with the Roosevelt administration, and after the Republicans chalked up large gains in the congressional elections (winning 81 new seats in the House and 8 in the Senate) liberals and conservatives had battled to a standoff. Congress had passed no major piece of reform legislation since the Fair Labor Standards Act of 1938. With the outbreak of war in Europe, preparations for defense rather than proposals for social betterment absorbed the energies of an increasing number of government officials. By the time the United States entered the war, New Dealers were fighting a rear-guard action against the onslaughts of conservatives in Congress.

In fact, liberal disillusionment after 1941 derived in part from the belief that war might breathe new life into social reform. Throughout the 1930s many reformers were less interested in how World War I had weak-

From *War and Society: The United States 1941–1945* by Richard Polenberg. Reprinted by permission of the publisher, J. B. Lippincott Company. Copyright 1972.
[1]"Defeatist Liberals," *New Republic*, CX (March 6, 1944), 302.

ened progressivism than in how, by allowing Americans to put aside the ethic of individualism, it had strengthened the movement. Only in 1917 and 1918 had large numbers of people been willing to accept full-blooded regulation of the economy; only then had planning in the national interest been possible. The war, Rexford Tugwell explained in 1939, had released Americans from the tyranny of the competitive system and gotten them to accept a form of "disciplined cooperation." Surely war had its terrible aspects, but "the fact is that only war has up to now proved to be such a transcending objective that doctrine is willingly sacrificed for efficiency in its service." Of course liberals were of two minds about the probable consequences of a future war: many pacifists feared that mobilization would lead to dictatorship, but it was not at all unusual for New Dealers to predict that social gains would be extended, for only in the event of war would men be "prepared to take the risks of the positive state."[2]

At first the war seemed to nourish these hopes, for it drew some reformers who had supported isolationism back into the New Deal fold and broke down resistance to the enlargement of presidential authority. A number of progressives had remained bitterly critical of the President's foreign policy until December 7, 1941, but Pearl Harbor removed some of their mistrust and improved chances for cooperation on domestic programs. One of Roosevelt's assistants, who had not spoken to Senator Robert La Follette, Jr. of Wisconsin for several months, dined with him "as soon as he voted correctly" on the declaration of war. "Bob is now 100 percent O.K.," he reported, "I am sure there isn't a thing Bob wouldn't do for the President right now." Just as the war enabled reformers to put aside differences over foreign policy, so it caused many Republicans to recognize, however grudgingly, that Roosevelt required sweeping powers to meet the emergency. Even while insisting that war not serve as a pretext for social reform, Herbert Hoover admitted, "To win total war President Roosevelt must have many dictatorial economic powers. There must be no hesitation in giving them to him and upholding him in them."[3]

Nevertheless, expectations founded on memories of World War I and on the mood of unity following Pearl Harbor were not fulfilled. Instead the war weakened American liberalism in many ways, some temporary and some lasting, some small and others large. The war obliged reformers to grant priority to military objectives, provided an excuse to liquidate certain New Deal programs, and revealed that powers lodged in the welfare state could be put to illiberal uses. The war raised other barriers to reform by creating pressure to cut domestic expenditures, to halt the inflationary spiral and to staff emergency agencies with businessmen.

[2]Rexford Tugwell, "After the New Deal," *New Republic*, CI (July 26, 1939), 324; Harold Laski to Roosevelt, December 17, 1942, Roosevelt Papers, PPF 3014.
[3]David K. Niles to Grace Tully, December 10, 1941, Roosevelt Papers, PPF 1792; Herbert Hoover, *Addresses upon the American Road: World War II* (New York, 1946), pp. 160–71.

Finally, by injecting new issues into the political arena, the war splintered the electoral coalition upon which Roosevelt had relied. This is not to say that the war invariably worked against the interests of reformers. It solved many problems which had baffled New Dealers and made possible the implementation of particular reforms—such as the GI Bill of Rights— that could be justified on military grounds. Nevertheless, the reform movement was in a weaker condition at the end of the war than at its start.

From the beginning, most liberals agreed to put aside social reforms that could interfere with the military program. Few protested when rural electrification was trimmed back to free copper for military purposes, or when the working day was lengthened in order to boost industrial output. "Progressives should understand that programs which do not forward the war must be given up or drastically curtailed," wrote David Lilienthal, head of the Tennessee Valley Authority. "Where a social service doesn't help to beat Hitler, it may have to be sacrificed," observed another reformer. "This may sound tough—but we have to be tough."[4] Roosevelt and his advisors took much the same approach. Although he believed that existing reforms should be preserved where possible and that others would undoubtedly be required when peace came, Roosevelt thought that "the weaknesses and many of the social inequalities as of 1932 have been repaired or removed and the job now is, first and foremost, to win the war." Even Bruce Bliven, an editor of the New Republic, concurred. "If it were true that continued devotion to the New Deal hampered the war effort, then the New Deal should be laid on the shelf."[5]

Of course the key to Bliven's remark was the word "if." Very often liberals denied that reform was incompatible with wartime requirements and argued instead that it would contribute to victory. New Dealers supported job training programs "not as a social gain, but as a wartime necessity," upheld collective bargaining on the grounds that it fostered industrial harmony, and defended payroll deductions in an expanded social insurance system as "an effective weapon in the wartime battle against inflation." Sometimes they carried this argument to the point where it seemed that every reform would help win the war because, by advancing social justice, it would make American society that much more worth defending. Again and again reformers employed military metaphors; in urging Roosevelt to sponsor a postwar economic plan Henry Wallace even suggested the title "Lend-Lease on the Domestic Front."[6] Reform, in a sense, was considered guilty until proven innocent. Liberals had to show how each reform was related to victory, and unless they could provide an ironclad case it stood slim chance of survival.

[4]David Lilienthal, The Journals of David E. Lilienthal, (New York, 1964), I, 43, Delia Kuhn to Archibald MacLeish, January 15, 1942, Pringle Papers.
[5]Roosevelt to Louis Brownlow, December 29, 1943, Roosevelt Papers, PPF 1820; Bruce Bliven, "Liberals Today and Tomorrow," New Republic, CVIII (May 17, 1943), 658–61.
[6]Robert F. Wagner, "Post War Security for All the People," Progressive, September 27, 1943; Wallace to Roosevelt, February 4, 1943, Roosevelt Papers, OF 4351.

Nothing better illustrates the way in which wartime needs forced a postponement of reform than anti-trust policy. Beginning in 1938 the Roosevelt administration had made a vigorous effort to enforce the Sherman Act. But by 1940 officials began to think twice about prosecutions that might hamper defense production and were quite reluctant, for example, to bring suit against large oil companies suspected of fixing prices and compelling service stations to handle their products exclusively. One New Dealer, admitting that antitrust action would not disturb gasoline deliveries, nevertheless feared that it might have an adverse "psychological effect" upon an industry vital to the production of synthetic rubber and hi-octane gasoline. After much hesitation the Justice Department decided to proceed with the suit. The Attorney-General, who still thought that "the question of national defense is more important than the settlement of the theory on which the oil industry is to operate," did not want his department to "be placed in the position of saying it will let down the bars." Also, he expected that the case "would sink into an argument between lawyers and disappear from the newspapers." That is exactly what happened.[7]

Once the United States entered the war, however, anti-trust prosecutions virtually ceased. Not only did businessmen receive immunity if the War Production Board certified proposed arrangements in advance as being in the national interest, but the demand to relax the law even for suspected violators proved irresistible. Although Thurman Arnold, who headed the Anti-Trust Division of the Justice Department, maintained that the Sherman Act did not diminish business efficiency and should be stringently enforced, most officials responsible for production believed that anti-trust actions antagonized businessmen and caused them to fritter away valuable time preparing legal defenses. Secretary of War Stimson came to consider Arnold a "self-seeking fanatic," and reported a prevalent feeling in his department that rigorous enforcement "frightened business" and had "a very great deterrent effect upon our munitions production." Harry Hopkins, voicing the general desire to suspend the anti-trust laws in certain instances, affirmed that the President would have to "take [Arnold] in hand and stop his interference with production."[8]

To settle the matter, Roosevelt called on Samuel I. Rosenman who, after listening to all sides, found a solution that gave Stimson most of what he wanted. Any anti-trust investigation, prosecution or suit that might obstruct vital production would, at the discretion of the Attorney-General and the Secretaries of War or Navy, be postponed until after the emergency. In the event of disagreement between Justice and War "a letter from Secretary Stimson would be controlling." Arnold had tried to salvage at least his right to initiate investigations (if not prosecutions) but met with no luck. On March 30, 1942 the President approved the agreement,

[7] *Minutes of the Advisory Commission to the Council of National Defense* (Washington, 1946), pp. 40–47.
[8] Stimson Diary, January 16, 1942; March 2, 1942; March 4, 1942.

pointing out that "the war effort must come first and everything else must wait." During the next few years twenty-five suits involving such concerns as Bendix Aviation, General Electric and ALCOA were deferred at Stimson's request, and early in 1943 Thurman Arnold moved from the Justice Department to the Circuit Court of Appeals. A few old-style progressives wailed that anti-trust enforcement stood in greater peril than "when the New Deal went off courting the NRA," but most accepted the need to subordinate the competitive ideal to wartime requirements.[9]

Similarly, meeting the manpower shortage took precedence over protecting child labor. The Fair Labor Standards Act of 1938 had, by providing for effective regulation of child labor in interstate commerce, capped a twenty-five year crusade by social reformers. But during the war youngsters poured into the labor market. From 1940 to 1944 the number of teenage workers jumped from 1 to 2.9 million; four times as many fourteen- and fifteen-year-old girls held jobs at the end of the war than at its start. Not only were more young people employed, but they were also performing heavier work. Fewer fifteen-year-olds ran errands and more worked in retail trade; fewer seventeen-year-olds were found in grocery stores and more on assembly lines. As a result, over a million teenagers dropped out of school.

Breaches of the child labor law occurred repeatedly. In North Carolina inspectors found more than twenty times as many violations in 1944 as in 1940. In New York the number of boys and girls illegally employed climbed by nearly 400 percent, and a survey of pinsetters in bowling alleys revealed that "boys as young as 9 years go to the alleys after school, eat supper in an upstairs or back room, and work until midnight on school nights and until 3 or 4 o'clock in the morning on Sunday." When violations of the law became too common, states simply watered down their laws. In 1943 fifteen states extended the hours that children might work, and the following year four others followed suit. Yet when reformers proposed a law banning the employment of anyone under sixteen during school hours or in any type of manufacturing, they agreed to permit "deferred effective dates" so as "to avoid any possible objection to the raising of State child-labor standards during the period of war production."[10]

Just as the war shouldered aside certain reforms, so it provided an excuse to abolish various New Deal relief agencies. During 1942 and 1943 Congress and the administration snuffed out the Civilian Conservation Corps, the Works Progress Administration and the National Youth Administration. In each instance the defense boom altered the character of the agencies' clientele, which had come increasingly to consist of those last to be hired—Negroes, women, very old and very young workers.

[9]"Anti-Trust Procedure Memorandum," March, 1942, Rosenman Papers; Richard Lee Strout, "The Folklore of Thurman Arnold," *New Republic*, CVI (April 27, 1942), 570–71.

[10]"New York State Campaign Against Child Labor in Bowling Alleys," *The Child*, IX (May 1945) 173–74; "A 16-Year Minimum Age for Employment," *ibid.*, (January, 1945), 107–09.

Then, wartime job openings and draft calls had reduced the agencies' importance still further. Consequently, while the CCC, WPA and NYA often tried to justify their continuation by undertaking projects of military value, they could no longer count on strong backing from the Roosevelt administration. The point at issue was not as much the function of relief in wartime as its role in the reconversion period that would follow. Reformers wanted to preserve these agencies in at least a skeletal form for future use. Conservatives thought they "should be dropped, not only for the duration of the war, but forever after."[11]

The first relief agency to walk the plank was in some ways the most popular. The Civilian Conservation Corps had always attracted broad political support, in part because it was run by conservative administrators and brought revenue to communities in which camps were located. As late as 1940 Congress had allocated more for the CCC than Roosevelt had requested. From then on the agency took an active role in national defense, ordering drill for enrollees, providing instruction in reading blueprints, and performing tasks for military reservations. Its director affirmed that the CCC contributed to the war by building up boys' stamina and accustoming them to barracks life. Nevertheless, by early 1942 enrollment fell sharply, reaching a low point in March of little over 100,000, just one-third of what it had been a year before. A Gallup poll found that public opinion had turned against continuation, CCC officials were themselves unsure about whether to go on, and the President no longer showed much interest. He suggested maintaining camps "for only very nominal purposes, such as looking after parks, historic places, and forests," and opening them only to boys below draft age, preferably those "with slight defects which might be corrected." In June 1942 the House voted not to grant any funds for the CCC, and the Senate barely approved a small amount. The compromise appropriation bill provided just enough to liquidate the CCC in an orderly manner.[12]

Unlike the CCC, the Works Progress Administration had been embroiled in controversy from its creation in 1935. Opponents of the New Deal had always opposed work relief, particularly for white-collar workers, and suspected that the WPA would create a political machine that would keep the Democrats in power indefinitely. But as wartime jobs opened up, the WPA experienced an abrupt decline, losing two-thirds of its enrollees in the year after Pearl Harbor. Conservatives saw a golden opportunity to abolish the agency and few liberals thought it worth defending. By mid-1942 one welfare official understood that "WPA's days are numbered," and most hoped merely that the program would last through the winter so as not to create hardships for "the Negroes, older workers, and women." In December 1942 Roosevelt asserted that a national work relief program was no longer needed and gave the WPA an

[11]John Taber to Ray P. Chase, January 15, 1942, Taber Papers.
[12]Harold D. Smith Diary, December 18, 1941; January 16, 1942; John Salmond, *The Civilian Conservation Corps* (Durham, 1967), pp. 200–217.

"honorable discharge." Although a few New Dealers believed that it deserved a "wartime furlough" instead, the WPA mailed its last relief check in April 1943, ten years after Roosevelt first took office.[13]

The National Youth Administration became a third casualty of the war. In much the same manner as the CCC had turned to wartime tasks, so the NYA after 1940 had stressed vocational training programs that contributed to national defense. Spokesmen for the agency asserted that "the N.Y.A. is now exclusively for defense training," and professed their readiness "to liquidate everything that does not have to do with the winning of this war." The NYA enjoyed the support of many businessmen, since it taught needed skills and simplified worker recruitment by bringing boys from widely scattered rural areas to a central location. According to one manufacturer, the NYA had taken "strong mountain boys" and provided work experience so that they were "shop broken" and ready to take their place on the production lines. Given this, the agency survived the 1942 session of Congress. But as NYA director Aubrey Williams admitted, obtaining an appropriation "really becomes a great game of tightrope walking."[14]

As the war progressed, the balancing act became impossible. Not only did the manpower shortage whittle down the NYA's clientele, but it ultimately forced manufacturers to hire untrained workers and provide instant on-the-job instruction. One official informed the President that "the pressure on production had changed the whole aspect of pre-employment training." As the need for NYA programs lessened, opponents of the agency took the offensive. State education officials, who had always disliked the NYA because it competed for funds and students, claimed that it opened the door to federal control of education. Arguing that the NYA "runs in competition with us and is not needed," they urged congressmen to "kill this octopus before it kills us."[15] Conservatives in Congress were eager to comply, for many regarded the NYA as a hotbed of radicalism. A Republican member of the House from New York reported his outrage at observing a Negro boy and a white girl walking side by side from an NYA training center in his home town; he also suspected that the school had destroyed property values in the surrounding area. By June 1943 pressures had grown to such an extent that Congress abolished the agency. Aubrey Williams attributed the action mainly to Republicans and "the school clique," which he likened to "a pack of wolves, nipping at the NYA's heels."[16]

[13]Florence Kerr to Hopkins, June 2, 1942, Harry Hopkins Papers; "Memorandum for Discussion," November 9, 1942, *ibid.*

[14]*Termination of Civilian Conservation Corps and National Youth Administration,* Hearings before the Committee on Education and Labor, U.S. Senate, 77th Congress, 2nd Session (Washington, 1942), pp. 115, 162, 511; Williams to Eleanor Roosevelt, April 14, 1942, Aubrey Williams Papers.

[15]Smith Diary, March 17, 1943; Earl E. Krum to John Taber, January 21, 1943, Taber Papers.

[16]John Taber to Charles A. Cannon, June 1, 1943, Taber Papers; Williams to James Richmond, July 6, 1943, Williams Papers.

In addition to shunting aside various reforms and putting New Deal relief agencies out of commission, the war demonstrated that the government might use its power in ways that reformers had never intended. Throughout the depression years, liberals had fought to expand government authority and had confidently assumed that this authority would be used for humane ends. But the war revealed that even well-intentioned programs were susceptible to other uses. "The United States Government is a vast machine that could be used for other purposes than national defense and furthering the common welfare," reflected Malcolm Cowley in 1943. He added ominously, "It is possible that a fascist state could be instituted here without many changes in government personnel, and some of these changes have been made already."[17] Although most reformers did not share these fears, the war at least raised questions in the minds of some about the benevolence of the state.

That federal authority could be a double-edged sword was nowhere more clearly illustrated than in the evacuation of Japanese-Americans from the West Coast, a process facilitated by a number of New Deal welfare agencies. The Farm Security Administration supervised the evacuees' agricultural property, the Federal Security Agency provided health services in the relocation centers, and former WPA personnel applied the knowledge gained in setting up work projects to administering War Relocation Authority camps. Nor could other reform agencies, even one so archetypical as the NYA (before its demise), be counted on to soften the blow. In the spring of 1943, still under heavy attack in Congress, Aubrey Williams refused to permit young Japanese-American citizens to leave the relocation centers in order to attend NYA schools. The issue, he remarked, was loaded with dynamite and his agency was too vulnerable.[18] The ease with which relief programs could serve the cause of relocation suggested that such a massive and efficient movement of people would have been immeasurably more difficult before the advent of the social service state.

The desire to trim nondefense expenditures loomed as another important obstacle to reform in wartime. As military costs mushroomed it became all the more difficult to justify spending for domestic programs not directly related to the war. Throughout the 1930s conservatives in Congress and spokesmen for the business community had favored a balanced budget; now that the war made gargantuan deficits necessary, they sought partial compensation by cutting back domestic spending. "The plausible argument that the nation cannot afford to buy both guns and social security," wrote one reformer, "is all the Roosevelt-baiters have left and they are making the most of it."[19] Republican victories in the 1942

[17]Malcolm Cowley, "The End of the New Deal," *New Republic*, CVIII (May 31, 1943), 729–32.
[18]Aubrey Williams telephone conversation with J. S. Samler, May 31, 1943, and with Dillon S. Myer, June 1, 1943, Williams Papers.
[19]T.R.B., "Washington Notes," *New Republic*, CVI (February 23, 1942), 269.

elections greatly bolstered the drive to prune costs. The call for economy, of course, often served as a cloak behind which various interest groups concealed more substantive objections to reform measures. This was made evident in the dissolution of the National Resources Planning Board, the erosion of the Farm Security Administration, and the unwillingness of Congress to extend social security and unemployment insurance benefits or to provide for comprehensive medical care.

Unlike New Deal relief agencies which grew less important as unemployment fell, the National Resources Planning Board could have exerted considerable influence over economic policy during the war and after. But the Board, which analyzed economic trends, formulated plans regarding resource utilization, and evaluated priorities for public works projects, was always subject to conservative suspicion. If anything, distrust of "long haired planners" increased early in 1943 when the NRPB proposed an elaborate postwar expansion of medical care, education, housing and social insurance to help "the degraded and impoverished of our country, the disinherited and despised." The Board's chairman, Frederic A. Delano, noted "a strong disposition in Congress to cut our appropriations to the bone," and although Roosevelt pointed out that planning saved money ("I am definitely opposed to the principle of 'Penny wise, dollar foolish'," he told party leaders) Congress in the spring of 1943 appropriated only enough for the NRPB to wind up its affairs.[20] Even one conservative member of the House thought that his colleagues might become too free in wielding the economy axe. "Having 'tasted blood', I am now a bit fearful that its zeal toward economy and toward disrupting New Deal agencies may be excessive and in the end injurious."[21]

That is exactly what occurred in the case of the Farm Security Administration. As with other reform agencies, the FSA had for some time emphasized its role in national defense. The agency claimed that by helping marginal farmers purchase land and equipment it boosted crop production. Its defenders praised the FSA as a "first-line war agency" that would "help in meeting the food needs of wartime America." One official, who insisted that he was "not normally disposed to place social considerations precedent to considerations of winning the war," nevertheless reasoned that farm workers were "the lowest paid, least organized group in the country," and deserved whatever protection the government could provide.[22] The FSA also retained a symbolic as well as economic value. "FSA is the very symbol of the New Deal for small farmers," commented one reformer. "It is the agricultural equivalent of the Wagner Act." Calvin

[20]"Charter for America," *New Republic*, CVIII (April 19, 1943), 542; Delano to Roosevelt, October 14, 1942, Roosevelt Papers, OF 1092; Roosevelt to Carter Glass, March 24, 1943, *ibid.*

[21]Sterling Cole to Ernest Merritt, February 22, 1943, Sterling Cole Papers.

[22]John Beecher, "Save Farm Security!" *New Republic*, CVIII (April 26, 1943), 561–63; John K. Galbraith to Leon Henderson, October 27, 1942, Leon Henderson Papers.

B. Baldwin, a staunch liberal who headed the FSA, boasted that it "has always been proud to be known as a New Deal agency."[23]

For a time the FSA's reform instincts found an outlet in the Mexican farm labor program. In 1942 farmers in Texas, California and Arizona had urged the government to allow importation of *braceros* to ease the labor shortage. In August the United States and Mexico reached an agreement which required American farmers to pay prevailing wage rates, absorb transportation costs, furnish housing and medical facilities equal to those available for American workers, and provide protection against periods of unemployment. For about a year the Farm Security Administration supervised the program, but American farmers complained bitterly that the agency imposed impossible standards. Landowners in the Southwest believed that the FSA consisted of "social uplifters" who "look to the guidance of [the Mexicans'] spiritual welfare, their entertainment, physical well-being and happiness, see that they are fairly well taken care of with food and housing." "I get tripped every time I turn around," groaned one Arizonan, "My Mexicans are all happy." Farm owners thought they should be trusted to provide decent facilities, and wanted the matter handled at the state level by the agricultural extension services with a minimum of interference. Congress moved in that direction in the spring of 1943 by requiring the approval of county agricultural agents before farm laborers could be transported across state lines. Then, on July 1, control of Mexican farm labor was transferred from the FSA to the War Food Administration.[24]

In addition, Farm Security faced a threat to its very existence from a band of hostile forces: southern conservatives who thought that the agency was controlled by "social gainers, do-gooders, bleeding-hearts and long-hairs who make a career of helping others for a price and according to their own peculiar, screwball ideas;" Republicans who considered the agency communistic because it required farmers "to sign agreements with the laborers to pay them certain amounts and to provide them with meals costing at least $1.00 a piece and nothing but the highest grade of delicacies—no veal, little pork, plenty of lamb and beef and chicken, all sorts of fresh fruits and fresh vegetables;" and established farm organizations such as the American Farm Bureau Federation whose leaders thought that the FSA "promoted socialistic land policies."[25] With these groups united under the banner of economy, Congress cut the FSA budget to ribbons, slashing it by 30 percent in 1942 and by 36 percent more the following year. Indeed, the 1943 appropriation of $111.7 million went through only after Baldwin promised to resign. Within a short

[23]*Farm Security Administration,* Hearings before the Select Committee of the House Committee on Agriculture (Washington, 1944), IV, 1553, 1557.

[24]James G. Patton to Roosevelt, April 8, 1943, Roosevelt Papers, OF 1568; Baldwin to Roosevelt, September 24, 1943, *ibid.*

[25]Sidney Baldwin, *Poverty and Politics: The Rise and Decline of the FSA* (Chapel Hill, 1968), p. 284; John Taber to Thomas Dewey, February 23, 1943, Taber Papers; *Farm Security Administration,* Hearings, II, 801.

time his place was taken by a former Democratic representative from North Carolina whom conservatives found unobjectionable. The FSA lingered on with its funds depleted, liberal leadership gone, and program much reduced.

In much the same way as the budget squeeze victimized the NRPB and the FSA, so it worked against congressional enactment of new social welfare measures. Throughout the war liberals in the administration pressed for reform of the social security and unemployment insurance systems so as to cover more workers and liberalize payments.[26] Many of their proposals were embodied in the Wagner-Murray-Dingell bill introduced in 1943 which would have set up a national insurance system to replace the existing federal-state arrangement, extended coverage to 15 million agricultural and domestic workers, and increased unemployment benefits. In addition it proposed a federal system of health insurance under which each worker's family could obtain medical and hospital care. The individual would select a physician from among those agreeing to participate, provided the doctor was willing to treat him. Although it did not cover dental treatment or maternity costs and was to be financed by employer and worker contributions, this was the most ambitious plan of health insurance yet proposed.

Such proposals, however, made no headway during the war. President Roosevelt occasionally spoke in favor of social welfare measures, but he lent no support to Wagner's legislative endeavors. On one occasion he asked Frances Perkins, who was preparing a speech in behalf of expanding social security, to emphasize "that this is not, what some people call, a New Deal measure." The President also recognized that health insurance was widely resented by doctors who saw in it the specter of socialized medicine. "We can't go up against the State Medical Societies," Roosevelt concluded, "we just can't do it."[27] The President undoubtedly assessed the balance of political forces correctly. Given the conservative mood in Congress, the opposition of the medical profession, and the rather widespread prosperity, there was little inclination to undertake potentially expensive new programs. Congress not only failed to broaden social security coverage, but from year to year it froze the rate of contributions at 1 percent thereby postponing a small scheduled increase.

If social welfare schemes stood little chance in wartime, proposals to help those on the bottom of the ladder stood even less. Although most Americans enjoyed higher incomes during the 1940s than ever before, for some the depression had never really ended. In 1944 ten million workers—one-fourth of those engaged in manufacturing—received less than 60 cents an hour. Moreover, white collar wages lagged far behind those of industrial workers. But the people who suffered most were those on

[26]Arthur Altmeyer to Isador Lubin, November 19, 1943, enclosing draft of "An Expanded Social Security System," Isador Lubin Papers.
[27]Grace Tully memorandum, February 18, 1943, Roosevelt Papers, PSF 21; John M. Blum, *From the Morgenthau Diaries: Years of War* (Boston, 1967), p. 72.

fixed incomes (such as the elderly on social security), state employees, and unskilled workers. Congressional committees investigating substandard conditions heard from a New York City sanitation worker, a Pittsburgh cleaning woman and a Boston nurse, none of whom could support their families. "I have no fresh meat for my family," lamented one woman who received 50 cents an hour for canning tomatoes and whose husband worked in an automobile plant. "We do not have milk; I cannot afford milk except for only the baby." In January 1944 a group of senators reported that twenty million Americans "dwell constantly in a borderland between subsistence and privation, where even the utmost thrift and caution do not suffice to make ends meet."[28]

Nevertheless, the Roosevelt administration opposed across-the-board wage increases on the grounds that they would increase inflationary pressures. When Senator Claude Pepper of Florida sought to aid those in the greatest distress by allowing the War Labor Board to permit voluntary wage hikes to 65 cents an hour (rather than the 50 cents allowed in 1944) he received a chilly response. Asserting that "you cannot wish 65 cents out of the air," WLB chairman William Davis suggested that raising the wages of the lowest paid was like tossing a stone into a pond: inflationary ripples would spread through the economy since, to preserve wage differentials, adjustments would be made all along the line. Higher prices would eventually rob the worker of any benefit. "Unfortunately," said Davis, "you cannot fix that substandard bracket in our present economy at the level which really represents a decent standard of living with security for the future." The President strongly endorsed this view. In defending his anti-inflation drive Roosevelt remarked that every group would have to accept a cut in its standard of living during the war. The government could do no more than see that "those on the lower rungs of the economic ladder are not ground down below the margin of existence."[29] Not until 1945 did the War Labor Board authorize a wage increase to 55 cents an hour, and then only in certain instances.

Having argued that the danger of inflation precluded gains for the working poor, the administration attempted to deal with the very rich by limiting salaries to $25,000. Roosevelt first advanced this idea in April, 1942 and after the Price Control Act passed in October he empowered Stabilization Director James Byrnes to hold salaries at $25,000 after taxes "insofar as practicable." But congressional opposition, particularly in the House Ways and Means Committee, soon put an end to the plan. A Treasury official noted that when he informed congressmen of his work on the limitation, "I received a Bronx cheer, and was told by many that I

[28]*Substandard Wages,* Hearings before a Subcommittee of the Committee on Education and Labor, U.S. Senate (Washington, 1945), pp. 86–89; *Wartime Health and Education,* Hearings before a Subcommittee of the Committee on Education and Labor, U.S. Senate (Washington, 1945), III, x–xi.

[29]*Substandard Wages,* Hearings, p. 245; *Wartime Health and Education,* Hearings, pp. 1233–43; Seymour E. Harris, *Inflation and the American Economy* (New York, 1945), pp. 360–63.

could spare myself that work."[30] In the spring of 1943, ignoring Roosevelt's pleas, the Committee attached a rider ending the salary limitation to a bill authorizing an increase in the public debt, and the President had no choice but to go along. In a sense the issue had greater symbolic than fiscal meaning: since maximum salaries were computed after taxes the limitation ordinarily affected earnings over $67,200; exceptions could be permitted to meet life insurance premiums, mortgage payments and contributions to charity; and income from interest or investments was not touched. At most the plan had affected some three thousand people. Even so, its repeal contrasted vividly with the treatment of those who eked out a marginal existence during the war.

Changes in the composition of the federal bureaucracy worked to the disadvantage of social reform no less than did the need to give priority to military projects, to limit domestic spending, or to curb inflation. During its early years the Roosevelt administration had drawn into government service a group of economists, lawyers, social workers and reformers motivated largely by the desire (in Rexford Tugwell's phrase) to make America over. But during the defense buildup a number of conservative lawyers and businessmen—such as Edward R. Stettinius, James V. Forrestal, Henry L. Stimson and Dean Acheson—began moving into Washington, and in the early 1940s the federal service underwent a major overhaul. Some New Dealers remained but usually their influence was greatly reduced. Many left government employment altogether: some enlisted in the armed forces, others became sacrificial offerings to congressional conservatives, and still others resigned when their objectives were frustrated or they became physically exhausted. Often their places were filled by business executives who possessed the skills needed to manage war production but who had little interest in social reform. As one observer explained, "The mere fact of passing from a state of peace into a state of war is marked by a change in the prestige of professions which is perhaps most clearly symbolized by the influx of production experts into Washington and the simultaneous exit of the social engineers."[31]

The new prestige accorded businessmen did much to refashion their attitude toward government. During the 1930s the business community had resented the Roosevelt administration not because it jeopardized capitalism, but because it deprived them of status and authority. It was not so much that New Deal policies were harmful as that businessmen felt they had literally no voice in decision making. This changed dramatically during the war. As the government called on industrialists to staff production agencies, business once again basked in the warm glow of public admiration. A chairman of the National Association of Manufacturers noted happily that "the public is turning again with confidence to business leaders." *Business Week* declared that the war had placed a premium on

[30]Randolph Paul to Samuel Rosenman, May 12, 1942, Rosenman Papers.
[31]Richard Rovere, "Warning to the Liberals," *Common Sense*, XI (August, 1942), pp. 266–68.

"business talents," that the administration could no longer afford the "amateurism" of "braintrusters and theoreticians," and, best of all, that businessmen were "moving up in the New Deal Administration, replacing New Dealers as they go." Since government was destined to play a cardinal role in economic affairs, it followed that businessmen should discard the idea that the state was their enemy and make sure it remained responsive to their interests. "The management men who have gone to Washington during the war should be the opening wedge for the participation of management men in peacetime government."[32] Politics had become too important to be left to the politicians.

Nothing infuriated liberals more than this steady movement of businessmen into positions of authority. "The New Dealers are a vanishing tribe," wrote James Wechsler, "and the money changers who were driven from the temple are now quietly established in government offices."[33] Reformers, however, saved their sharpest darts for the "dollar-a-year" men. To recruit executives for national defense, the government often permitted them to remain on their company's payroll for they might otherwise refuse to sacrifice their normal incomes in order to accept temporary federal employment. Ultimately, dollar-a-year men made up three-fourths of the War Production Board's executive force. Even though such employees were supposedly prohibited from ruling on cases directly involving their own firms, liberals claimed that they looked after their own interests. But at bottom the issue was less one of individual selfishness than of the fundamental outlook and ideals of an entire class of governmental administrators. Reformers saw clearly enough that war had bestowed power on many men who held the New Deal in horror and were likely to make judgments based on their past experience.

World War II weakened liberalism in still another respect: it raised issues that ruptured the New Deal coalition. Throughout his presidency Roosevelt had tried to hold together such diverse groups as southern white farmers, urban blue collar workers, middle-class intellectuals, and members of ethnic and racial minorities. Like every political coalition this one had always contained unstable elements, and signs of strain were apparent after 1937 when rural elements balked at proposals to aid northern industrial groups. The war both exacerbated existing tensions and introduced new ones. Foreign policy was one source of division: the administration found it increasingly difficult to retain the loyalty of Irish-Americans as a result of its collaboration with the Soviet Union, and of Polish-Americans after the Yalta settlement. Civil rights was yet another problem: as wartime manpower shortages forced the federal government to support, even in limited fashion, equal employment opportunities for

[32]Frederick C. Crawford, "A Better America Through Freedom of Enterprise," in National Association of Manufacturers, *A Better America* (New York, 1944), p. 3; *Business Week*, November 13, 1943, p. 116; October 9, 1943, p. 108.

[33]James Wechsler, "The Last New Dealer," *Common Sense*, XII (May, 1943), 163–64.

Negroes, southern whites talked openly of bolting the Democratic party. But most of the difficulty stemmed from the competition between interest groups at a time when the government had to withhold economic favors rather than hand them out. For example, the imposition of price controls on agricultural products provoked a dispute between farmers who favored high food prices and consumers worried about their weekly budgets. By setting the farmer's interest against that of the urban dweller the war made it impossible not to alienate some part of the New Deal's constituency.

Similarly, the war caused some liberal intellectuals to re-examine their attitude toward the labor movement. During the 1930s reformers had occasionally criticized union tactics but had warmly endorsed labor's goals of union recognition, job security and improved conditions. Then the war enormously complicated what had formerly seemed a simple matter of justice for the underdog. As unions gained members and workers' conditions improved, the problems posed by disruptive strikes, racially exclusive membership policies, and inflationary wage demands became more difficult to resolve. A prominent liberal told Victor Reuther of the United Automobile Workers that if the demands of striking workers were met, "it will be at the expense of some other group. Higher wages will not result in greater production of consumers goods as heretofore." The *New Republic*, noting that labor "has the highest real wages, the greatest extent of employment and the best working conditions it has had in its history," suggested that the time had come for unions to turn away from their "immediate interests" and concern themselves instead with liberalizing American national life. While the war did not disrupt the alliance between liberals and the labor movement, it surely subjected it to severe strain.[34]

As they observed the setbacks dealt to social reform in the early 1940s, liberals quite naturally grew pessimistic about the future. Many concluded that a postwar depression would occur and became obsessed with the menace of domestic fascism. Often they expressed such fears in terms bordering on the apocalyptic. "America is today more reactionary in its prevailing mood than any other country where the fascists are not openly in power," wrote one. "The counterrevolution is gathering its forces in America."[35] Despite these complaints the war did not in all respects impair the reform movement. Not only did it solve some pressing social problems, but it demonstrated the efficacy of Keynesian economics, inspired reforms related to labor efficiency and troop morale, and provided an opportunity to incorporate into the liberal program ideas which had largely been ignored in the 1930s.

"What are we liberals after?" asked a writer in *Common Sense* in Sep-

---

[34]Thomas Amlie to Victor Reuther, May 16, 1942, Union for Democratic Action Papers; "War Thoughts on Labor," *New Republic*, CVIII (January 25, 1943), pp. 103–104.

[35]Max Lerner, *Public Journal* (New York, 1945), p. 382.

tember 1943. "Do we just want words which will run our way in neat ideological packages? Or do we want a better break for the common man?" Since the latter was surely the case, liberals would have to recognize that the war meant a higher standard of living than any had dreamed possible a few years before. "The honest minded liberal will admit that the common man is getting a better break than ever he did under the New Deal." The war, in fact, pushed farm income to new heights, reduced tenancy as individuals left the land for factory jobs or enlisted in the armed services, strengthened trade unions, and literally ended unemployment. Although not everyone shared equally in the new prosperity, wartime hardship where it existed differed qualitatively from depression hardship: it was not a matter of having no job, no food, and no place to live but rather of having less nutritious food, poorer housing and lower wages than people thought they deserved. In 1943 the Women's Christian Temperance Union in Illinois failed to find a single needy family to whom it could distribute Christmas baskets.

The war, moreover, exerted a modest levelling influence. Because the well-to-do paid heavy taxes and goods were rationed, class differences were felt somewhat less keenly. "Rockefeller and I can now get the same amount of sugar, gasoline, tires etc., etc., etc.," said one reformer, "and the etc's will soon fill many pages."[36] Between 1939 and 1944 the share of national income held by the wealthiest five percent of the American people declined from 23.7 to 16.8 percent. The pyramid of social stratification was by no means entirely flattened, but far fewer could be found at the very bottom. In that sense, the war remedied problems that had plagued reformers even before the crash of 1929.

Since it was abundantly clear that government spending had created this prosperity, Keynesian economic thought acquired new converts. Followers of Keynes asserted that fiscal policy, in the form of deficit spending and the control of taxes and interest rates, held the key to prosperity. By stimulating investment and boosting purchasing power, they said, the government could insure high levels of employment. This argument, which a growing number of New Dealers had found appealing in the late 1930s, now seemed wholly substantiated. "The war has proved to us that it is possible to have full employment," wrote Alfred Bingham. "It was achieved by making available to the government sufficient spending power to put all our productive resources to use." If the government could spend vast sums for war, surely it could spend a fraction of that amount for constructive social purposes in peacetime. Keynesian economics became sanctioned fiscal policy with the Employment Act of 1946, an early version of which had been introduced in 1944. Although watered down considerably in that it did not establish methods of dealing with future downturns or instruct the President to lift federal expenditures to a level necessary to insure full employment, the act recog-

[36]Stuart Chase, "New Deal Dead—So What?" *Common Sense*, XI (September, 1943), 385; Thomas Amlie to James Loeb, May 12, 1942, UDA Papers.

nized the responsibility of the federal government for the prevention of mass unemployment. "We have seen the last of our great depressions," said Chester Bowles, "for the simple reason that the public [is] wise enough to know it doesn't have to stand for one."[37]

The war afforded greater scope to reformers in the area of housing. From 1940 to 1945 millions of Americans moved to new homes, many to be near defense plants. To ease the strain of migration, the government often assumed responsibility for housing defense workers (as well as for providing health facilities and day care centers for the children of working mothers). In February 1942 Roosevelt created the National Housing Agency which, along with other production and manpower boards, determined the nature and location of the necessary dwellings. In all, public and private sources provided housing for more than nine million migratory war workers and their families. The government spent $2.3 billion for this purpose, much of which necessarily went for temporary facilities. Even though building standards were diluted to conserve materials and manpower, government construction of low-cost housing far exceeded anything contemplated before the war.

Since most people did not live in public projects, it was essential to prevent landlords from taking advantage of war workers by hiking rents. In March 1942 the Office of Price Administration froze or rolled back rents in twenty defense areas; in April three hundred additional areas were included, and eventually 86 million tenants benefited. Wartime rent control proved both popular and successful. Unlike businessmen who could frequently evade price control by turning out a new product and finding a customer willing to pay the price, landlords dealt with relatively unalterable products and with tenants who moved quickly to obtain OPA assistance when threatened by a rent hike or eviction. Of course means were devised, legal and illegal, to get around rent control. Since commercial rents were not affected landlords attempted to convert dwellings to business purposes. Even worse, tenants were obliged to give a nonreturnable deposit, purchase furniture already in the apartment, or assume responsibility for repairs. Nevertheless, rents paid in large cities rose only fractionally after OPA controls took effect.

To a much greater extent than war workers, soldiers and veterans benefited from social legislation. Although broad-gauged proposals for national health insurance made no headway, maternity and pediatric care were provided for families of servicemen in the lowest pay grades. More than one million mothers and infants eventually received medical, hospital and nursing care; at its peak the program covered one of every seven births in the United States. Then in the fall of 1943 the President called for liberal unemployment, social security and education benefits for veterans. In January 1944, after several bills had been introduced along

[37]Alfred Bingham, *The Practice of Idealism* (New York, 1944), pp. 81–82; Chester Bowles to Wallace, September 15, 1944, Wallace Papers.

these lines, the American Legion proposed an omnibus measure thereafter known as the GI Bill of Rights. It sailed through the Senate by a unanimous vote in March, and then made its way more slowly through the House where it was modified to suit John Rankin of Mississippi, chairman of the Committee on World War Veterans' Legislation. Rankin feared that overly generous education or unemployment benefits might weaken the incentive to find work. "We have 50,000 negroes in the service from our State," he said, "and in my opinion, if the bill should pass in its present form, a vast majority of them would remain unemployed for at least a year, and a great many white men would do the same thing." Rankin succeeded in partially diluting the measure, but as signed by the President in June 1944 it provided generous educational benefits, readjustment allowances for veterans during the transition to civilian life, and guarantees of mortgage loans.[38]

The GI Bill of Rights revealed much about the character of wartime social reform. In many ways the bill proved an exception to the rule: in this instance, congressmen—whether from gratitude, considerations of troop morale, or knowledge that financial outlays would not begin until the war's end—were willing to distribute benefits denied to other groups. Unlike the Wagner-Murray-Dingell health insurance bill or the activities of the Farm Security Administration, veterans' legislation affronted no major interest group. On the contrary, it had the backing of a powerful lobby headed by the American Legion, which saw a chance to put returning veterans in its debt and was anxious to centralize services in the Veterans' Administration rather than see them divided among various government bureaus. Moreover, the bill passed only after John Rankin had whittled down some of its most liberal features by tightening eligibility requirements for educational grants. Above all, the GI Bill of Rights was construed wholly as a veterans' measure rather than as part of a broader scheme of social reform. New Dealers had wanted to link veterans' benefits to expanded social insurance, aid to education and home loans for the entire population, but had met with no success.

If liberals failed to provide most Americans with the advantages offered to veterans, the war nevertheless brought into prominence ideas which had either not been part of the reform tradition or had been regarded as inessential. The depression had fastened attention on problems of economic security, unemployment, business regulation and conservation of natural resources. Given these concerns, reformers had paid scant regard to health insurance, federal aid to education, and civil rights. But as the war cleared away economic problems, each was incorporated into the liberal platform. Roosevelt accepted the proposition, first advanced by members of the National Resources Planning Board, that the political liberties guaranteed by the Constitution needed supplementing by an

[38]David R. B. Ross, *Preparing for Ulysses: Politics and Veterans during World War II* (New York, 1969), p. 108.

Economic Bill of Rights, that the right to adequate medical care and a good education was no less important than freedom of speech or trial by jury. Liberals also asserted more positively that Negroes as well as whites were to enjoy these benefits. In the 1930s a man like George Norris could oppose an antilynching bill and still be counted a liberal in good standing; by 1945 support for civil rights had become an acid test of one's liberal credentials.

The relationship between the war and social reform depended on reformers' goals and the degree to which those goals contributed to the military or economic conduct of the war. To the extent that American liberalism was identified with expanding the scope of governmental activity in behalf of underprivileged groups, it lost strength during the war. Liberals had relegated many reforms to a back seat, had seen New Deal projects dismantled and wartime agencies taken over by businessmen, and had found that pressure to prevent inflation often precluded assisting the poor. Yet the war also had a more positive long-range effect, for it solved old problems even as it created new ones. By liberating the economy from the grip of depression, the war permitted more attention to be paid to other issues—federal aid to education, civil rights, medical insurance and a compensatory fiscal policy—that would comprise much of the liberal agenda for the next twenty years.

John Morton Blum
"THAT KIND OF A LIBERAL": FRANKLIN D. ROOSEVELT AFTER TWENTY-FIVE YEARS

A cultural and class gap existed on the subject of Franklin D. Roosevelt while he lived. Among historians today there is sometimes a generation gap which marks their attitudes towards his presidency. It is likely that few historians born since Roosevelt's inauguration agree with very many of John Morton Blum's judgments of F.D.R.'s accomplishments. Blum has not written an apologia; none is required. Rather, he asks his readers to consider the numerous forces which provided Roosevelt with a plausible logic for his policies. He obliges us to inquire if Roosevelt's shortcomings were really due to his time or to America's institutions instead of to Roosevelt himself.

Perhaps Roosevelt's greatest problem was his inability to anticipate the consequences of his actions; also, he is being viewed from the "presentist" perspective of modern historians who ascribe many of today's ills to yesterday's "presentist" politics. Only grudgingly do some historians born during or since Roosevelt's administration admit to his social justice intentions and successes. Blum suggests that our perspective of the New Deal has been distorted by current events; we, like Roosevelt, are prisoners of contemporary turmoil.

After a quarter of a century, the manner has receded in national memory, and with it so has the man. Americans under forty—most Americans, that is—cannot hear the voice that spoke the words which history records. Few under forty can evoke a personal experience of long depression ("I see one-third of a nation ill-housed, ill-clad, ill-nourished") or of sudden war ("Yesterday, December 7, 1941—a date that will live in infamy"). Few have a sense of a living Franklin Roosevelt in their past. He lives for them, if he lives at all, only in history, which strips from his past, as from any past, much of its passion, much of its gaiety, much also of its distorting sentimentality, and some of its immediate truth.

If the past is largely prologue, then Roosevelt's past and that of his contemporaries opened avenues leading to an awful present. Twenty-five years after his death young Americans see their country drifting toward the edge of a new recession, see most men in high public office indifferent about the poverty and prejudice that divide the nation and unconcerned about the power of huge corporations nurtured by federal military spending but readily accountable to no one. They see the United States mired in an unjust, destructive war, its grandeur committed to corrupt and undemocratic governments, its wealth wasting in an unending weapons race and an incessant hedonism. In the perspective of that present, young critics especially have found Roosevelt the captive rather than the master of depression, timid in his ventures in reform, callous toward the sufferings of persecuted people, and disingenuous in his pleas for peace and freedom. Yet the present mood, no less distorting than sentimental memories, casts Roosevelt in a different world from that he ever knew.

The world he knew as President was pervaded by the Great Depression of the 'thirties with its attendant hardships. There was no general affluence, no plenitude of funds or goods to be distributed to needy people. Recovery, eluding the New Deal's various efforts, occurred incidentally, not as a product of deliberate national policy but in response to heavy federal spending for defense and war. In theory at least the failure to achieve recovery was unnecessary. Had Roosevelt understood economics, he might in theory have built business confidence and thus stimulated private investment, or alternatively have championed countercyclical spending at many multiples of the volume of the peacetime deficits actually incurred. In fact, the circumstances of the 1930's, the relatively primitive level of economic intelligence, the prevailing hostility to business and industry, and the constrictive possibilities of politics all militated against those theoretical solutions.

Only a minority even of professional economists embraced Keynesian theory until late in the decade. Their attempts to explain the new economics did not quickly persuade the large majority of businessmen and congressmen, who clung instead to the prudential folklore of outmoded analyses even after the experience of war provided ample documentation for Keynes's case. Indeed the proponents of the Employment Act of 1946 met strong resistance on the Hill. Roosevelt, for his part, had moved belatedly, more by hunch than comprehension, to Keynesian formulations, first during the budget crisis of 1938 when he accepted the counsel of the spenders in his official circle ("it is up to us to create an economic upturn"), again in 1945 when he approved the basic outline of the Employment Bill that Congress weakened in the following year. He had moved faster and farther than most Americans of his generation. He had learned from his mistakes, precisely as he had learned, after his adventures in buying gold in 1933, to find a better basis for monetary policy. Roosevelt never understood economics any more than he understood atomic physics. He was not an intellectual; few Presidents have been. But he had a respect for intellectuals, including economists, and a searching zest for new ideas. Too few Presidents have shared those traits.

Recovery failed partly because Roosevelt was resolved to advance his objectives in social reform. He was prepared on his own terms to cooperate with industry but not to boost business confidence if boosting entailed special tax favors or permissive government. Herbert Hoover's reiterated reassurances had not spurred investment. More important, the practices of the business and investment communities during the 1920's did not commend the practitioners for favor. Roosevelt was not content with rhetoric ("money changers ... in the temple of our civilization" ... "royalists of the economic order"). The regulatory agencies the New Deal created, each in some measure confined by compromises characteristic of the legislative process, nevertheless for a time imposed refreshingly strict standards of behavior on their charges. Only after Roosevelt's death did appointments to those agencies lead to the substitution of genial collusion for vigorous vigilance, just as appointments to the Supreme Court seem now to be about to bend the law away from justice.

More than regulation, Roosevelt's labor and tax policies made him enemies on his right. Gradually he became a champion of the unions. He and his advisers in 1933 contrived the National Recovery Administration to bring more order and more government planning to national economic life. Though industry soon dominated planning within the NRA, the provisions of the act also strengthened the union movement and its emerging new and militant leadership. That stimulus, intensified by the Wagner Act, assured unions, for the first time in American history, of a fair chance under the law to bargain collectively with employers. The President, it was said of Roosevelt as it could be said of few others ever in his office, wanted men to join the unions. Since his time, the terms of labor law and the quality of labor leadership have changed to the detriment of American workers but, in his day, labor organizations enjoyed their sunniest and most creative season, while federal fair labor standards and unemployment and old age insurance—innovations Roosevelt sponsored—provided the foundations for a still unfinished structure of equity and security for the laboring force.

Roosevelt sponsored, too, a succession of controversial revenue acts. Given the New Deal's modest level of spending, advancing tax schedules impeded economic recovery. But taxation, for Roosevelt, was as much an instrument for reform as for revenue. The legislation he signed in 1935-1937 lifted income and estate taxes in the higher brackets, closed many of the loopholes through which the wealthy were escaping taxes, increased corporate taxes, and attempted major corporate reforms by imposing an intercorporate dividend tax and a short-lived undistributed earnings tax. Roosevelt meant to soak the rich to help the poor. He achieved less than he wanted to partly, as the critics on his left complained, because he fought less doggedly than he might have, but largely because Congress gave him much less than he asked for. Indeed in 1943 he took the unprecedented step of vetoing a revenue bill because, as he said, it provided "tax relief . . . not for the needy, but for the greedy."

Yet Roosevelt was not and never claimed to be a radical. He was a reformer, a meliorist, much in the tradition of the progressives of the early twentieth century, one of whom he had been as a young man. Like them, he intended to reform capitalism in order to preserve it, to enlarge and strengthen the middle class rather than to abolish it. ("I am that kind of a liberal because I am that kind of a conservative.") He moved therefore to protect farms and homes from foreclosure by providing government loans at reduced rates, loans that also increased the liquidity of banks that held mortgages either defaulted or in arrears. So, too, federal insurance of bank deposits protected depositors from loss and banks from runs. While helping those who owned property to retain it, the New Deal also generated a gradual leveling effect as labor policy moved blue collar workers toward middle-class income and status, and agricultural policy assured many farmers first of a tolerable and later of a comfortable standard of life.

The urban unemployed had the hardest road to travel. In contrast to any previous President, Roosevelt accepted the obligation of the federal government to provide assistance to the destitute. There was never enough relief, never enough money appropriated to hire all those who needed jobs or properly to care for all the shivering and hungry. But as they developed, the relief programs hired more and more men, and hired them increasingly in jobs related to their talents and aspirations as lawyers, accountants, engineers, artists, writers, teachers, actors. The New Deal's relief policies ("We are poor indeed if this Nation cannot afford to lift from every recess of American life the dread fear of the unemployed that they are not needed in the world"), sometimes faltering in execution, rarely adequate for unemployables, pointed to the large goals Roosevelt defined for a more prosperous, postwar America—the rights of every family to a decent home, to necessary medical care, to a decent education; the right his generation especially cherished "to a useful and remunerative job."

As his kind of liberal, his kind of conservative, Roosevelt took for granted the need to operate within the tolerances of the American political system and consequently to build not for eternity but for a year or two or ten ahead, when building would have to proceed again. As a tactician, he did not want to tie his hands, he liked to remain on a twenty-four-hour basis, he was ready to concede what he considered marginal in order to gain what he deemed essential. By the standards of a later generation, on some issues his concessions outweighed his gains.

So it was with racial matters. Roosevelt tended not to think in racial terms. He approached questions of Negro rights from a political rather than an idealistic angle. He responded to Negro leaders sympathetically but evasively. Accordingly the New Deal assisted Negroes only in limited ways. Government under Roosevelt ceased being lily-white. The executive departments desegregated their facilities, and particularly in Washington, increasing numbers of Negroes found permanent federal jobs, though disproportionately in menial or clerical roles. In some Northern states, Negroes received a considerable though not an equitable share of relief, and one major relief program trained young Negroes for skilled jobs until Congress eliminated its funds. But Roosevelt delayed establishing the Fair Employment Practices Committee until he was pushed into it. Without reflection, he permitted discrimination against Negroes within the Civilian Conservation Corps and by the Tennessee Valley Authority. Fearful that a Southern filibuster would tie up "must" legislation, he continually avoided taking a strong stand for an anti-lynching bill. For their part, Southern congressmen had no trouble amending the Relief Act of 1935 so as to make appointments of senior administrators subject to senatorial consent, a provision that assured rewards for deserving Democrats everywhere and the triumph in the South of Jim Crow in the distribution of relief.

His spotty record on racial issues reflected Roosevelt's sense of priorities. Questions of political economy commanded his attention until 1940. During the years of war, his preoccupation was victory, to which he subordinated various democratic objectives, often on the basis of supposedly expert but dubious advice. To the dismay of Eleanor Roosevelt, he accepted the hollow argument of the War and Navy Departments that desegregation of the armed forces would impede the progress of the war. He also followed the Army's lamentable advice in incarcerating the Japanese-Americans. Similarly, on the basis of his judgments about the mood of Congress and the politics of the Middle East, he tolerated the State Department's devastating delays in finding asylums for European Jews threatened with extinction by the Nazis. Yet Roosevelt's humanity, projected in his spontaneous warmth, won him the trust and love of men and women who had reason for impatience with those public acts.

When his personal impulses clashed with his sense of political possibilities, Roosevelt suffered seasons of caution or indecision. Detesting Hitler, he foresaw the dangers Naziism posed to Europe and to peace. But he also recognized, as in degree he shared, the disenchantment of Americans with the First World War and their reluctance again to be embroiled. Yielding to that mood, which dominated Congress, Roosevelt until 1940 put forward no significant policy contingent upon public approval to retard aggression or to preserve world peace. Within the area of his executive discretion, he made occasional, inconclusive gestures toward those ends. Concern for the balance of power in Europe and Asia motivated his recognition of the Soviet Union in 1933. His desire to buttress France brought him in 1936 to support technical changes in monetary and tariff policy he had previously opposed. He interpreted neutrality legislation to the advantage of China and of Loyalist Spain. After the Munich conference, he stretched his interpretations further so as to encourage French and British purchases of American military aircraft. But his first bursts of effective energy came only with the fall of France when his constituency at last recognized the vulnerability of the United States. Then in quick succession came the sale of surplus arms to England, the destroyer deal, lend-lease, the use of the American navy to convoy ships as far as Iceland, and the incremental embargo against Japan.

By the summer of 1941, those limits drawn, Roosevelt's energy abated. By then he had settled in his mind upon the policy of assisting the British and the Russians in the war in Europe first, the Chinese only secondarily, and of continuing, as fast as possible, to arm the United States, still woefully unprepared to fight. There Roosevelt halted. To those eager for outright war against the Axis, he seemed unsure of himself, drifting. Pearl Harbor mobilized his energy again, as it mobilized the temper of America, until then manifestly anti-Axis but still wistfully anti-war.

Roosevelt did not plan Pearl Harbor, an unparalleled disaster for the United States. American officers, civilian and military alike, had misinterpreted the MAGIC intercepts which, if accurately interpreted, would have removed the surprise element in the attack. But those officers were not traitors. They simply erred, just as loyal men in Norway, France, Great Britain, and the Soviet Union had erred in failing accurately to read the evidence of incipient German movements before those movements caught them by surprise.

Roosevelt's policies, however, did challenge Japanese ambitions. Had

he raised no objections to the Japanese war against China or Japanese
expansion into Southeast Asia, Japan would not have chosen to attack.
If the American embargo had not reduced Japan's access to supplies of
strategic materials, Japan would probably not have decided to attack in
1941. War came in the Pacific because the Japanese government, committed to its purposes, wholly understood American opposition to them
and believed it could prevail by starting a war it expected to win.

By insisting upon the independence of China, Roosevelt demanded
more than the resources of the United States could guarantee, but before
and after 1941, he committed only a fraction of those resources to the
Chinese. Even that fraction was wasted by the weak, undemocratic, and
corrupt government of Chiang Kai-shek. In spite of growing doubts about
Chiang, Roosevelt retained more confidence in the possibility of guiding
him than conditions warranted. There was no ready alternative. Repeated
American efforts failed to bring Chiang to necessary social and political
reforms. The United States could not engage in a full-scale land war in
Asia, or in the deliberate subversion of Chiang's regime. Blindly, the
Generalissimo raced to his own destruction which the Japanese had be-
gun by their invasion and the Communists completed by force of arms.
Roosevelt's tactic failed, for Chiang was a weak instrument for achieving
the independence or guiding the development of China. But unlike most
statesmen in the West, Roosevelt realized that a strong and independent
China would occupy a crucial place in postwar politics.

He realized, too, that the winning of the war and the preservation
of the peace depended upon the cultivation of cooperation with the
Soviet Union as well as with Great Britain. Yet jealous of American interests, he conceded to Russia and England only those matters he deemed
expendable for the sake of victory. He shaped the Bretton Woods agreements to the economic advantage of the United States. He looked forward
to the ultimate independence of India and of other British and European colonies, but he pressed for that eventuality only as far as he believed he could without disrupting the Anglo-American alliance. Similarly, he never agreed to Russian expansion in eastern Europe. But
because he recognized the indispensable contribution of Russian armies to
the waging of the war and the enormous costs the Russians bore, he
pushed his subordinates to facilitate lend-lease aid to Russia and he
shared Stalin's impatience with British hesitations about the cross-channel
invasion. He also welcomed the prospect of Russian engagement on the
Asian front where the Japanese, until Yalta and later, seemed capable of
prolonged resistance to American offensives.

Roosevelt did not foresee, much less invite, the cold war. On the contrary, he planned after an armistice rapidly to remove American forces
from Europe and Asia. He expected also, perhaps with too little sensitivity for the feelings and prerogatives of smaller nations, to base postwar
stability, within the framework of the United Nations, upon the influence
and continuing cooperation of four major powers—the United States, the

Soviet Union, the United Kingdom, and China. Those expectations over-estimated Russian friendship and British strength, and underestimated the aspirations of colonial peoples, the distress of Europe, and the mutual suspicions of governing authorities in Washington and Moscow. Perhaps Roosevelt overestimated most of all his own ability to improvise, to patch things over, once the war was won, until the gradual realization of his expectations dispelled the suspicions that threatened them.

While the war raged, Roosevelt was so intent on victory that he made some decisions that worried the Soviet Union and challenged the identification of the United States with democratic forces and causes, with the very freedoms he had pronounced. So, in two revealing in-stances—American reliance on Darlan and later Peyrouton in North Af-rica, and American collaboration with Badoglio in Italy—the United States chose partners whom French and Italian democrats distrusted and disliked. The advocates of those partnerships excused them on the ground of military necessity. Roosevelt agreed, just as he had agreed on the same ground to the War Department's opposition to racial desegre-gation. As Commander-in-Chief he felt, apparently, that he had no choice. Still, he incurred long-range costs to international amity and to social justice, causes he intended to promote.

Those decisions and others like them persuaded Roosevelt's critics that he was a master of duplicity. He was not that. Rather, his priorities, by no means inappropriate to the exigencies of his time, entailed costs less necessary and more cruel than he let himself perceive. He was, after all, a statesman, not a saint; a politician, not a pamphleteer; a man whose chosen role put a premium on doing. He disciplined his consciousness in order to protect his essential capacity to act from the complicating coun-sels of his democratic sympathies. And though not without occasional miscalculations, he succeeded in being his kind of a liberal, his kind of a conservative.

For most Americans over forty ("This generation . . . has a rendezvous with destiny") he still lives in their past. A Lackawanna train in April 1945 on which some dozen homewardbound commuters cheered the death of that bastard in the White House. ("They are unanimous in their hatred for me—and I welcome their hatred.") A small ship swinging into Tulagi harbor where a message told the incredulous crew that Roosevelt had died. "Who the hell is President," a teen-age sailor wondered. He recalled no other President. ("Let me assert my firm belief that the only thing we have to fear is fear itself.") For those over forty there remain that open Ford, that old gray hat, that tilted cigarette, that wave and grin, those words and their familiar cadence: "The test of our progress is not whether we add more to the abundance of those who have much; it is whether we provide enough for those who have too little." "More than an end to war, we want an end to the beginning of all wars." After a quarter of a century, there is that past, and in those words it speaks di-rectly to the present.

Ewing Galloway

IV
HEATED PEACE, COLD WAR

"The ordeal of the twentieth century—the bloodiest, most turbulent era of the Christian age—is far from over," Adlai E. Stevenson warned in accepting the Democratic nomination for President in 1952. "Sacrifice, patience, understanding and implacable purpose may be our lot for years to come. Let's face it. Let's talk sense to the American people. Let's tell them the truth: that there are no gains without pains; that this is the eve of great decisions, not easy decisions like resistance when you are attacked, but a long, costly, patient struggle against the great enemies of men—war and poverty and tyranny."

How should we interpret this statesman's ambiguous rhetoric in the light of past, present, and future events? Stevenson's Churchillian eloquence, admirable as a call for national abnegation, requires clarification to scholars as it must have to his listeners. The significance of his statements is not diminished by the fact that Stevenson never attained the Presidency. Stevenson was one of those few men in public life whose words are repeated by others because he could articulate so well what lay in the hearts and minds of more active but less expressive men. Eight years later Senator Eugene McCarthy urged Democrats to nominate Stevenson for President a third time because, with pronouncements like this, he had made them proud of their party.

At the time that Stevenson called for Americans to sacrifice, thousands of our soldiers were giving their lives in Korea without necessarily understanding the purpose of the venture. Nor did Americans at home suffer their losses with patience and confidence in our cause. This was part of the ordeal to which Stevenson referred: the nation made war against an enemy whose intentions did not constitute a direct threat to American security. America's intervention in the hostilities had not followed the constitutional process of a congressional declaration. Even an anti-communist like Senator Robert A. Taft was troubled enough to dissent with President Harry Truman's commitment of American soldiers to a United

194

Nations "police action," even as he concurred with the administration's announced goal of thwarting Communist aggression. Limited wars and collective security failed to make sense to many Americans. With his oblique plea for "patience . . . and implacable purpose," was Stevenson cautioning Americans that they would face similar conflicts in the years to come?

An affirmative answer to that question suggests that since 1945 there has been a continuity in American foreign and domestic policies which revolves around anti-communism. The nation faced the ordeal of sustained military ventures abroad at the same time as an internally expanding welfare state. Nonetheless, most of the sacrifices, policymakers believed, could be isolated outside of the country while the nation enjoyed the benefits of peacetime stability. A series of commitments involved us in affairs around the globe. The Truman Doctrine committed United States military assistance to governments in nations which were resisting Communist-led insurrections. The Marshall Plan bolstered the economic strength of western European nations whose infirmities, it was feared, made them prey to insurgent Communists. Then the United States supplanted its economic assistance with the first peacetime military alliance in its history, the North Atlantic Treaty Organization. Also, Point Four economic assistance, it was hoped, would stabilize the former colonies in Asia and Africa as the Marshall Plan had done in the European mother countries.

By 1948, the bipartisan cold war policy had been developed. The pattern for the containment of expansionist Communism throughout the world called for economic and military assistance to allies and permanent mobilization of our armed forces to intervene in behalf of those who could not resist the "Red Menace" by themselves. Moreover, the American economy was stimulated by spending which the foreign aid given our allies had generated. The Truman Presidency promised all this plus anti-communism and social reform at home.

From 1945 to 1960 a bipartisan foreign policy elicited few dissenters, but the basic dilemma of democracies remained as it had since the time of the ancient Greeks: could a democracy prosecute wars overseas without undermining liberties at home? Could a democracy behave like an empire? In order to succeed, would it pay the price of regimentation? If it failed in its foreign ambitions, would the result be domestic turmoil?

American leaders gambled that limited wars could be fought, a military establishment sustained, and foreign aid given with a minimum of civilian disturbance. Presidents Truman and Eisenhower enlarged what the latter called a "military-industrial complex," minus the austerity which characterized the homefront in World War II. Military spending spurred production, and prices soared with few government controls to check them. Generally speaking, politicians refused to tamper stringently with the economy lest they disturb interest groups and evoke a challenge to the consensus foreign policy. As I. F. Stone observed, the cold war "created an atmosphere which [made] it comfortable to drift on to catastrophe."

Indeed, the cold war at its hottest produced some of the strangest contradictions known to the American system. It was a bad time for conventional wisdoms. Businessmen who swore that the high American standard of living depended upon a stable, low price structure earnestly contributed to an escalating inflation. Many avid free enterprisers scorned government intervention in the economy while they reaped huge profits from government contracts. Workers railed against the rising cost-of-living which their higher wage demands contributed to. The Eisenhower administration boasted of limiting defense expenditures even as it pursued a foreign policy destined to require a bigger military establishment. Amid higher mass consumption, widespread American poverty became more obvious. The greatest extension of civil rights to Negroes magnified the years of denial and the injustices that remained. In the name of domestic tranquility the Civil Rights Revolution of the fifties encountered indifference and repression.

Was this what Stevenson had intended? After the 1949 Communist victory in China, Republican and Democratic politicos vied with each other as to which party was more anti-communist at home and abroad. At its most virulent in McCarthyism, anti-communism threatened a disuse of the liberty to dissent in American society and fueled the political process to the near-exclusion of other issues. The long, costly, and implacable struggle against communism which Stevenson and others invoked often obscured the truth behind the great decisions of the time. Thus, the 1950 debate over recognition of the de facto government in China was, in the words of I. F. Stone, "between one set of men blinded by their preconceptions and another set of men too fearful politically to look at truths they would otherwise recognize." As the sixties dawned, war and poverty and tyranny seemed to be proliferating. There had been few gains and more pains and the greatest ordeal lay ahead.

Walter LaFeber

OPEN DOORS, IRON CURTAINS (1945)

Walter LaFeber is concerned with the attitudes and policies which conditioned the postwar international power complex. The cold war, he argues, did not grow in a vacuum but rested "on a foundation of a half-century of Russian-American distrust and apprehension." Taking into account the designs and trepidations of the two countries in 1945, LaFeber's interpretation of the origins of the cold war is devoid of villains in a conflict which had numerous victims.

The total nature of World War II rendered helpless every major nation with the exceptions of Russia in the East and the United States in the West. Despite their awesome power, American leaders were uneasy. They felt responsible for the protection of American interests in western Europe against a Communist nation which believed that its World War II victories required the imposition of its system upon the conquered nations. Americans believed that the Soviets initiated events to which the West had to respond. Soviet hegemony of eastern Europe foretold a threat to the balance of power. Its police state in Poland occasioned Churchill's epithet "Iron Curtain" for the new Communist states of eastern Europe. But not all Americans subscribed to Churchill's bipolar views. Was Soviet expansion beyond its pre-World War II frontiers merely a security need, as a few government officials like Henry Wallace and scholars like D. F. Fleming believed? Or was it what American policymakers feared—the prelude to overt military action against or subversion of western European capitalism? Interpretations of Soviet intentions var-

ied widely, but a consensus attributed to the Soviets the most malevolent of motives.

Then, too, interpretations of the cold war depend upon an initial understanding of American ambitions. LaFeber suggests that Americans were not merely responding to Soviet thrusts. Their behavior was determined in large measure by a world view which did not require a Communist antagonist; the Soviet threat merely rationalized American activities. The cold war policy was actually a continuation of earlier U.S. policies. American dogma and interests, according to LaFeber, dictated a hemispheric sphere of interest in the Americas and a demand elsewhere for equal economic and political opportunities for Americans. This meant that the United States sought to bar the expansion of the Soviet Empire while dismantling the British Empire. In 1945, however, only the Soviets were strong enough to resist American universalism. If the reader accepts this interpretation, does he believe that the cold war was inevitable?

It was October 1945 and war had never ended. The new issue of Russia's leading doctrinal journal, *Bol'shevik*, warned its readers that Marxists must not lapse into pacifism, since the "imperialist struggle," which ignited World War II, continued to rage. The Soviet Union, *Bol'shevik* proclaimed, would never retreat from wars waged "for the liberation of the people from landowning, capitalist slavery." In Washington, meanwhile, President Harry S. Truman delivered a speech larded with references to America's monopoly of atomic power. In one sentence the President attacked Russia's tightening hold in Eastern Europe: it is one of the "fundamentals" of American policy, Truman announced, that "We shall refuse to recognize any government imposed upon any nation by the force of any foreign power." A week later, M. Vjacheslav Molotov, People's Commissar for Foreign Affairs, answered Truman. Peace cannot be reconciled with an armament race "preached abroad by certain especially zealous partisans of the imperialist policy," Molotov admonished. "In this connection we should mention the discovery of atomic energy and the atomic bomb."[1]

As the *Bol'shevik* editorial illustrated, the triumphant wartime alliance had already split on ideological, economic, and political issues. The Truman and Molotov speeches explained the immediate causes of the split: the dropping of an iron curtain by the Soviets around Eastern Europe,

From Walter LaFeber, *America, Russia and the Cold War, 1945–1966.* Reprinted by permission of John Wiley & Sons, Inc.

[1] *Bol'shevik* (August, 1945), especially pp. 48–59; Harry S. Truman, "Restatement of Foreign Policy of the United States," *Department of State Bulletin,* XIII (October 28, 1945), 653–656; Vjacheslav Molotov, *U.S.S.R. Foreign Policy* (Shanghai, 1946), pp. 7–8.

and the determination of the world's sole atomic power to penetrate that curtain. At the Potsdam Conference, a month before Japan surrendered, Churchill blurted out to Stalin that "an iron fence" surrounded parts of Eastern Europe. "All fairy-tales!" Stalin blandly replied. Months earlier, however, American officials had arrived at Churchill's conclusion. On April 12, 1945, Harry S. Truman, Vice-President of the United States, former Missouri politician and Senator, and a man who was to become known as one not reluctant to make decisions, suddenly became President of the United States. Truman's knowledge of foreign policy issues was pitifully weak, partly because his predecessor, Franklin D. Roosevelt, had seldom invited his opinion on international problems. Truman evidently learned quickly about Soviet moves in Eastern Europe; in any case, he made a rapid policy decision. Eleven days after becoming President, Truman invited Molotov to the White House and proceeded to give the Russian a stern lecture against trying to lower an iron fence around Poland. An astonished Molotov retorted, "I have never been talked to like that in my life." "Carry out your agreements," Truman replied, "and you won't get talked to like that."[2]

The roots of Truman's complaint went back at least to the nineteenth century. Since becoming a major world power in the 1890s, the United States had viewed anything in the world resembling Stalin's iron fence as incompatible with American objectives. An open, free world had no such divisions. Russia had historically been a chief offender in this regard. American officials had faced problems similar to Truman's, not only with the signing of the Nazi-Soviet Pact of 1939 or after the Bolshevik Revolution threatened to spread over Eastern Europe in 1917–1920, but during the first major clash of American and Russian interests in the 1890s. At the end of that decade the United States, having expanded westward across a continent and a great ocean, and Russia, sweeping eastward through Siberia, confronted one another on the plains of China and Manchuria.

It was a presentiment of events half a century later. Their policy differences sprang from the American determination to keep China politically sovereign and whole for purposes of exploitation by the burgeoning United States industrial complex, while the Russians, who could not economically compete on such terms, tried to assure themselves political leverage and markets by creating exclusive spheres of influence. The Czar, like the Soviets in 1945, also attempted to create buffer states between Russian soil and the ambitions of Great Britain, the United States, and especially Japan. After several years of cold war, Japan broke the Czar's power in the Far East in the Russo-Japanese war of 1904–1905.

The Japanese then set off on their own career of empire. This climaxed in a conflict caused in large measure by the Japanese determination to

[2]Harry S. Truman, *Memoirs. Volume One: Year of Decisions* (Garden City, N.Y., 1955), p. 82.

spread their own type of fence around China while the United States insisted on an open-door policy. In Europe, Great Britain further isolated Germany by joining the Franco-Russian alliance. When this realignment of power led to World War I, the United States faced the terrible choice that would continually haunt its officials in the twentieth century. Colonel Edward House, President Woodrow Wilson's closest advisor, defined the alternatives in August 1914: "If the Allies win, it means largely the domination of Russia on the Continent of Europe; and if Germany wins, it means the unspeakable tyranny of militarism for generations to come."[3]

The danger posed to American interests by Russia's possible domination of Europe immeasurably worsened in 1917 when the immense potential of Russian national power was abetted by an ideology supposedly driven by historical law and dedicated to world revolution. The Allies first tried to topple the Lenin government with force. Intervention between 1918 and 1920 by British, Japanese, and American armies, however, somberly demonstrated the futility of this kind of preventive war; the Russian people reacted against the foreign armies with a renewed and stronger allegiance to the Bolshevik government. Meanwhile, Woodrow Wilson's fear that Bolshevism would thrive in war-ravaged Europe became real in 1919 when Communist governments came to power for short periods in Hungary and a part of Germany and threatened other European nations. At the Versailles Peace Conference in 1919, the victorious Allies, aware that armed intervention had not brought the Russian Communists to their knees, tried another approach. With the shadow of Lenin and Trotsky overhanging every discussion, the Western powers, as young, embittered Walter Lippmann phrased it, created a *cordon sanitare* across Central and Eastern Europe to isolate Russia. Lippmann argued instead for a "sanitary Europe," warning that the use of such states as Poland, Rumania, Czechoslovakia, and Jugoslavia to separate the Russian peoples from the West could never develop into a long-range solution.[4]

Wilson coupled this reconstruction of Central Europe with a declaration of August 10, 1920, which indicated that the United States hoped to mellow or, preferably, break up the Bolshevik regime with a policy of nonrecognition. Other Western nations, however, refused to follow this lead. The British opened formal trade relations with Russia in March 1921. A major Soviet breakthrough followed a year later when the two outcasts, Germany and Russia, reached agreement on several important issues in the Rapallo Pact. This and the Nazi-Soviet Treaty of 1939 proved that regardless of any ideological division, Germany and Russia could readily compromise and join hands when they thought it was in their common interest. In February 1924, the British recognized the Soviet government *de jure* and set off a chain reaction of recognition by nearly all major powers except the United States.

[3]Quoted in Arthur S. Link, *Wilson: The Struggle for Neutrality, 1914–1915* (Princeton, 1960), p. 48.
[4]Walter Lippmann, *New Republic* (March 22, 1919), supplement.

Americans by no means ignored the Soviets. A United States Relief mission distributed over sixty million dollars worth of aid to the Russians in the early 1920s. American businessmen, encouraged by Secretary of Commerce Herbert Hoover, surged into the Russian market. Between 1925 and 1930, trade between the two nations amounted to nearly $100 million, or twice the prewar figure; this was rather remarkable, given the failure of the State Department to recognize that the Soviets officially existed. The trade declined rapidly in 1931 and 1932, and urged on by demands of American businessmen for formal political relations, Franklin D. Roosevelt finally extended recognition in November 1933. (Perhaps Roosevelt worried about how Americans would receive the news; he had the Soviet delegation arrive in Washington at the same time that Prohibition was being lifted.)

The Russians welcomed recognition. They cared less about increased trade, however, than about cooperating with the United States to stop Japanese aggression in the Far East. Roosevelt refused to respond to this Russian appeal, and the State Department assured the Japanese that opening relations with the Soviets contained no hidden meaning for Japanese policies in Asia.[5] The New Deal maintained this policy of no-cooperation throughout the decade, receiving strong support from many American liberals, even former Communists, who in the post-1936 period became bitterly disillusioned with Communism after Stalin began his bloody purges and signed the Nazi-Soviet Pact. After the war, these liberals would not forget their earlier disenchantment with the "God Who Failed."

Hitler's invasion of Russia in June 1941 forced a four-year partnership upon the Soviets and Americans. Despite the wartime cooperation and the goodwill generated by $9½ billion of lend-lease materials sent to Russia, conflicts erupted over war strategies and plans for the postwar peace. In 1942 and 1943, Churchill and Roosevelt indicated readiness to open a second front in Western Europe. Their backs to the wall, the Soviets seized upon these indications as ironclad pledges. When the Allies invaded North Africa and Italy, thus stalling the second front invasion until mid-1944, Stalin became increasingly suspicious and resentful. Nor did the Russian dictator care for the Anglo-American refusal to assure him that after the conflict the Soviet borders would essentially be those recognized by the Nazi-Soviet treaty, that is, that the Baltic states and parts of Poland, Finland, and Rumania would be absorbed by Russia. The United States instead asked Stalin to wait until the end of the war to settle those territorial problems. As the conflict came to a close, American policy-makers realized that these issues would have to be discussed in the context of a new world balance of power, since the Allies had destroyed Germany and Japan, two nations which historically had blocked Russian expansion in Europe and Asia.

The Cold War consequently developed on a foundation of a half cen-

[5]Stanley K. Hornbeck to Secretary of State Cordell Hull, Oct. 28, 1933, and Hornbeck to William Phillips, October 31, 1933, 711.61/333, Archives of the Department of State, Washington, D.C.

tury of Russian-American distrust and apprehension. These early years, especially the shock of depression and disillusionment in the 1930s, forged four major assumptions upon which the United States built its initial post-World War II foreign policy.

Washington officials first assumed that foreign policy grew directly from domestic policy; American actions abroad did not respond primarily to the pressures of other nations, but to political, social, and economic forces at home. Policy-makers could consider the economic the most important of these forces, a not unreasonable conclusion given the national crisis endured in the 1930s. The ghosts of Depression Past and Depression Future led officials to a second assumption: the post-1929 quagmire had been prolonged and partly caused by high tariff walls and regional trading blocks which had dammed up the natural flow of foreign trade. Such economic dislocation had inexorably led to political conflicts which, in turn, had ignited World War II. Free flow of exports and imports were essential. Third, the United States, quadrupling its production while other major industrial nations suffered severe war-time damage and forced liquidation, wielded the requisite economic power to establish this desired economic community. The use of this type of power, moreover, would allow the United States and the world to deemphasize military power and return to peace-time conditions. Finally, Washington policy-makers determined to use this gigantic economic power. Unlike the 1930s, the United States would not sit on the side-lines; indeed, it could not afford to do so.

One week after Japan surrendered, Secretary of State James F. Byrnes elaborated upon these four assumptions. "Our international policies and our domestic policies are inseparable," he began. "Our foreign relations inevitably affect employment in the United States. Prosperity and depression in the United States just as inevitably affect our relations with the other nations of the world." Byrnes expressed his "firm conviction that a durable peace cannot be built on an economic foundation of exclusive blocs ... and economic warfare.... [A liberal trading system] imposes special responsibilities upon those who occupy a dominant position in world trade. Such is the position of the United States." In announcing the American intention to reorder the world, he uttered a warning as well as a policy assumption: "In many countries throughout the world our political and economic creed is in conflict with ideologies which reject both of these principles. To the extent that we are able to manage our domestic affairs successfully, we shall win converts to our creed in every land."[6] John Winthrop had not expressed it more clearly at Massachusetts Bay. Only now the City Upon a Hill had been industrialized and internationalized.

American officials hoped that this process would primarily occur

[6]*Documents on American Foreign Relations, VIII* (1945–1946), edited by Raymond Dennett and Robert K. Turner (Princeton, 1948), pp. 601–602; the best historical treatment of this developing view is in Lloyd C. Gardner, *Economic Aspects of New Deal Diplomacy* (Madison, Wisconsin, 1964).

through the United Nations, the World Bank (the International Bank of Reconstruction and Development), and the International Monetary Fund. The World Bank had a treasury of $7.6 billion (and the authority to lend twice that amount), which would guarantee private loans given to build facilities in war-torn Europe and the underdeveloped areas. The International Monetary Fund possessed a fund of $7.3 billion to stabilize currencies so that multilateral trade could be conducted without sudden currency depreciation or wide fluctuations in exchange rates, two ailments which had almost destroyed the international economic community in the 1930s. The United States hoped that such international agencies would minimize exclusive and explosive nationalisms and maximize economic and political interchange. Of course, there was one other implication of this policy: American economic power necessarily made the United States the dominant force in these organizations. In March 1946, Secretary of the Treasury Fred Vinson became the first chairman of the Board of Governors of both groups.

At home, the Truman Administration moved rapidly to implement this multilateral approach. Congress renewed the Reciprocal Trade Agreements Act of 1934, a powerful lever in lowering tariff walls at home and abroad. Conversely, the Export-Import Bank, since 1934 the central American agency in extending *bilateral* overseas credits for the purchase of American exports, received notice that its $3.5 billion authorization would terminate in mid-1946. At that point, Congress wanted the Bank's functions picked up by the new United Nations organization, the World Bank, and the International Monetary Fund. Rapid demobilization of American armed forces also fitted into the pattern. Pressured by the public demand to "bring the boys back home," determined to use peaceful economic pressures instead of military force to reorder the world, and disturbed by the long string of wartime unbalanced budgets, the President reduced a 3.5 million-man army in Europe to 500,000 men in less than ten months. If American interests demanded the quick use of military force, the Administration could exploit its monopoly of the atomic bomb. That was the not-so-hidden stick back of America's economic carrot.

Bernard Baruch caught the essence of the American tactics: if the United States can "stop subsidization of labor and sweated competition in the export markets," the elder statesman exulted in March 1945, and prevent the rebuilding of war machines in the world, "oh boy, oh boy, what long-time prosperity we will have."[7] Amidst such excitement, however, one question plagued American officials: would all the former Allies play the game according to American rules? Within a year after the German surrender, France and Great Britain gave most of the appropriate pledges.

[7]Bernard Baruch to E. Coblentz, March 23, 1945, Papers of Bernard Baruch, Princeton University Library, Princeton, New Jersey.

France cooperated despite the fierce independence of Charles de Gaulle, President of the French Provisional Government, and despite nearly two centuries of conflict between French and American political interests in both the New and Old Worlds. French dependence upon American aid demanded that de Gaulle swallow his pride and travel to Washington in August 1945 to ask for a one billion-dollar loan. After nine months of hard negotiations, the United States granted the money, receiving, in return, French promises to curtail governmental manipulation and subsidies, which had given French producers and exporters advantages in the international market. This agreement perfectly fitted Byrnes' dream of the postwar world, but it missed the roots of Franco-American conflicts. French and American officials continually clashed over occupation policies in Germany, and de Gaulle insisted on reestablishing the French colonial empire in Southeast Asia despite strong pressure from Washington to keep the area independent and open to the capital of all nations. ("I told him," Baruch recalled of a conversation with de Gaulle, "what the Mormons had done for Utah which was practically wilderness when they reached there."[8])

The British proved even more compliant, since, unlike the French, they fell into line politically as well as economically. Long-suffering England had little choice. Two wars had destroyed the shipping and export industries, which had traditionally paid for the importation of over half of England's food staples and nearly all of its raw materials except coal. Despite nationalization of some key industries by the newly elected Labour Government of Clement Attlee, and despite the importation of 300,000 Italian and German prisoners of war to serve as laborers, Britain faced a trade deficit of nearly $1.5 billion in 1946. The United States responded in December 1945 by signing a loan agreement for about $3.8 billion to be paid back with an annual interest which would approximate 1.6 percent. (The British had hoped to obtain a larger loan interest-free.) In return, the United States exacted stiff concessions. The weary British dismantled much of their Imperial Preference system, promised that the pound sterling and the Imperial trade would move throughout the world with a minimum of restrictions, and received severe warnings from Washington about further nationalization of industry. Assistant Secretary of State William Clayton, who negotiated the agreement, confided to Baruch, "We loaded the British loan negotiations with all the conditions that the traffic would bear."[9]

Triumphant economically, the State Department began to move against British political policies in Europe. In October 1944, Churchill had shown some doubt about American plans for an open, multilateral world when he traveled to Moscow and worked out with Stalin a deal which gave Russia control of Rumania, Bulgaria, and Hungary and assured Great

[8]"Memorandum for James F. Byrnes," August 27, 1945, Baruch Papers.
[9]"Memorandum for Mr. Baruch" from William Clayton, April 26, 1946, Baruch Papers.

Britain a free hand in Greece. The two men agreed to split control of Yugoslavia between them. The United States immediately disavowed these negotiations, but Russian armies in Eastern Europe and ruthless British suppression of a revolt in Greece (in which Stalin did not raise a hand) made the American disavowal academic. United States opposition, however, never wavered. A State Department memorandum of late June 1945 informed Truman that although spheres of interest did in fact exist in both Eastern Europe and the Western Hemisphere, "Basic United States policy has been to oppose spheres of influence in Europe. . . . American policy must be attuned to events in Europe as a whole. . . ."[10]

This memorandum exposed a central problem in American diplomacy, for while Washington firmly set itself against spheres of interest in Europe, it moved to strengthen its own sphere of interest in the Western Hemisphere. Unlike its policies elsewhere, however, the State Department did not attempt to achieve this through economic tactics. The economic relationship with Latin America and Canada could be assumed; none had to be developed. During the war most Latin American nations linked themselves closely with the North American economy by feeding cheap raw materials to war industries. After the war, and despite American promises to the contrary at the Mexico City Conference in February 1945, Latin American economic needs were neglected in Washington while American money and goods flowed to Europe.

Economically, the United States failed to meet its first postwar test with the problems of an underdeveloped area. An inauspicious revival of Roosevelt's "Good Neighbor" approach, this failure also heralded the crisis to come in the post-1954 era when the newly-emerging nations forced their way toward the top of the State Department's list of priorities. In 1945–1946, the problem was different: how could the United States reconcile its general multilateral, open-door-to-all approach elsewhere with its traditional policy of maintaining Latin America as its own sphere of influence? The answer lay in Article 51 of the United Nations Charter. This provided for collective self-defense through special regional organizations to be created outside of the United Nations, but under the principles of the Charter. Latin American officials had pushed for this provision in the hope of regaining the preferential position in American policy that they had enjoyed during the 1930s. Washington policy-makers had other reasons. These were best explained by Arthur Vandenberg, Republican Senator from Michigan, architect of the bipartisan approach to postwar foreign policy, and former "isolationist" turned "internationalist."

How far Vandenberg had turned is debatable. He fervently believed in the internationalization of the Atlantic Charter freedoms framed by

[10]Department of State, *Papers Relating to the Foreign Relations of the United States: The Conference of Berlin (Potsdam)* (Washington, 1960), I, 262–264.

Roosevelt and Churchill in 1941, particularly the freedom of "all peoples to choose the form of government under which they will live." These principles, Vandenberg grandiloquently proclaimed in 1945, "sail with our fleets. They fly with our eagles. They sleep with our martyred dead." And they must be had by all, especially those in Eastern Europe. His growing fear of the Soviet Union weakened his hope that the United Nations, encumbered by the Russian veto in the Security Council, could effectively enforce these freedoms. The Western Hemisphere, however, could be protected. Teaming up with Assistant Secretary of State Nelson Rockefeller, Vandenberg formulated Article 51. "We would," Vandenberg candidly explained, no longer "have to depend exclusively on the Security Council" in American affairs.[11] The Senator wanted the best of both worlds: exclusive American power in the New and the right to exert American power in the Old.

This view was not a radical departure from pre-1941 policies. United States objectives in Latin America remained the traditional goals of the Monroe Doctrine: order, exclusion of extra-hemispheric influences, and equal economic opportunity for United States citizens. These terms, however, became increasingly interchanged with the phrase "anti-communism." Article 51 provided a weapon which might ward off "communism" in the short run. For the long run, a comprehensive economic and social reform program was needed, and given Latin American dependence upon the United States, the program's success would depend upon help from Washington. The United States was not interested in such a program and would not be for more than a decade. Europe came first. In the meantime, Vandenberg and other American officials were content to preserve American freedom of action in the hemisphere through Article 51.

With considerably more brutality and less regard for the formalities of the United Nations Charter, Joseph Stalin also constructed his postwar policy upon the necessity of maintaining freedom of action in spheres he considered vital for Soviet economic and strategic requirements. Within a year after Hitler's demise, American open-world diplomacy crashed against Stalin's iron curtain, and only Vandenberg's vehicle of Article 51 remained to cart away the pieces.

Regardless of the threat, whether economic or atomic, Stalin had reasons for not lifting the curtain. For strategic and psychological purposes, he divided Germany and then maintained buffer states between Germany and the Soviet Union. The Soviet peoples and leaders alike viewed almost everything in their lives through the memories of the horrors that struck from 1941 to 1945.[12] The Germans "will recover, and very

[11]Arthur H. Vandenberg, Jr. (ed.), *The Private Papers of Senator Vandenberg* (Boston, 1952), pp. 134, 187.

[12]Ralph K. White, "Images in the Context of International Conflict," in *International Behaviour*, edited by Herbert C. Kelman (New York, 1965), p. 271

quickly," Stalin observed at a banquet in April 1945. "Give them twelve to fifteen years and they'll be on their feet again. And that is why the unity of the Slavs is important."[13]

Such predictions were confirmed in Stalin's mind by his own peculiar interpretation of Marxist-Leninist doctrine. All Soviet rulers have cloaked their policies, no matter how divergent, with this doctrine, and, in the post-1945 years, have used it not only to rally the Soviet people against foreign threats, but to rationalize the power of their regime and silence internal dissent. To outside observers, doctrine can consequently act as a weather vane; once officials have decided upon a policy, they justify it with appropriate doctrine, and the doctrinal changes then indicate policy changes.

Stalin's use of this doctrine in 1945 differed little from the dogmas used during the bitterest East-West confrontation between 1937 and 1941. Perhaps this similarity resulted in part from the remarkably stable membership of the Politburo (the policy-making body of the Central Committee of the Communist Party), whose membership in 1945 was almost exactly that of 1939. The similarity could also be ascribed to Stalin's belief that his warnings in the 1920s and 1930s regarding capitalist encirclement of the Soviet Union had proved accurate. The war-time alliance with the West apparently did not dent Stalin's outlook. His views of Western democracy, the danger of capitalist encirclement, the inevitability of war, the nature and sources of imperialism, and the impossibility of disarmament evidently changed very little between 1939 and 1945.

Soviet journals muted these beliefs during the German onslaught of 1941–1942, for Stalin was shrewd enough to ask the Russians to sacrifice themselves for "Holy Russia," not for the Communist party. The old dogmas began to reappear with the Red Army victories of 1943 and arguments among the Allies regarding the second front and postwar boundaries. By 1944 and early 1945 Soviet articles, for the first time since 1941, explored, with appropriate Marxist terminology, the importance of unemployment in the United States. In April 1945, Eugene Tarle, a leading Soviet academic figure, told a Moscow audience that Anglo-American contributions to the Great Patriotic War had consisted of little more than goodwill.[14]

With his doctrinal house more orderly, Stalin consolidated his personal power by raising his close associate, Lavrentia Beria, chief of the Secret Police, to the rank of Marshall of the Red Army, and promoting himself to Generalissimo. Red Army officers, who controlled the only power

[13]Milovan Djilas, *Conversations with Stalin* (New York, 1961), p. 114.
[14]John S. Curtiss and Alex Inkeles, "Marxism in the U.S.S.R.—The Recent Revival," *Political Science Quarterly*, LXI (September, 1946), 349–364; Frederick C. Barghoorn, "Great Russian Messianism in Postwar Soviet Ideology," in Ernest J. Simmons, editor, *Continuity and Change in Russian and Soviet Thought* (Cambridge, Massachusetts, 1955), p. 541.

capable of challenging Stalin's control, slowly disappeared from public view.[15] In August 1945, rumors circulated that Stalin would shortly announce a new Five-Year Plan. Such a plan would cut two ways for the Soviet dictator, since its required regimentation would maximize his own power, while compelling the Russians to resurrect rapidly their war-torn economy.

These same objectives were accomplished by the Red Army's occupation and consequent communization of Eastern Europe. Doctrinal demands and neurotic personal ambition partly explained Stalin's policies in this area. But the overriding requirement dictating this policy was the Soviets' need for security and economic reconstruction. Here Stalin's dilemma became strikingly evident. If he wished quick economic reconstruction, he would need American funds, since the United States possessed the only sufficient capital supply in the world. To obtain those funds, however, Stalin would have to loosen his control of Eastern Europe, allow American political and economic power to flow into the area, and consequently surrender what he considered to be the first essential of Soviet security. Through absolute control of Eastern Europe, Stalin might obtain both security and, through forced drafts upon those European economies, the economic resources needed for Soviet reconstruction. Russia had lost one quarter of her capital equipment, 1700 towns, 70,000 villages, nearly 100,000 collective farms and more than twenty million dead during World War II. In 1945 Soviet steel production sank to only one eighth the amount of American production. Control of Poland, Rumania, Hungary, Bulgaria, and East Germany (as well as the Baltic States which Stalin had absorbed in 1940, and Manchuria in the Far East) enabled the Soviets to drain vast quantities of goods and laborers to refurbish their economy. Stalin imposed a communist system over most of these areas, not because the historical inevitability of Marxism had come to pass, but because, in the Russians' view, both their security and economic requirements could be found in such a system, and the success of the Red Army presented a unique opportunity to act. As Stalin remarked in the spring of 1945, "Whoever occupies a territory also imposes on it his own social system."

For American policy-makers dedicated to creating a Western-democratic world built on the Atlantic Charter Freedoms, Stalin's moves posed the terrible problem of how to open the Soviet empire without alienating the Soviets. Given their assumptions of how the postwar world must work, Washington officials had little choice but to attempt to stop the descent of the curtain around Stalin's domains. Otherwise the world would be divided, as in the late 1930s, into separate and hostile blocs. In these dilemmas lay the roots of the Cold War.

The first test came in Poland. During the darkest days of 1941 and

[15]Raymond L. Garthoff, *Soviet Military Policy, A Historical Analysis* (New York, 1966), pp. 42–44.

1942 when the German armies drove toward Moscow, Stalin insisted to Western officials that after the war Soviet security required the annexation of large areas of Polish soil. Consequently, when the Russians formally agreed in early 1942 to the Atlantic Charter's provision that "all peoples" have the right "to choose the form of government under which they will live," Stalin added a significant reservation: "Considering that the practical application of these principles will necessarily adapt itself to the circumstances, needs, and historic peculiarities of particular countries, the Soviet Government can state that a consistent application of these principles will secure the most energetic support on the part of the government and peoples of the Soviet Union."[16] The first half of the reservation clearly indicated that the Soviets had no intention of allowing the history of 1919–1939 to repeat itself; if they could gather the requisite power, Eastern Europe and particularly Poland, across which German armies had invaded Russia twice in less than twenty-five years, would come under *de facto* Soviet control. American diplomats attempted to soften this policy at the Moscow Conference in October 1943 and again at Yalta in February 1945, but the Russians refused to yield.

When, therefore, the discussions at Yalta reached the substantial question of the composition of the Polish government, the Soviets announced that the basis of that government would be the Communist-controlled Lublin group. This move threatened largely to exclude from power the Polish government-in-exile which had lived in London during the war; that regime had angered Stalin by demanding that Poland regain its pre-1939 boundaries. Churchill and Roosevelt finally acquiesced in Stalin's two demands that Russia receive large areas of eastern Poland, and that the Polish government be reorganized on the basis of the present provisional government which was dominated by the Lublin group. The British and American leaders, however, did not believe that this agreement gave the Soviets a veto power over the future course of Poland, although the Russians proceeded to interpret the understanding in precisely those terms. Churchill and Roosevelt also thought they had scored by getting Stalin's signature on the "Declaration of Liberated Europe," a document that soon became a highly contentious issue in Soviet-American relations. In the "Declaration," the three powers agreed to destroy all Nazism and Fascism, to follow through on the Atlantic Charter principle of allowing the liberated peoples to create their own democratic institutions, and to hold "free elections" at the "earliest possible" time. The important debates centered upon the crucial phrases that would explain how these laudable objectives were to be reached, and here the Soviets got their way. Instead of accepting an American suggestion to insert a phrase that would establish machinery to carry out these principles, Molotov succeeded in including a simple promise that,

[16]Martin Herz, *Beginnings of the Cold War* (Bloomington, Indiana, 1966), pp. vii-viii and, for the following account in which I have drawn heavily from Herz's analysis, see pp. 50, 69, 176, and particularly Chapter IV of his book.

if problems arose, the three powers would "take measures for the carrying out of mutual consultation." In such "consultation," unanimous agreement would have to be reached for further action; that is, the Soviets could veto any new Western moves in Poland and Eastern Europe.

Critics have attacked these agreements on the grounds that American officials surrendered Eastern Europe to Russia at Yalta, and that the Russians broke their word. The critics cannot easily have it both ways and actually cannot argue either way with any consistency. Churchill and Roosevelt did not surrender Poland; given the presence of the Red Army in Poland, the nation was not theirs to surrender. The two Western leaders were playing for the highest stakes with weak hands. They hoped to keep the game going and maintain some form of Russian cooperation until their hands could be strengthened with postwar American economic power. On the other side, the Russians argued that they did not break these agreements, at least not until they believed they were forced to do so in the post-1946 years. They held "mutual consultations" (although this did not mean that such consultations necessarily would lead to different policies), and they allowed "free elections" (although the Russians were extremely careful to insure that "free" in this case was compatible with their view of Soviet security requirements).

The Soviet approach to East European governments varied. In Rumania, which had been an ally of Hitler and whose troops had actually invaded Russia, the Soviets first attempted to rule through a government in which the Communists were a minority. Two weeks after Yalta, however, Stalin issued a brutal ultimatum demanding that the Communist party obtain power within two hours to restore "order" or else Russia would "not be responsible for the continuance of Rumania as an independent state." On the other hand, the Soviets held elections which allowed a non-Communist government to gain power in Hungary, suffered an overwhelming defeat in elections in the Russian-controlled zones of Austria, supervised elections in Bulgaria, which satisfied British if not American officials, and agreed to acquiesce in the coming to power of an independent, non-Communist government in Finland (a nation against which the Russians had fought a bloody war in 1939–1940) if that government would follow a foreign policy friendly to Russia. Historical events, particularly the two German invasions, led Stalin to place Poland in the same category as Rumania, not Finland.

Soviet concern over Western attitudes toward Eastern Europe grew in March 1945 when, at the same time that Americans demanded a voice at Warsaw, reports reached Stalin that United States officials were considering the negotiation of a secret surrender of German forces in Italy. These reports contained barely enough truth so that Roosevelt was unable to relieve Stalin's fears that the Americans were cooperating with German efforts to move Nazi armies from Italy to the Soviet front. In 1944–1945, moreover, the United States had effectively excluded Russian representation from the key commission which controlled the Italian occupation. The Soviets later used this precedent to exclude Americans from a similar commission in Rumania. Another bitter Soviet-American dispute erupted over voting procedures in the new United Nations organization.

These arguments sharpened the feelings over the crucial Polish question. In a letter of April 24 (the day after the Molotov-Truman confrontation noted at the beginning of this chapter), Stalin answered Anglo-American complaints about Russian actions in Poland by observing that "Poland borders on the Soviet Union, which cannot be said about Great Britain or the U.S.A. . . . I do not know," he continued, "whether a genuinely representative Government has been established in Greece, or whether the Belgium Government is a genuinely democratic one. The Soviet Union was not consulted when those Governments were being formed, nor did it claim the right to interfere in those matters, because it realizes how important Belgium and Greece are to the security of Great Britain." The Soviet dictator concluded: "I cannot understand why in discussing Poland no attempt is made to consider the interests of the Soviet Union in terms of security as well." Stalin held fast to his views on the Provisional Government and on territorial boundaries that gave Russia a huge section of Poland. He recompensed the Poles by moving their boundary to the Oder-Niesse rivers, well inside eastern Germany.

By the time the Potsdam Conference met in July 1945, the United States recognized the Soviet-controlled Polish government, but throughout the summer and autumn attempted to weaken Soviet control by using relief materials and equipment badly needed by the Poles to force Poland to accept, as the State Department said, "a policy of equal opportunity for us in trade, investments and access to sources of information."[17] This policy failed before it could ever get under way, and the failure left an enduring mark on postwar American policy. Vandenberg had drawn the appropriate conclusion as early as the Yalta Conference. The Polish settlement there "was *awful*," he had written; if anything ruined the new United Nations, it would "be the ghost of Poland."[18] Stalin had drawn his own conclusions.

A greater test began in Germany. At Yalta, the Big Three agreed to govern Germany temporarily after the war by dividing it into four sections: Russia would control the northeastern provinces between the Oder-Neisse and Elbe rivers, Britain the northwest, and the United States the southern areas. France later received control of two Rhineland states in the American sector. Each area was to be governed individually by the military commanders of each power. Together, the commanders formed the Allied Control Council which, by unanimous decision, would lay down rules for reuniting Germany. The rub lay in the requirement of unanimity, since the powers were badly split on policy objectives.

In the early months of the Cold War, the United States and Great

---

[17]Department of State, *Potsdam, I*, 715, 784–785.
[18]Vandenberg to Baruch, February 15, 1945, Baruch Papers.

Britain hoped to keep Germany politically whole and, after destroying her war-making potential, restore industry to a self-supporting level; the Allies would thus not have to expend their own resources to keep Germany alive. The Soviets, supported in large part by the French, preferred a politically-divided, economically-weakened Germany. Stalin's tactics included demands for huge reparations to be taken out of the German industrial complex. He liked the figure of $20 billion with $10 billion going to Russia. At Yalta, Roosevelt agreed that the $20 billion figure might be the starting point for negotiations, but during the summer of 1945, American and Russian delegates meeting in Moscow failed to reach agreement on this crucial question.[19] The collapse of these talks forced the issue to be worked out at Potsdam where it became part of a deal: the West essentially surrendered the disputed Oder-Neisse area by allowing Poland to "administer" those lands, and the Anglo-Americans took a long step toward their goal of making Germany self-sufficient by winning Russian assent to a proposal which gave the Soviets 25 percent (instead of a fixed figure) of German capital equipment from the Western zones. Fifteen percent of this, however, was to be exchanged for agricultural products from the Soviet sector. In their own zone, the Soviets received *carte blanche,* and now that their opportunities in the Western areas had been sharply cut, they accelerated their divestment of industrial machinery and laborers from eastern Germany.

By the end of 1945, chances for a united, open, and self-sufficient Germany had largely disappeared. The French adamantly opposed any central administration. In the Soviet zone Stalin destroyed the Prussian landlord class, nationalized industry, and forced political parties to accept Communist control. In the American zone, General Lucius Clay, head of the American Military Government in Germany, pushed for the raising of German industrial production until the State Department on December 12, 1945 allowed the ceiling placed on that economy at the Potsdam Conference to become a minimum instead of a maximum level. Clay's arguments received strong support from important American industrialists. Alfred P. Sloan, President of General Motors, reminded Bernard Baruch (who wanted to keep Germany under tight control) of General Motors' accomplishments in prewar Germany ("it was frequently passed on to us by the German Economic Ministry that we had contributed much to the expansion of industry in Germany") and urged loose controls over all but war industries so that Germany would once again become attractive to American investors.[20] Throughout Germany, the Allied Control Council lost power, and American, French, British, and Russian commanders assumed supreme authority in their zones.

Little else was possible, for as Stalin had remarked, each occupying

[19]"Summary of Procedure of Allied Commission on Reparations," Vol. 19-A, Papers of Richard A. Scandrett, Cornell University Library, Ithaca, New York.
[20]Sloan to Baruch, November 30, 1945, Baruch Papers.

power imposed its own system on its area. The division of Germany was set. Poland and Eastern Europe were sinking behind a Soviet iron curtain. The question now became: how would the world's most powerful nation respond to these frustrations of its dream for the postwar world?

Ronald Steel
PAX AMERICANA

The United States, despite its fetish for the middle of the political road in domestic politics, has been accused of emotional extremism in foreign affairs. This contradiction is somewhat explained by our pragmatic domestic outlook as opposed to our excessively moralistic view of world affairs. Before World War II Americans righteously called themselves isolationists; however, the aggression of the thirties and forties made the word "isolationist" an invective in the succeeding decades. Thus Americans became staunch believers in the worth of collective security in order to perpetuate their ideals. But, inquires Ronald Steel, did American policy in the cold war exhibit a taste for foreign intervention that far exceeded the principles of a democratic society? Beginning with the most altruistic of motives, did our policy-makers educate the public and its representatives to endorse the worst of all multinational endeavors—an empire, a Pax Americana?

Steel contends that despite our anti-imperial tradition, the United States has erected one of the great empires of modern time. Supporters of U.S. cold war policies deplore the validity of the term "empire" to characterize the American response to aggression in Asia. Also, some argue that imperial behavior does not connote a formal empire. Is Steel overly simplistic and plain wrong in insisting that ideology has overcome national interest in deciding our Asian policies? Does Steel's depiction of errant idealism contradict LaFeber's analysis of American objectives in 1945? Does he overlook a pre-cold war historical pattern which necessarily leads to a Pax Americana?

We in this country, in this generation are—by destiny rather than choice—the watchmen on the walls of world freedom.

JOHN F. KENNEDY

The United States, delighting in her resources, feeling that she no longer had within herself sufficient scope for her energies, wishing to help those who were in misery or bondage the world over, yielded in her turn to that taste for intervention in which the instinct for domination cloaked itself.

CHARLES DE GAULLE

A Taste for Intervention

"Sometimes people call me an idealist," Woodrow Wilson once said as he stumped the country trying to drum up support for the League of Nations. "Well, that's the way I know I am an American. America, my fellow citizens, . . . is the only idealistic nation in the world." Wilson, whose career is a tragic example of what happens when idealism is divorced from political realism, never spoke a truer word. America is an idealistic nation, a nation based upon the belief that the "self-evident truths" of the Declaration of Independence should be extended to unfortunate peoples wherever they may be.

For the first 170 years of our national existence, however, we were content to make this a principle rather than a program of action. America was, in John Quincy Adams' phrase, "the well-wisher to the freedom and independence of all," but "the champion and vindicator only of her own." With the exception of Mexico, the Philippines, and a few brief adventures in the Caribbean, our national idealism did not go abroad in search of new fields to conquer. The great European war of 1914-1918 entangled us more against our will than by design. We entered it under the banner of idealism when neutrality became difficult, and we left Europe in disillusionment when power politics reared its ugly head at Versailles. Never again, we said. And never again we did, until the Japanese dragged us into a global war by the attack on Pearl Harbor.

From that time on, American idealism was transformed into a plan. The Word was given Flesh by the mating of American military power to a native idealism. For the first time in its history the nation had the ability to seek its idealistic goals by active intervention rather than merely by pious proclamation. The result was twin crusades, one in Europe, one in Asia: one to restore freedom to the West, one to bring it to the East. But the passing of one tyranny in Europe saw the rise of another; the defeat of Japan gave way to the resurgence of China. The triumph of the Second World War marked not the end of our labors, but only the beginning. It transformed a philosophical commitment to the principles of free-dom and democracy into a political commitment to bring them about. American idealism was the foundation; American power was the in-strument to achieve the ideals. From 1945 on, we were no longer simply the "well-wisher" to the world; we were its "champion and vindica-tor" as well. The moral purity of American isolationism gave way to the moral self-justification of American interventionism.

The change from the old isolationism to the new interventionism flowed almost inevitably from the Second World War. The unavoidable war against fascism revealed the bankruptcy of isolationism and destroyed the illusion that America could barricade herself from the immoralities of a corrupt world. It also provided the means for the dramatic growth of American military power which made the new policy of global interven-tionism possible. As a result of her participation in the war, America became not only a great world power but *the* world power. Her fleets roamed all the seas, her military bases extended around the earth's periph-ery, her soldiers stood guard from Berlin to Okinawa, and her alliances spanned the earth.

The Second World War threw the United States into the world arena, and the fear of communism prevented her from retreating. The old iso-lationism was buried and discredited. The crusade that was the war against fascism gave way to the new crusade that was the cold war against communism. Roused to a new sense of mission by the threat of Soviet communism, eager to bring her cherished values to the masses of man-kind, a bit infatuated with the enormous power she possessed through the unleashing of the atom, America quickly accepted—and even came to cherish—her new sense of involvement in the fate of the world. The world of the early postwar era may not have been the One World of Wendell Willkie's dream, but America felt a unique sense of responsibility about its welfare.

A reaction to the old isolationism, the new globalism forced Americans to realize that they could no longer escape involvement in an imperfect world. But because the cold war, like the Second World War, was con-ceived as a moral crusade, it inflated an involvement that was essentially pragmatic into a moral mission. Since we were accustomed to victory in battle and were stronger than any nation had ever been in history, we be-lieved that the world's problems could be resolved if only we willed hard enough and applied enough power. Convinced of the righteousness of our cause, we became intoxicated with our newly discovered respon-sibilities and saw them as a mandate to bring about the better world we so ardently desired. American military power, consecrated by the victory of the Second World War and reconfirmed by the development of the atomic bomb, joined forces with the power of American idealism to in-augurate a policy of global interventionism.

This policy of interventionism is not only military, although we have intervened massively throughout the world with our military power. Our intervention has also been economic and political. We have funneled nearly $120 billion of American money into foreign aid since the Second World War—to bring about changes in other countries that would reflect our ideals or advance our interests. We have intervened in the politics of other nations as well, trying to push some into new alignments, trying to remake the social structures of others, and helping to overthrow the governments of not a few. America, whether most of us realize it or not, has become the interventionist power par excellence. Whether we consider this to be commendable or deplorable, it is certainly undeniable.

For the past quarter-century the United States has—at a great financial, human, and even emotional cost—been pursuing a foreign policy designed to promulgate American values. This ambition inspired the policy of "containment" that followed the Second World War, and provided the rationale for a series of military involvements. Seeking universal peace and condemning war as a means for settling political grievances, America has, nonetheless, been an active belligerent in two major land wars since 1950 and the sponsor of a series of military interventions—a record unmatched by any other power. America did not enter these wars from a sense of adventure, or a quest for territorial gain, or an effort to retain distant colonies, but rather from a desire to contain communism and protect the values and boundaries of the "free world." "What America has done, and what America is doing now around the world," President Johnson declared at Catholic University a few months after he ordered the bombing of North Vietnam, "draws from deep and flowing springs of moral duty, and let none underestimate the depth of flow of those wellsprings of American purpose."

Who, indeed, would underestimate them? But to estimate them highly is not necessarily to understand them, or to find them always wise. The moral inspiration of America's involvement in foreign wars is undeniable. But it has also posed a terrible dilemma for American diplomacy, one which is rarely acknowledged openly and is often not even clearly recognized. It is the dilemma of how American ideals can be reconciled with American military actions—and, perhaps even more grave, of how American values can be made relevant to a world that seems not to want or even respect them. However deep the wellsprings of moral duty to which President Johnson refers, the means chosen to transfer these values to a recalcitrant and often unadmiring world has troubled many thoughtful Americans. American presidents have spoken in the most noble rhetoric of the need to defend freedom wherever it may be threatened and of the indivisibility of our responsibility to protect other nations from external (and even internal) aggression. Yet the pursuit of this aspiration has frequently led others to believe that our motives may be self-justifying and tinged with hypocrisy.

The United States has become an interventionist power, indeed the world's major interventionist power, without most Americans quite realizing how it happened or its full implications. Intervention has been the dominant motif of American post-war foreign policy, but the purpose, and even the methods, of this intervention have been concealed in a miasma of rhetoric and confusion. In the belief that we were containing or repelling communism, we have involved ourselves in situations that have been morally compromising, militarily frustrating, and politically indecisive.

The commitment to interventionism as a guiding principle has made it exceedingly difficult to distinguish between necessary and spurious motives for intervention—to determine which actions have a direct relation to the nation's security, and which merely represent wish-fulfillment on an international scale. In this respect it reflects a traditional weakness in American policy—a penchant for grandiose principles at the expense of a cool assessment of national interests, which has led the nation into painful involvements as a result of bold gestures carelessly made. The warning of John Quincy Adams has lately been forgotten in the intoxication of heady moral obligations, obligations which no one asked us to assume, and whose purpose we do not often understand. This is not the fault of the public but of its leaders, who are often tempted to use slogans to justify their actions, and then become prisoners of them. "American statesmen," as the historian Dexter Perkins has written,

> have believed that the best way to rally American opinion behind their purposes is to assert a moral principle. In doing so, they have often gone far beyond the boundaries of expediency. And perhaps it is fair to say that in underemphasizing security, they have helped to form a national habit which unduly subordinates the necessities of national defense to the assertion of lofty moral principles.[1]

The rhetoric of our cold-war diplomacy rests upon the indivisibility of freedom, the belief in self-determination, the necessity for collective security, and the sanctity of peaceful reform as opposed to violent change. These are not bad ambitions, but nowhere does this noble rhetoric seem to be in touch with the crass reality of the world as it is. Freedom, we have learned, is not only divisible between nations but subject to a hundred different interpretations. One man's freedom, all too often, is another man's exploitation. Self-determination can be a formula for political instability, and one which it may not always be in our interests to further. Collective security, as applied to our postwar military pacts, has never been much more than a polite word for a unilateral guarantee by the United States to protect her clients. Even this is now being shattered by the break-up of the cold-war alliances. The commitment to peaceful social change by constitutional processes has now collided with the reality of revolution and disorder throughout much of the world.

[1] Dexter Perkins, *The United States and Latin America.* Baton Rouge: Louisiana State University Press, 1961, p. 19.

With every expansion of our commitments, there has been a corresponding expansion of our official rhetoric. Statesmen, unable to adjust our limited means to our unlimited ends, have committed us to goals beyond the capacity of the nation to carry out. They have done this not because they are knaves intent on foreign adventurism, but because they have been carried away by the force of their own rhetoric. Infused by the belief that nothing is unattainable so long as the cause is just, and fortified by reliance on America's awesome military power, they frequently confuse the desirable with the attainable. In doing so, they commit the nation to ends that cannot be achieved, and thereby breed a national frustration that nags at the roots of American democracy. "To some extent," in the words of a Senate committee dealing with problems of national security, "every postwar administration has indulged our national taste for the grand and even the grandiose." Because the source of this comment is not one which is normally unreceptive to the application of American military power, its conclusions deserve quotation at greater length:

> The idea of manifest destiny still survives. Officials make sweeping declarations of our world mission, and often verbally commit the Nation to policies and programs far beyond our capabilities. In this way expectations may be created at home and abroad that are certain to be disappointed and that may result in a squandering of our power and influence on marginal undertakings. We may also find ourselves entangled in projects that are incompatible with the real needs of other peoples, or are, in some cases, actually repugnant to them. To some extent every postwar administration has indulged our national taste for the grand and even the grandiose.
>
> Our ability to think up desirable goals is almost limitless; our capabilities are limited. We still have much to learn about the need to balance what we would like to do with what we can do—and to establish intelligent priorities.
>
> The "can do" philosophy accords with American folklore, but even the United States cannot do everything. In policymaking, also, the assumption tends to be made that "we can find a way." We can do a lot, but our power is limited and the first claimant on it is the American people. According, it must be rationed in accordance with a responsible ordering of national interests.[2]

The alignment of national goals with national interests—of our desires with our needs—is the most pressing task facing American diplomacy. It is a task that has become increasingly urgent with each expansion of our commitments. These commitments are to be found in a tangle of regional alliances, military pacts, verbal agreements, and even unilateral decisions. They can all, to one degree or another, be traced back to the Truman Doctrine of March 1947, when the United States made the ambiguous offer to defend threatened nations from aggression, whether direct or indirect. This led, through the back door of the European Recovery Pro-

---

[2]*Memorandum of the Subcommittee on National Security and International Operations of the Committee on Government Operations*, U.S. Senate, 89th Congress, 1st session, 1965, pp. 2–3.

gram, to NATO, under which the United States is pledged to the defense of most of Europe and even parts of the Near East—from Spitzbergen to the Berlin Wall and beyond to the Asian borders of Turkey. From there the commitments become more vague, the situations more ambiguous, the countries themselves less crucial to American security.

From the seeds of the Truman Doctrine and the precedent of NATO came the Middle East Resolution, under which Congress gave President Eisenhower permission to protect the Arabs against communism; the CENTO and SEATO treaties that John Foster Dulles constructed to fill in the alliance gap from Iran to the Philippines; the ANZUS treaty with Australia and New Zealand; special defense arrangements with Japan and Korea; an unwritten obligation to protect India; the pledge for the defense of the entire western hemisphere under the Rio Pact; various peace-keeping functions under the United Nations; and, most recently, the Tonkin Gulf Resolution, a blank check given by Congress, allowing President Johnson to intervene as he saw fit in Southeast Asia. Early in 1970 the United States had more than 1,000,000 soldiers in 30 countries, was a member of 4 regional defense alliances and an active participant in a fifth, had mutual defense treaties with 42 nations, was a member of 53 international organizations, and was furnishing military or economic aid to nearly 100 nations across the face of the globe. Put all this together and it leaves us, in James Reston's words, with "commitments the like of which no sovereign nation ever took on in the history of the world."

These entanglements were justified as a response to events. The United States became involved in the defense of Western Europe because the defeat of Nazi Germany brought Stalin's armies into Central Europe. In Asia the disintegration of the Japanese Empire brought Russia into Manchuria and the United States into Japan, Okinawa, South Korea, and Taiwan. Later we advanced into Indochina when the French, despite our financial and military support, were unable to retain their Asian territories. We had no intention of virtually annexing Okinawa, of occupying South Korea, of preventing the return of Taiwan to China, of fighting in Indochina, or of remaining in Western Europe. If one had said in 1945 that twenty-five years later there would be 225,000 American soldiers in Germany, 50,000 in Korea, and a half million Americans fighting in Vietnam, he would have been considered mad. Yet so accustomed are we to our global commitments that we take this remarkable situation for granted.

Although the postwar vacuums are receding—with the resurgence of China, the recovery of Japan, and the revival of Europe—our commitment remains unchanged. We are still playing the same role of guardian that we played twenty years ago, when America and Russia were the only important powers in the world. Our diplomacy has not kept pace with the changes in the world power structure, and we are engaged far beyond our ability to control events. The result has been a dangerous gap in our foreign policy between our involvements and our means—between what we would like to accomplish and what we can reasonably hope to accomplish.

In a way it could be said that our foreign policy has been a victim of its own success. In the decision to rebuild and defend Western Europe, the United States acted with wisdom, humanity, and an enlightened conception of her own interests. The military alliance with Western Europe worked successfully because there was a clear community of interests between America and her allies. When we built our bases in Europe and sent our own soldiers to man the front lines, it was in the knowledge that we agreed with our allies on the dangers they faced and on the means by which they should be met. We came not as an army of occupation or as foreign mercenaries, but as friends joined in a common cause. We turned our back on the isolationism of the 1930s, put the American frontier right up to the Brandenburg Gate in Berlin, pledged our atomic weapons to the defense of our allies, added our own soldiers as guarantors of this pledge, and accepted the risk of nuclear devastation. We took this terrible risk because we had to: because neither strategically nor culturally could we accept the loss of Western Europe to our adversaries. The goal we sought in Western Europe in the early postwar period had three qualities essential for military intervention: it was vital to our interests, it was within our means to achieve, and it had the support of those we were trying to protect.

The difficulty, however, arose when the principles underlying NATO and the Marshall Plan were applied indiscriminately throughout the world—when it was assumed that the success of the Atlantic alliance could be duplicated in countries which shared neither our traditions, nor our interests, nor even our assessment of the dangers facing them. Too often American diplomacy has been engaged in the effort to create miniature NATOs and Marshall Plans with countries that have only recently shaken off the yoke of Western rule, that are at a greatly inferior stage of economic and political development, that are as suspicious of us as they are of our adversaries, that are endemically poor and unstable, and that usually greet us as unwanted manipulators rather than as welcome friends.

If our policies were judged by a cold calculation of national interest, a good many of them might have been scrapped long ago. If the struggle with Russia were merely over geographical spheres of influence, if the cold war were nothing more than old-fashioned power politics on a global scale, our commitments could have been cut and our involvements drastically limited. But the cold war has not been simply a struggle of giants for supremacy; it has also been an ideological contest for the allegiance of mankind. Or so it has seemed to its leading participants. It is because we feel ourselves embroiled in a much greater struggle that we are involved in the sustenance and security of some hundred countries, that we have replaced the old isolationism with a sweeping policy of interventionism and are today fighting yet another land war in Asia.

We are there because we feel ourselves to be pledged to a worldwide struggle against communism, because we see ourselves as the defenders of freedom and democracy in the contest against tyranny, because we are, in President Kennedy's words, "by destiny rather than choice, the watchmen on the walls of world freedom." But this role of watchman is not, for all President Kennedy's noble rhetoric, imposed by destiny. It is imposed by ourselves and subject to whatever limitations we choose to put upon it. It can provide the excuse for our playing the role of global gendarme, or serve as a guideline for a measured calculation of the national interest. No task of global omniscience is imposed upon us that we do not choose for ourselves.

As we face the obligations of our global commitments, we are becoming aware of our inability to impose our will upon events or to structure the world into the form we believe it should take. We have the power to destroy most human life on the planet within a matter of minutes, yet we cannot win a guerrilla war against peasants in black pajamas. We are so rich that we can retain an army in Europe, fight a war in Asia, dispense billions in foreign aid, and increase our national wealth by $30 billion a year. Yet we cannot adequately deal with the decay of our cities, the pollution of our atmosphere, the disintegration of public services, the growing hostility between whites and blacks, and the inadequacy of our educational system. Nor, despite the fact that we have dispensed nearly $120 billion abroad during the past twenty years, have we been able seriously to alleviate the poverty and hopelessness in which most of the world's population lives. We have assumed the responsibility for creating Great Societies at home and abroad, but we have not been able to bring this goal into line with our interests or capacities.

As a nation we have what General de Gaulle uncharitably labeled "a taste for intervention." Applied intelligently and with restraint, as in Western Europe after the war, this taste has done credit to our nation and served its interests. But expanded indiscriminately and without measure, it has involved us in struggles we do not understand, in areas where we are unwanted, and in ambitions which are doomed to frustration. Intervention is neither a sin nor a panacea. It is a method, and like all methods it must be directly related to the end in view. Otherwise it is likely to become an end in itself, dragging the nation down a path it never intended to follow, toward a goal it may find repugnant.

Too often our interventions have seemed to be imposed upon us by abstract theory rather than by a cold assessment of political realities. We have found ourselves involved in areas—the Congo the day before yesterday, Santo Domingo yesterday, Vietnam today, perhaps Thailand tomorrow—where our presence has sometimes exacerbated rather than alleviated the problem, and where it was not within our power to achieve a solution. Interventionism, as a principle of foreign policy, has not served us noticeably well in recent years. But it is a principle to which we are deeply committed: in NATO and its sister pacts, CENTO and SEATO;

in the Alliance for Progress; in the Rio Pact and the OAS; in foreign aid; in Southeast Asia; and in any nation which may be taken over by communists, whether from the inside or the outside. It has fostered a staggering program of involvements and it could easily lead us, at it already has in Vietnam, into conflicts whose extent we cannot possibly foresee.

We are in very deep in Europe, in Korea and Japan, in Thailand and Vietnam, in Latin America, and in the entire nexus of underdeveloped countries which are tottering between various forms of authoritarianism. This is an American dilemma: the dilemma of how to use power—sometimes economic power in the form of tractors and dollars, sometimes raw military power in the form of soldiers and napalm—for the achievement of ends which American leaders declare to be morally desirable.

The answer to that dilemma has eluded us ever since we plunged wholeheartedly into the world arena a generation ago and acquired, in a bout of moral fervor, a string of dependencies stretching around the globe —an empire, in short. It is an empire the scope of which the world has never seen, and which we, to this day, have scarcely begun to recognize ourselves.

The American Empire

If the British Empire, as Macaulay once said, was acquired in a fit of absent-mindedness, the American empire came into being without the intention or the knowledge of the American people. We are a people on whom the mantle of empire fits uneasily, who are not particularly adept at running colonies. Yet, by any conventional standards for judging such things, we are indeed an imperial power, possessed of an empire on which the sun truly never sets, an empire that embraces the entire western hemisphere, the world's two great oceans, and virtually all of the Eurasian land mass that is not in communist hands.

We are the strongest and most politically active nation in the world. Our impact reaches everywhere and affects everything it touches. We have the means to destroy whole societies and rebuild them, to topple governments and create others, to impede social change or to stimulate it, to protect our friends and devastate those who oppose us. We have a capacity for action, and a restless, driving compulsion to exercise it, such as the world has never seen. We have a technology that is the wonder of the world, an energy that compels us to challenge the obdurate forces of man and nature, and an affluence that could support whole nations with its waste. We also have a taunting sense of insecurity that makes it difficult for us to accept the limitations of our own remarkable power.

Although our adventure in empire-building may have begun without regard to its consequences, it could not have occurred at all had it not appealed to a deep-rooted instinct in our national character—an instinct to help those less fortunate and permit them to emulate and perhaps one day achieve the virtues of our own society. There was nothing arrogant in this attitude; indeed, it was heavily tinged with altruism. But it did rest upon the belief that it was America's role to make the world a happier, more orderly place, one more nearly reflecting our own image. We saw this as a special responsibility fate had thrust upon us. Standing alone as the defender of Europe, the guardian of Latin America, the protector of weak and dependent nations released from the bondage of colonialism, possessing the mightiest military force in history, an economy productive beyond any man had ever known, and a standard of living the envy of the world—we naturally became persuaded of the universal validity of our institutions, and of our obligation to help those threatened by disorder, aggression, and poverty.

We acquired our empire belatedly and have maintained, and even expanded, it because we found ourselves engaged in a global struggle with an ideology. When we picked up the ruins of the German and Japanese Empires in 1945, we discovered that we could not let them go without seeing them fall under the influence of our ideological adversaries. Struggling against communism, we created a counter-empire of anticommunism. This counter-empire was built upon the idealism enshrined in the charter of the United Nations, the altruism exemplified by the Marshall Plan, the cautious improvisation of the Truman Doctrine, and the military arithmetic of the NATO pact. It spread to Korea and the Congo, to Pakistan and Vietnam, and to a hundred troubled spots where inequality bred grievances, disorder, and instability. We came to see the world as a great stage on which we choreographed an inspiring design for peace, progress, and prosperity. Through American interventionism —benignly where possible, in the form of foreign aid; surgically where necessary, in the form of American soldiers—we hoped to contain the evil forces from the East and provide a measure of hope and security for the rest of mankind. We engaged in a kind of welfare imperialism, empire-building for noble ends rather than for such base motives as profit and influence. We saw ourselves engaged, as Under Secretary of State George Ball declared shortly after we began bombing North Vietnam, in "something new and unique in world history—a role of world responsibility divorced from territorial or narrow national interests."[3]

But there are good economic reasons for our interest in the political stability of the underdeveloped countries, for American prosperity in part depends upon access to their raw materials. With only 6 per cent of the world's population, the United States consumes one-third of the world's production of bauxite, 40 per cent of its nickel, 36 per cent of its chrome, 25 per cent of its tungsten and copper.

While we did not acquire our empire for profit, "history," as Arnold Toynbee has observed,

[3]George Ball, "The Dangers of Nostalgia," *Department of State Bulletin*, April 12, 1965, pp. 535–36.

RONALD STEEL

tells us that conquest and annexation are not the only means, or indeed the most frequent and most effective means, by which empires have been built up in the past. The history of the Roman Empire's growth, for instance, is instructive when one is considering the present-day American Empire's structure and prospects. The principal method by which Rome established her political supremacy in her world was by taking her weaker neighbors under her wing and protecting them against her and their stronger neighbors; Rome's relation with these protégées of hers was a treaty relation. Juridically they retained their previous status of sovereign independence. The most that Rome asked of them in terms of territory was the cession, here and there, of a patch of ground for the plantation of a Roman fortress to provide for the common security of Rome's allies and Rome herself.[4]

Although the desire to defend other nations against communism is not an imperial ambition, it has led this country to use imperial methods: establishment of military garrisons around the globe, granting of subsidies to client governments and politicians, application of economic sanctions and even military force against recalcitrant states, and employment of a veritable army of colonial administrators working through such organizations as the State Department, the Agency for International Development, the United States Information Agency, and the Central Intelligence Agency. Having grown accustomed to our empire and having found it pleasing, we have come to take its institutions and its assumptions for granted. Indeed, this is the mark of a convinced imperial power: its advocates never question the virtues of empire, although they may dispute the way in which it is administered, and they do not for a moment doubt that it is in the best interests of those over whom it rules. A basically anti-colonial people, we tolerate, and even cherish, our empire because it seems so benevolent, so designed to serve those embraced by it.

But, many will ask, have we not been generous with our clients and allies, sending them vast amounts of money, and even sacrificing the lives of our own soldiers on their behalf? Of course we have. But this is the role of an imperial power. If it is to enjoy influence and command obedience, it must be prepared to distribute some of its riches throughout its empire and, when necessary, to fight rival powers for the loyalty of vulnerable client states. Empires may be acquired by accident, but they can be held together only by cash, power, and even blood. We learned this in Korea, in Berlin, and in Cuba; and we are learning it again in Vietnam. Whatever the resolution of that tragic conflict, it has once again shattered the recurrent illusion that empires can be maintained on the cheap.

Our empire has not been cheap to maintain, but we have never conceived of it as an empire. Rather, we saw it as a means of containing

[4]Arnold Toynbee, *America and the World Revolution*. London: Oxford University Press, 1962, pp. 29–30.

communism, and thereby permitting other nations to enjoy the benefits of freedom, democracy, and self-determination. This was particularly true in the vast perimeter of colonial and ex-colonial states which offered an enticing field for communist exploitation—and also for our own benevolent intervention. With the European colonial powers weakened and discredited, we were in a position to implement our long-standing sentiments of anti-colonialism. Opposed to the efforts of France, Britain, and Holland to regain control of their Asian colonies, we actively encouraged the efforts of such nationalists as Nehru, Sukarno, and Ho Chi Minh to win the independence of their countries.

However, once the war-weakened European powers finally did leave their colonies, we discovered that most of the newly independent nations had neither the resources nor the ability to stand on their own. With a very few exceptions, they were untrained for independence and unable, or unwilling, to exercise it in ways we approved of. Having proclaimed self-determination as a moral principle valid on every continent and in every country, we found ourselves saddled with the responsibility for some of its consequences. As a result, we stepped into the role left vacant by the departed European powers. In many of the new states we performed the tasks of an imperial power without enjoying the economic or territorial advantages of empire. We chose politicians, paid their salaries, subsidized national budgets, equipped and trained armies, built soccer stadiums and airports, and where possible instructed the new nations in the proper principles of foreign policy. We did this with good intentions, because we really did believe in self-determination for everybody as a guiding moral principle, and because we thought it was our obligation to help the less fortunate "modernize" their societies by making them more like ours. This was *our welfare imperialism,* and it found its roots in our most basic and generous national instincts.

But we also plunged into the economic primitiveness and political immaturity of the new nations because we saw them as a testing-ground in the struggle between freedom and communism, the cataclysmic duel that was to determine the fate of the world. Carried away by the vocabulary of the cold war, we sought to combat communism and preserve "freedom" in whatever area, however unpromising or unlikely, the battle seemed to be joined. Confusing communism as a social doctrine with communism as a form of Soviet imperialism, we assumed that any advance of communist doctrine anywhere was an automatic gain for the Soviet Union. Thus we believe it essential to combat communism in any part of the globe, as though it were a direct threat to our security, even in cases where it was not allied to Soviet power. Our methods were foreign aid, military assistance, and, where all else failed, our own soldiers.

But while this policy was valid in Europe, where there seemed to be a real threat of a Soviet take-over and where our allies shared our feelings about the danger facing them, it was less reasonable throughout most of the ex-colonial world. There the ruling elites were worried not so much by communism as by the real or imagined "imperialism" of the Western powers. They were not particularly committed to our advocacy of free speech and democracy, having never experienced it themselves, and they were totally mystified by our praises of capitalism, which in their experience was associated with exploitation, bondage, and misery. Insofar as they thought about communism at all, they could not help being drawn to a doctrine to which the Western powers were opposed. Western antipathy in itself was a major recommendation.

Most of these new nations have genuinely tried to keep out of the struggles among the great powers. They are anti-colonial and suspicious of the West by training and instinct. But they also have not wanted to compromise their neutrality by too close an association with the communists. Insofar as communist doctrine has seemed to offer a solution for their problems of political authority and economic development, they have been receptive to it—as a doctrine. But where it has been allied with Soviet power, they have uniformly resisted it, because it represents a threat to their independence. Most of the new nations, therefore, have tried to tread a path between the conflicting demands of East and West.

Some of them, of course, have been led by clever men who learned to take advantage of our phobias. They found that a threat to "go communist" would usually win large infusions of American foreign-aid funds, just as a threat to "join the imperialists" would inspire Russian counter-bribes. They learned, with the agility of Ben Franklin at the court of Louis XVI, how to manipulate our obsessions, seek out sympatic ears in Congress and the Pentagon, and conjure up terrible happenings that were about to befall them. The twin doctrines of communism and anti-communism became tools by which they could secure outside help to build up their feeble economies and gain a larger voice in world affairs.

These nations cannot really be blamed for any of this. Being poor, they naturally wanted to secure as much outside assistance as they could, and played upon the anxieties of the great powers to do so. They thus served their own interests and pursued legitimate objectives of their foreign policy. What was less natural, however, was that we permitted ourselves to be manipulated by those who had so little to offer us. We allowed this because we feared that the new nations would fall under the influence of communism. Just as they were inspired by sentiments of anti-colonialism, so we were inspired by an equally powerful anti-communism. It provided the stimulus which led the United States to a massive postwar interventionism and to the creation of an empire that rests upon the pledge to use American military power to combat communism not only as a form of imperialism, but even as a social doctrine in the underdeveloped states. The foundation of this American empire can be traced back to the threat to Europe as it existed more than twenty years ago.

The American empire came into being as a result of the Second World War, when the struggle against Nazi Germany and imperial Japan brought us to the center of Europe and the offshore islands of Asia. With Russian troops on the Elbe and with the governments of Western Europe tottering under the strain of reconstruction, it seemed that only American power could halt the spread of communism. Consequently, the United States intervened to meet this new European danger, first with economic aid under the Marshall Plan, and then with direct military support under NATO. This was a necessary and proper response to a potential threat, although the emphasis on military over economic support has been sharply debated by historians. However, even before the Marshall Plan was announced, and two years before the NATO pact was signed, the United States laid down the guidelines for its intervention in Europe—and ultimately throughout the world—in the Truman Doctrine of March 12, 1947. Urging Congress to grant $400 million to help the Greek royalists fight the communist rebels, and to enable the Turks to defend themselves against Russia, President Truman declared: "It must be the policy of the United States to support free peoples who are resisting attempted subjugation by armed minorities or by outside pressure."

While such military aid may have been necessary to prevent Greece and Turkey from falling into the communist camp, the language in which the Truman Doctrine was cast implied a commitment far beyond the communist threat to those nations. Had it been confined to the containment of Soviet power, the Truman Doctrine would have expressed a legitimate American security interest. But by a vocabulary which pledged the United States to oppose armed minorities and outside pressure, it involved us in the containment of an ideology. In so doing, it provided the rationale for a policy of global intervention against communism, even in areas where American security was not involved. What was, as Kenneth Thompson has written, "a national and expedient act designed to replace British with American power in Central Europe, was presented as the defense of free democratic nations everywhere in the world against 'direct or indirect aggression.' It translated a concrete American interest for a limited area of the world into a general principle of worldwide validity, to be applied regardless of the limits of American interests and power."[5]

President Truman probably did not envisage the extreme ends toward which this policy would eventually be applied. While he argued that the United States could not permit communism to overturn the status quo by aggression or armed subversion, he put the emphasis on economic assistance and self-help. And he assumed that our efforts would be made in conjunction with our allies. What he did not intend, at least at the time, was unilateral American military intervention in support of client states threatened from within by communist-inspired insurgents. He did not suggest that the Greek civil war should be fought by Ameri-

[5]Kenneth Thompson, *Political Realism and the Crisis of World Politics: An American Approach to Foreign Policy*. Princeton: Princeton University Press, 1960, p. 124.

can troops, nor did he seriously contemplate the bombardment of Yugo-slavia, from whose territory the Greek communist rebels were being supplied. The language of the Truman Doctrine was sweeping, but its application was limited. It grew into a policy of global interventionism only with the later acknowledgment of America's imperial responsibil-ities.

Historically speaking, the Truman Doctrine was essentially an ex-tension of the Monroe Doctrine across the Atlantic to non-communist Europe. Just as the Monroe Doctrine was designed to maintain the nine-teenth-century balance of power between the New World and the Old, so its twentieth-century counterpart was meant to prevent communism from upsetting the political balance between East and West. Where the former used British seapower to serve the security interests of the United States, the latter used American economic and military power to protect non-communist Europe and thereby defend American interests. The im-plied limitations of the Truman Doctrine were, however, swept aside by the communist attack on South Korea and the resulting assumption that the Russians were prepared to resort to a policy of open aggression. The extension of the Truman Doctrine to cover the Korean war set the stage for its expansion into a general commitment to resist communism everywhere, not only by economic and military support, but by direct American mili-tary intervention where necessary. The alliances forged by Dulles were based upon this premise, and even the war in Vietnam is a logical corollary of the Truman Doctrine.

The old limitations of spheres of influence, treaty obligations, and Con-gressional consent are no longer relevant in cases where the President should deem it necessary to launch a military intervention. As Dean Rusk told a Senate committee: "No would-be aggressor should suppose that the absence of a defense treaty, Congressional declaration, or United States military presence grants immunity to aggression."[6] As a hands-off warning by an imperial power, this statement is eminently logical. It does, however, take us into waters a good deal deeper than those chartered by the Truman Doctrine. By indicating that the United States would not feel itself restricted even to the military treaties it has with more than forty nations, the Secretary of State implicitly removed all inhibitions upon a Presidential decision to intervene against communism wherever, whenever, and however it is deemed necessary.

Behind the warning of Secretary Rusk lies the belief that American military power is so great that the old considerations of national interest —which confined a nation's military interventions to areas deemed vital to its security—are no longer necessary. The growth of American military power—the enormous array of weapons, the awesome nuclear deterrent, the largest peacetime standing army in our history, and an economy that dominates the world—has apparently convinced many in Washing-

[6]Dean Rusk, Statement to the Senate Preparedness Subcommittee, *The Washington Post*, August 26, 1966.

ton that "the illusion of American omnipotence," in D. W. Brogan's famous phrase, may not be an illusion. The old feeling of being locked in a closet with Russia appears to have vanished and to have been replaced by the conviction that America alone has world responsibilities, that these are "unique in world history" and justify a policy of global interventionism. If this is not an illusion of omnipotence, it might at least be described as intoxication with power.

Although we consciously seek no empire, we are experiencing all the frustrations and insecurities of an imperial power. Having assumed a position of world leadership because of the abstinence of others, America has not been able to evolve a coherent concept of what she wants and what she may reasonably expect to attain in the world. She has not been able to relate her vision of a universal order on the American model to the more limited imperatives of her own national interests. She is a territorially satiated power, yet plagued by terrible insecurities over her global responsibilities and even over her own identity. America has rejected the old tradition of abstinence and isolationism without having been able to find a new tradition that can bring her interests into line with her ideals.

One of the expressions of this insecurity has been the emergence of anti-communism *as an ideology,* rather than as a reaction to the imperial policies followed by the Soviet Union and other communist powers. This counter-ideology of anti-communism has been both internal and external, reflecting our anxieties about ourselves and about our position in the world at large. As an external anxiety, anti-communism arose from the frustrations of the early postwar period and the disappointments of a terrible war which brought a terrible peace. To possess a military power unequaled in human history, to have marshaled an atomic arsenal capable of eradicating an enemy in a matter of hours, to have no conscious political ambitions other than to spread the virtues of American democracy to less fortunate peoples—to experience all this and still not be able to achieve more than stalemate in the cold war has been difficult for many Americans to accept. The transformation of adversaries into demons followed almost inevitably.

Anti-communism as an ideology was a response not only to stalemate abroad, but also to the insecurities of life at home, where traditional values had been uprooted. To those whose sense of security had been destroyed by the extreme mobility of American life, who felt threatened by the demands of racial minorities for equality, and who were humiliated by the impersonality of an increasingly bureaucratized society, ideological anti-communism served as a focal point of discontent. It could not allay these anxieties, but it could explain them in a form that was acceptable to those who saw as many enemies within the gates as they did outside. The McCarthyism and the witch-hunts of the 1950s, which so debased American intellectual life and spread a blanket of conformity over the government, were a reaction to this insecurity, acts of self-exorcism by a people tormented by demons.

Plagued by domestic anxieties and faced with external dangers that defy the traditional virtues of the American character—an ability to organize, to solve problems, to get things done by sustained energy and determination—the American people have been deeply shaken throughout the whole postwar period. They have had to accept the frustrations of stalemate with Soviet Russia and learn to live in the shadow of atomic annihilation, where the very survival of America is threatened for the first time in her history. This is a situation which, after the traumas of the 1950s, we have now learned to accept with resignation, and even with a certain equanimity. But it is one which breeds deep-rooted anxieties of the kind expressed on the radical right. These frustrations conflict with the most basic elements of Americanism as a secular faith. To challenge this faith is to commit a kind of heresy, and it is as a heretical doctrine that communism has been treated in this country. This is comprehensible only if we accept the fact that Americanism is a creed, that, as a British commentator has observed,

> America is not just a place but an idea, producing a particular kind of society. When immigrants choose to become Americans they are expected to accept the political values of this society, associated with the egalitarian and democratic traditions of the American Revolution. As an immigrant country, perhaps only Israel is comparable in the demands it makes for the acceptance of an ideology as well as a territorial nationality. Consequently American patriotism is more readily identified with loyalty to traditional political values; ... the reverence paid to the American Constitution and the basic political principles of the American revolution encourages the tendency to believe that all failures of the political system must be blamed on corruption, conspiracy or some external enemy. Communism has uniquely provided both an internal and external threat.[7]

Pampered by a continent of extraordinary riches, insulated from political responsibility in the world for longer than was healthy, her soil untouched by war for more than a century, spoiled by an economy which produces a seemingly inexhaustible wealth, flattered by an unnatural dominion over temporarily indigent allies, America has found it difficult to bring her political desires into line with her real needs. We think of solving problems rather than of living with them, and we find compromise an unnatural alternative to "victory." These attitudes are a reflection of our frontier mentality, of the cult of individualism, and of a national experience where success is usually the ultimate result of a major effort.

We have fought every war on the assumption that it was the final war that would usher in universal peace. We believed that every adversary was the architect of a global conspiracy, and that break-up of the cold-war military blocs—these are the central realities of our time. Yet our diplomacy remains frozen in the posture of two decades ago and mesmerized by a ritual anti-communism that has become peripheral to the

[7]Robert Stephens, *The Observer* (London), July 19, 1964.

real conflict of power in today's world. We are in an age of nationalism, in which both communism and capitalism are ceasing to be ideologically significant, and in which the preoccupations of our diplomacy are often irrelevant. We are the last of the ideologues, clinging to political assumptions that have been buried by changing time and circumstance, a nation possessed of an empire it did not want, does not know how to administer, and fears to relinquish. We live in a time of dying ideologies and obsolete slogans, where much of what we have taken for granted is now outdated, and where even the political condition that has dominated our lives—the cold war—may now be over.

W. W Rostow
THE NATIONAL INTEREST

Walt Whitman Rostow, it is often noted, has led a double life as economic historian and counselor of state. He has written several books proposing American policy towards the Soviet Union and Communist China in the 1950s and interpreting the influence on international politics of the stages of economic growth. The United States in the World Arena, from which this reading is taken, was first published in 1960. The following year Rostow served briefly as Deputy Special Assistant to President Kennedy for National Security Affairs, moved over to the State Department where he headed the Policy Planning Council until 1966, and returned to the White House as Special Assistant to President Johnson until 1969. Rarely has a theorist enjoyed such opportunities for the practical application of his concepts.

Rostow's prominence in the executive branch gives special significance to his interpretation of America's national interest during the cold war. He is succinct and incisive about the necessity to confront world communism. In this passage Rostow is both an economic historian and an advocate of cold war strategy, but it is the latter role which stands out. As an economic historian, he sees the world as consisting totally of Eurasia and the United States: America is only an island adjacent to the Eurasian continent, whose control is our dominant interest. As a policy planner, he emphasizes mutual dependencies and interrelationships: military successes engender ideological gains; victory in one nation portends a triumph over its neighbor (a view popularly known as the domino theory). Rostow's conceptualization of American power is important if historians are to appreciate a liberal's view of the world in the cold war.

A Definition

It is the American interest to maintain a world environment for the United States within which American society can continue to develop in conformity with the humanistic principles which are its foundation. This definition, in terms of the progressive development of the quality of American society, would, of course, include the physical protection of the country; but the protection of American territory is viewed essentially as a means to a larger end—the protection of a still-developing way of life.

The operative meaning of this definition derives from the geographic position of the United States. For no substantial period in the nation's history has the American interest been automatically assured by geographic isolation. Contrary to a mythology which still strongly affects American attitudes and the nation's performance, the American interest has been chronically in danger from the late eighteenth century forward. This danger arose and continues to arise from the simple geographic fact that the combined resources of Eurasia, including its military potential, have been and remain superior to those of the United States— Eurasia being here defined to include Asia, the Middle East, and Africa as well as Europe.

The United States must be viewed essentially as a continental island off the greater land mass of Eurasia. Various combinations of power in Eurasia have been and remain a potential threat to the national interest. American independence was achieved in the eighteenth century only because Americans could exploit a conflict between Britain and France. A united Britian and France could have stifled the American Revolution. During the nineteenth century the nation expanded and consolidated American power on the North American continent and in the Western Hemisphere by exploiting the power conflicts of Eurasia; and in the twentieth century the United States has been thrice placed in jeopardy, and instinctively sensed that jeopardy, when a single power or combination of powers threatened to dominate Western Eurasia, Eastern Eurasia, or both.

There is, then, much of the whole sweep of American history which denies the notion of an America safely isolated by act of God and geography; and there is nothing fundamentally new in taking the American relationship to the power balance in Eurasia as central to the nation's security problem.

The Dual American Interest in Eurasia

If the problem of the national interest is viewed as a question of protecting not only the nation's territory but also its basic values as a society, it follows that the United States has two distinct but connected interests in Eurasia. Since the combined resources of Eurasia could pose a serious threat of military defeat to the United States, it is the American interest that no single power or group of powers hostile or potentially hostile to the United States dominate that area or a sufficient portion of it to threaten the United States and any coalition the United States can build and sustain. But under modern conditions of communication, there is a second threat to the nation's interest. Whatever the military situation might be, a Eurasia coalesced under totalitarian dictatorships would threaten the survival of democracy both elsewhere and in the United States. It is, therefore, equally the American interest that the societies of Eurasia develop along lines broadly consistent with the nation's own ideology; for under modern conditions it is difficult to envisage the survival of a democratic American society as an island in a totalitarian sea.

Three Clarifications of the American Ideological Interest

This proposition must be immediately clarified in three respects.

First, the United States need not seek societies abroad in its own image. The United States does have a profound interest that societies abroad develop and strengthen those elements in their respective cultures that elevate and protect the dignity of the individual as against the claims of the state. Such elements of harmony with the Western democratic tradition exist in different forms everywhere; and they have been strengthened by the attractiveness of the Western democratic example at its best, notably by the example of British parliamentary government, the American Revolution, and the values on which American society was erected. But the forms of legitimately democratic societies can vary widely.

Second, the democratic process must be viewed as a matter of aspiration, trend, and degree, not as an absolute. The value judgments which underlie the political, social, and economic techniques of Western societies might be summarized as follows:

1. Individual human beings represent a unique balancing of motivations and aspirations which, despite the conscious and unconscious external means that help shape them, are to be accorded a moral and even religious respect. The underlying aim of society is to permit these

individual complexes of motivations and aspirations to have their maximum expression compatible with the well-being of other individuals
and the security of society.

2. Governments thus exist to assist individuals to achieve their own
fulfillment, to protect individual human beings from the harm they
might do one another, and to protect organized societies against the
aggression of other societies.

3. Governments can take their shape legitimately only from some
effective expression of the combined will and judgments of individuals
on the basis of one man, one vote.

4. Some men aspire to power over their fellow men and derive satisfaction from the exercise of power aside from the purposes to which
power is put. This fundamental human quality in itself makes dangerous
to the well-being of society the concentration of political power in the
hands of individuals and groups even where such groups may constitute
a majority. *Habeas corpus* is the symbol and, perhaps, the foundation of
the most substantial restraint—in the form of due process of law—men
have created to cope with this danger.

From Plato on, political scientists have recognized that men may not
understand their own best interest, and, in particular, that they may
be short-sighted and swayed by urgent emotions in their definition of
that interest. As between the individual's limitation in defining wisely
his own long-run interest and his inability wisely to exericed power over
others without check, democratic societies have broadly chosen to risk
the former rather than the latter danger in the organization of society,
and to diminish the former danger by popular education, by the inculca-
tion of habits of individual responsibility, and by devices of government
which temper the less thoughtful political reactions of men.

From this definition the democratic element within a society emerges
as a matter of degree and of aspiration. The pure democratic concept is
compromised to some extent in all organized societies by the need to protect individuals from each other, by the need to protect the society as a
whole from others, and by the checks required to protect the workings of
the society from man's frequent inability wisely to define his own long-
run interest. Even when societies strive for the democratic compromise, the balance between liberty and order which any society can achieve
and still operate effectively, and the particular form that balance will
take, are certain to vary. They will vary not only from society to society
but also within each society in response to the state of education of its
citizens and the nature of the specific problems it confronts as a community at different stages in its history.

It is evident that some present societies have not had and do not
now have the capability of combining effective communal action with a
high degree of what is here called the democratic element. Both history
and the contemporary scene offer instances of governments in which the

balance of power is heavily in the hands of the state rather than in the hands of the individual citizens who comprise it.

The legitimate American ideological interest is not that all societies become immediately democratic in the degree achieved in the United States or Western Europe, but that they accept as a goal a version of the democratic value judgments consonant with their culture and their history and that they move toward their realization with the passage of time.

Now a third clarification of the American ideological interest. Since the American interest does not require that all societies at all times accept democratic values and move toward their achievement, the nation is concerned not with total ideological victory, somehow defined, but with the balance and trend of ideological forces in Eurasia. Therefore, the application of the limited, but real, margin of American influence on the course of other societies can and should be selective. Given the nation's geographic circumstance, its history, and the quality of its society, the American interest demands, in a sense, that Americans be crusaders; but the American ideological crusade must be tolerant, long term, and directed toward areas of importance where the nation's margin of influence may be effective. The United States is concerned not with absolutes but with the direction of political trend in Eurasia.

Current Threats from Eurasia

In more specific geographic terms, it is a persistent interest of the United States that no single power or power grouping militarily dominate either Western or Eastern Eurasia.

In Western Eurasia the threat of such an outcome is posed by the possible absorption within the Soviet empire of East Germany and Eastern Europe. The threat would become a reality should West Germany be drawn into the Soviet power orbit; and the threat would be made acute by the ideological defection of Italy, France, or both. In the East the threat of such an outcome is posed by the close alliance of the Soviet Union and Communist China. In Asia there are two major centers of power, Japan on the one hand and India on the other, the latter being key to the complex stretching from Indochina around to Pakistan. In Asia the threat to the American interest would become virtually a reality should either Japan or India be lost to the Free World.

At the present time the intentions and capabilities of the Communist Bloc pose two threats to the United States—a military threat and an ideological threat. These threats are clearly related; the ideological loss of India, for instance, would raise important military problems; the military loss of northern Indochina has raised important problems of ideological orientation throughout Southeast Asia. But the two American interests are not and should not be considered identical. The time necessary and the kind of effort required to cope with the military threat are likely to differ from those required by the ideological threat. The military threat to South Korea was dealt with in a few years; defeating the ideological threat to South Korea may prove a creative Free World task for a generation.

The Interweaving of Power and Ideological Interests

If this view of the American interest is correct, the debate which has been proceeding in the United States over recent years as to whether the nation's interests should be defined in power terms or in terms of the ideological principles to which American society is attached is a somewhat misguided debate. This is so in two respects.

First, if the essential American interest is to preserve a world environment within which its chosen form of democratic society can persist and develop, then the nation's stake in the ideological and political balance in Eurasia is as legitimate as its interest in the military balance of power in Eurasia. Two national efforts, one military and the other political, interacting intimately, must go forward together as part of a total effort to protect the interests of American society.

There is a second sense in which the debate appears misguided. It appears to be a characteristic of American history that this nation cannot be effective in its military and foreign policy unless it believes that both its security interests and its commitment to certain moral principles require the nation to act. From the Spanish-American War to the present, the nation has acted effectively only when both strands in its interest were believed to be involved—in the Spanish-American War itself, in the First and Second World Wars, in the effort to reconstruct and defend Western Europe in 1947–1950, in the early phases of the Korean War.

When idealism alone seemed to be the basis for the positions taken, the nation did not back its play, as, for example, in Wilson's ideological formulation of the American interest at Versailles. Equally, the nation has not been effective when confronted with situations where its power interests might be involved but where a persuasive moral basis for American action was not present. The notion of American imperialism, popular in certain American circles at the turn of the century, died quickly when it confronted the abiding American instinct in support of political independence in the case of the Philippines and elsewhere. Similarly, a major reason why the United States was ineffective in the Indochina crisis of 1954 was that it was then extremely difficult simultaneously to deal with the Communist menace and to disengage from French imperialism in that area; and in the summer of 1956 the United States was gravely inhibited in dealing with Nasser because, among other reasons, his claim to national sovereignty over the Suez Canal had a certain resonance in the American image of its historic meaning on the world scene as the friend of those struggling for independence.

The wisdom of American policy in Indochina and at Suez is, of course, debatable. Moreover, a nation's belief that its ideals are or are not involved is by no means an unambiguous criterion for performance. Nevertheless, it is unrealistic to expect American society—given its history and values—to perform in terms of pure power criteria.

The components in the American ideological interest can, then, be distinguished and summarized in the following three propositions:

1. The ideological loss of key areas in Eurasia would have major military consequence for the United States.

2. Apart from its military consequences, the ideological loss of the balance of power in Eurasia would, under modern conditions, have major adverse consequences for the quality of American society and for the viability of the humanistic principles which underlie it.

3. Among the qualities of American society threatened by the loss of the ideological balance of power in Eurasia would be the historic sense of American democratic mission on the world scene, present since the nation's founding, which has given to American life much of its moral worth, its distinction, and its forward momentum.

The art of American statesmanship is to formulate and to sustain courses of action which harmonize in specific settings abiding American interests and abiding American ideals, steadily preserving the dual power balance in Eurasia, preventing by forehanded effort the emergence of such crises as those which hitherto have been required to evoke a major American effort at self-preservation.

The requirements of protecting the military balance of power and developing the ideological balance of power will not always converge. Foreign policy is full of painful choices. There may be times when in order to maintain military positions action must be taken which will conflict with the norms of the American ideological interest; and there may be occasions when it will be proper to take military risks to permit movement toward ideological objectives. But in the world of 1958 and beyond there are many more points of convergence than are now being exploited. If the dual character of the national interest—as a democratic island off a potentially threatening Eurasian mainland—is accepted, and if the interrelations of the two objectives are perceived, courses of action still appear open to the United States which will protect and sustain the quality as well as the existence of the nation's life in the face of current and foreseeable challenges.

The United States and the Decline of Nationhood

Among those challenges is the problem of using American power and influence to tame military force by effective international accord; for the nature of modern weapons in a context other than American monopoly is a danger to the national interest sufficiently grave to justify acceptance of important constraints on the nation's sovereignty. Put another way, it is a legitimate American national objective to see removed from all nations—including the United States—the right to use substantial military force to pursue their own interests. Since this residual right is the root of national sovereignty and the basis for the existence of an international arena of power, it is, therefore, an American interest to see an end to nationhood as it has been historically defined.

The pace at which means of communication are now under development argues, further, that the present nations of the globe will move into relations of increasing intimacy and interaction.

Between them, the urgent imperative to tame military force and the need to deal with peoples everywhere on the basis of an accelerating proximity argue strongly for movement in the direction of federalized world organization under effective international law. And, should effective international control of military power be achieved, it might prove convenient and rational to pass other functions upward from unilateral determination to an organized arena of international politics.

It is not easy or particularly useful to peer far beyond the time when this great human watershed is attained. Nevertheless, it can be said that the American regional interest would still continue to embrace elements from the long sweep of the past. Convergent and conflicting relationships of geography, of cultural connection, of economic interest would in substantial measure be simply transferred from a setting where military force enters the equation of negotiation to one of global domestic politics. When the great conference has ended and the freely moving inspectors take up their initial posts from one end of the world to the other and the nightmare passes, the agenda of international politics will look not unfamiliar. Much in the historic relation of the United States to the balance of affairs in Eurasia will remain. There will be, however, a special dimension to global politics with special meaning for Americans—the problem of so conducting the world's affairs as to avoid a dissolution of the federal machinery and civil war.

Samuel Lubell
THE MAN WHO BOUGHT TIME

Both William Howard Taft and Harry Truman followed Roosevelts in the Presidency, but unlike Taft, Truman emerged from the shadow of his predecessor to play his own role as President. To attribute this difference solely to their different times and circumstances is to do a disservice to

Truman. He possessed too much political acumen to be a President other than the activist he was. Of course, Samuel Lubell's assertion that Truman's accomplishments were the consequences of "skills and energies . . . directed to standing still" can be disputed, but not convincingly. Truman deserves to be celebrated for his negative action: at a time when others signaled retreat, his holding action became a victory. By pressing ahead for progressive social programs when conservatives insisted upon dismantling those gained in the previous decade, Truman secured New Deal legislation before the Eisenhower administration ratified the liberal program. And, not at all incidentally, he temporarily preserved the New Deal coalition and liberalism's hazy consensus.

That his tenure was not a great debacle is in part a measure of Truman's talents. He came to the White House as a "Missouri Compromise" heir to a man who had been elected overwhelmingly four times. Few leaders possessed Truman's talent for orchestrating national politics in spite of a personality that enraged people more readily than gratifying them. He took the Democratic party from unavoidable defeat in 1946 to a spectacular victory in 1948 that presaged the Democratic congressional majorities which have prevailed since 1954. He charted the course for cold war policies which had little deviation for almost twenty years. Political exigencies underpinned both his applaudable and deplorable actions, whether the leadership of an incipient civil rights movement or a noxious anti-communist domestic crusade; in both instances he set aside personal reservations in order to achieve the desirable electoral result.

Does Lubell believe that the nation could afford programs designed for maximum voting impact? Did shrewd politics produce good policy?

The Truman Riddle

When the Seventy-fifth Congress reconvened in January, 1938, most of the Senators were dismayed to find that the first order of business before them was the antilynching bill. Particularly among those Senators whose constituencies straddled Northern and Southern prejudices the prospect of having to vote on the proposal stirred much anguish. As one of these Senators explained to a leader of the Southern opposition, "You know I'm against this bill but if it comes to a vote I'll have to be for it."

This Senator went on to recall how a favorite uncle had served in the Confederate Army and how his mother still associated all Republicans with the "redleg" abolitionists who had helped make the Kansas-Missouri border a guerrilla battlefield during the Civil War period. "All my sympathies are with you," the Senator fervently declared, "but the Negro vote in Kansas City and St. Louis is too important."

Turning to go, Senator Harry S. Truman added almost wistfully, "Maybe the thing for me to be doing is to be playing poker this afternoon. Perhaps you fellows can call a no quorum."

This episode is related here for the first time in print, not to raise doubts about President Truman's sincerity in the matter of civil rights—of that more later—but because it brings into focus so clearly the essential political qualities which made Truman President and which remained the key to his whole administration. Few Presidents seemed more erratic and puzzling to their contemporaries; yet few occupants of the White House ran more consistently true to form.

Truman was commonly pictured as "a little man" hopelessly miscast for the "biggest job in the world." Yet how many of our Presidents gave the historians more to write about? Almost any one of a number of his actions would have made his Presidency memorable—the dropping of the first atomic bomb, the Truman Doctrine of resistance to communism, the Marshall Plan, the Berlin Airlift, his spectacular election triumph in 1948, his abandonment of the tradition of "no entangling alliances" with the signing of the North Atlantic Defense Treaty, our armed intervention in Korea, the firing of General Douglas MacArthur.

The strange thing about these precedent-shattering actions is how basically unchanged things were left. After seven years of Truman's hectic, even furious, activity the nation seemed to be about on the same general spot as when he first came to office.

Consider the three principal conflicts which dominated the Truman years and whose interweavings formed the fabric of our times:

Domestically, our economy trembled with the alternating fevers and chills of threatened inflation and threatened depression, even as it did when World War Two ended. The cold war with Russia continued to pursue its malarial course, now and then sinking into endemic concealment, only to flare up in blood-letting recurrence. Although both the Wallaceites and Dixiecrats were discredited in 1948, the civil war inside the Democratic party raged on relentlessly through Truman's entire administration.

Nowhere in the whole Truman record can one point to a single, decisive break-through. All his more important policies reduced themselves to one thing—to buying time for the future. Far from seeking decision, he sought to put off any possible showdown, to perpetuate rather than break the prevailing stalemate.

The mystery of where Truman was heading can be answered simply. All his skills and energies—and he was among our hardest-working Presidents—were directed to standing still.

This persistent irresolution can hardly be blamed on a lack of personal courage. A less courageous—or less stubborn—man, in fact, would not have been so resolutely indecisive. It took courage to order American troops into Korea. It also took courage to dismiss General MacArthur at a time when the Republicans were howling so furiously for Secretary of State Dean Acheson's English mustache. Characteristically, both these moves, each so bold in itself, neatly neutralized themselves into a policy of limited action.

This faculty for turning two bold steps into a halfway measure—no mean trick—was Truman's political hallmark. If it applied solely to our relations with the Soviets one might conclude that it was the only shrewd course left between an inability to make peace and an unwillingness to go to war. But the same middle touch could be seen in Truman's handling of domestic political and economic problems. When he took vigorous action in one direction it was axiomatic that he would contrive soon afterward to move in the conflicting direction. In the end he managed to work himself back close to the center spot of indecision from which he started.

In the fight against inflation, for example, Truman warned again and again of the calamitous consequences of uncontrolled price rises and, just as repeatedly, he followed these warnings with actions which aggravated the dangers of inflation. When World War Two ended, he eloquently called for holding the line against inflation to avoid another boom and collapse such as followed World War One. Still, despite the enormous backlog of spending power left over from wartime savings and profits, Truman supported repeal of the excess profits tax, wage increases and liberal credit policies, all of which pumped still more money into the economy.

Again, when Truman called a special session to enact the Marshall Plan, he demanded legislation to control prices. When the Korean War broke out, however, he pointedly refrained from requesting price control powers, even while asking for the broadest authority to mobilize the economy. Why did he seek price control in 1948 but not in 1950? Could it have been that in 1948 he requested legislation which he knew would not be enacted so he could blame the Republican-controlled Congress for whatever happened, while in 1950 he feared that price powers *would* be given him, leaving him no alibi for failing to check the rise in living costs?

Even after Congress forced price control powers on him, Truman delayed acting for several months, while wholesale prices leaped 14 per cent and the real value of every defense dollar was cut by one fifth. By the spring of 1951, with the renewal of price control at issue, Truman had once again donned the armor of the champion of the voting consumer.

There is a good deal more behind this curious jerkiness which characterized Truman's administration than the politician's common desire to face both ways at the same time. Partly it can be attributed to Truman's personality. Where Franklin Roosevelt radiated serene self-confidence, Truman seemed afflicted by an inner sense of inferiority. It might have been an outgrowth of the shyness forced on him as a child because of nearsightedness, or of the financial failures of his father who lost the family farm speculating on the grain market and was reduced to the job of night watchman, or of Truman's own business reverses and his lateness in getting into politics. Thirty-eight years old when he ran for his first political office, he was fifty when he won his seat in the U.S. Senate. On reaching Washington he felt his inadequacy so keenly that he announced he intended to go to law school at night.

Whatever the psychological reason, Truman's personality seemed to demand that he alternate between crafty caution and asserting himself boldly, even brashly, as if proving something to himself. His usual instinct appeared to be to play things close to his vest, but periodically he had to unbutton his vest and thump his chest.[1]

Many of his explosive flare-ups probably were forced by his irresolution in allowing situations to build up until drastic action became unavoidable. With the RFC and Internal Revenue Bureau frauds for example, he let matters drift for months until it became clear that a major scandal was in the offing and only then instituted his own "shake-up."

The real key to Truman's determined indecision, however, is the fact that he was the product of political deadlock. It was because stalemate fitted his nature so snugly that he became President. Truman can be considered a "political accident" in the sense that Roosevelt's death brought him to the White House. But there was nothing accidental about his being in the line of succession. Only a man exactly like Truman politically, with both his limitations and strong points, could have been the Democratic choice for Roosevelt's successor.

How Presidents Are Made

The ruthless, Darwinian process of natural selection which Truman had to undergo to reach the White House was provided by the fierce struggle between the President and Congress which burst into the open early in 1937 with Roosevelt's proposal to pack the Supreme Court and which has continued to the present.

Roosevelt's winning a third and fourth term has obscured the fact that the last major measure of a New Deal nature which he was able to get through Congress was the Wages and Hours Law in mid-1938. With the failure of the attempted purge of the more conservative Democratic Senators and the Republican gains in the 1938 Congressional election, the anti-New Deal coalition came into undisputed control on Capitol Hill.

---

[1] After he left the White House, Truman spoke out bluntly and sharply on every possible occasion, but this was not how he operated as a President.

After that Roosevelt never could work his will with Congress. Through the power of veto, he usually could hold the rebellious Congress in check. Congress, for its part, was able to block any Roosevelt proposal it disliked.

That this President-Congress deadlock did not paralyze the effective functioning of the government can be credited largely to the development of a new profession in Washington—that of the so-called "border-state" politician, who undertook to act as political brokers between the White House and Capitol Hill.

Although many members of this bloc actually came from the border states, the label really represented a state of mind. In favor of Roosevelt's foreign policy, the border Democrats were middle of the roaders on domestic issues. They leaned more toward the farmer than toward labor, but still were not antilabor. In fact, they consciously made a point of remaining acceptable to both the liberals and conservatives, to both the isolationists and interventionists.

Theirs was the balance of compromise, which they employed to mediate between the Democratic extremes, being careful never to throw their influence finally on one side or the other. Probably the most effective single member of the group, until his elevation to the Supreme Court, was South Carolina's Jimmy Byrnes, whose talents were admirably suited to cloakroom negotiation.

In many ways this border-state bloc, which included Senators like Dick Russell of Georgia and Carl Hatch of New Mexico, constituted the real locus of political power in Washington. Roosevelt soon learned what Truman discovered, that to get any proposal through Congress required the approval of these middle-of-the-road Democrats. Throughout Truman's administration whenever the border-state Democrats swung their influence against the Administration it got beaten.

By political geography and personal temperament, Truman was a typical border-state Senator. Campaign biographies usually describe him as having been one of Roosevelt's most faithful supporters and in his first year in the Senate Truman did go down the line for every New Deal measure. But in the struggle within the Democratic party, which developed during Roosevelt's second term, Truman had a way of straying in and out of both camps.

He backed the resolution introduced early in 1937 by Byrnes condemning sit-down strikes. Although supporting Roosevelt on packing the Supreme Court, Truman voted for Pat Harrison of Mississippi for Senate majority leader against Alben Barkley, the White House choice. A regular member of John Garner's convivial "Board of Education," Truman supported the Vice-President's efforts to block a third term.

Garner had calculated that a majority of the 1936 convention delegates consisted of postmasters, marshals, internal revenue collectors, and other federal officeholders, plus their relatives. Hoping to deprive Roosevelt of this support, Garner contrived the Hatch Act, which barred federal officeholders from political activity. Truman supported the Hatch Act. Early in 1940 he issued a statement, "I am not for anyone for a third term."

Nor was Roosevelt especially friendly toward Truman. Several times Truman complained to James A. Farley, then Democratic National Chairman, of being treated unfairly on patronage matters. Roosevelt preferred to consult with Missouri's Governor Lloyd Stark, who was planning to oppose Truman for the Senate. Late in 1939 Roosevelt tried to get Truman to withdraw in Stark's favor by offering him a $10,000-a-year appointment to the Interstate Commerce Commission.

Truman has described the 1940 Democratic primary as the crucial battle of his entire political career. With Boss Pendergast in jail, the Kansas City organization could not be counted upon for its usual ingenious vote. Truman had no funds of his own for campaign purposes—he couldn't even prevent the family farm from being foreclosed.

One noon at lunch in the office of Edward Halsey, then secretary of the Senate, Truman complained of his difficulties in raising funds for radio talks and political advertising. Byrnes was at the same table. In 1938 Byrnes had taken the lead in opposing Roosevelt's efforts to purge some of the more conservative Senators like Walter George, Bennett Clark, Millard Tydings, Pat McCarran and Guy Gillette. Although Truman was not being openly purged by Roosevelt, Byrnes still felt that no President should interfere in Democratic primary contests. Byrnes sought out Bernard M. Baruch, who had helped finance the fight against the purge, and interested him in Truman's behalf.

Up to this time, Bennett Clark, then senior Senator from Missouri and now a federal judge, had been on the fence taking no active part in the campaign. When Clark decided to support Truman, he also went to Baruch for campaign funds. Again, Baruch contributed generously.

Truman's biographers have made much of his loyalty to those who stuck with him in 1940, like Harry Vaughan and Secretary of the Treasury John Snyder. Yet, during the 1948 campaign, when Baruch refused to join a Democratic fund-raising committee, explaining that he never had accepted such a post before, Truman upbraided Baruch with the taunt that politics was not a one-way street. That action hardly jibes with the legend of Truman's code of unswerving loyalty to his political friends.

It was Baruch, moreover, who sparked the idea which inspired Truman's successful 1948 campaign strategy. Shortly after the Republican Convention, Baruch suggested to Truman that he call the Republican-controlled Congress back into special session, thus providing an arena in which the Republican performance could be matched against the newly drafted Republican platform. Truman was so enthusiastic over this suggestion that he sent Clark Clifford to New York City to discuss the idea more fully with Baruch on the eve of the latter's departure for Europe.

That Baruch should have been interested in Truman by Byrnes, who became a leader of the anti-Truman opposition within the Democratic party, must surely rate as one of the more ironic footnotes in American political history. The irony deepens in view of how the famous Truman Defense Investigating Committee came to be set up.

Early in 1941 Representative Eugene Cox of Georgia, an uncompromising Roosevelt foe, began demanding an investigation of defense spending. The prospect of an inquiry headed by Cox, a zealot by nature, sent shivers through the heads of the defense agencies. One day Roosevelt explained the concern of the Army and Navy to Byrnes, without referring to Cox by name. "I can fix that by putting the investigation into friendly hands," Byrnes assured the President. Under its rules, Byrnes explained, the House could not authorize an investigation for a week but the Senate could act in a few hours.

Some weeks earlier Truman had introduced a resolution for an investigation, which had been referred to the Committee on Audit and Control which Byrnes headed. Calling Truman to his office, Byrnes asked him why he had introduced the resolution? Truman explained that some Missouri contractors were complaining that the big companies were getting all the defense construction contracts. A little pressure on the War Department, he felt, would be a good thing.

"What would you do if the resolution were reported out?" Byrnes asked.

"I know there isn't a chance in the world of your reporting it out," Truman replied. "But if you did I wouldn't conduct the investigation in a way that would hurt defense. You could count on me for that."

Shortly afterward the resolution was reported out and, although no one dreamed it, a new President was in the making.

Truman's able management of the Defense Investigating Committee transformed him into a figure of national importance, earning him a reputation for honesty and fearlessness. What was not widely appreciated was how adroitly Truman appealed to both Democratic factions. Since his Committee's reports were sharply critical of the defense agencies the conservative Democrats were pleased, as were the Republicans. Since the "military" was a favorite committee target the New Dealers also were gratified. An informal understanding existed between the Truman Committee staff and Donald Nelson, the chairman of the War Production Board. Whenever Nelson ran into particular difficulty with the War or Navy departments, he would "leak" his troubles to the Truman Committee, which would then bring pressure on the military.

While the Truman Committee was conducting its able investigations, the attrition of the wartime "Battle of Washington" was steadily shifting the political balance against Roosevelt in favor of Congress. A variety of factors entered into this—the off-year Republican gains in 1942; the vengeful fury of the isolationists who, although supporting the war, drummed constantly with criticism of home front bungling; the failure to bring prices and wages under control; the feuding and squabbling among the government administrators; also the rising resistance in various quarters to wartime restrictions.

In the case of the rubber crisis, the rumbling resentment on Capitol Hill broke through with the passage of a bill which would have disrupted the whole mobilization machinery by setting up a separate rubber administrator independent of Donald Nelson. Roosevelt vetoed the measure. But, confronted with the likelihood that his veto would be overridden, he called upon Baruch, Harvard president James B. Conant, and Karl Compton, then president of the Massachusetts Institute of Technology, to investigate the situation. Their report, unsparing in criticizing the administrative responsibility, saved Roosevelt's veto.

The following month Roosevelt pulled Byrnes off the Supreme Court and made him "assistant president" with an office in the White House. The political significance of this action was largely overlooked. It meant that Congress had gained the ascendancy in Washington. After that, the overhanging political question facing the administration became how to come to terms with the dominant coalition in Congress.

Significantly, all of the new administrators Byrnes brought in either had served in Congress or were acceptable on the Hill. Scrappy Leon Henderson gave way as price administrator to Prentiss Brown, a former Senator. Marvin Jones, a former Congressman, was appointed Food Administrator. Fred Vinson, later to become Chief Justice of the Supreme Court, was brought off the Court of Appeals and named Director of Economic Stabilization.

It was hoped that Vinson, who had been a highly popular member of the House Ways and Means Committee, would be able to charm Congress into accepting a stiff tax bill. When Vinson appeared to request $10,500,000,000 in additional taxes, his former colleagues listened to him with obvious good humor. They laughed at his jokes and chuckled when, in his colloquial way, he took out his lead pencil to do some figuring. But when it came time to write the tax bill they ignored everything Vinson had said.

Only about two billion dollars in new taxes were voted. When Roosevelt vetoed the bill, condemning it a bit too pungently perhaps, the Senate rose in front page revolt. Barkley resigned as majority leader, rebuking the President who made hasty amends. Ironically, few of Roosevelt's actions were more conservative in the true meaning of the term or more justified in the national interest than this veto of so obviously inadequate a tax bill. The Senate, though, was less concerned with the merits of its tax position than with showing Roosevelt who was boss.

Further weakening Roosevelt's influence with Congress were the victories of American arms abroad. That may sound like a paradox. But since a two-thirds vote of the Senate would be needed to approve any peace treaty, Roosevelt had to edge closer to the views of Senator George and Senator Arthur Vandenberg, the Republican leader, who headed the conservative coalition in the Senate. Also, with the war's end in prospect, the struggle over who was to control the political destinies of postwar America broke forth in savage earnestness.

To make sure that the future of America would be shaped without benefit of New Deal planning, the Senate killed the National Resources Planning Board. Instead it created its own Postwar Planning Committee, vigilantly headed by George and Vandenberg, which was determined to stamp "conservative" on every postwar policy.

But the problems of war and peace could not be separated so cleanly. Since war contracts were already being canceled, reconversion policies had to be laid down while the war was still on. The Senate, though, bristled jealously at any suggestion of Administration action. Searching for some means of bridging the paralyzing deadlock of suspicion, Roosevelt asked Baruch to prepare a report on reconversion policies. In formulating some of the policies, as in the contract termination law, what Baruch and his associate, John M. Hancock, really did was to negotiate a treaty of peace between Congress and the Executive, as if they were foreign powers.

By the time the 1944 Democratic convention opened in Chicago, the balance of Washington power had shifted so strongly that Roosevelt's running mate had to be acceptable to the conservative Democrats in the Senate. Henry Wallace, on whom Roosevelt had soured before the end of the 1940 campaign, was never really in the running. He served as a stalkinghorse behind whom labor and the big city delegates could hold their votes and bargaining power. The logistics of the Battle of Washington required that the Vice-Presidency go to one of the border-state Democrats who had made a veritable profession of reconciling the warring Democratic wings. The real choice lay between Byrnes and Truman, who had gone to Chicago to nominate Byrnes.

Three principal objections were raised to Byrnes. Negro leaders opposed him as a Southerner. Ed Flynn, the Democratic boss closest to Roosevelt, argued that Byrnes would "hurt the ticket" since he had been converted from Catholicism. Then, as "assistant president," Byrnes had been too forceful for the liking of some labor leaders.

Truman's record, by contrast, could hardly have been more shrewdly tailored to the needs of a compromise candidate. Usually a safe administration vote, he enjoyed the asset of having been opposed for re-election by Roosevelt, which reassured the more conservative Democrats. He had supported Roosevelt in the World Court and Neutrality battles, yet two of the Senate's leading isolationists, Burton Wheeler and Bennett Clark, were the men Truman usually looked to for political guidance. Although acceptable to labor, Truman had opposed the sit-down strikes and had voted for the Smith-Connally antistrike act, but not to override Roosevelt's veto of it.

Truman had voted for price control but against the wartime limitation of $25,000 a year on salaries. He had favored all relief appropriations but had helped kill the WPA theater project.

In nominating Truman the embattled Democrats actually were voting to keep the line of succession to the Presidency from passing to either the Northern or Southern Democrats. The 1948 convention found the deadlocked Democrats in the same plight—with the same result. When the Philadelphia convention opened, the clamor to ditch Truman was joined in by such factional rivals as Dixiecrat Southerners and the Americans for Democratic Action, by James Roosevelt and big city bosses like Jacob Arvey of Chicago and Frank Hague of Jersey City. Their unanimity in desiring to get rid of Truman was surpassed only by their inability to agree on anyone to take his place.

This same necessity to preserve the precarious balance within the party dictated the nomination of Barkley, another border-state Senator, as Vice-President.

The Red Queen

Compromise made Truman President and—despite the controversies he stirred, the officials he fired and the terrible-tempered letters he wrote —compromise remained the unswerving objective of his Presidency. If this has been obscured it is because of a failure to appreciate that the only form of compromise possible in Truman's administration was stale-mate.

Broadly speaking, any middle-of-the-road politician faces one of two prospects. He can allow himself to be torn in two by the forces he is attempting to conciliate. Or he can draw strength from both irrecon-cilable extremes by playing one off against the other. In view of Tru-man's Senate record it is not surprising that he followed the latter course.

His role was to raise all issues but to settle none. He repeatedly pressed vigorous recommendations on Congress knowing they would be rejected—not only on inflation control but on civil rights and repeal of the Taft-Hartley Law. During the 1948 campaign he could think of send-ing Justice Vinson to Moscow on a "peace mission," not long after he had publicly denounced the Soviet leaders as men whose word could not be trusted. One doesn't have to question Truman's sincerity to observe that he appeared happiest when able to make a dramatic show of activity, secure in the knowledge that nothing much was going to happen.

Harsh as that estimate may sound it was Truman's claim to greatness. There is much to be said, after all, for the mariner who, knowing that he cannot quiet the storm, contrives somehow to stay afloat until the storm has died down of itself. The major problems Truman grappled with were mainly inherited. All were fearfully difficult, perhaps impossible of har-monious solution. As the President of the last center of hope in the world,

Truman could hardly confess helplessness. Unable either to reconcile or to ignore the forces in conflict, he tried to stall them off hoping that time would make decision unnecessary.

The contradictions in Truman's actions vanish when one appreciates that actually he dreaded moving too far in any direction, of doing too much or too little. Even his acrobatic economics find their consistency in the fact that he was afraid of both rising and falling prices. When prices went up, Truman wanted them to come down. When they started down, as in 1949, he would become frightened of a possible recession and start up the government's inflationary credit engines. Truman's apologists may contend that this is what is known as a "managed economy" —but the motivating force was to put off politically painful economic adjustments.

Similarly, in foreign affairs Truman would lash out boldly when his hand was forced, as in Korea. When it came to seeing things through, however, he would drag action, as if hoping for something to turn up to make it unnecessary to go too far. Not for two years after the North Atlantic Defense Pact was signed was anything much done to implement it, although in the interval the Soviets exploded their first atomic bomb. So leisurely was the timetable for mobilization laid down in 1950, that it really represented a gamble that the Soviet Union did not intend to go to war. Our slow rate of rearming could be justified only on the basis of faith in Stalin's desire for peace.

If over the course of his Presidency Truman's personal standing rocketed up and down like a roller coaster, it was not because he, himself, was so erratic, but because of changes in the stresses and strains of the forces in conflict.

As the costs and frustrations of continued stalemate grew more burdensome the middle ground on which Truman pitched his political tent tended to crack and crumble. The tensions of office told on him personally as, like Alice's Red Queen, he had to run ever faster in order to stand still. In the glaring light of threatened showdown, all his weaknesses became mercilessly exposed—the wavering evasions, the lack of any policy for achieving decision.

But if that was the source of his weakness, it also explains his astonishing recoveries from the abysmally low levels of public esteem to which he fell at times. The choices of action which Truman tried to evade were all extremely difficult ones, such as splitting the Democratic party or letting the economy run loose to find its natural level, or precipitating a showdown with the Soviets which might cause them to back down but could also bring on war. Truman's constant gamble was that the American public, when confronted with the unpleasant implications of decisive action, would prefer to continue with his policy of calculated drift.

The secret of Truman's political vitality was that he shrewdly planted himself on the furiously dead center of stalemate to which irreconcilables must repair if they are to make a bargain. Whenever the balance of the raging conflict shifted in favor of conciliation, Truman inherited the situation. But could the stalemated forces be held at arm's length indefinitely? Eventually wouldn't they wrench apart whoever stood in the middle?

There we have the essential drama of Truman's Presidency. It was the drama of a man fighting stubbornly and, yes, courageously, to avoid decision. Whether, in standing against these pressures, Truman was a pitiful or heroic figure cannot be answered finally today. Although his place in history is set, as the man who bought time, one all-crucial question remains unanswered:

In whose favor has time been working?

Has time been operating to strengthen the cause of peace? Or has it been giving the Soviet Union a breathing spell to overcome its weaknesses and amass the strength to make an eventual war bloodier and more difficult to win?

Has time been working to invigorate and stabilize our economy or has it been merely piling the inflationary bricks ever higher for a bigger crash?

Has time, in its not always obvious workings, been managing to bring into existence the conditions which will consolidate the Democrats as the nation's majority party? Or have its clashing elements been driven ever more hopelessly apart until they must split?

In short, have the processes of time in these atomic-riven days been of a self-healing or a cancerous nature?

If the verdict of history vindicates Truman,[2] he will rate as one of our greatest Presidents, as much for what he did not do as for what he did. If the verdict proves hostile, Truman is likely to appear as another James Buchanan, who also considered himself a crafty, dexterous politician, but who wasted the last remaining years of conciliation and left the White House with his own party ready to break up and a disunited country drifting into bloody war.

Whatever the judgment of the future, it should be clear that Truman was incapable of breaking the stalemate which gripped us and was probably even unwilling to try. Deadlock was the essence of the man. Stalemate was his Midas touch.

This same question was bound to dominate any administration that succeeded Truman's. Could this deadlock be broken or were we fated to continue to drift in irresolution?

Before attempting to answer that question it would be well to examine this stalemate carefully. In existence since 1938, it has been no simple thing to be resolved by a mere change of tenants in the White House. Nor has this deadlock been solely political in any narrow sense of the

---

[2]By 1965 the verdict of history seemed to favor Truman on domestic issues and in Europe but remained a question mark in Asia.

word. The harsh fact we face is that virtually all of the major political, social, and economic strands of our times have become twisted into one Gordian knot which seems to defy either unraveling or cutting.

There can be no question that the American people have been treading knee-deep in one of the gravest political crises in our history. In my judgment that crisis can be summed up roughly in these terms:

The overhanging threat of war requires a strengthening of the Presidency. Only through Presidential leadership can national unity be achieved, a coherent foreign policy formulated and the resources of the nation mobilized to meet the needs of the cold war. Yet, domestically, the prevailing political currents are directed at weakening Presidential power. This attack on the Presidency does not arise primarily out of misgivings over the personal capacities of the individual holders of the office, although that may be a factor. Mainly the conflict stems from the fact that the Presidency has become the symbol of the political revolution wrought by Roosevelt, while Congress has become the symbol of the counterrevolution which has been seeking to reverse the New Deal.

That is not to imply that the New Deal revolution was good and the counterrevolution is bad. The issues involved are not that simple. My point is that at a time when the threat of atomic war makes political unity desperately urgent, the heritage of political conflict which Roosevelt left continues to divide the nation.

Politically, we are passing through a perilous twilight period. So torn and divided is the established majority that the compromise of mutual frustration is the only harmony its clashing elements can find. Yet, there is no party realignment in sight which promises to bring a new majority into existence. At a time when the capacity of government to achieve decision was never more important, indecision appears to be what holds together our party balance.

Whatever the result of the 1952 election this problem will remain— can the American people overcome their internal dissensions sufficiently to re-establish an effective political majority? This unity will not be achieved merely through some dramatic appeal to patriotism. If many Americans today would weaken the powers of government, it is because they fear how those powers may be used domestically.

Behind all our fitful political tossings, I believe, stirs this search for a new domestic political balance. Essentially it is an effort to reconcile the many changes wrought by the Roosevelt Revolution. In the chapters which follow we will trace through these changes in terms of the major elements which comprise the Roosevelt coalition. We will follow this coalition through three successive stages, showing:

First, how this coalition emerged, from origins not generally appreciated, to become the new, normal majority party in the country.

Second, how it came to be deadlocked in self-conflict by its own successes and, in the process, stalemated the Roosevelt Revolution. In brief, what the New Deal did was to give the rival Democratic elements the strength with which to fight one another for control of the Democratic party.

Third, how the cold war thrust up new issues which aggravated the tensions within the coalition to the breaking point.

Must the Roosevelt coalition be smashed before the national unity that is so sorely needed can be attained? Can the Republicans build a new coalition which can deal with the problems of this time of troubles?

Michael Rogin
McCARTHYISM AS MASS POLITICS

The major question in any consideration of Joe McCarthy and the "ism" he called forth is how aberrant a phenomenon they were in American politics. Certainly, anti-communism antedated McCarthy's discovery of its power and had been a primary force in domestic and foreign politics since 1945. Within a bipartisan consensus, the major issue of the period was whose anti-communism would prevail: the liberal's or the conservative's? As a conservative Republican, McCarthy flogged the liberal Democratic administration with the anti-communist whip. In the controversy that followed conservatives overlooked Truman's own campaign against bureaucrats suspected of being "soft" on the Reds. The administration was chastened enough by the Communist victory in China to go to war in Korea lest it be accused of "losing" more Asian terrain to Red aggression. Liberals supported measures taken against "security risks" in sensitive government positions. Yet, try as the liberals and their congressional allies might, Joe McCarthy, Richard Nixon, and others of the Republican Right pre-empted the anti-communist issue and blamed the Democratic Left for Communist gains in East Europe and China. Right wing Republicans stamped liberals as "pink" for sympathies bordering upon the Red ideology, liberal disclaimers notwithstanding.

In this reading Michael Rogin argues that McCarthyism remained primarily a conservative Republican phenomenon. McCarthy's following, however, represented a broad sector of American society. Liberal politicians were rendered ineffectual when they concurred with militant anti-communism but accused the Junior Senator from Wisconsin of hitting the wrong targets with the wrong weapons. Few Democrats dared to say that anti-communism might be an inflated issue. Accordingly, some liberals endorsed repressive measures like the Internal Security Act of 1950 and thereby became accomplices to McCarthyism. But McCarthy insisted that libertarian objections to his methods were prissy; fighting authoritarianism demanded authoritarianism, and civil liberties went by the board in that phony war. The liberals' horror at being branded "fellow-travelers," a crime in the right-wing book, seemed almost comic to McCarthy and his cohorts. In the end, liberals were saved by the grossness of McCarthy, his lack of real political power in the Senate, and the electorate's indifference to an increasingly tiresome cry of "wolf."

Yet it remained for historians to discover which people McCarthy appealed to during 1950–1954, why they believed his charges, and why liberals foundered in establishing anti-communist credentials. Finally did McCarthy have a lingering impact upon policy decisions in the sixties? Or, to put it another way, did McCarthyism need McCarthy?

The Elites

Conservative Republican activists provided McCarthy with the core of his enthusiastic support. In addition, groups ranging from Catholic Democratic workers to conservative southern senators contributed to McCarthy's power—the workers by verbal approval in the polls, the senators by their actions and silences in Washington. Having examined the contribution of the masses to McCarthyism, we turn now to the elites.

The pluralists argue that McCarthy was not simply attacking Communists, but also had as his targets the eastern, educated, financial, political, and intellectual elite. There is merit in this view; nevertheless, McCarthy enjoyed the support of some wealthy and influential political elites, and even some of those he attacked played a role in augmenting his power. The existence of a powerful Republican right wing, the new appeal of the issues of communism and foreign policy, and McCarthy's own tactical brilliance raised McCarthyism to a place of national prominence. But there was more to McCarthy's success than this. The response of a variety of political elites—by no means simply allies of the Wisconsin senator—enabled him to harness himself to the everyday workings of American politics. Those already part of this machinery often did not approve of McCarthy. Some, like moderate Republicans in their battle with the Democrats, congressmen in their battle with the executive, newspapers in their search for news, thought they could use him.

From *The Intellectuals and McCarthy* by Michael Paul Rogin. Copyright The M.I.T. Press. Reprinted by permission of the publisher.

Others, like southern Democrats, saw no need to treat McCarthy differently than they treated other senators. Still others, moderate Republicans in their desire for party unity, liberal Democrats in their desire
for reelection, were afraid of him. Political and psychological reasons
made a variety of political elites anxious to avoid a confrontation with
McCarthy. Until it became clear to them that McCarthyism was more
than politics as usual, they failed effectively to challenge it.

We have already pointed to the importance of the political structure in
influencing McCarthy's mass support. Regardless of attitudes toward
civil liberties and even toward McCarthy in the abstract, traditional political
allegiances kept the workers in the Democratic Party in the 1950's and business and professional men in the GOP. McCarthy's "mass" appeal did not
register directly in politics because many who supported him cared more
about the Democratic Party, the New Deal, their trade unions, or their
wives and families than they cared about McCarthy. They therefore did not
break their traditional political habits.

Just as the political structure limited the sustenance McCarthy could
derive from the grass roots, so it influenced the behavior of political elites.
We look now at conservative Republicans and GOP moderates, at
the Senate and the southern Democrats, at the press and at the liberals.

Most of those who mobilized behind McCarthy at the national level
were conservative politicians and publicists, businessmen, and retired
military leaders discontented with the New Deal, with bureaucracy,
and with military policy. Of nineteen businessmen in the leadership of
the Ten Million Americans mobilizing for McCarthy, only one had inherited wealth.[1] These men had been part of the Republican right wing
before McCarthy; they were joined by an occasional ex-agrarian radical
like Burton Wheeler. Numbers of former Marxist intellectuals such as
Louis Budenz, James Burnham, and John Chamberlain became McCarthy publicists, but they lacked political influence or popular support.
The political conservatism of the elite supporters of McCarthy ran
the gamut of domestic and international policy.

We have already discussed the historical reasons for McCarthy's conservative support. The evolution of politics in the Middle West and
the nation had had two political consequences for conservatives. They
were in heretofore unprecedented positions of political power at the
state level and political weakness at the national level. Their desperation is suggested by Taft's famous advice to McCarthy, "If one case
doesn't work, then bring up another."[2] This political elite sustained Mc-
Carthy. It helped dramatize his issues and fight his fights. Conservative
Republican activists provided money and enthusiasm for the Senator's

---

[1] Cf. Paul E. Breslow, "The Relationship between Ideology and Socio-Economic
Background in a Group of McCarthyite Leaders" (unpublished Master's thesis, Department of Political Science, University of Chicago, 1955), pp. 82–103.

[2] Quoted in Nelson Polsby, "Towards an Explanation of McCarthyism," *op. cit.*,
p. 263.

cause. In Wisconsin, for example, McCarthy did not mobilize the mass of voters. But he did mobilize the local elites of the Republican Party. The near-hysterical enthusiasm with which they identified with the Senator gave the movement its emotional intensity. The regular Wisconsin Republican organization—in an action almost unprecedented in American politics—put up a candidate to oppose Wisconsin's other incumbent Republican senator because he had not voted against McCarthy's censure.

How to explain the mentality of these McCarthy supporters? Lipset, analyzing American politics as a conflict between values of achievement and egalitarian populism, argues that political excesses such as McCarthyism derive from America's egalitarian strain.[3] Thus it is argued that Britain was spared a McCarthyite episode because the populace had deference for its established leaders. But a more important difference between Britain and the United States on this score is the character of conservative politics of the two countries. The British example suggests by comparison what American conservatives were willing to do.[4] Certainly these conservatives were unrestrained by aristocratic traditions, but to ascribe this to populist values rather than to the capitalist-achievement ethic is perverse. In a Protestant, competitive society, an individual can blame only himself for failure, and the fear of failure appears at all levels of the social structure. The attendant insecurities and frustrations will often produce conspiracy theories, scapegoat hunting, and terrible resentments. McCarthy was supported by the activists of a party that emphasizes free enterprise, achievement, and individual responsibility. The politics of these people seems more sensibly explained by their preoccupations with achievement and failure than by their populistic concerns.

McCarthy, however, was not simply another conservative Republican. Mundt, Wherry, and a host of other right-wing Republicans had sought to dramatize the communism issue, but only McCarthy succeeded. And McCarthy succeeded while the others did not in part because of his thoroughgoing contempt for the rules of political controversy. This contempt stemmed partly from his career pattern. McCarthy came from relatively low social origins, and was elected to the Senate without either the inherited status position of some senators or the record of political or professional accomplishment of others. In the period from 1947 to 1956, this was true of only 4 percent of America's senators. Moreover, McCarthy did not conform to Senate folkways; thus he voted with small minorities against large majorities more than most of his colleagues. Clearly, McCarthy had less commitment to established norms than other

---

[3] S. M. Lipset, *The First New Nation, op. cit.,* pp. 1–2, 262–273, 318–343.

[4] There were, of course, other reasons for the absence of something similar to McCarthyism in Britain. Unlike America, Britain was not entering the world stage as a preeminent power for the first time. The Communist "menace" was much more salient in America. But McCarthyism arose out of the response of American elites to these new challenges, not primarily out of the response of American masses.

conservative Republicans; in fact, his career pattern and behavior in the Senate resembled Langer's.[5]

It is important to stress McCarthy's uniqueness, but the pluralists stress it for the wrong reasons. McCarthy's significance as an individual did not derive from new alliances he personally mobilized to assault the social fabric. It lay rather in the fact that he personally, not the masses or even elites behind him, did tremendous damage and wielded great power. And this personal power in large part derived from his willingness not to play by the rules—he was, after all, an extremist. But without the issue of communism and without the enthusiasm he evoked from right-wing Republicans who did conform to Senate folkways and orthodox career patterns, he would have been merely what Langer was—a maverick without influence.

Moderate Republicans were clearly less enthusiastic about McCarthy than the conservative wing of the party, yet without their support as well McCarthy would have been far less powerful. Eastern and moderate Republicans and their allies desired political power, and were also genuinely concerned about the Communist question. For a long time, they acquiesced in McCarthy's power. Viereck writes that McCarthy's targets were not the Communists, but those who had always stood for the rule of law and moderation, like Senator Watkins.[6] By the time Watkins headed the committee which recommended McCarthy's censure, he was an anti-McCarthy pillar of strength. Earlier, however, he had been one of many Republican signers of a statement attacking the Truman administration and the Gillette committee investigation of McCarthy. The official Republican leadership did not sign this pro-McCarthy statement, but Watkins and other future McCarthy critics did.[7]

There are other examples of support for McCarthy by moderate Republicans. Senator Carlson, an Eisenhower Republican, hammered hard at the Communist issue during the early 1950's. He called McCarthy's 1952 primary victory a "great victory."[8] Later that year, Eisenhower deleted a favorable reference to General Marshall from a Wisconsin campaign speech under McCarthy's pressure. After his victory, the President decided that the use of his office to attack McCarthy would split the Republican Party and aid the Democrats. A timid chief executive, Eisenhower also wanted to avoid making enemies, particularly in Congress. Orders went out telling members of the administration not to criticize

[5]Cf. Donald R. Matthews, *U.S. Senators and Their World* (New York: Random House, Vintage Books, 1960), pp. 64–66, 254–255 and letter from Professor Matthews to the author.

[6]Peter Viereck, "The Revolt Against the Elite," in Daniel Bell (ed.), *The New American Right, op. cit.,* p. 111.

[7]Frank Kendrick, "McCarthy and the Senate," *op. cit.,* p. 145.

[8]*Ibid.,* pp. 173–174; K. E. Meyer, "The Politics of Loyalty: From La Follette to McCarthy in Wisconsin: 1918–1952" (unpublished Ph.D. dissertation, Department of Political Science, Princeton University, 1956), pp. 90–91.

McCarthy—and those like Stassen who did were publicly humiliated. In appointing a McCarthy man as Personnel Officer, Eisenhower gave the Senator an effective veto over appointments to the State Department. He made every effort to avoid a fight with him over the army. "Among the opponents of McCarthy in the administration (and he also had friends)," reports one chronicler, "the view was that McCarthy should be handled behind closed doors." If McCarthy benefited from airing his charges to the public, he benefited also from moderate unwillingness to combat him openly.[9] By 1954 moderate Republicans were appeasing McCarthy because they feared splitting the party more than because they hoped they could use him. But in both cases McCarthy was able to capitalize on existing political alliances. He had succeeded in harnessing respectable elites and respectable institutions, to which the populace paid deference.

McCarthy's popularity itself in large part depended on his moderate Republican support. Before the 1952 elections gave the GOP control of the Senate, most Americans had not heard of McCarthy and only 15 percent had a favorable opinion of him. By the middle of 1953, McCarthy had sent Cohn and Schine to Europe, had control of a Senate committee, and had been legitimized by the Republican Party; 35 percent of the population approved of him. Having achieved the instruments of Senate power and publicity, McCarthy could keep his name before the public day after day.[10]

In this achievement, he was aided not only by the moderate Republicans but also by the Senate and by the press. Seniority gave McCarthy his committee chairmanship, and Senate traditions permitted him virtually unchecked power. Individual senators were unwilling to interfere with committee prerogatives or with the power of McCarthy as chairman, since their own personal influence depended in large part upon their own committee positions. Many senators also feared that interferences with McCarthy's activities as an individual senator could later rebound to their disadvantage; they feared creating unpleasant precedents. The famed individualism encouraged by the Senate thus worked to McCarthy's advantage.[11]

Moreover, McCarthy capitalized on congressional-executive rivalry. Al-

[9]Cf. Michael Straight, *Trial by Television*, *op. cit.*, p. 140. Cf. also Norman A. Graebner, *The New Isolationism* (New York: Ronald Press, 1956), p. 199; Telford Taylor, *Grand Inquest* (New York: Simon and Schuster, 1955), pp. 114–123; Aaron Wildavsky, "Exploring the Content of McCarthyism," *The Australian Outlook* (June 1955).

[10]Dwaine Marvick (in personal conversation) has suggested some relevant findings from survey data on members of the John Birch Society in California. The Birchers justify their views by pointing to prestigious members of their local communities who are also Birchers. As in support for McCarthy, deference can be more important than anti-elitism.

[11]Cf. Frank Kendrick, "McCarthy and the Senate," *op. cit.*, pp. 317–323; Aaron Wildavsky, "Exploring the Content of McCarthyism," *op. cit.*

ways a factor in American politics, this institutional conflict was at its height in the McCarthy period. The growing power of the executive, attributable to the New Deal and to the importance of foreign policy, produced congressional concern over the decline in congressional prerogatives and prestige. Relations were further strained by the presence in Washington of New Deal administrators, so different in outlook from the more particularistic, locally oriented congressmen. McCarthy tried to make himself the champion of congressional power and at least succeeded in exploiting the executive-congressional rift.[12]

The Senate in the McCarthy period was dominated by conservative Republicans and southern Democrats. About the former enough has already been said. The southern Democrats, embodying the institutional traditions of the Senate, were unwilling to jeopardize the prerogatives of an individual senator or of the Senate as a whole. As McClellan of Arkansas remarked, "I do not want to do unto one of my colleagues what I would not want him to do unto me under the same circumstances."[13] Southern senators were not pro McCarthy. But they were perhaps not unhappy to see their northern liberal colleagues and the Fair Deal administration embarrassed. (Reprisals from the populist masses hardly worried these safe-seat senators, particularly since southerners opposed this Catholic Republican in the polls.)

Without the newspaper treatment he received, McCarthy's impact would have been far milder. Large numbers of newspapers, particularly outside the major metropolitan centers, actively supported him.

The respectable press opposed the Wisconsin senator, which suggests to the pluralists McCarthy's absence of elite backing.[14] But McCarthy benefited from their treatment of him in the news columns. Desiring to dramatize the news, the wire services featured McCarthy's activities without regard to their importance. Stories and headlines gave the impression that charges were facts.[15] Even *The New York Times* fostered the myth that McCarthy's investigations had some connection with demonstrated espionage. The coverage of the other anti-McCarthy press was no better. McCarthy's popularity in the polls reached its all-time high during the well-publicized Fort Monmouth investigations.

Eventually *The Times* realized that McCarthy had taken them in. Columnist Peter Kihss concluded a series of articles setting the record straight (lacking the prominence of the earlier stories) with the observation,

For the newspapers Fort Monmouth has been a lesson that will not be quickly forgotten, but the reading public should understand that it is difficult if

---

[12]Aaron Wildavsky, "Exploring the Content of McCarthyism," *loc. cit.*
[13]Quoted in *ibid.*
[14]Daniel Bell, "Interpretations of American Politics," in Daniel Bell (ed.), *The New American Right, op. cit.*, p. 25; Leslie Fiedler, "McCarthy," *op. cit.*, p. 13.
[15]Cf. Jack Anderson and Ronald W. May, *McCarthy the Man, The Senator, The Ism* (Boston: Beacon Press, 1952), pp. 266–270.

not impossible to ignore charges by Senator McCarthy just because they are usually proved exaggerated or false. The remedy lies with the reader.[16]

Thus newsmen like politicians sought to lay the blame for McCarthy's prominence on the public and argue that their own hands were tied. Newsmen like Kihss often justify their activities by saying that they print the news and the news is what happens. To understand the role of the press in the McCarthy period one must realize that a figure who gains notoriety sells more papers, and that to ignore such a figure is to risk losing sales to competing publishers.[17]

Finally, many prominent liberals failed actively to oppose McCarthy. Here McCarthy could feed upon feelings of guilt and insecurity pervading the nation's capital. Democratic politicians and government bureaucrats had to adjust to replacing the Popular Front, the New Deal, and the wartime Soviet alliance with the new cold war attitudes. This change weakened the will of the elites to resist McCarthy, since they felt vaguely guilty of his accusations.[18] In addition, liberal politicians were simply afraid of McCarthy's power to retaliate at the polls. They saw Millard Tydings oppose McCarthy and go down to defeat in 1950, William Benton attack him and lose his Senate seat in 1952. The evidence suggests that although McCarthy may have contributed to Tydings' defeat he had no impact on Benton's. Certainly his power at the polls was greatly exaggerated.

Nevertheless, Lippmann and others argued at the time that liberals had lost the confidence of the country over the issues of communism and foreign policy which sustained McCarthy and that only the moderates and conservatives could stop him. If this argument is true, it cuts both ways. For if the moderate Republicans and southern Democrats had this power, why did they not exercise it earlier? McCarthy's influence and his popularity reached their heights during the Eisenhower administration. If moderates and conservatives can take credit for McCarthy's defeat, they must share a large portion of the blame for his successes.

The failure of American elites to confront McCarthy immeasurably enhanced his power. This unwillingness cannot be explained as a response to mass pressures. But if these existed in the minds of observers of McCarthyism, surely they were also in the minds of the political actors themselves. If the populist attitudes of the masses did not enhance McCarthy's power, what of leadership fear of popular pressure? Shils, for example, argues that a "populist" system of authority weakens the will of elites in America. Political leaders lack confidence in themselves, it is alleged, because the value system promotes suspicion of independent leadership. The environment of the legislator makes him too willing to

[16]Cf. Reinhard Luthin, *American Demagogues, op. cit.*, pp. 293–294.
[17]Cf. Nelson W. Polsby and Aaron B. Wildavsky, *Presidential Elections* (New York: Scribner's, 1964), pp. 40–46.
[18]This point was suggested, in correspondence, by Nelson Polsby.

accede to real or imagined popular whims. In this view, the people may not seek to wreak their passions against the body politic, but the politicians, victims of populist rhetoric, will accede to demands which seem to speak for popular passions. Where the politician can look to other sources of authority besides the people—institutions, established procedures, groups, values—he can be more autonomous.[19]

About the desire for elite autonomy more will be said subsequently.[20] We can agree now, however, that one would have preferred elites whose will to resist McCarthy had been firmer. But to blame this weakness on a populist system of authority, holding out pluralist values as alternatives, is too simple a view. An urge to give in to real or imagined popular passions is not a democratic virtue. But the question is not the attitudes of the people in the abstract or the attitudes of the leaders about the people in the abstract. The question is what one wants protection against. Groups often use "populist" rhetoric to insulate themselves from popular control. They may speak of the grass roots to protect their bailiwicks against outside, popularly supported political leaders. A wider political constituency, often sustained by "populist" rhetoric and appeals to principle, can strengthen political leadership against group pressure. It can help political elites confront such figures as McCarthy. The relation between populism and pluralism is more complex than is suggested by the image of practical and procedure-conscious organizations opposed to ideological and authoritarian masses. The "masses" did not produce McCarthyism in America, and groups and their leaders alone did not save us from him.

Consider first the specific reasons for elite tractability, called forth by the nature of McCarthy's issue. Other movements—agrarian radical ones for example—have played on a populist system of authority without achieving anything like the inroads and the power of McCarthy. Racist Governor George Wallace captured the support of masses of northern, urban whites during the 1964 presidential primaries without hindering the passage of a pending civil rights bill. But McCarthy's situation was uniquely favorable. On the one hand, he benefited from the nondivisiveness of his issue: many groups, elites, and institutions were for "Wall Street," the railroads, or "the interests," but no one was for communism. But at the same time, McCarthy could capitalize on divisions and insecurities within the elite structure. Wallace was up against a northern elite consensus on civil rights (created, paradoxically enough, by mass Negro pressure). But McCarthy fed upon Republican suspicion of Democrats, Democratic anxieties about their past policies, and a mood of temporization and passivity in Washington.

Second, here as elsewhere the symbiosis between "populism" and prag-

---

[19]Cf. Edward Shils, *The Torment of Secrecy, op. cit.,* pp. 46–47, 102–109.
[20]This argument is developed more fully in the following chapter.

matism cannot go unnoticed. One might blame elite weakness on the instrumentalism and pragmatism of political leaders, which made them less willing to stand up for principle and more willing to give in to the line of least resistance. It was easier to remain silent than to oppose McCarthy, so many remained silent. Individuals did not want to risk their personal gains by opposing the Wisconsin senator. Perhaps the business orientation and narrow self-concern in the society make politicians unwilling to stand up for the commonweal. The principled politics feared by the pluralists might have been an asset here.

Third, institutional restraints and traditional allegiances may be alternatives to populist values, but they augmented McCarthy's power. The Senator capitalized on the routine politics of the political stratum—Senate traditions, executive-legislative rivalry, Republican party loyalty, anxiety to keep disputes out of the limelight. The general unwillingness of American politicians to assume responsibility for controversial actions became increasingly bizarre during the years of McCarthy's hegemony. This monumental insistence that politics continue as usual is surely a classic example of the banality of evil.

One would have hoped for a greater presidential appreciation of the dignity of the executive branch. One would have welcomed greater respect for the rule of law and for individual rights. Yet when Eisenhower finally fought for executive dignity and the rule of law, he had to resort to the instruments of publicity and open confrontation. Only with the publicity of the Army-McCarthy hearings did American politicians gain the confidence and integrity openly to oppose and then to ignore McCarthy.

Temporization and surrender having failed, the Eisenhower administration finally challenged McCarthy directly. Big businessmen who had heretofore supported the Senator began to back away, as he attacked their administration and an institution (the army) with which they identified.[21] After the censure, the Senate "club" would have even less than usual to do with him.[22] The respectable press, allegedly forced to publicize McCarthy's charges because they were news, stopped giving him coverage. Meanwhile, the Korean War had ended, and the tensions of the cold war eased. Observers agree that McCarthy's influence then reached a low point from which it never recovered. All McCarthy had left was the support of those in the populace basically hostile to American society. Undaunted, perhaps even encouraged by his attacks on the institutions in American life from which they were alienated, these anomic "masses" continued to support the Wisconsin Senator. They had no more influence on his power than they had ever had. When McCarthy became a real antagonist of the institutions which conservatives

---

[21]Charles Murphy, "McCarthy and the Businessmen," op. cit., pp. 100, 216.
[22]Cf. William S. White, Citadel (New York: Harper, 1965), p. 137.

repeated—the Republican Party, the Senate, and the Army—he lost influence both among moderately conservative political leaders and among the population at large. As McCarthy became "radical," he lost his hold on American politics.

William L. O'Neill
A DULL DECADE

Coming of age in the fifties was not so arid an experience as some pundits have advised us. To be sure, it lacked the excitement of the liberated sixties and seventies. The generation which went to college after 1953 lingered in a twilight period, being too young to identify with the World War II generation and too old for the war babies. It reached maturity too late to be drafted for the Korean War and too soon for Vietnam. Many of the college men in that generation viewed military service as a strategic withdrawal from society while they read, thought, and traveled at the expense of Uncle Sam; unlike many of their younger brothers of the sixties, they did not fear the draft as Russian roulette. College students in the fifties were not alienated from their society, but they were not necessarily enamored with the America that confronted them. In fact, they deplored its materialism, conformity, and injustice. That these collegians were a silent generation did not signal their assent; they were bewildered, and they had been taught to fear.

It is true that in the fifties certain ideas were taboo and that reading of them was proscribed. Even so, college students read Lenin and Marx if only to fulfill class assignments. They did not study Marcuse, but C. Wright Mills served as a more readable and empirical revolutionary. They relished Mort Sahl's iconoclastic political humor, and some reveled in the poetic profanity of Allen Ginsberg's Howl. McCarthyism, for them, was a double-edged sword: it inhibited many students and dared some to investigate excluded ideas for themselves. Pariah cultures within our society which had been visited only by dilettantes gradually were included in the era's popular culture. Students discovered the Negro idiom by embracing a hybrid rock and roll music. It became increasingly conventional to deplore conventionality. Students in the fifties were not candid about sex even though they were free enough to make their elders wonder about the looseness of the younger generation. Parents, the youth of the thirties, deplored their children's lack of idealism. William L. O'Neill writes that in the fifties "Students did not look forward to a life of challenge, high adventure, and great profits, but rather to one of modest achievement, numerous fringe benefits, and a reasonable security."

Considering the three economic recessions of the affluent society, could young people's expectations be so different from those of their intimidated parents? Perhaps too few committed themselves to social crusades, but most rejected the foreign crusades for the ideal of democracy which the World War II generation imposed upon the students of the sixties. Many celebrated the advent of Fidel Castro; many went to law school to become the civil rights lawyers who demanded equal protection of the law for Negroes in Mississippi; and others earned doctorates in the social sciences in order to teach and write about America "like it is."

A decade after their graduations, most of the students of the fifties admitted their admiration and even envy for the emancipated young people of the sixties. They admitted that by comparison their college years had been a "very boring time."

The Nineteen Fifties

Even for those who lived through it, the decade of the 1950s (that is, the period that began around 1948 and ended in 1960 or 1961) has an aura of unreality. Could we really have believed that J. D. Salinger was a writer of great moral power and acumen? Did we honestly think America ripe for subversion? Was Elvis Presley actually considered a threat to established morals? Alas, these and other views, which now seem ludicrous at best, were held not only by the uninformed and unenlightened but by people of taste and intelligence as well. How is such a peculiar state of affairs to be explained?

To begin with, the Cold War had a depressing effect on American morale. World War II had been a great and terrible event, yet it had also been a reassuring one. The struggle was plainly and unambiguously fought between the forces of good and evil. Truth crushed to earth rose again and overcame error with fire and the sword. Both the physical power and the ideology of fascism were destroyed. Even more, all this was accomplished with little sacrifice, while the high level of American prosperity during the war was further evidence of divine favor. The Cold War changed all this. Russia's emergence as the chief threat to world peace and freedom, or so it was thought, retrospectively discredited the wartime coalition and, to a degree, the war effort itself. Unlike Nazism, communism seemed to have a broad and persistent popular appeal. The accomplishments of Soviet Russia, the rise of large Communist parties in Europe and elsewhere, and, most of all, the revolution in China undermined American self-confidence. While abroad the nation increasingly reacted to communism as if the challenge it posed was chiefly military, at home the threat was perceived differently. An excessively concrete foreign policy based on guns and money was matched by an excessively abstract domestic response concerned mainly with ideas. This reaction was based on the premise that communism had to be defeated ideologically as well as militarily. America needed to win what was commonly described as "the war of ideas." But in the nature of things, ideological warfare had to be waged mainly at home. It was easy to send troops to Europe and guns to Formosa; it was very difficult to get foreigners to read *Time* magazine, the *Saturday Evening Post*, and other vehicles of American popular thought. Thus, except for certain feeble propaganda efforts, the war of ideas was confined pretty much to our own mass media.

Considering how practical Americans are supposed to be, the great polemics of the 1950s were extraordinarily abstract. They generally revolved around two concepts, "totalitarianism" and "democracy," which everyone agreed were what the Cold War was all about. Democracy got rather short shrift. It had something to do with Abraham Lincoln, telephones, and air-conditioning, but its virtues were more taken for granted than analyzed. Totalitarianism, on the other hand, was exhaustively discussed. What made people want to "escape from freedom"? Was there such a thing as an "authoritarian personality"? (Indeed, there probably was, at least in America, judging by the classic study on this subject by T. W. Adorno and others, *The Authoritarian Personality*.) A vintage example of this genre was Eric Hoffer's *The True Believer*, which purported to demonstrate by the use of maxims, aphorisms, and the author's numerous and interesting personal prejudices how the weak-willed were seduced into worshiping false political gods. Although the book was in no way marred by factual evidence, and assumed everything that normally demands proof, it was vastly popular.

The effects of this mighty stream of literature condemning wrong thoughts and those who held them were profound. Most dramatic were the trials and investigations of the late forties and early fifties—the great witch-hunts. Nominally these efforts were directed against disloyal acts. In reality they were attempts, often successful, to proscribe false opinions. The best evidence for this is the absurd grounds on which so many prosecutions were based. Apart from a handful of legitimate espionage cases, none of which seriously compromised national security, most victims of the anti-red hysteria were guilty of little more than poor judgment. In the celebrated Hiss case, for example, the point at issue was whether or not Alger Hiss, while an officer of the Department of

State in the 1930s, had passed some classified documents to Soviet agents. Robert Oppenheimer, invariably described as "the father of the A-bomb," was denied a security clearance for opposing development of the hydrogen bomb. Most victims were chosen because they had once belonged to the Communist party or its front groups in, usually, an open and legal fashion. Sometimes they were attacked through their associations with suspected communists, or, as the phrase went, "fellow travelers." As their behavior was neither treasonous nor criminal, few were convicted on account of it. What could be done, however, was to publicize their opinions and associations in ways that subjected them to public humiliation and made them, as teachers, government workers, and especially entertainers, virtually unemployable.

In principle, of course, the Bill of Rights protected Americans from prosecution for their opinions, but it offered no defense against this sort of persecution. Moreover, the courts tended to accept broad definitions of the national security and narrow definitions of individual rights. Thus, injured persons could not usually secure a redress of their grievances, no matter how false the charges raised against them. And congressional committees could "try" an individual without the usual legal safeguards. Many liberals acquiesced in the suppression of dissent. Some were scared of being caught up in the popular mania themselves and joined the mob lest it turn on them. Others were convinced that the handful of Soviet sympathizers in America were a great enough menace to warrant extreme action. This faith in the power of American communism continued even after the American Communist party was effectively destroyed, its leaders jailed, and its apparatus riddled by FBI informers in the early fifties.

In theory, liberals were governed by Sidney Hook's famous maxim, "Heresy yes, treason no." But in an atmosphere where the power of totalitarian ideas was taken for granted, the distinction broke down. Whatever sophistries were advanced to explain why a given person should be jailed or fired from his job, it was clear to the average American that ideas, not actions, were being penalized. Having been assured by liberal and conservative anti-communists alike of the awful potency of false opinions, thousands of communities felt justified, even obliged, to search out and destroy the sources of ideological contagion. Teachers were fired, textbooks scrutinized for un-American ideas, and libraries censored. Even mild criticisms of American society opened one to attack, so few were made. Those liberals who supported the anti-communist crusade, for whatever reason, were themselves weakened by it. At a time when Presidents and cabinet officers were accused of treason, no liberal could be above suspicion, however strident his denunciations of communists and fellow travelers. After Henry Wallace's futile presidential campaign of 1948, and after the empty rhetoric of Harry Truman's Fair Deal died away, this intimidating atmosphere brought the process of reform pretty much to a halt.

The Cold War had other consequences for American life and thought.

The attack on false ideas spilled over into an attack on all ideas. Adlai Stevenson's chief handicap as a presidential candidate in the 1950s was his status as an intellectual, or an "egghead," to use the era's favorite term. Many critics and social scientists came to accept this distrust of ideas as, in some measure at least, desirable. It was compared favorably to the European infatuation with ideas which allegedly had produced fascism and communism. The true American philosophy, it could now be seen, was pragmatism—which somehow always seemed to mean either selling out one's highest principles or operating largely on the basis of snap judgments. Problem-solving, an attribute of pragmatic men, was highly admired, but few problems were solved. As it turned out, what Daniel Bell called "the end of ideology" was not necessarily the beginning of wisdom. The denigration of intellect encouraged schools to place socialization ahead of education. The repudiation of moral passion and utopian politics enfeebled public life and generated a peculiar body of social thought.

Criticism did not, however, entirely die. On the left, C. Wright Mills produced several brilliant and passionate books, notably *The Power Elite*. At the other extreme, Russell Kirk, a fugitive blossom in the rank garden of reactionary thought, produced his first-rate study *The Conservative Mind*. These men, who combined a straightforward partisanship with high standards of intellectual rigor, were not typical of the fifties, however. More representative was William Whyte's *The Organization Man*, which argued that variety and originality were giving way in every sphere of American life to conformity. A common type was emerging in business, government, and education. Everywhere the bureaucrat was replacing the pioneer. Even domestic life reflected this, for the new suburbs were but extensions of the corporate structure. This theme, and variations of it, dominated intellectual discourse in the fifties. Perhaps the most searching example of the genre was David Riesman's *The Lonely Crowd*. This book was rooted in that obsessive concern, typical of the period, with what was usually called "the national character." Riesman suggested that the nineteenth-century Americans were indoctrinated with a fixed set of values which, once absorbed, enabled them to move through life with certainty and sureness. The image he used to describe this "inner-directedness" was the gyroscope. Victorian man kept an even keel, regardless of circumstances, because his moral guidance system was invariable. Modern man, on the other hand, was "other-directed," instructed in relative moral principles and dependent on his peer group for direction. Instead of a gyroscope, he was fitted with a radar set.

This vein of criticism had several interesting features. Because it was neither reactionary nor progressive it did not point to any particular course of action. Indeed, it was programmatically sterile to the point of absurdity. William Whyte concluded his forceful critique of the organizational (we would now say corporate) society by showing how to cheat on personality tests.   Otherwise, he had no important suggestions to make. *The Lonely Crowd,* after exposing the other-directed man, ended with a pious hope that someday a better type, the "autonomous man," would emerge and the American character assume a more pleasing shape. These formal studies were reinforced by novels like Sloan Wilson's *The Man in the Gray Flannel Suit* (which was to the fifties what *Babbitt* had been to the twenties) and by journalistic exposés such as Vance Packard's *The Hidden Persuaders.* This last indicates another effect of the social criticism of the 1950s. In the absence of a program there developed in some quarters a kind of centrist scapegoating. If a plan for reforming American society could not be found, one could at least pinpoint the source of decay. Usually this turned out to be the advertising industry. Madison Avenue, home of many large advertising agencies, came to occupy the position once held by Wall Street in the mythology of popular social criticism. It stood for everything meretricious and corrupt in American life. Peopled entirely by men in three-button suits who carried attaché cases and drank martinis (or the even more sinister gibsons), it was the evil center of a giant, if amorphous, conspiracy which was converting a nation of eagles into a nation of hogs.

This is not to say that the advertising industry was in any respect admirable, but only to point out that the attack on it was characteristic of the fifties: the symptoms were mistaken for the disease. The real problems of the fifties were the same as those of the sixties, except almost no one could see them. The racial crisis, the urban crisis, even the war in Vietnam were building at the very time when Madison Avenue, automobiles with garish tail fins, and rigged television quiz shows occupied the critics' attention. The key issues were seen as essentially moral ones. Was the national moral fiber being undermined? (Strictly speaking, of course, fibers fray, but in the fifties moral fiber was always in danger either of being undermined or eroded.) Was abundance destroying those virtues that had made the country great? Did the youth of today lack the idealism of their predecessors (i.e., the middle-aged men asking this question)? Matters of this sort could neither be resolved nor made the basis of rational policies. The public discourse was thus mired in a welter of fuzzy generalizations. Once again, an era that proudly claimed to be pragmatic and unideological showed itself to be obsessed with abstract, not to say ethereal, propositions. When a handful of American prisoners of war defected to China, or when a member of a distinguished family of intellectuals was found to have conspired with the producers of a TV quiz show, these events were instantly recognized as signs of the general rot. To combat it people were urged to go to church more often, vote for General Eisenhower, and read books like Norman Vincent Peale's *The Power of Positive Thinking.*

In retrospect the era's problems were distressingly concrete. John Kenneth Galbraith made this clear in *The Affluent Society* which, while it appeared at the end of the fifties and used those protective mechanisms of wit and irony demanded by the times, anticipated the future's concerns. Galbraith argued that what ailed America was not private richness but public poverty. While private transportation (especially the auto industry) was given every sort of encouragement, public transit languished. While private housing was subsidized by government-guaranteed loans and burgeoned at a fantastic rate, public housing was neglected. During the Eisenhower years especially, a modified laissez faire (modified in the sense that government now underwrote a great variety of private enterprises) was pursued at the expense of all those social ills from which a profit could not be extracted. What C. Wright Mills called the "higher immorality" dominated life in the United States. Slums were ignored and caution urged upon civil rights workers lest "Southern moderates" become alienated. But most Americans had never had it so good, as politicians tirelessly reminded them.

In fact, domesticity was what the fifties were really all about. The decline of politics as a serious enterprise was accompanied by the privatization of everyday life. In a real sense the family became the chief unit of that private sector whose demands Galbraith spoke against. The neo-Victorian revival of family life in the fifties was, like the baby boom that accompanied it, unexpected and almost inexplicable. It was rooted in a demographic revolution of immense proportions. From the Civil War to World War I the trend had been toward smaller families. People married later and, partly because of this, had fewer children. At first, alarmists had raised the cry of "race suicide." The basic American stock, they warned, was on the verge of extinction through birth control, while the immigrant birthrate was rising. Simple arithmetic showed that if immigrants multiplied and Yankees subtracted, the former would soon overcome the latter. In the 1920s this particular anxiety faded (even though contraceptive devices were at last available) because immigration was restricted. Moreover, it was becoming evident that as immigrants improved their socio-economic status they tended to have fewer children. In the 1930s the marrying age rose sharply and the birthrate fell, as wedlock and paternity became luxuries that the economically depressed could ill afford. Even the divorce rate, which had been rising for almost a century, declined. World War II provoked a wave of sudden marriages followed in due course by a crop of babies. No one was surprised by this. In part it was thought to be a consequence of war-generated emotions, partly also a result of the new prosperity that allowed people who had deferred marriage in the thirties to consummate their relationships. Everyone was certain these changes were temporary, and that in the postwar era normal demographic patterns would be re-established. This was why the Census Bureau's director, in an article for the *New York Times Magazine*, estimated in 1946 that the population would not reach 163 million until 2000 A.D. No one was prepared, therefore, when the wartime pattern persisted into the 1950s. The marrying age for both men and women dropped, the birthrate soared. In the 1960s these trends finally began to reverse themselves, but by then almost an entire generation had passed.

What caused such an extraordinary phenomenon we do not really know. These great demographic movements remain as mysterious and little understood as the nature of life itself. Between the 1920s, a prosperous time when the population grew slowly, and the 1950s, when the population exploded, something of importance had happened at which we can only guess. One possibility is that the prosperity of the fifties was so much greater than that of the twenties that for the first time in perhaps a century large numbers of middle-class people felt able to indulge themselves in the luxury of large families. This does not, however, explain why they chose to spend their surplus on children as against other kinds of luxuries. A better guess concerns the changing roles and expectations of women in the past century. If we assume that women determine family size—a big assumption, for here also little is known—then a solution does offer itself. The middle-class family declined in size during the years—roughly from 1860 to 1920—when women were demanding, and to a degree getting, a larger measure of freedom. They entered the colleges and the professions, obtained jobs in large numbers, gained the vote, formed a great variety of volunteer associations, and in many other ways secured public rights that conflicted somewhat with their private obligations as mothers. Working women married later than those who did not work. College graduates married later still. We do not have to strain very hard, then, to argue that a cause-and-effect relationship existed between women's expanded public role and their diminished private role. In certain areas the connection was obvious. During the nineteenth century about half of all women college graduates never married. Later, as more women went to college, the ratio changed, but for years higher education correlated positively with spinsterhood.

In the 1920s, however, a counterreaction began. The percentage of women earning college degrees peaked. In 1920, 47 per cent of all students in institutions of higher learning were women; by 1950 they accounted for only 30 per cent of the student body. In 1930, 40 per cent of all bachelor's degrees were awarded to women, but in 1956 only a third of the recipients were female. In 1920 one out of every seven doctorates was given to women, but in 1956 women earned less than one out of ten. Similarly, the percentage of women professionals declined. While the female sector of the work force continued to grow, that growth was concentrated at the bottom of the occupational hierarchy. It had always been known that marriages and careers for women were not easily reconciled, but until the 1920s women increasingly chose the latter over the former. After 1920 the balance tilted, with marriages gaining the advantage over careers.

Almost certainly this reactionary development was stimulated by what Betty Friedan, in her admirable polemic, has called *The Feminine Mystique*. The feminist movement had defeated the nineteenth-century precept that "woman's place was in the home" by demonstrating that women could fill a great many other places just as well. Although the stream of propaganda directing women to marry early and raise numerous children never dried up entirely, and many women continued to observe its tenets, by 1920 feminism appeared to have won the war of ideas. But at the very moment of triumph, feminism was undone by a successful counterattack which used new ideas to advance the old principles. Emancipated individuals had demanded sexual freedom to liberate women from the tyranny of marriage. In the 1920s readers of Sigmund Freud argued that true sexual freedom took place within marriage, and, indeed, that motherhood was essential to real fulfillment. Feminists had sought to refute the old idea that child-rearing was woman's only duty by showing that women could enjoy the same accomplishments as men. Now they were overcome by the argument that women were completely unlike men and could achieve satisfaction only by living in harmony with their biological compulsions. Housekeeping became "domestic science," and businessmen eager to expand their markets advanced the notion that modern homemakers were actually managers of the family system, equal in skill and status with professional executives. With this positive effort came the charge that women who did not remain faithful to their feminine natures, who persisted in competing with men in the outside world, were victims of "penis envy," or its dread counterpart, "the castration complex."

Of course, women did not give up their public aspirations and return to domesticity because of the feminine mystique alone. Domestic life became more attractive, we can fairly assume, because by the 1920s women had accumulated enough practical experience to know that the joys of struggling in the marketplace were not so agreeable as feminists had led them to suppose. Many women found only routine jobs which were hardly worth the sacrifices they demanded. Others discovered that, even after they became fully qualified professionals, advancement was more difficult for them than for comparably equipped men. Also in the twenties the reform and service enterprises that had engaged masses of women in the Progressive era had grown stale and no longer commanded the enthusiasm of active young women. At this point, then, marriage and family life, cleansed, as it was thought, of their old imperfections by modern technology and more enlightened customs, took on a new lustre. This general response began in the twenties, was obscured by the thirties, but matured in the postwar era. Once middle-class women conceded that motherhood was their highest duty and most fulfilling role, the domestic explosion of the 1950s was inevitable.

The revival of domesticity affected many areas of the national life. After reaching an all-time high in 1946, the divorce rate fell sharply. The marriage rate and the birthrate shot up. The marrying age declined. "Going steady," as exclusive dating among adolescents was called, rose in popularity and became a kind of pseudo marriage that often led to the real thing. Families with large numbers of small children demanded separate houses with contiguous play areas. This promoted the development of great real estate subdivisions. The "tract," with its hundreds, even thousands, of similar dwellings, each with its own yard, became the standard form of middle-class and upper lower-class housing. Tracts were invariably located outside of cities, thus accelerating urban deterioration by taking the most important bloc of taxpayers out of the city while increasing the demand for urban transportation facilities. Tracts were usually closed to the flood of nonwhites pouring into the cities, thus the slums grew, imposing further strains on underfinanced city administrations and forcing increases in property taxes which accelerated the suburban movement. The federal government contributed its bit by subsidizing, especially through G.I. and FHA home loans, suburban construction, and later by subsidizing urban expressways which enabled larger numbers of people to live in tracts while working in the cities. More and more private automobiles washed into the city, poisoning the air and reducing the tax base further as expressways and parking lots displaced more productive facilities. An expanding population and a diminished living area put great pressure on the slums. No private housing was built for low-income people, and public housing projects usually did not meet the needs even of those people who were displaced by their construction.

While this was going on the American people were preoccupied with what one popular women's magazine called "togetherness." "The family that prays together stays together," it was said, and families did, in truth, more praying than ever before. Or at least they went to church more often. The percentage of people who manifested a denominational affiliation increased. The burgeoning suburbs were festooned with new churches, which became as characteristic of life in the tract as the car pool, the shopping center, and the new elementary school. The automobile came fully into its own. Suburbs everywhere were poorly serviced by public transit authorities, so men commonly drove to work, singly or in combinations, and wives had to spend an important part of their time driving themselves and their children about. In fact, to live comfortably in the suburbs families really needed two cars, and, as more families bought them, the air became more poisonous and the traffic snarls more numerous and complex.

These developments did not escape notice. In two witty books, *The Crack in the Picture Window* and *The Insolent Chariots,* John Keats attacked the twin pillars of suburban life. Innumerable writers drew attention to the cloying domesticity, the smugness and self-satisfaction, the sterile homogeneity, and the aesthetic shortcomings of tract housing. None of the criticisms did the slightest good. For one thing, when the residential construction boom started in the late forties, it had to meet the needs of an entire generation. There had been no homebuilding since the twenties, and many Americans were frantic to escape their aging quarters. Whatever its flaws, tract housing was an improvement over what most new suburbanites were accustomed to. For another thing, they genuinely liked their new houses. This was a point that intellectuals and hardened city dwellers had difficulty in grasping. To their eyes the tracts were ugly and barren, the houses cheaply constructed, and the lots on which they stood offensively small. But the occupants loved them. Critics predicted that the tracts would degenerate into suburban slums. Some did, but more often the owners repaired their houses' defects, enlarged and improved them, and planted trees and shrubs, so that today the original subdivisions are more valuable, and much more attractive, than when they were first built.

Another feature of suburban life that escaped critics was the way in which the tracts satisfied their residents' needs for proprietorship and community. These are old wants in America. The pioneers pushed west in order to become freeholders, and the desire to own house and land, the visible symbol of independence, is deeply imbedded in the American character. City dwellers, living in apartments and using public transit facilities, typically own nothing at all by these standards. For many, therefore, the suburban movement replicated the essential American experience by which the dependent Easterner became the freeholding Westerner. The pioneers had also sought community. They built schools and churches, formed social and political organizations, and developed an intricate community life. The city is, by comparison, a social wasteland. New Yorkers are fond of pointing out that they have lived in the same apartment building for twenty years without ever getting to know their neighbors. Dedicated urbanites are horrified at the thought of living in the open, as it were, and of knowing everything about their neighbors while their neighbors know everything about them. But for many people this was a principal virtue of the tracts. Here too the pioneer social experience could be imitated, schools and churches built, neighborly ties formed, and the dense infrastructure of small American communities reproduced. The social life of suburbia became, in fact, much more complex and demanding (or rewarding) than urban life. The PTA flourished, as did volunteer political organizations like the League of Women Voters, the Americans for Democratic Action, and the John Birch Society.

The search for community probably also accounts for another baffling aspect of the fifties, the religious revival. Through the first half of the twentieth century religion was on the defensive almost everywhere in America. Science had, it seemed, discredited the church's claim to truth, while the school, the welfare agency, and other public institutions had usurped many of its traditional functions. In the postwar era, however, church membership increased strikingly, and, in consequence of it, religion gained a new dignity and importance. A variety of reasons were advanced to explain this surprising development. The horrors of war and the strains of a nuclear peace undermined men's faith in science and reason as the sole guides of conduct and the only conduits of knowledge.

In these terms the religious revival was an emotional reaction against a world suddenly grown too terrible for solitary man to bear. Considering that most church growth took place in the suburbs, whose pleasures we have just described, this explanation somehow lacks authority. Other explanations concerned doctrine: for example, that the neo-orthodoxy of Reinhold Niebuhr was more intellectually satisfying to Protestants than the theologies it displaced. But the most striking feature of postwar Christianity was the ecumenical movement and the suppression of doctrine which it entailed.

This suggests that the new institutional strength of the churches *was* a function of suburbia; that it was produced by the same drives which built the schools. Church membership was a mark of community solidarity and stability. At a time when there was so much talk of "atheistic" communism, it was also a badge of good citizenship. Religion was good for children too. It strengthened their character and helped them resist the temptations of a materialistic age. The churches may sometimes have seemed irrelevant in an urban context, but in suburbia they had several useful functions, and it made perfectly good sense to support them. The churches, it must be said, made excellent use of their opportunities. Although it was awkward for them to preach against the very affluence that created them, they did so all the same. They provided much of the institutional support for the civil rights movement that emerged in the late fifties. And by joining together in all those cooperative ventures that flowed out of the ecumenical spirit, they helped heal many old wounds from the sectarian past. It was, in fact, just this new spirit that made possible the election of a Roman Catholic President in 1960.

One of the most extraordinary features of the postwar era was the degree to which young people accepted the values of their elders. The dedication of bourgeois America to personal security and sociability produced a generation with strongly middle-aged attitudes. In high school the emphasis was on successful peer relations and becoming, as it was said, "educated for life." The life to which young people were educated was generally one of docile citizenship and earnest consumption. In college the physical sciences and humanities declined, while practical fields like business and engineering rose. About half of the male college graduates went into business, mainly big business. When William H. Whyte investigated this situation he discovered that the appeal of big business derived from the student's perception of it as a kind of private welfare state. Students did not look forward to a life of challenge, high adventure, and great profits, but rather to one of modest advancement, numerous fringe benefits, and a reasonable security. The functional hero of *The Man in the Gray Flannel Suit* perfectly represented their aspirations when he turned down an important promotion because it would interfere too much with his family life. By all accounts, college men looked forward to the same comforts and moderate prosperity that their fathers enjoyed, while college women aspired only to relive their mothers' lives.

The young were not, of course, wholly contented. From time to time the placid campus suffered "panty raids," as attacks on female dormitories by young men in pursuit of underwear were called. Such acts usually were viewed indulgently by the authorities, who regarded them as mere pranks. Once in a while indignation was voiced at the racial and religious prejudices of fraternities and sororities. On the whole, however, most complaints concerned what student editors always called the "apathy" of what had become known as the "silent generation." The protests and demonstrations of yesteryear were nostalgically recalled by professors and administrators who would later have to eat their words. Even when the young were visibly disturbed, however, they found it impossible to say why. The silent generation's most significant folk hero was James Dean, who starred in a motion picture called *Rebel Without a Cause.* In it he played an unhappy young man who expressed himself by driving his automobile in a dangerous manner. The film intimated that society had failed him in some undisclosed way, but the message was vague and without point. So was Dean's premature death in a sports car accident. In death as in life, James Dean symbolized the aimless resentments of submerged youth during what was, after all, a very boring time.

V
AN INHERENTLY
PRECARIOUS CENTURY

John F. Kennedy was elected to the Presidency in 1960 on his promise to "get America moving again." The image of a dormant nation alerted and surging toward a progressive goal stirred Americans to excited anticipation. It heralded a departure from the apparent lethargy and complacency of the Eisenhower years and promised that the country would be instilled with the dynamism of energetic and enthusiastic youth. Like Stevenson before him, Kennedy grandiloquently called Americans to arms in a national crusade against the enemies of mankind. Although it remained to be proven that war could be exorcised by war, Kennedy prepared the nation mentally for renewed sacrifices. What practical course did he have in mind?

Kennedy had three general goals. First, in order to avoid a repetition of the three Eisenhower recessions, he had to stabilize the economy and increase its growth rate. Kennedy's strategy was founded upon the Keynesian conviction that the annual economic growth of 3 per cent experienced under the Republicans would result in stagnation. As the first President to embrace a frankly Keynesian governmental manipulation of the economy, Kennedy advocated a 7 per cent tax credit for capital investment, a general tax cut, and expanded public investment. Inflation was to be stabilized at a 1 to 2 per cent increase through the cooperative efforts of business and labor and the moral persuasion of the White House. Businessmen, accustomed to having their own way under a Republican President and deeply suspicious of organized labor's favored role in the Kennedy administration, were hostile to the youthful Democratic Chief Executive. Kennedy's economic advisers and spokesmen vainly tried to persuade big businessmen that the President's policies were designed for business' benefit. Not until the laissez faire candidacy of Barry Goldwater in 1964 threatened to deprive businessmen of the government's largesse did businessmen turn in large numbers to the Democratic party.

The second Kennedy goal complemented the first. Asserting that the quality and quantity of the nation's defense lagged behind Russia's, Kennedy planned to increase spending on the military establishment, which, he asserted, had been neglected by the parsimonious Republicans. During the 1960 campaign, Kennedy blamed Eisenhower's tight-fisted economic and defense policies for a "missile gap" between the United States and the Soviets, with the U.S. suffering the disadvantage of fewer long-range missiles in its arsenal. The Cuban Missile Crisis of 1962 proved, however, that the reverse was true.

Nevertheless, the real Kennedy objectives lay with the less visible conventional military structure. Our missiles were useless against guerrilla victories by Communist-led national liberation forces in Asia, Africa, and Latin America. Therefore, it became imperative that the massive retaliation of atomic weapons yield to the concept of a flexible deterrent. In the fifties, a group of army generals led by Matthew Ridgway, Maxwell Taylor, and James Gavin had assailed the Eisenhower administration's reliance upon a "bigger bang for the buck"—bombers carrying nuclear weapons as an economical defense of United States interests. The generals had argued that America needed instead a "sky cavalry," a mobile infantry employing helicopters to fight limited wars in places like Southeast Asia, where we believed U.S. interests were being "nibbled to death." The Kennedy people embraced the generals, whose tactics so well suited the Democrats' plans for overseas activities stressing counterinsurgency warfare plus expanded defense spending to spur economic growth. While research and development turned out a host of new types of helicopters and numerous other innovative weapons for guerrilla warfare, little was denied to air force bomber and navy carrier advocates. When Eisenhower left the Presidency in 1961, he warned against a massive "military-industrial complex"; two years later the Eisenhower defense budget seemed puny compared with Kennedy's, and the economy appeared ready to soar from the infusion of defense dollars. Both the liberal economists and the generals had achieved a considerable growth record.

A third goal of the Kennedy administration was social justice for America's disadvantaged groups. Notwithstanding the Warren Court's decision in 1954 that racial segregation was unconstitutional, the Eisenhower administration had remained indifferent to the civil rights movement. Integration proceeded slowly in southern schools, while segregation accelerated in the North. John Kennedy recognized that millions of Negro voters waited to be mobilized in their own behalf and in that of the Democratic Party. He and his brother Robert anticipated that if barriers to Negro voting were removed, black power at the polls would open racial opportunities in education, housing, and labor. Likewise, the administration noted the writings of Michael Harrington and others who spotlighted the hard-core poor in an affluent society and introduced relief programs for the unemployed and new Social Security benefits for the elderly.

Kennedy maintained bipartisanship and consensus in foreign policy. He perpetuated the strategy he had inherited from Truman and Eisenhower: containment in Europe and counterinsurgency elsewhere. Mobile armed forces gave Kennedy a weapon with which he hoped to resist Communist guerrilla incursions, and Indochina provided a theater for testing the effectiveness of the forces. At the time of the President's assassination, November 22, 1963, 16 thousand American troops aided their South Vietnamese proxies against indigenous Vietnamese Communist and nationalist forces.

Kennedy's successor, Lyndon Johnson, faced an apparently imminent military defeat in 1965 unless American soldiers supplanted the hapless South Vietnamese. Reasoning that a test of Communist and American wills for control of Indochina had reached a climax, Johnson sent a half million Americans to fight against what he saw as a spread of communism engulfing all of Asia. More years of fighting resulted in the end of American escalation in 1968 and the election of Richard Nixon to succeed Johnson amid widespread discontent with the war and its attendant problems. Nixon applied the carrot of a phased withdrawal of American troops over a few years and the stick of expanding the war to Cambodia and Laos before he gradually neutralized hostility to the war in 1970. Peace negotiations begun in 1968 dragged on until late 1972. By no means, however, was Nixon able to silence antiwar sentiment at home. As his "Vietnamization" program continued into 1971, more Americans doubted that Nixon really intended to withdraw completely from Indochina. Many in Congress suspected that if America left, our surrogate government in Saigon would fall, an event to which Nixon would never reconcile himself.

Then, in the summer of 1971, Nixon startled America with the announcement that Presidential Assistant Henry Kissinger had visited Communist China to arrange for a future visit there by Nixon himself. For over twenty years the United States and China had maintained stern positions of hostility, the U.S. denying the Chinese any diplomatic recognition or entry into the United Nations. That policy had had no firmer advocate than Richard Nixon, and, thus, the anti-communist logic of United States politics made him the most unlikely person to change the policy. With a possible rapprochement with China in the works, and her seating in the U.N. a fact, what did this portend for U.S. strategy in Indo-China?

Amid reports of an impending armistice in Vietnam, President Nixon won a landslide re-election in 1972. Yet his electoral triumph did not bring peace until after some of the heaviest bombing of the war. Nineteen seventy-three brought official peace to Vietnam while battles and bombing continued to rage elsewhere in Indochina. At home the nation concerned itself with the worst inflation in over twenty years. Nixon's victory had been construed by the administration as a mandate to destroy the social gains of Lyndon Johnson's Great Society program, but a Democratic Congress prepared for a fight in its defense. The second Nixon administration began with greater uncertainty than it had anticipated.

Robert Lekachman
KENNEDY, JOHNSON, AND KEYNES

Keynesian economists enjoyed a heyday in the sixties. They emerged from their academic strongholds to be welcomed by Democrats as the prophets of prosperity. Their fiscal precepts promised a new era in governmental manipulation of the economy. By encouraging investment, they expected to enlarge the gross national product with only a minimum of controlled inflation. The Democratic party adopted that strategy, and it worked for a while. By 1965, Detroit's motor industry enjoyed a rare condition called "overemployment": more jobs were available than there were jobless seeking work. But the Vietnam war and industry's lack of cooperation with the federal government made inflation control precarious in the mid-sixties. The union and corporation self-restraint which John Kennedy counted on to stabilize wages and prices was not forthcoming after 1962.

In addition to the economic boosts contributed by the war, investment spending, and a tax cut, Kennedy added the stimulus of the space program, and Johnson contributed federal funds for education. Communities which had postponed building schools and hospitals and other social projects for just such a boom found that a rise in prices at 5 per cent per year robbed their dollars of purchasing value, thereby limiting the number of services they could provide. Cities, counties, and states frantically raised their taxes but never collected enough revenue to fulfill their social obligations. Local and state income taxes took money from workers on the job, while sales taxes afflicted them in the stores. By the seventies, some sales tax rates hit 7 per cent. Tragically, local and state governments never had sufficient funds and services continued to be restricted by rising costs. The education boom of the sixties tapered off sharply in the seventies. Home building, which had soared in the sixties, slowed in the seventies as interest rates made credit hard to obtain. More highly trained Americans found fewer available jobs. Regardless of how the war in Asia turned out, the American economy was the loser.

Robert Lekachman, a Keynesian economist, published a celebration of "The Age of Keynes" in 1965. The war had not yet taken its toll of the economy, but the misdirection of resources had become apparent. In this selection he analyzes President Johnson's "Great Society" program and distinguishes neatly between its rhetoric and prospective reality. The events of those years cause us to wonder if it is possible for the United States to wage simultaneous wars against insurgents abroad and poverty at home without invoking politically hazardous wage and price curbs or excess profits taxes.

In the calm which has followed a new national consensus, it is possible to see at last that Keynesian economics is not conservative, liberal, or radical. The techniques of economic stimulation and stabilization are simply neutral administrative tools capable of distributing national income either more or less equitably, improving the relative bargaining position of either unions or employers, and increasing or decreasing the importance of the public sector of the economy. Keynes's personal history and the early affiliation of liberals and radicals with Keynesian doctrine have obscured this vital point. In the United States, the fact is that two Presidents and two Congresses have chosen to stimulate the country's economy not by expanding public activity but by encouraging more private activity. Indeed, every tax reduction diminishes the federal government's relative share of the gross national product and correspondingly increases the relative importance of the private economy. Each tax cut contains the implicit proposition that dollars released to private discretion achieve benefits more valuable than could be attained by public expenditures of the same amount. Quite probably expressing a national preference, President Kennedy and President Johnson have placed a large bet on the capacity of business to produce the right goods in the right quantities and to distribute them to the right people.

The 1964 presidential campaign disguised this as it did other issues. Promoting neither himself nor public enlightenment, Mr. Goldwater ran a straightforward pre-Keynesian campaign. In it he advocated, *inter alia,* less federal spending, further tax reduction, and budgets balanced in all save extraordinary circumstances, of which recession was not one. He opposed labor "monopolies" and attacked the public use of fiscal policy as a stabilizing tool. It was all too consistent with a Senate voting record which featured opposition to the Reciprocal Trade Agreements Act, the Kennedy Trade Expansion Act, agricultural price supports, social security protection, medicare, minimum wage legislation, and all the other "interferences" in free markets which the enemies of liberty (Republican as well as Democratic) had forced upon the country. Under the circumstances President Johnson had no political reason to advance a detailed economic program or to discuss the genuine issues which now confront him and his constituents.

The major economic question which faces Americans in the Keynesian era is no longer a matter of whether modern fiscal policy should or should not be employed. For the reasonable, this is an issue finally resolved. It has been superseded by a much harder set of choices dependent on social valuations more complex than the simple preference of prosperity to depression, growth to stagnation, and progress to retrogression. These are the choices which were foreshadowed by the controversy in the Kennedy administration over the best way to stimulate the American economy. When a President and a Congress acknowledge the need for fiscal stimulus, *how* should this stimulus be supplied? The practical choice, the major social valuation, and the continuing political argument focus upon the two routes to economic expansion which are open, the twentieth-century liberal route and the twentieth-century conservative alternative.

The modern economic conservative is no longer a budget balancer; he is perfectly willing to recognize deficiencies in aggregate demand as they present themselves. He may well accept the current diagnosis that the economic malaise of the 1950s and early 1960s was the consequence of insufficient private investment and a tax structure which withdrew the fruits of economic expansion too quickly and too copiously from the pockets of consumers and entrepreneurs. Defining the problem in this fashion, the conservative expansionist is prone to pin his hopes on a refashioning of the federal tax system and periodical infusions of fiscal stimulus in the shape of additional tax reductions. He is likely to be wary of large expenditures on social welfare and still suspicious of the enlargement of federal influence. Nevertheless, more and more he esteems the federal government as a partner in business prosperity.

As many of the preceding portions of this volume suggest, the thrust of two Democratic Presidents' legislative programs and administrative actions has been at the least consistent with the expectations of modern economic conservatives. The familiar roster of liberalized depreciation, investment tax credit, reduced corporate income tax rates, moderated personal tax progression, and excise tax alteration all have amounted to direct or indirect attempts to stimulate business confidence, enlarge private investment, and emphasize the significance of private economic production. The Kennedy and Johnson appointments to the federal regulatory agencies and the Cabinet, and the decision to vest control of the communications satellite in private corporate hands, are additional acts of solicitude for business feelings and preferences. It is accurate rather than invidious to term the faith of modern businessmen commercial Keynesianism, and it is only sensible to welcome the perception by intelligent businessmen that private activity can be aided by a government sympathetic both to business and to high employment. Commercial Keynesianism is a giant step beyond older policies preferred by the business community.

Nevertheless, the opposing contemporary position also has its just claims. The liberal expansionist stance owes a debt to the Galbraith of *The Affluent Society,* the Harrington of *The Other America,* and the unemployment analyses of Charles Killingsworth. Liberal expansionists unite in denying that commercial Keynesianism is capable of meeting adequately the economic challenges of the next decade. By itself expansionary policy will not prepare the nation for a changing labor market.

One of the major concerns of liberal expansionists is the slow growth of manufacturing employment and output. Computers and servomechanisms are eliminating unskilled, semi-skilled, and even skilled positions. Education requirements for steady employment are rising too sharply to allow much hope for many of today's unemployed. The uncertainties and dangers of the new market for human skill and energy are such that even advocates of tax reduction perceive that their favored device is less than the whole answer to unemployment. Testifying on poverty in 1964, Walter Heller phrased the position eloquently: "open exits mean little to those who cannot move—to the millions who are caught in the web of poverty through illiteracy, lack of skills, racial discrimination, broken homes, and ill health—conditions which are hardly touched by prosperity and growth." On this front the alarmists insist upon the imminence of a transformation of production and employment larger in scale and more devastating in impact than the Industrial Revolution of the eighteenth century. Such is the diagnosis advanced by the signers of the Manifesto of the Ad Hoc Committee on the Triple Revolution, among them Michael Harrington and Gunnar Myrdal. But even the more cautious structural analysis of Charles Killingsworth implies the need for a good deal more than the simple stimulation of aggregate demand by tax reduction.

Clearly the persistence of poverty, the presence of structural unemployment, and the looming menace of automation all demand specific programs of public intervention. So also does the fact, in the Galbraithian view, that Americans allocate far too many resources to private activity and far too few to public purposes. What concerns Galbraithians is the number of places in the United States like Perry County, Kentucky, whose teachers start at a salary of $74.42 a week; Washington, D.C., whose Ludlow Elementary School contains one washbasin for its 260 students and whose General Hospital compels indigent patients to wait even in emergencies three to six hours before they can see a doctor; and even rich New York City, whose decades of experiment with public housing have not eliminated the slums of Harlem. Liberal expansionists are convinced that the nation's schools, houses, hospitals, and social services will never be so high in quality as its automobiles, cosmetics, and detergents until large amounts of resources are shifted from low-priority private uses to high-priority public uses. The practical import of the judgment is that in a time of prosperity as in a time of recession, the role of the federal government should increase, not decrease.

Therefore, whether they emphasize poverty, structural unemployment, or the starvation of the public services, liberal expansionists favor public spending over tax reduction. It is exactly at this point in the practical politics of fiscal policy that they part company from conservative expansionists. Since each time taxes are reduced it is harder to achieve larger federal appropriations, liberal expansionists must in logic be the opponents of tax cuts and the friends of larger expenditures on urban redevelopment, regional rehabilitation, vocational education, manpower retraining, public recreation, aid to education, and low-cost, federally assisted housing. Liberal expansionists dislike tax reduction because they perceive it as the inevitable competitor of the superior policies which assist the unemployed young, the victims of segregated education, the technologically displaced, and the miserably housed.

The art of democratic politics often lies in blurring the issues, not sharpening the definitions as intellectuals are fond of doing. It would be naive to expect a successful President to define his program in clear-cut ideological terms. Moreover, final judgments upon functioning political leaders are risky. As this is written, Lyndon Johnson has been President in his own right only a year and a half. The ultimate shape of his own program preferences and accomplishments will depend on many factors, a number of them outside any President's control. The urgencies of foreign affairs, the necessities of the defense establishment, the temper of Congress, and the behavior of the economy are among the important variables which will influence presidential economic policy. Any present assessment must be provisional, the more so because 1965's Great Society legislation contains sufficiently varied emphases to permit of a number of different sequels during the next three or possibly seven years of President Johnson's administration. All the same it is useful to examine Mr. Johnson's unusually varied program up to now in the framework of liberal and conservative expansionism.

To begin with, the President's policies are often continuations of Kennedy, Truman, or even Roosevelt initiatives. The lines of development between the Kennedy and the Johnson years are particularly numerous. Originated by President Kennedy, the tax cut was enthusiastically embraced by President Johnson. The preliminary plans for the War on

Poverty had already been laid by the Kennedy staff before President Johnson adopted the War on Poverty as the initial identifiable program of his own new administration. President Kennedy had urged Congress to enact medicare and aid to education. Assisted by a huge Democratic majority, President Johnson pressed the measures through Congress. The wage-price guidelines which appeared first in *The Economic Reports* of the Heller Council of Economic Advisers have been reiterated by the Council headed by Gardner Ackley.

It is style rather than legislative substance which separates the two Democratic Presidents. That Mr. Johnson has won business confidence seems to be the joint consequence of the demonstrated success of fiscal policy and Mr. Kennedy's apparent "hostility" and Mr. Johnson's evident sympathy to businessmen and their problems. The tragicomedy of President Kennedy's relations to the business community has already been told. In the months which preceded the assassination, there were signs that the President and business were moving toward reconciliation. Still, it is doubtful whether even proper courtesy between businessmen and their President could have been achieved. Rapport seemed a distant hope. A recollection of Theodore Sorensen's may exemplify the feelings on both sides. Mr. Sorensen cites the President as commenting caustically to him after addressing the Business Council that this was the only audience which did not stand when the President of the United States entered the room.

Birthplace, experience, and temperament have combined in President Johnson to produce a different set of feelings. Like any other successful Texas politician, Mr. Johnson, first as Congressman and then as Senator, had to reach an accommodation with the major economic interests of his region. Although Lyndon Johnson entered Congress as a New Dealer, the personal protégé of Franklin Roosevelt, and voted consistently for New Deal measures, he sought also to protect the tax advantages of his state's oil interests. Moreover, in his own private affairs, he entered into partnership with his wife in one of the period's more speculative industries—television. The texture of Mr. Johnson's personal experience equips him to understand concretely, directly, and intimately the financial and tax difficulties of ordinary businessmen. His experience also gives him insight into the way businessmen regard the regulatory agencies and the federal bureaucracy. His past activities have developed in him a taste for business company and business conversation. The presidency is a great symbolic office, and these small details of its present occupant's career can have large consequences.

One of them indeed has been the unexampled extent of business approbation of Mr. Johnson. It has been a long time since so conservative an organ as the *Monthly News Letter* of New York's First National City Bank could say publicly the kind of thing it said of this Democratic President's 1965 congressional program, that "These reports and messages indicate a marked evolution toward a more pronounced pro-business attitude, combined with an increasing stress on free enterprise and market competition in the allocation of resources."

The body of messages and reports which the writers of the encomium were commending were portions of the Great Society program. They offer an excellent opportunity to examine the quality of the expansionary program of this activist President. The chance is the better because the 1965 Congress was more nearly under the complete control of the chief executive than any has been since 1933. President Johnson made full use of his fortunate situation to press through Congress an unusually varied list of measures, covering topics ranging from highway beautification to immigration reform. Even though this legislative program is not the President's final word, it is an impressive first chapter.

Let us consider its elements. The documents which sound the major legislative themes are the budget message and *The Economic Report of the President*. The latter began with an account of the successes of the past twelve months. Nineteen sixty-four had been a year of expansion in which employment had risen by a million and a half, the gross national product had increased from $584 billion to $622 billion, corporate profits had continued a four-year ascent, and personal income per capita (after taxes) had touched $2,288 per year, up 17.5 percent in just four years. Any administration would have pointed proudly to another characteristic of its stewardship—the price stability which had accompanied economic expansion.

In allocating the credit, *The Economic Report* tactfully began with the "businessmen, workers, investors, farmers and consumers" whose investing, spending, and planting decisions had combined to stimulate economic growth. Then came the last partner, "Government policies which have sustained a steady, but non-inflationary growth of markets." The President stated his belief "that 1964 will go down in our economic and political history as the 'year of the tax cut.'"

From the attractive economic record President Johnson drew a semi-Keynesian lesson, that "Purposeful expenditure, stimulative tax reductions, and economy in government operations are the three weapons which, if used effectively, can relieve our society of the costs and consequences of waste." How the President intended to use the first two weapons rapidly emerged in his concrete legislative proposals.

The "stimulative tax reductions" included the remainder of the reductions already mandated under the 1964 tax measure—some $3 billion in personal tax benefits and another $1 billion in corporate tax remissions. The new tax item substantially reduced some excise taxes and eliminated a good many others. In combination these tax changes were a continuation of the fiscal stimulus initiated in 1964 by the passage of the Tax Reduction Act.

The "purposeful expenditure" list was an interesting agglomeration. It included enlargements of old programs like social security and the War on Poverty as well as initial financing for some new programs. The latter were a varied lot—aid to education, the rehabilitation of Appalachia, the construction of regional medical centers, rent subsidies, and medical assistance to the aged. Although so many programs were new (as objects of legislation if not of repeated proposal), requests for increased spending amounted to only a modest total. In fact, as a fiscal exercise, what unified this program of tax reduction and welfare extension was a constraint—the President's promise that both tax benefits and welfare spending would be financed out of the normal growth of an expanding economy. Both types of benefits depended upon the capacity of a growing economy to create a fiscal dividend each year to be distributed to its citizens.

Emphatically, the architects of this legislative design did not intend to reallocate the community's resources in the direction of greater public influence. During his first two budgets, President Johnson's insistence on not exceeding the $100 billion expenditure mark attested to the importance which he attached to keeping government activity within limits. It appears likely that the President would have recommended still greater fiscal stimulus in each of the budgets if he had not been restrained by his concern for the size of federal spending. That concern was itself related to the President's wish to retain within the boundaries of his political consensus the business support which he had won. In the end the implicit check on the size of social welfare expenditure delimited the amount of intervention that the business community was willing to accept.

The President's choices between tax reduction and larger spending continued to emphasize the former. Even after 1964's major tax surgery, the President offered new benefits in 1965 and intimations of future reductions in personal income levies. Only the escalation of the Vietnam war transformed administrative discussions and created the possibility of tax increases. As a result, even though the 1965 congressional record was startlingly enlightened by comparison with earlier congressional performances it remained true that the combined increases in old social programs and initial appropriations for new ones amounted to less than the reductions in personal income taxes, corporate imposts, and excises.

From the standpoint of the liberal expansionist, this was bad enough, but the distribution of the tax benefits and even the new public spending raised still livelier apprehensions for him. Like 1964's tax harvest, much of 1965's improvements would be realized by prosperous corporations and wealthy individuals. Reduced corporate income tax rates generated additional dividends and capital gains which flowed for the most part to upper-income investors. The same group would enjoy a very large percentage of the gains from additional reductions in personal income taxes. Some portion of reductions in excise taxes would be retained as extra profits by corporations which were already turning in highly satisfactory earnings records.

The design of the expenditure programs also raised a number of questions about who precisely benefits from welfare policies besides the direct recipients of assistance. The interests of specific business groups sometimes appear to influence the shape of programs as much as the needs of the ostensible beneficiaries. Thus, the major innovation of the 1965 omnibus housing measure, the rent subsidy plan, undoubtedly enables a number of families, ineligible under other programs, to escape the slums and move into a decent environment. At best rent subsidies modestly promote housing integration. However, local governments have long known that under such programs financial benefits accrue to landlords and builders, helping them maintain the existing structure of building costs and apartment rentals. This is another way of saying that the rent subsidies tend to support the existing customs of an industry usually considered backward in both its technology and its social practices.

The Appalachian program raises somewhat similar issues. No reader of Harry Caudill's affecting *Night Comes to the Cumberlands* will question that most of Appalachia's inhabitants live in abject misery, nor that public help is unqualifiedly desirable in a region that has manifestly lost a grip on its own troubles. All the same, it is hard not to pause and wonder why the most expensive of the components of the administration program is a major road-building effort. Certainty on its merits is not easy, for in the long run, new roads in the appropriate places may indeed open the region to the tourist trade, promote the internal mobility of labor, and encourage industrialists to establish new plants. However, what appears all too likely in the short run of the next few years is that the road contractors will reap the major gains. There will be little immediate increase in local employment because of the highway construction. By now road-building has become so skilled a trade and uses so much expensive equipment that much of the labor force employed on the new Appalachian highways will be imported from other more prosperous regions.

Not even the poverty program is totally exempt from the same reservation, that it contains an excessively generous tendency to distribute some portion of the available largess to the unneedy. The ample scale on which local poverty officials are paid has already aroused a quantity of sour humor about the identity of the program's major beneficiaries. This point may be comparatively minor administratively though it is surely significant psychologically. However, it can reasonably be argued that high salaries attract abler and more inventive human types into social welfare specialties than the social service bureaucrats who now dominate the field.

A more serious question about the goals and strategies of the War on Poverty concerns the participation of major corporations like Litton Industries, Philco, and International Telephone & Telegraph in poverty ventures which they define as commercial opportunities. These and other firms have signed up as operators of new job camps for unemployed youths. Although there is no reason to quarrel with the sincerity of either portion of a Litton executive's remark that "We got into the poverty war for two reasons, one the opportunity to serve the community, the other the business opportunity," serious issues are tied up in business sponsorship of training programs. Will the training become a variety of publicly subsidized preparation for semiskilled jobs with little future in the sponsoring corporations? Will a firm's concept of training necessarily or even usually coincide with the interests of either the trainees or the community? Will the commercial limitations of even the best-intentioned business ventures really lead to the social transformations which in its more visionary moments the poverty program promises? Once more it is difficult not to wonder whether the Administration program, intentionally or unintentionally, does not offer as many benefits to the successful as prospects for the poor, the rejected, and the hopeless.

Under the circumstances it is not astonishing that many businessmen have extended substantial support to the administration's housing, poverty, and regional development plans. Thus far, at any rate, the total outlays required are small enough to be financed from that portion of the growth of federal tax receipts not pledged to tax reduction. The programs are so constructed as to favor existing agencies and interests. To their credit, a generation of more sophisticated business leaders have come to see that active fiscal policy and limited social welfare improvements are themselves conducive to business prosperity. Perhaps still more to their credit, many businessmen have come to identify themselves sufficiently with their employees to recognize a common interest in higher wages and steady employment.

When all this is said, the administration's program can be realistically appraised only within the context of a consensus whose limits are defined by the business community, not by trade union leaders or liberal intellectuals. In some areas these limits are narrow. In 1965, the repeal of Section 14(b) of the Taft-Hartley Act, the section enabling the individual states to outlaw union shop agreements, was put at the top of the AFL-CIO's legislative agenda. Congress, which cheerfully passed a variety of Great Society proposals, stopped abruptly at the presidential request for the deletion of Section 14(b), and repeated its action at the start of 1966's congressional session. A similar reluctance to raise minimum wages and extend coverage to migratory farm workers and other unsheltered groups attests to the reluctance of influential portions of the business community to shift the existing balance between labor and industry.

Possibly the best illustration of all brings us back to the continuing shortage of low-income housing. This is a huge problem. As President Johnson sketched its dimensions, "In the remainder of the century . . . urban populations will double, city land will double and we will have to build in our cities as much as all that we have built since the first colonist arrived on these shores." As the President went on to observe, the cities are already overcrowded, the nation contains "over nine million homes, most of them in cities, which are run down or deteriorating," and "many of our central cities are in need of major surgery to overcome decay." The concluding sentence of Mr. Johnson's diagnosis—"The old, the poor, the discriminated against are increasingly concentrated in central city ghettos"—is both accurate and eloquent enough to command the agreement of most students of city affairs, not to mention the unfortunate city residents themselves.

Just here appears most glaringly the gap between the accurate description of a large problem and the means which the limits of business-defined consensus permit to be used. Although the 1965 Housing Act contains many commendable features, including the rent subsidy innovation, it fails at two crucial points. The amounts allocated to the rent subsidy program are very small, as are the benefits that the big cities, the accepted focus of the problem, can anticipate in 1965, 1966, and 1967. New York City, for example, can expect no more than 3,500 units of low-income housing each year. Indeed, Mrs. Hortense Gabel, in 1965 the City's rent control administrator, observed that the federal government planned to spend less on all housing programs in New York City than it did four years earlier in 1961.

No one denies that improving housing and eliminating slums are enormously complex matters, made more difficult by the accumulation of past failures and the existence of contemporary prejudices. Nevertheless, successful advancement requires the creation of a huge, expensive, and coordinated program of urban renewal and public housing— and a willingness to upset comfortable commercial, union, and political practices. In the past the failures of urban renewal measures have flowed partly from the perversion of the program into a series of subsidies to luxury builders, real estate speculators, and business promoters; partly from municipal decisions to set the quite legitimate expansion needs of great universities like Chicago and Columbia ahead of the equally legitimate (and much more acute) housing requirements of displaced residents; and partly, perhaps mainly, from the circumstance that adequate quantities of public housing—attractively designed, socially mixed, and suitably located—were never supplied. In New York the consequence has been that at the end of a generation-long boom in private construction, there is still no decent place where most Negroes and Puerto Ricans can live. Though unenviable, this is a record readily matched by Chicago, Philadelphia, Los Angeles, Saint Louis, and Detroit.

Thus, in relation to need, the administration program is minute, far below Senator Robert A. Taft's goals for a smaller population and a poorer nation two decades ago. Yet where consensus is the objective, existing practices must be respected, and benefits are likely to accrue according to the relative weight of the different groups joined together in mutual accommodation. The real if very limited benefits to the poorly housed which present programs offer are provided in ways which please the construction industry, assist middle-income families also, elevate banking profits, enlarge city real estate tax rolls, and unfortunately leave in their present plight the mass of wretchedly sheltered urban slum-dwellers. This judgment is less a moral statement than a summary of the fact that in this important sphere, established practices and social objectives are in conflict.

Even medicare, the triumph of an aspiration thirty years old, has its conservative, prudential aspects. A complex piece of legislation, this is the first extension of major significance to social security since the passage of the Social Security Act in 1935. Benefits to the elderly are enlarged, and existing child health and aid to dependent children programs are expanded. But the basic innovations are in the medical provisions. Henceforth social security pensioners are automatically entitled to payment of the expenses of hospitalization, posthospital care, nursing home treatment, and home health visits. Moreover, a voluntary supplementary plan pays the bulk of medical and surgical costs incurred in clinics, homes, and medical offices.

In 1967 the program's first full year of operation, the entire medicare package will cost about $6 billion—$2.2 billion for the basic health care plan, an additional $1 billion for the supplementary plan, $2.3 billion for increased social security benefits to the elderly, and the remaining $500 million for the liberalization of existing public assistance programs. Particularly by comparison with recent social welfare spending, the scale of the new measure is generous. More welcome yet are the relief from anxiety and the gain in human dignity finally accorded the old. That this program has taken so long in the coming detracts nothing from its very substantial merits.

However, this legislation also contains certain checks on benefits and on their extension to other age groups. Throughout, financing is exceedingly conservative. A case in point is the voluntary program. The premiums set are $3 per month per covered individual, adjustable upward as medical costs rise. Rise they will. If the precedent of the postwar history of Blue Cross premiums holds true, the elderly must anticipate rapid increases in these initially modest premium payments. Worse still, other portions of the program will be financed overwhelmingly by increases in payroll taxes, which are now scheduled to rise to 5.5 percent *each* for employer and employee in the next fifteen years. This bite will be the more ferocious because soon the first $6,600 of earned income will be assessed instead of the $4,800 now taxed.

Reliance upon payroll taxes has unfortunate consequences. Fiscally, these taxes are as much a drag on economic expansion as any other impost. From the standpoint of social fairness, they are inequitable, regressive imposts which will remove smaller percentages of total income from those who will earn over $6,600 each year than from those who will earn less than that sum or derive their income from property. This rise in payroll taxes, coupled with recent decreases in personal and corporate income tax rates and progressions, involves a shift toward greater inequality of income distribution after taxes. Finally, the reinforcement of the precedent that social security benefits are to be financed only out of social security payroll taxes renders it exceedingly difficult to extend the benefits of medical protection to other age groups. Further increases in payroll levies may well arouse the opposition of ordinary wage earners on whom these deductions are an irksome present burden.

What can be achieved by the consensus of the major interest groups in the United States is very substantial. The flood of legislation in 1965 verified the possibility of moderate improvement within the fiscal limits set by business predominance in the administration coalition. In short, conservative expansionism is really capable of making American society tolerable for most Americans. Nevertheless, its limitations are such, its powerful tendencies to favor the prosperous are so dominant, and its suspicion of the public sector is still so strong that it will take a more vigorous path of government action, the road of liberal intervention, to convert even an enlightened commercial community into a Great Society—to move from Keynesian fiscal policy to the Keynesian vision of a rational community.

Newsweek

THE TROUBLED AMERICAN: A SPECIAL REPORT ON THE WHITE MAJORITY

As the sixties passed into the seventies, it became increasingly evident that a prime casualty of the Indochina War was the average American. Concerned with throttling an armed Asian insurgency, American leaders inadvertently had given voters cause for an electoral insurrection. It is difficult to articulate American grievances of this time: they were too numerous and diverse. It is enough to say that Americans rarely had felt so beset by a rising tide of societal ailments. Race remained a chief issue, but drugs, crime, the war, taxes, inflation, and public services were also major concerns. Established power groups struggled to retain their pre-

ferred status against newcomers who craved a fair share of a dwindling economic pie. Ethnic, economic, and community organizations invaded government at all levels to protect and promote their interests. Organized and unorganized groups shared deep frustration, even if their reasons for anguish had little in common.

It seemed that all Americans who were not well-to-do were militant; the poor and the working class were not the only alienated Americans. The new middle class, its rising expectations unfulfilled, felt cheated. White-collar workers shed old inhibitions and organized unions, and so did professionals like teachers. They had learned that those who paid the most taxes per capita and earned the least wages in American society were the unorganized. Business and labor unions had combined for three decades to pass the financial burdens of World War II and the cold war along to Americans who were not organized. While the industrial core of the system had been relieved of considerable tensions, crises merely had been transferred to other sectors and postponed for other times.

The following is a good journalistic compendium of the various ills which beset "middle America." Although parts of it are grounded upon interpretations of respected social scientists, it does not pretend to be a scientific sampling or analysis. The selection's chief attribute is the overview it gives of American attitudes and repressed complaints. America in its bicentennial decade had become a nation under siege; its undefinable internal adversaries boded a new revolution. Stability and harmony never seemed more remote. Diversity, once the most special and celebrated aspect of America, threatened the American community with hostility and chaos. The melting pot had evolved into a dreaded cauldron. Had liberalism and the American Dream dissolved into war between the police and certain ethnic groups? Perhaps the question pivoted not so much around whether a President could bring us together as it did around whether we wanted to be brought together.

All through the skittish 1960s, America has been almost obsessed with its alienated minorities—the incendiary black militant and the welfare mother, the hedonistic hippie and the campus revolutionary. But now the pendulum of public attention is in the midst of one of those great swings that profoundly change the way the nation thinks about itself. Suddenly, the focus is on the citizen who outnumbers, outvotes and could, if he chose to, outgun the fringe rebel. After years of feeling himself a besieged minority, the man in the middle—representing America's vast white middle-class majority—is giving vent to his frustration, his disillusionment—and his anger.

"You better watch out," barks Eric Hoffer, San Francisco's bare-knuckle philosopher. "The common man is standing up and someday he's going to elect a policeman President of the United States."

How fed up is the little guy, the average white citizen who has been dubbed "the Middle American"? Is the country sliding inexorably toward an apocalyptic spasm—perhaps racial or class warfare or a turn to a grass-roots dictator who would promise to restore domestic tranquillity by suppressing all dissent and unrest? To get a definitive reading on the mood of the American majority, NEWSWEEK commissioned The Gallup Organization to survey the white population with special attention to the middle-income group—the blue- and white-collar families who make up three-fifths of U.S. whites.

The survey, bolstered by reports from NEWSWEEK correspondents around the country, suggests that the average American is more deeply troubled about his country's future than at any time since the Great Depression. The surface concerns are easy to catalogue: a futile war abroad and a malignant racial atmosphere at home, unnerving inflation and scarifying crime rates, the implacable hostility of much of the young. But the Middle American malaise cuts much deeper—right to those fundamental questions of the sanctity of work and the stability of the family, of whether a rewarding middle-class life is still possible in modern America.

America has always been the most middle-class of nations, the most generous and the most optimistic. But the pressures of the times have produced confused and contradictory impulses among the people Richard Nixon likes to call "the forgotten Americans." Himself a prototypical expression of the middle-class majority ("These are my people," he says. "We speak the same language"), the President presides over a nation nervously edging rightward in a desperate try to catch its balance after years of upheaval.

The reassertion of traditional values has festooned millions of automobile windows with American-flag decals, generated nationwide crusades to restore prayers to the schoolroom, to ban sex education, to curb pornography. The uneasy new mood has also spawned a coast-to-coast surge to law-and-order politicians—one of them a roly-poly Malaprop named Mario Procaccino, who may oust America's most outspokenly progressive mayor, John V. Lindsay, in New York City, once the Athens of American liberalism.

For the Negro, the turn in the tide can have the most momentous consequences. More and more American institutions are opening their doors to Negroes—mostly as a result of the social momentum generated in the Kennedy-Johnson years. Still, with the Nixon Administration setting the tone, the country seems to be retreating from active concern with its black minority—as the nation did nearly a century ago with the demise of Reconstruction. Self-reliant or self-delusive, the trend to separatism among younger blacks only intensifies the withdrawal. More ominous, even well-educated liberal whites have begun once more to speak openly of genetic differences between the races, an intellectual vogue before the turn of the century. "One has to consider the evidence that the Negro may be inherently inferior to the white and incapable of competing with him," says an MIT professor. "Look at the ones who have succeeded—they're almost all light-colored."

Such talk is only the tip of the iceberg. All around the country—especially among blue-collar workers—whites feel increasingly free to voice their prejudices and their hostility. "Everybody wants a gun," reports a community worker in a Slavic neighborhood in Milwaukee. "They think they've heard from black power, wait till they hear from white power —the little slob, GI Joe, the guy who breaks his ass and makes this country go. Boy, he's getting sick and tired of all this mess. One day he'll get fed up and when he does, look out!" A sign of the times: near-violent demonstrations by white construction workers enraged by Negro job demands in Pittsburgh last month and again last week in Chicago.

NEWSWEEK's survey yielded provocative evidence of a deep crisis of the spirit in Middle America—but so far, at least, no real indication of outright rebellion. The average white American feels relatively optimistic about his own personal prospects, but he fears that the country itself has changed for the worse, that it will deteriorate further in years to come, that his government is not coping with its problems, that America's troubles may be so overwhelming that the nation may not be able to solve them at all. He thinks the war in Vietnam is America's most pressing concern right now, feels it was probably a mistake to send American troops to fight it, but has no clear idea how to get them home with honor. He gives President Nixon a generally favorable rating (highest in the South) and is inclined to prolong the new President's honeymoon, but he shows no deep enthusiasm for Mr. Nixon.

He bitterly opposes much of what is happening in the country. The Middle American complains that standards of morality have declined and that the exploitation of sex and nudity in the mass media erodes morals further every passing day. He is relentlessly opposed to violent tactics by blacks and campus radicals and believes that the police should have more power to curb crime and unrest. Out of perversity or ignorance, he is convinced that Negroes actually have a better chance to get ahead in America than he does and that any troubles blacks suffer are probably their own fault. Yet he does not reject black aspirations altogether. And, despite his rejection of campus revolutionaries, the average white has a favorable attitude about young people and thinks much of their criticism of the society is warranted. Perhaps most encouraging of all, the middle-class American wants the government to start moving on the nation's domestic ills. Even though he grumbles that taxes are too high, he would favor spending money on such programs as training for the unemployed and housing for the ghetto poor.

The statistics flesh out only one dimension of the story, of course. For all the essential stability the numbers indicate, the people of Middle America talk with eloquent bitterness or forlorn resignation about the state of the nation. There is a strong strain of fear in their conversation. "The honest person doesn't stand a chance because of what the Supreme Court has done," a Boston cabbie complained to a NEWSWEEK correspondent. "People are scared and they've changed. Ten years ago if you were getting beaten up you could expect some help. Now people just walk by—they're afraid for their lives." In Inglewood, Calif., a dentist wonderingly recalls a confrontation with a booted band of motorcyclists: "When the light changed they didn't move off so I blew my horn. One of them yelled, 'What do you want, you old son of a bitch?' I was so scared and nervous I didn't even get their license numbers."

There is a pervasive feeling of being cheated by the affluent society. "Why, I can't even afford a color-TV set!" explodes a Los Angeles plumber. And there is the conviction that the government has its priorities wrong. "They spend $50 million to send a f------ monkey around the moon and there are people starving at home," growls a Milwaukee garage man.

But most of all there is a sense of loss and neglect. No hero to millions of Americans in life, John F. Kennedy has been elevated in death to an almost magical place in the hearts of his countrymen. "Kennedy put the spirit back in people," says a factory hand in Tyler, Texas. "He would have done some good if they would of gave him some time and hadn't killed him." And, feeling himself the spokesman of the oppressed majority, a hard-hatted San Francisco construction worker gripes: "The niggers are all organized. So are the Mexicans, even the Indians. But who the hell speaks for me?" Adds Paul Deac, head of the National Confederation of American Ethnic Groups: "We spend millions and the Negroes get everything and we get nothing."

Resentment over compensatory programs for blacks feeds the Middle American's sense of himself as the ultimate victim. The experts typically disagree over whether the middle-class white is as victimized by the society as he feels himself to be. Some contend that the white reaction is a rational response to the squeeze of taxes and inflation (despite big wage increases the average factory worker's real income has declined $1.09 per week in the past year) and the authentic danger of rising crime. Others point out that Middle Americans tend to ignore the large government subsidies they get in such benefits as tax write-offs for mortgage interest payments; still others say unrealistic expectations are bred by the myth of affluence. "Middle-class people," says University of Michigan philosopher Abraham Kaplan, "look around and say, 'We've entered paradise and it looks like the place we just left. And if this is paradise why am I so miserable?'" Then, says Kaplan, they look for scapegoats among those who are attacking middle-class values.

Indeed, the most deeply rooted source of the white American malaise is the plain fact that middle-class values are under more obdurate attack today than ever before. "The values that we held so dear are being shot to hell," says George Culberson of the government's Community Relations Service. "Everything is being attacked—what you believed in, what you learned in school, in church, from your parents. So the middle class is sort of losing heart. They had their eye on where they were going and suddenly it's all shifting sands."

The sands are shifting beneath all the familiar totems—the work ethic, premarital chastity, the notion of postponing gratification, and filial gratitude for parental sacrifice. Middle-class folk, says philosopher Kaplan, are infuriated by college demonstrations because they "upset their image of what college is—a place where there are trees, where the kids drink cocoa, eat marshmallows, read Shakespeare and once in the spring the boys can look at the girls' underthings." Says radical writer Paul Jacobs, once a union organizer: "The notion of work that they had been brought up to deify is being undermined by the young people. The hippies, Woodstock, all those broads walking around with their boobs bouncing. Not only do young people do it, but the media seem to approve it and the upper class does these things, too." Television is the most subversive enemy of the old ways. "Through television," says Anthony Downs, a consultant to LBJ's riot commission, "we are encouraging, on the consumption side, things which are entirely inconsistent with the disciplines necessary for our production side. Look at what television advertising encourages: immediate gratification, do it now, buy it now, pay later, leisure time, hedonism."

Beyond that, TV enhances the Middle American's feeling that he is enveloped in a chaotic world he never made and cannot control. "You have violence and sex and drugs on television," says Chicago psychiatrist Dr. Jarl Dyrud, whose patients are mostly drawn from the middle class. "You have the news about the Vietnam war, the protests of the kids on campus, the protests of the blacks. It's hard to escape any more." "Every time you turn around, there's a crisis of some sort," says community organizer Saul Alinsky, a brassy anti-Establishmentarian now concentrating his efforts on white communities. "You have the black crisis, the urban crisis—it's just one goddam crisis after another. It's just too much for the average middle-class Joe to take. There's always something else to worry about. But the worst thing about it for the middle class is that they feel powerless to do anything about anything."

The more precarious a family's hold on economic security, the more menaced it feels by the pressures of black militancy and inflation. The government estimates that it costs at least $10,000 a year for a family of four to maintain a moderate standard of living—yet 26.3 million white families fall below that level. And, despite nine consecutive years of prosperity, many a breadwinner can't forget the specter of the wolf in the carport. "Blue collar and white collar alike still live too near 'layoffs,' 'reductions,' 'strikes,' 'plant relocations' to be personally secure," says former HUD Under Secretary Robert Wood, now head of the Harvard-MIT Joint Center for Urban Studies.

With little equity but his mortgaged home and his union card, the white worker is especially resistant to integration efforts that appear to threaten his small stake in the world. "I believe that an apprenticeship in my union is no more a public trust to be shared by all, than a millionaire's money is a public trust," one worker wrote to The New York Times. "Why should the government . . . have any more right to decide how I dispose of my heritage than it does how the corner grocer disposes of his?" "Second-generation people inherit from their parents a reverence for their own home," says Rep. Roman Pucinski, a Chicago Democrat who takes the pulse of his district each Saturday. "The Polish have a word, grunt—a base, a foundation. They know integration has to come, but their big concern is property values."

The hunt for scapegoats goes beyond the blacks to their allies: the liberal white elite. Many lower-middle-class whites feel that an unholy alliance has grown up between the liberal Establishment and Negro militants to reshape American life at their expense. School busing to achieve integration, for example, is probably the least popular social nostrum of the 1960s. And the Kerner commission's well-publicized conclusion that "white racism" is the basic cause of black riots touched off howls of indignation. "They resent their leaders' hypocrisy," says Paul Jacobs, "—especially the rich liberal politicians who send their own kids to private school."

There has always been a streak of anti-intellectualism in Middle America. It bubbles to the surface when the country feels itself betrayed—as it did in the days before Joe McCarthy's rampages. All through the late 1960s, liberals and radicals have been predicting a revival of know-nothingism. So far, it has failed to materialize to any great degree—although George Wallace did his best last year with his diatribes against "pointy heads" and such enemies of the common man. Today, a growing sense of betrayal undoubtedly is percolating in many middle-class hearts. The anti-middle-class bias of college radicals contributes to the problem. "Many of the young people see middle-class people as nothing but a bunch of big-bosomed, beer-drinking, drum-and-bugle-corps types," says Rep. Allard Lowenstein, who tries to keep up his contacts both on the campus and in his middle-class Long Island district.

S. I. Hayakawa, who became something of a Middle American folk hero by suppressing demonstrations at San Francisco State College last year, thinks the educated elite is dangerously out of touch with the middle-class masses. "You and I," he tells a visitor, "can live in the suburbs and demand integration in the schools downtown. We can make the moral demands and someone else has to live with them. We can say the war in Vietnam is a dirty, immoral act while our children are in college, exempt from the draft. The working people's children are in Vietnam and they're praying for victory. They want to believe America is right."

More bluntly, Eric Hoffer rages: "We are told we have to feel guilty. We've been poor all our lives and now we're being preached to by every son of a bitch who comes along. The ethnics are discovering that you can't trust those Mayflower boys."

Hoffer's observation is symptomatic of the new mood of ethnic chauvinism taking hold in Middle America. "The rise of Negro militancy," says Congressman Pucinski, "has brought a revival of ethnic orientation in all the other groups." The hard truth is that the celebrated American melting pot has never worked quite so well in life as in nostalgic myth. As Nathan Glazer and Daniel P. Moynihan pointed out six years ago in "Beyond the Melting Pot," Americans tend to maintain their sense of ethnic identity far more tenaciously than was once supposed. One result of the new white nationalism is a greater willingness to express anti-black feelings—intensified by Negro job competition. "They've always been anti-Negro," says one old union hand. "But they've never been pressured to say it publicly before."

In the current atmosphere, liberal groups are devoting new attention to the hyphenated American. The American Jewish Committee has conducted substantial research on the subject, and Americans for Democratic Action is making a major thrust to try to keep ethnic voters in the Democratic coalition. "Any politician who ignores 40 million ethnics is a fool," says Leon Shull, executive director of the ADA. Paul Deac, of the Washington-based ethnic lobby, is trying to pry anti-poverty money and other considerations for his people from the Administration. "Right now, the ethnic vote is up for grabs," insists Deac. "Our people are as gun-shy of the Republicans as of the liberal Democrats. If the Republicans grab the opportunity they can forge an alliance with ethnics and remain in power for a long time."

Except for the Italians, few of the nation's later immigrant groups have had much use for the Republican Party. And no one can say for certain how successful Richard Nixon will be if he tries to entice ethnic voters into his new centrist coalition. The President's strong anti-Communist stand over the years—and his recent trip to Rumania—are likely to enhance Mr. Nixon's appeal. Just such a thrust is at the heart of a GOP battle plan devised by Kevin P. Phillips, a 28-year-old Justice Department aide, in a much-discussed book called "The Emerging Republican Majority." As Phillips envisages it, the Republicans could cement their hold by building an alliance based on the South and the traditional heartland, and whites disgruntled by Democratic "social engineering." The President professed last week not to have read the book. And basically, Mr. Nixon will stand or fall on his over-all ability to convince America that he can end the war, reorder priorities and bring greater stability to the U.S.

On that score, the President seems to have a number of advantages.

"Nixon is tremendously reassuring to middle-class Americans," says sociologist Robert Nisbet of the University of California at Riverside. "If you started out to design a human being who would be an answer for this kind of person in this kind of time, you couldn't design a better one than Nixon. His kind of corny, square, ketchup-on-cottage-cheese image is very reassuring to these people." What's more, says Brandeis University historian John Roche, who was once LBJ's intellectual-in-residence, government—Nixon style—has reduced the level of disorder in America. "The edge is already off," says Roche, "because the election of Nixon put into office people who are not going to be responsible for demonstrations. There will be no great riots—you don't riot against your enemies but against your friends, because you know your friends don't shoot. [Attorney General John] Mitchell means business."

Even if he should end the war and further cool the ghettos and campuses, the President faces the more fundamental problem of giving the white majority a greater sense of participation and reward in the life of the society. And he must somehow accomplish this while maintaining the nation's commitments to its non-white minorities, especially the Negroes. "The ethnic groups, the Irish and the Jews don't want to penalize the Negro but they feel strongly that the rules they came up with should apply," says Roche. "To change rules now is basically unfair."

"We need more programs for Mr. Forgotten American," says a Washington liberal. The fact is, however, that very little thought has gone into the problems of the white middle class. Foundations and think tanks have primarily been concerned with the plight of the minorities. A turnabout of sorts is under way. The Harvard-MIT Joint Center for Urban Studies has made Middle America its target subject for the new year, and the Ford Foundation plans to focus some of its attention on the middle class. Concrete ideas are sparse. Mitchell Sviridoff, Ford's vice president for national affairs, speaks rather vaguely of expanding medicaid programs and of retraining the middle-aged white worker trapped in a dead-end assembly-line job.

But the underlying necessity is to find the national resources to help both the majority white and his non-white counterpart. "We've stimulated the minorities to believe that something is going to happen for them. If we slow down, as we have, their frustrations will be so seriously exacerbated that they will be pushed to more militant behavior," argues Sviridoff. "Then the majority will be pushed to more repressive behavior and we will have an absolutely impossible situation on our hands."

Some think that the problem goes far beyond the reach of even the most imaginative government. "When the hippies go to Woodstock," says Paul Jacobs, "they are building a new community of their own. The worker's community is disintegrating. He doesn't know where to find a new one. So he keeps harking back to the old days and the old values.

But it is not possible to go back. And there is no new community to re-place the old."

Can Middle America somehow create a new pluralist community to satisfy its new needs? On the answer to that question rests much of the destiny of the nation in the years ahead.

HOW IT FEELS TO BE CAUGHT
IN THE MIDDLE

There's racial problems, money problems, more crime ... Everything has gone to pieces.

—A Kalamazoo, Mich., housewife

In this harvest season of 1969, that is the voice of Middle America —the white middle class, the backbone of the country, the people who have taken to thinking of themselves as "forgotten."

NEWSWEEK's special poll of white Americans, conducted by The Gallup Organization in an unusually wide sampling of public opinion, found the white majority profoundly troubled—but not, as some have sug-gested, on the brink of violent rebellion. There is a heavy undertone of resentment—a dark suspicion that the rules are being changed in the middle of the game, that the dice are loaded in somebody else's favor. But at bottom, the mood adds up to a nagging sense that life is going sour—that, whatever is wrong, the whole society somehow has lost its way.

This new pessimism has serious implications for the nation, because Middle America, in a real sense, *is* America. For the NEWSWEEK survey, Gallup interviewers talked to 2,165 adults comprising a cross-section of the entire white population (which, in turn, is almost 90 per cent of the total population). The sample included a middle-class group large enough for detailed analysis: 1,321 Americans with household incomes ranging from $5,000 to $15,000, representing 61 per cent of the white population.

By themselves, the Middle Americans are a majority of the nation— and the strength of their opinions outweighs their numbers. In the NEWS-

WEEK Poll, the attitudes of the middle-income group showed hardly any significant variation from those of the total white group on any question.

As the Middle American sees it, his country is beset by a sea of troubles. The war in Vietnam oppresses the nation—nearly two out of three of those polled cite it as one of America's top problems. "I don't like a war where there couldn't be a winner," complains an electrician in Mineral Wells, Texas. There is the endless, abrasive racial crisis, mentioned by 41 per cent. "We could have a civil war," warns a county employee in Stanwood, Wash. There are the nagging pocketbook issues: inflation erodes everybody's pay check, and 78 per cent think Federal taxes are just plain too high. There is crime and delinquency and a gnawing feeling of powerlessness. The government, says a Chicago truck driver, "doesn't know I exist—or care." And there is a sense that solid old values are crumbling. "Seems like we have lost respect for ourselves," says a housewife in Bellefontaine Neighbors, Mo.

Save for the war, the nation's brooding is almost exclusively inward. Only 2 per cent of the sampling thought to mention nuclear war as a problem facing the country; fewer than 1 per cent listed Russia or Red China. But the internal discontents are as varied as they are pervasive. "This sex education shouldn't be in the small grades, like I heard they're going to have," said the wife of a laborer in South Bend, Ind.

For all that, most middle-class Americans expect to prosper in coming years. Nearly two-thirds of the sampling feel that five years from now they will be at least as well off as they are today—or better off. But they are afraid they will enjoy it less. Fully 46 per cent agree that the nation has changed for the worse in the past ten years. Opinion splits on whether the United States can solve its problems at all. Fifty-nine per cent believe that the danger of racial conflict is on the rise—and 58 per cent feel that the United States, on the whole, is likely to change for the worse in the years ahead.

Middle America itself is hardly monolithic; its over-all statistical unity conceals many shadings of opinions. The biggest differences match educational levels. Thus, people who went to college tend to have better jobs, earn more money and be more tolerant on racial issues and less disturbed by youth protests. Those whose education ended in grade school tend to hold blue-collar jobs—and to be financially insecure and angry over the accelerating pace of social change. The educational split was neatly shown by a question asking whether the United States is becoming too materialistic. Some 54 per cent of those who had gone to college agreed—but only 36 per cent of the grade-school group would go along.

Other significant divisions of opinion stem from age, sex and region of the country. Women, for instance, tend to be less hawkish than men on Vietnam. Westerners worry most about drugs and air pollution. And surprisingly, adults under 30 tend to disapprove of modern youth more vehemently than do people aged 30 to 55.

Despite these internal differences, however, Middle America is united in its discontent—and, increasingly, sees itself as an oppressed majority. "I think the middle class is getting the short end of the stick on everything," says a computer technician from Brooklyn. "The welfare people get out of taxes, and so do the rich," says a construction foreman in Baltimore. "The middle-class family is just forgotten."

The worst frustration is the war in Vietnam. It is, by now, a war that has come very close to home; 55 per cent of the NEWSWEEK Middle American sampling said they were personally acquainted with someone who had been killed or wounded in Vietnam. Yet people are frankly and bitterly confused as to the conduct of the war, the reasons for American involvement and what should be done next.

There is general agreement on only one thing: that the war is not going well. Only 8 per cent believe that the U.S. and South Vietnam are winning. One in five said the war was being lost, and two-thirds of the sampling opted for the euphemistic "holding our own." Nearly three in five said the U.S. was justified in intervening in the war—but 70 per cent argued that, justified or not, the nation should have kept its sons at home.

At the extremes, hawks and doves were almost evenly divided. Approximately one in five said that the U.S. had "no right or reason" to fight

LOOKING AHEAD: PESSIMISM

	Agree	Disagree	No Change
The U.S. has changed for the worse over the past decade	46%	36%	13%
The danger of racial violence is increasing	59%	26%	12%
The U.S. is likely to change for the worse over the next decade	58%	19%	14%
The U.S. is less able to solve its problems than it was five years ago	40%	40%	16%

Undecided omitted

WANTED: "LAW AND ORDER"

	Yes	No
Local police do a good job of preventing crime	78%	16%
Police should have more power	63%	35%
Suspects who might commit another crime before they come to trial should be held without bail	68%	23%
Black militants have been treated too leniently	85%	8%
College demonstrators have been treated too leniently	84%	11%

Undecided omitted

THE BLACKS: TOO MUCH, TOO SOON?

**Do Negroes today have a better chance or
worse chance than people like yourself—**

	Better	Worse	Same
To get well-paying jobs?	44%	21%	31%
To get a good education for their children?	41%	16%	41%
To get good housing at a reasonable cost?	35%	30%	27%
To get financial help from the government when they're out of work?	65%	4%	22%

Undecided omitted

in Vietnam; one in four said it was "our right and duty." In volunteered opinions, however, the strongest expressions were hawkish, with 21 per cent urging a more aggressive, fight-to-win policy. "I can't figure it out," complained a retired sand-and-gravel dealer in Fort Loramie, Ohio. "If you can't go into North Vietnam, what's the use of fighting? If you hit me and go into the next room and I can't follow, what the hell's the use?" "Don't bomb here, don't bomb there—it's a cuddly war," snapped a nurse who lives in East Keansburg, N.J. "They should blast them all and come home."

In contrast, the dovish opinions sounded oddly uncertain; opponents of the war cited passionless arguments on the theme that the U.S. should not have been involved in the first place, or that it was time for the war to end. "I can't remember when we started fighting there," said 22-year-old William H. Neumann Jr., manager of a restaurant in Sarasota, Fla., "but I do think we should have been out a long time ago." One of the most curious findings of the survey was the almost total absence of moral arguments against the war. Despite the clamor of the most vocal doves over the past four years, only a handful of the sampling argued that the war was simply wrong. Instead, opinions both pro and con were thoroughly pragmatic; as a New York City housewife phrased her case: "There's nothing to be gained."

On issues closer to home, the Middle American is considerably more emotional. He is in a financial vise, with inflation and rising taxes threatening what precarious security he has—and to make this threat worse, black Americans are demanding an ever-greater economic share.

Resentment of Negroes is at once the most obvious and the most complex note in the new mood of Middle America. It is not outright racism, in the sense that Negroes are hated because they are black. As recently as 1966, a NEWSWEEK survey found white Americans agreeing, by more than 2 to 1, that Negroes were discriminated against and deserved better. Fully 70 per cent of whites then said that, like it or not, they would probably be living in integrated housing in five years' time—

and there was a similarly grudging acceptance of black gains in jobs and education. But with this acceptance went a strong feeling among whites that Negroes were trying to win too much, too fast—and this attitude is as strong as ever.

Recent progress for Negroes—particularly in jobs, education and housing—has come partly at the expense of the middle class. What's worse, some black demands and white-liberal rhetoric have focused on the concept of reparations for years in discrimination—an idea that Middle America sees simply as a new form of reverse discrimination. "I see the Negro stepping on my rights," said a finance manager in Los Angeles. "He is asking for more than is justifiably his."

Whatever the facts of the case, a substantial minority of white America professes to believe that the black man already has the advantage. More than four out of ten in the sampling said Negroes actually have a better chance than whites to get a good job or a good education for their children, and nearly two-thirds said Negroes got preference in unemployment benefits from the government. "The Negroes think they are having a disadvantage, which is not true," said Mrs. John Tiedje, in Clarksville, N.Y. Ludicrous as the idea sounds to Negroes, many Middle Americans are convinced that police and the courts give blacks especially lenient treatment: "It looks," said an oil-refinery worker in Galena Park, Texas, "like whites don't have the rights that Negroes do."

Blacks are also perceived by many as morally different from whites: they don't seem to live by the rules of the basically Puritan white middle class. "They are given jobs by good companies and they don't work," says a New York policeman. "The backers of the Negro are making them think that we owe them jobs, and we owe them housing, food, money, for nothing." This attitude is astonishingly widespread; 73 per cent of the NEWSWEEK sampling agreed that blacks "could have done something" about slum conditions, and 55 per cent thought Negroes were similarly to blame for their unemployment rate. What's more, nearly four out of five declared that half or more of the nation's welfare recipients—who tend to be thought of mainly as Negroes—could earn their own way if they tried.

With such basic attitudes, it is hardly surprising that Middle America shows little enthusiasm for what it thinks of as sacrifice to advance the black cause. In education, for instance, only 2 per cent of those polled favored busing to improve racial balance in the schools. In fact, only one out of four favored further integration at all. Given their choice, nearly two-thirds would either improve Negro schools or let blacks run their own schools.

Even this attitude is not unalloyed bigotry. Unfashionable as it is to credit racial rationalizations at face value, much white middle-class opposition to integration reflects a genuine fear that the quality of education may deteriorate. And for all his resentment at black activism, the Middle American still has a basic sympathy for the Negro's aspirations.

BLACK SCHOOLS—OR MIXED?
What should be done about Negro
demands for better education?

Improve schools where Negro children go	40%
Move toward integration	25%
Let Negroes run their own schools	24%
Integrate schools by busing children	2%
Ignore demands because they are not justified	3%

Undecided omitted

Significantly, nearly seven out of ten agreed that at least some of the demands presented by Negro leaders were justified. Equally to the point, the same proportion also agreed that "it will take some time" to meet the demands.

White America's prejudice is most obvious when it comes to the crime problem—which large numbers automatically associate with Negroes. "We are really afraid," said a North Carolina woman, "with the colored right in our backyard." Asked to define "law and order," an investment adviser in King of Prussia, Pa., said, "Get the niggers. Nothing else."

Crime, the survey showed, is considered one of the nation's most serious problems—but oddly enough, it is generally thought to be worse in somebody else's backyard. Only 10 per cent of the sampling volunteered crime in their own listing of the nation's problems, and fewer than half considered it a serious issue in their own communities. Yet nearly two-thirds checked it off as one of the worst problems facing the cities—and suburbanites were more likely to think so than city dwellers themselves.

Despite the furor over crime in recent months, only three in ten said they had changed their habits to protect themselves; those few were mainly locking doors and windows formerly left unlatched. And despite widespread reports of an arms buildup, only 4 per cent volunteered that they kept guns to protect themselves, and fewer than 1 per cent said they had installed burglar alarms. Others mentioned tear-gas guns and judo lessons. "We've started feeding an ugly dog," reported David Ingraham, owner of a service station in Clarksville, N.Y.

Nearly four out of five are satisfied with their local police, reporting that the officers do a good job of preventing local crime. Nonetheless, 63 per cent of the sampling said police didn't have enough power in dealing with suspected criminals, and more than two-thirds agreed that judges should have the right to deny pretrial bail to suspects considered likely to commit a crime while on the loose—a crime-fighting step of dubious constitutionality.

A significant minority worried that more police power could bring on a police state—"Hitler had law and order," observed Mrs. Marjorie Runner, a San Francisco housewife. But the majority of those polled were convinced that thugs were getting too many breaks. To most people, the possibility of added police power offers no conceivable threat to anyone but wrongdoers. "Behave yourself and there's no problem," declared a construction worker in Wichita, Kans. "I think of law and order as what I do."

If crime is a threat to the Middle American's safety, the much-publicized youth rebellion is an equally real challenge to his self-esteem. Whether picketing on campus or parading barefoot in hippie regalia, the younger generation seems to be telling him that his way of life is corrupt, his goals worthless and his treasured institutions doomed. Logically enough, a good many middle-class citizens tend to resent the message. "It's horrible. They are going to the dogs," said Mrs. Cecil L. Davis of Wichita Falls, Texas. The overwhelming majority in the poll made it clear that they had little sympathy for the outright rebels among the younger generation; 84 per cent said campus demonstrators had been treated too leniently, and nearly three out of five said the demonstrators had little or no justification for their actions.

Nonetheless, most Middle Americans make a clear distinction between youthful rebels and the greater number of what they think of as normal youngsters. "These college rioters should be put in concentration camps," said Herbert R. Parsons Jr., a furniture store manager of Peru, Ind. "But by and large, the majority are fine young people." Some 59 per cent of those polled agreed that their impression of most young people was favorable.

And in his heart, the Middle American isn't all that sure that even the rebels are altogether wrong. Some 54 per cent of those polled, in fact, agreed that young people were not unduly critical of their country, and that criticism was actually needed. But this sentiment reflects not so much tolerance of the young as a deep-seated fear that the whole system is somehow failing, that the quality of life is declining and that the middle-class citizen's own place is no longer secure.

This painful awareness that things just aren't what they used to be is at the bottom of the nation's new discontent. "Conditions are changing for the worse," mused a farmer from Bald Knob, Ark. "Conditions are unstable, and getting worse." Solid old values seem to be deteriorating; seven-tenths of the sampling agreed that people now were less religious than they were five years ago, and 86 per cent said sexual permissiveness was undermining the nation's morals. "I really worry sometimes about this country, if we don't change our ways and return to religion," said another farmer in Timmonsville, S.C.

And this erosion of values extends to the interpersonal links that foster security and stability in any society. Only 39 per cent of those polled feel most people "really care" what happens to strangers. About the same percentage said it wasn't likely that anyone would help them if they were robbed on the street in their own neighborhoods. More

U.S. SPENDING: NEW PRIORITIES

On which problems do you think the government
should be spending more money—and on which
should it be spending less money?

	More Money	Less Money
Job training for the unemployed	56%	7%
Air and water pollution	56%	3%
Fighting organized crime	55%	3%
Medical care for the old and needy	47%	5%
Fighting crime in the streets	44%	4%
Improving schools	44%	7%
Providing better housing for the poor—especially in the ghettos	39%	13%
Building highways	23%	14%
Defense expenditures	16%	26%
Space exploration	10%	56%
Foreign economic aid	6%	57%
Foreign military aid	1%	66%

than half said they put only "some" trust in the news media and the Federal government to tell the truth about what was going on; some 30 per cent said they had little trust or none at all. But however skeptical, Middle Americans feel increasingly powerless to shape their own destiny. In the face of the complexity of the modern world, a bare half of the sampling thought they should have any say in their country's defense and foreign policy. "We are not well-informed enough to give solutions," said a Chicago accountant.

What the middle class does want is stability—or at least the illusion of stability. If change is inevitable, in race relations, for example, it should come without upheaval. "I think Negroes have justified reasons," said the wife of a utility serviceman in St. Paul, Minn., "but they are going about it in the wrong way with the wrong leaders."

In such a national dilemma, it would be natural for people to turn on their leaders—and there is, to be sure, no lack of grumbling in Middle America about the government. Only 24 per cent of the sampling said the government was doing a "good" or "excellent" job of dealing with the nation's problems; two-thirds said "fair" or "poor."

The grumbling is loudest, of course, over the pocketbook issues of taxes and inflation. Despite the vaunted prosperity of the nation during the 1960s, one out of every four middle-class Americans said the rising cost of living had forced a cutback on purchases; another 44 per cent said they were just managing to stay even. Nearly eight out of ten said Federal taxes were too steep, and 59 per cent thought local taxes excessive. "We had to sell our home because our taxes were too high," said G. W. Loenstein, a retired grocer in Oakland, Calif.

For the most part, however, the middle class has a weary sort of tolerance for their elected representatives. "It's not really the government's fault," said Thomas Silevitch, a Christmas-tree-bulb maker in Dorchester, Mass. "The government can't solve everyone's problems." Asked to rate President Nixon's performance in office, nearly half of the sampling—49 per cent—gave him favorable marks, with 31 per cent less enthusiastic and only 15 per cent downright critical. There was no great yearning for another leader; only 12 per cent thought the country would be better off with George Wallace at the helm, and a bare 10 per cent thought Hubert Humphrey would do better. But there was little enthusiasm for Mr. Nixon. In fact, people had a tendency to praise him with faint damns, explaining their ratings by saying that he had done all right so far, or seemed to be working for peace. "He is doing the best he can with the ability he has, which I don't think is too much," said a housewife in Jacksonville, Fla.

Whatever its resentments and frustrations, then, Middle America is not about to take to the barricades—or even to slump into mulish apathy. Indeed, the most encouraging finding of the NEWSWEEK Poll is the extent to which people are willing to seek fresh solutions; a clear plurality of 48 per cent agreed that "we need to experiment with new ways of dealing with the nation's problems." Even the celebrated tax revolt turns out, on close scrutiny, to be a paper dragon. The chief complaint is not so much the level of taxation but rather that the government has its priorities wrong. "Nobody has the right to take a hard-working man's money and waste it, but they all do," said Mrs. Margaret Donovan, a housewife in Albany, N.Y. "Our money just isn't used right."

By a clear margin, the middle class is more concerned with solving problems than with governmental economies. Asked how the government should use any unexpected surplus in revenues, fully 48 per cent said the money should go to improve conditions in the country; only one in three favored a tax cut, and 16 per cent wanted to reduce the national debt. In specific terms, the sampling favored added spending for such programs as job training, pollution control, medicare, slum housing and crime control. But a good many thought money was being wasted in foreign aid and defense spending—and even in the afterglow of the moon landing, fully 56 per cent thought the government should spend less on space.

In the end, this willingness to tackle the nation's problems tempers Middle America's pessimism. "Change is not bad," said John King, a Mississippi cattle raiser. "But there may be a period of time when things worsen before we settle on a course again." In the long run, said the owner of a printing shop in Cleveland, "I have great confidence in our ability to find the right answers. We're great opportunists and improvisers." A touch of malaise may be fashionable, and all very well for a while, but it goes against the Middle American grain. If something has gone wrong, it will simply have to be fixed; after all, says a San Diego aircraft inspector, "We won't just sit around and let the country go down the drain." And in this troubled harvest season, the hope is that his is the real voice of the country.

IN POLITICS, IT'S THE NEW POPULISM

In Minneapolis, a policeman named Charles Stenvig becomes mayor by rolling up an astounding 62 per cent of the vote against the experienced president of the City Council. In New York, Mayor John Lindsay and former Mayor Robert Wagner, both liberals of national stature, bow to obscure interlopers in their parties' mayoral primaries. In Boston, grandmotherly Louise Day Hicks, whose crusade for the "forgotten man" and against school busing carried her within an inch of City Hall two years ago, leads a big field in the upcoming City Council elections. And in Newark, a onetime construction worker named Anthony Imperiale, master of karate, the bowie knife and a fleet of 72 radio cars that regularly patrol the city's white neighborhoods, confidently maps his campaign to win next year's race for mayor and "get rid of every quisling" in sight.

This is the year of the New Populism, a far-ranging, fast-spreading revolt of the little man against the Establishment at the nation's polls. Middle America, long counted upon to supply the pluralities on Election Day, is beginning to supply eye-opening victories from coast to coast. The over-all political cast of the country remains mixed, to be sure. The freshman crop of U.S. senators elected just last year, for example, includes a significant share of conventional liberals and moderates. Only a fortnight ago, a Negro candidate topped the field in the Detroit mayoral primary, and progressive Lindsay may yet eke out a victory in New York next month. But—especially in close-to-home city politics—the frustrated middle-class majority has increasingly been turning to newfound champions drawn from its own ranks.

The seeds of popular rebellion have been long implanted beneath the surface of liberal hegemony. Even as John Kennedy and Lyndon Johnson held sway in Washington, Barry Goldwater astounded the political pros with his temporary seizure of the GOP, Ronald Reagan carried the banner of the "citizen politician" from the movie lots to the California Statehouse, and George Wallace and Lester Maddox found that fulminations against "those bureaucrats" was a sure path to popularity both in the South and, to some extent, in the rest of the nation.

But this was the year that the phenomenon finally broke the surface with a series of municipal victories impossible to dismiss as regional aberrations. And this was the year that the New Populism began to be seen more clearly for what it really is.

It is not, most politicians now agree, simply a burst of racist backlash. Though sheer bigotry has certainly played a part in fueling the little man's revolt, part of his resentment of the black man is traceable to his sense of desertion by a government that appears preoccupied with Negroes' needs and inattentive to his own. Liberals who have shouted "racism!" at white response to the black revolution are now beginning to realize that this oversimplifies the impulses involved and bolsters Middle America's mounting impression that liberals neither understand nor sympathize with lower-middle-class whites.

And it is not simply a swing to the political right. Though the New Populists have unquestionably turned conservative on law enforcement, they show few signs of wanting to scrap the social reforms—medicare, aid to education, and social security improvements—wrought by the liberal left. "It's a swing against anarchy," says liberal Congressman Allard Lowenstein, and indeed the disgruntlement with the progressives seems to stem far more from their permissiveness than from their programs.

Perhaps, most of all, the New Populism is a quest for recognition. "People felt that nobody was representing them and nobody was listening," says Minneapolis's Charlie Stenvig. "They felt alienated from the political system, and they'd had it up to their Adam's apples on just about everything. So they took a guy like me—four kids, an average home, a working man they could associate themselves with. They just said, 'Lookit, we're sick of you politicians'."

Stenvig was, indeed, a paragon of Middle America: the son of a telephone company employee, a Methodist of Norwegian stock, a graduate of a local high school and a local college (Augsburg), and an up-through-the-ranks detective on the police force. His opponent, by contrast, was almost pure Establishment: the son of an investment banker, a graduate of Stanford and Harvard Law, and a resident of the fashionable Kenwood suburb.

In his campaign, Stenvig pounded away at the privileged bastions of suburbia—he pledged to "bring government back to the citizens of Minneapolis and away from the influence of the golden West out there in Wayzata"—a priviledged enclave on the city's fringes. To low-income whites, the suburbs are where the liberals live. "The liberal preaches from his lily-white suburb," explains United Auto Workers official Paul Schrade, "while the worker usually lives on the borderline of the ghetto.

The workers are on the front lines of the black-white conflict and resent the advice of rear-echelon generals."

Minneapolis's workers relished Stenvig's assault on the suburbs—"He told those rich guys to go suck a lemon," chortles one local auto mechanic —and as mayor he has kept up the attack. He has protested the financing plan for a new hospital on the ground that the suburbs would not pay enough of the tab, and he has staffed city jobs with what he calls "just average working people."

A few of these appointments have aroused the only controversy in what most people in Minneapolis agree has been an extremely hard-working, well-intentioned municipal administration. Antonio G. Felicetta, vice president of the regional joint council of the Teamsters union, created a citywide sensation recently when he delivered some pungent remarks in his new role as a member of the city Commission on Human Relations. "I'm not going to take any bulls---," he announced to a local journalist. "If there are any grievances, I sure as hell would want to see them taken care of. But I sure as hell wouldn't want to give 'em [welfare recipients] half my goddam paycheck when I'm working and they're sitting on their asses." Felicetta was promptly denounced as a "card-carrying bigot" by a group of Minneapolis blacks, but he also received a torrent of phone calls saying "That's the way, Tony, sock it to 'em."

Middle America's radical right has always delighted in such tough words—and deeds. Newark's Tony Imperiale became an instant folk hero in these circles when he organized a band of white vigilantes in the wake of the disastrous summer riots in 1967. And last week, as he looked ahead to the day when he becomes mayor, he made plain that official investiture will not change his tune. "If any militant comes into my office, puts his ass on my desk and tells me what I have to do," he vowed, "I'll throw his ass off the wall and throw him out the door."

There is little question that Tony—38 years old, 5 feet 6¾ inches high and 260 pounds thick—is capable of doing just that. As he drove his volunteer ambulance—part of his vigilante patrol—past the corner of Mt. Prospect Street and Bloomfield Avenue in Newark's rugged North Ward one evening recently, he recalled an example of the sort of direct action he favors: "We came down here one night with eight guys and kicked the crap outa 22 junkies. Each time we came back to slap them around they lessened in ranks and finally took the hint." Imperiale keeps an arsenal of about 40 serviceable guns in his house, including a 14-inch-barrel scatter-gun stowed behind the couch (there have already been two attempts on his life).

Imperiale is a bit too rough-and-ready for the taste of most other politicians of the New Populism. And outside the South, most of them would disclaim any ideological kinship with Dixie's two most prominent contributions to the movement, former Alabama Gov. George Wallace and incumbent Georgia Gov. Lester Maddox. But Wallace, whose Presidential campaigns of 1964 and 1968 featured attacks on "pointy-headed intellectuals" and "briefcase-toting bureaucrats" that gave his appeal a di-

mension beyond sheer racism, claims paternity for much of the movement. "My vote was only the tip of the iceberg," he says. "There's others
I'm responsible for: Stenvig, Mayor Yorty of Los Angeles, two mayoral
candidates in New York. They were making Alabama speeches with a
Minneapolis, Los Angeles and New York accent. The only thing they
omitted was the drawl."

One of the things that draws the Populists together is their common
wistfulness for the "old values," for traditional verities and styles of life
that somehow seem to have gone awry. Lester Maddox, for example,
likes to think of himself as part of "the mainstream of the thinking of the
American people: the achievers, the success-makers, the builders, the
individuals who like to set their own goals and accept the challenges."
A number of Middle America's politicians also like to brandish the cru-
sader's cross. "God is going to be my principal adviser," declares Charlie
Stenvig, and Mary Beck, a 61-year-old Detroit councilwoman who placed
a strong third in last month's mayoral primary, dedicated her campaign
newspaper "to the laws of God and man."

When Populists brood on the agonies of contemporary society, a certain nostalgia for a simpler life is never far from the surface. "I was born
in a little town of 6,000 people," recalls Democrat Mario Procaccino, who
appears to be leading Lindsay and a conservative Republican in the
New York mayor's race. "We respected our parents, our teachers, and
our priest or man of the cloth. We had respect for men in public office.
We looked up to them . . . "

Procaccino frequently exhibits another characteristic of this new political breed: emotionalism. He wept when he announced his candidacy.
Occasionally he takes his wife, Marie, and his daughter, Marierose, for
an evening visit to the top of the Empire State Building. "I look out over
the city and say to myself, 'What's the matter with these people? Why
can't they get together?' " Many middle-class voters seem to warm to these
displays of feeling, perhaps because they themselves are so upset, perhaps because they sense that their government has been run recently by
soulless technocrats spouting bureaucratic jargon or political cant. "I
like him because he's so emotional," beamed one housewife to her neighbor as Procaccino campaigned through Queens last week. "Any tears he
sheds, you know he has heart. He doesn't fear to shed them and they
bring the people closer to him."

Mayor Sam Yorty of Los Angeles is another extremely warm-blooded
politician, endowed with a coloratura stumping style that ranges between
acid vituperation and passionate enthusiasm. Ever since the Watts riots
of 1965, he has concentrated the former on militants and the latter on
guardians of law and order. This approach proved immensely popular
in last spring's mayoral election, when he won an upset victory over Negro challenger Thomas Bradley. "Personally, I like the way Yorty shoots
off his mouth too much," said one white-haired old man at Los Angeles's recent 188th birthday party at the Hollywood Bowl. "He'll do

a better job for me than the other guy keeping down crime and taxes."

Yorty is an interesting case history in the shifting course of Middle America's mainstream. During the 1930s, he was a New Deal liberal, espousing such progressive programs as a 30-hour workweek. In the '40s, he took up the cause of zealous anti-Communism, and now he is sounding the alarms of law and order. He is no political newcomer— he has been running for office ever since 1936—but today's disgruntled voters seem willing to reward the old pros provided they step to the new beat.

More often, however, Middle America is turning to new political faces, even when they don't look exactly like the one in the mirror. Its latest champion, S. I. Hayakawa, the feisty little professor of English who is now president of San Francisco State College, is not by nature a man of the people. "I've been, all my life, the kind of intellectual highbrow I disapprove of," he admits. But his uncompromising suppression of radical disruption at San Francisco State last fall suddenly vaulted him into political prominence: he began being mentioned as a possible opponent next year of Republican Sen. George Murphy, he started a statewide round of speechmaking, and a recent Field Poll gave him a higher popularity rating than either San Francisco Mayor Joseph Alioto or California's former Democratic Assembly Speaker Jesse Unruh.

The yawning gap between the intellectual and the common man, between the governors and the governed, lies at the heart of the New Populism, and one of the first to discern it was Louise Day Hicks of Boston. A 50-year-old attorney from the predominantly Irish wards of South Boston, she pitched her 1967 mayoral campaign toward "the forgotten man," stressed the school-busing issue—and very nearly won. "I represented the alienated voter," she said last week in the midst of her new City Council campaign, "and that's who I'm representing now, except that the number has grown." Busing is no longer her main issue—some of her liberal opponents, in fact, now agree with her that the state busing law is unworkable. Now she concentrates her fire on higher taxes, declining municipal services and a government that, she contends, "is only concerned about the rich and the poor" and not about the man in the middle who pays the bills.

"The only thing saving this country," Mrs. Hicks says, "is the affluence that the middle class is feeling. But they don't realize the purchasing power is gone. When they do realize that, we're in for real trouble. There'll be a revolt—not violence, because the American people won't resort to violence, but they are going to speak up in a way to be heard."

In fact, they are already speaking up, and there is no reason to believe that November's elections will show a muting of their voices. "These people today are in revolt," warns Chicago Congressman Roman Pucinski. What's more, the middle class has become keenly aware of its political muscle and how to apply it. "The public is so much smarter than when I first started in politics," marvels Ken O'Donnell, JFK's special assistant who is running for the 1970 Democratic nomination for governor of Massachusetts. "Then it was no issues: just vote Democratic, vote Republican, and how to help your friends. What Gene McCarthy did was open the eyes of the people that they are the country. Before, it had been assumed that you couldn't bring a President down, that you couldn't fight the system. The McCarthy movement showed that you could do it after all."

The New Populism, as a matter of fact, seems to some analysts part of the same phenomenon as the New Politics. Eugene McCarthy and Robert Kennedy were trying to achieve on a national scale essentially the same goal that Charlie Stenvig and Louise Day Hicks have set on the municipal level: to bring new faces and new forces into play in the political arena, to mobilize the amateurs against the political pros, to return power to people whose interests and whose voices, they believed, had been too long ignored. Of course, the McCarthy-Kennedy movement was headed in a liberal direction, while the New Populism is exhibiting a rightward bent. And the fact is that several of its new champions seem to be helping to foment, not just reflect, the public's bitterness. Still, the two movements share some common impulses, which may explain the startling number of voters who felt a kinship with both Bobby Kennedy and George Wallace during last year's campaign.

It is still much too soon to say how long the New Populism may last or what direction it may take. It has cast itself loose from the traditional political parties, neither one of which seems to hold its favor, and it has lost faith in the programs and pieties of traditional liberalism. As George Wallace puts it, "The great pointy heads who knew best how to run everybody's life have had their day." Frustrated, fearful and confused, Middle America is stirring itself to seek out new pathways, and the nation has already begun to reverberate with the commotion of its search.

Richard M. Scammon
INTO THE '70s—A GOP DECADE?

Middle America decides who sits in the White House and it is in the dreams—and nightmares—of the middle class that the Republicans and Democrats will seek the victory formula for 1972 and 1976. Right now neither party is sure just what that formula may be.

The problem for the Republicans is simple enough, even if the answers aren't. For 1972 their hopes rest on the ability of the Nixon Administration to form a new coalition of the center—detaching at least some of those voters who would have been oriented to Roosevelt a generation ago and who supported Humphrey last year. Such a GOP coalition would have its own right wing (mostly in the South) and its own left (the Eastern Seaboard). It would not be a sharp move to the right. A militantly conservative line might attract some of George Wallace's 9.9 million supporters from the last election. But it would alienate other voters—and ignore the many populist characteristics of the Wallace vote. Mr. Nixon is much more likely to seek a new center coalition, and if he can forge such a consensus he will win.

The Nixon people know American political history. They know that outside the old Confederacy their party held general political sway for a long generation before the Great Depression and the success of Roosevelt in 1932. From the vote in 1896, when an earlier Middle America swung away from free silver and Bryan to the hoped-for stability of McKinley, right up to Roosevelt there was a long pattern of Republican rule.

But under Roosevelt a new coalition came to power in America. Save for the personalist Eisenhower years, that coalition kept power until a year ago. Even the voting in 1968 was in many ways a reaffirmation of the old Roosevelt coalition minus the South. Well-to-do and well-educated voters went Republican, despite rumbles of discontent among their young, while the poor went Democratic. Middle America split. Catholic and Jewish voters remained in the FDR pattern, voting more heavily Democratic than Protestants, while the Northern small towns and the countryside voted Republican, again in the pattern of the later years of the Roosevelt coalition. With the Negro vote going overwhelmingly to Humphrey, white Middle America edged to Mr. Nixon, but not overwhelmingly.

If the GOP is to succeed in making 1972 a triumph of the New Republicanism, it will have to break out of the tight political alignment of postwar America. The Republicans will have to make 1972 another 1896, with Middle America shifting as decisively to the GOP column three years hence as it did when challenged by Bryan nearly 75 years ago.

The attitudes within Middle America are a key to the probable planning of the Republicans in the '70s. These attitudes are not especially "liberal," as that word is used today. Indeed, a recent sounding of opinion in the bellwether state of California indicates that only 24 per cent of its citizens now label themselves "liberal" as against "middle-of-the-road" (27 per cent) or "conservative" (42 per cent). But neither are Middle America's attitudes hidebound, far right or reactionary.

Specifically, then, where might Republicans look to widen their slim half-million plurality of 1968 to 5 million or 8 million or 10 million in 1972? One of the most immediate tests, even with the 1972 voting more than three years away, is how people react to President Nixon. The

NEWSWEEK Poll found the great majority positive: 79 per cent of the national total is favorably or moderately disposed to the President, only 16 per cent negative.

Statistically, Mr. Nixon registers a "highly favorable" rating among about one-third of the people of Middle America. Men rate the President a bit higher than women, older people somewhat higher than the young, Southerners higher than the rest of the country. Nowhere does the "highly favorable" rating fall below 30 per cent or rise above 37 per cent. Mr. Nixon's "unfavorable" ratings range from 5 per cent in the South to just over 18 per cent in the big cities. In every category the top of the Nixon scale considerably outweighs the bottom, with the mass remaining in the middle.

The potential political implications of these ratings are clear to me. All these groups did *not* vote Republican in the same proportions in November 1968. If blue-collar workers are not reacting in a markedly different way to President Nixon than are traditionally Republican upper-middle-income business and professional people, then the new GOP target is very obviously the manual worker.

Of course, Presidential ratings three years before the event may not have much to do with voter opinions on Election Day in 1972. Still, the groups who now approve of Mr. Nixon, but who did not support him last November, seem logical recruits for Republicans seeking to win in 1972 —and beyond. In the larger sense, though, almost all of Middle America remains a Republican target. Many in Middle America are workers who have "exploded" into the middle class in the economic "great leap forward" since 1945, and many of these are trade-union members. Others are small-business men and salaried people. But, they all share in today's widened concept of the middle class. If the Nixon party can develop meaningful lines of communication to these "forgotten Americans," it may well be able to enlarge its share of Middle American strength to build itself into a virtually unassailable position in the 1970s.

Such lines of communication are not just questions of specific policies such as welfare reform, social-security increases, housing and education. Many of these are areas in which Democrats can be just as convincing as Republicans, perhaps more so. There are also important questions of style, for most of Middle America is not only middle class, it is strongly pro-middle class. Unlike upper-middle-class student rebels, the great majority does not reject middle-class values; it defends those values. The majority wants to better its situation, not overturn it.

In forming political opinion in these terms the Republicans may be the beneficiaries of Democratic mistakes. If the Democratic image in the 1970s is basically one of a party oriented away from the center, toward beard and sandal rather than toward crew cut and bowling shoe, then it seems very likely that President Nixon and the Republicans will establish a dominant position in American politics—perhaps not for a generation, as the party did after McKinley, but at least for a decade.

I doubt that the Democrats will make that mistake. Middle America controls our politics—and Middle America basically inclines neither left nor right. A swerve by the Democrats to the far left in the 1970s would end as disastrously as did 1964's right-wing adventure for the Republicans. And the Democrats have one great advantage—they remember the Goldwater experience.

Politicians are not only articulate, they are literate. They can read, and they read election statistics very clearly. While the Nixon Republicans are making every effort to win more of Middle America and to build a long-term base for their party, the Democrats will be trying just as hard to pull together the components of success as they knew them from 1932 through Lyndon Johnson—and, it might be added, almost through Hubert Humphrey's race as well. It seems likely that the real test of the Republicans' effort to move a bit more of Middle America their way will lie as much with the Democrats as with the Republicans themselves. If the Democrats can bridge their internal problems, they may well keep their share of Middle America, perhaps even move on a bit and win in 1972. But if they can't—and especially if they move away from the center—the '70s seem destined to be a Republican decade.

Leslie H. Gelb
VIETNAM: THE SYSTEM WORKED

Four years after Secretary of Defense Robert McNamara commissioned an internal study of his department's role in Southeast Asia since 1945, The New York Times *published excerpts of it. Although its publication in 1971 occasioned a controversy as to whether old documents were historical and belonged in the public domain or were still classified secret and belonged only to government files, the major issue remained American cold war policy and action in Southeast Asia.*

The published papers contained numerous revelations about the origins and conduct of the war, many of them apparently confirming allegations by anti-war critics. The study suggested that the United States had not blundered into a Vietnamese "quagmire," as many in the nation's press had characterized our involvement. Indeed, evidence in the Defense Department's files showed a continuity of policy development through the Eisenhower, Kennedy, and Johnson administrations. It portrayed escalation from 1963 to 1965 as part of a calculated "scenario" for the purpose of denying victory to guerrilla insurrectionaries. Not the war itself, but Washington's deception of the American public shocked most Americans who were unaware of their government's strategy and tactics for involving the United States in an Asian conflict. Even in retirement, the Johnson administration was plagued with a "credibility gap."

The nearly forty-volume study, including interpretive text and portions of departmental and military documents, had been assembled by a team of civilian defense strategists. The press called it "the Pentagon Papers," although defenders of America's Vietnam policy labelled it "the McNamara Papers"; General Maxwell Taylor titled it "the Gelb Report," in reference to Leslie H. Gelb, the research team's coordinator. This article was published before Daniel Ellsberg, a conscience-stricken member of the Gelb committee, leaked the report to the Times. *With insight gained from his vantage point, Gelb synthesizes the war's history.*

The "Pentagon Papers," as the Times *noted when it began publication, is far from a complete history if only because the study's perspective is limited to that of one government agency. Nevertheless, it sharpens our critical judgment of events while carrying the potential hazard of reading too much between the lines. It remains to be seen if greater historical importance than was apparent in 1971 will be attached to the "Pentagon Papers" in future studies.*

The story of United States policy toward Vietnam is either far better or far worse than generally supposed. Our Presidents and most of those who influenced their decisions did not stumble step by step into Vietnam, unaware of the quagmire. U.S. involvement did not stem from a failure to foresee consequences.

Vietnam was indeed a quagmire, but most of our leaders knew it. Of course there were optimists and periods where many were genuinely optimistic. But those periods were infrequent and short-lived and were invariably followed by periods of deep pessimism. Very few, to be sure, envisioned what the Vietnam situation would be like by 1968. Most realized, however, that "the light at the end of the tunnel" was very far away—if not finally unreachable. Nevertheless, our Presidents persevered. Given international compulsions to "keep our word" and "save face," domestic prohibitions against "losing," and their personal stakes, our leaders did "what was necessary," did it about the way they wanted, were prepared to pay the costs, and plowed on with a mixture of hope and doom. They "saw" no acceptable alternative.

Reprinted by permission of *Foreign Policy* and the author.

Three propositions suggest why the United States became involved in Vietnam, why the process was gradual, and what the real expectations of our leaders were:

First, U.S. involvement in Vietnam is not mainly or mostly a story of step by step, inadvertent descent into unforeseen quicksand. It is primarily a story of why U.S. leaders considered that it was vital not to lose Vietnam by force to Communism. Our leaders believed Vietnam to be vital not for itself, but for what they thought its "loss" would mean internationally and domestically. Previous involvement made further involvement more unavoidable, and, to this extent, commitments were inherited. But judgments of Vietnam's "vitalness"—beginning with the Korean War—were sufficient in themselves to set the course for escalation.

Second, our Presidents were never actually seeking a military victory in Vietnam. They were doing only what they thought was minimally necessary at each stage to keep Indochina, and later South Vietnam, out of Communist hands. This forced our Presidents to be brakemen, to do less than those who were urging military victory and to reject proposals for disengagement. It also meant that our Presidents wanted a negotiated settlement without fully realizing (though realizing more than their critics) that a civil war cannot be ended by political compromise.

Third, our Presidents and most of their lieutenants were not deluded by optimistic reports of progress and did not proceed on the basis of wishful thinking about winning a military victory in South Vietnam. They recognized that the steps they were taking were not adequate to win the war and that unless Hanoi relented, they would have to do more and more. Their strategy was to persevere in the hope that their will to continue—if not the practical effects of their actions—would cause the Communists to relent.

Each of these propositions is explored below.

I. Ends: "We Can't Afford to Lose"

Those who led the United States into Vietnam did so with their eyes open, knowing why, and believing they had the will to succeed. The deepening involvement was not inadvertent, but mainly deductive. It flowed with sureness from the perceived stakes and attendant high objectives. U.S. policy displayed remarkable continuity. There were not dozens of likely "turning points." Each postwar President inherited previous commitments. Each extended these commitments. Each administration from 1947 to 1969 believed that it was necessary to prevent the loss of Vietnam and, after 1954, South Vietnam by force to the Communists. The reasons for this varied from person to person, from bureaucracy to bureaucracy, over time and in emphasis. For the most part, however, they had little to do with Vietnam itself. A few men argued that Vietnam had intrinsic strategic military and economic importance, but this view never prevailed. The reasons rested on broader international, domestic, and bureaucratic considerations.

Our leaders gave the *international* repercussions of "losing" as their dominant explicit reason for Vietnam's importance. During the Truman Administration, Indochina's importance was measured in terms of French-American relations and Washington's desire to rebuild France into the centerpiece of future European security. After the cold war heated up and after the fall of China, a French defeat in Indochina was also seen as a defeat for the policy of containment. In the Eisenhower years, Indochina became a "testing ground" between the Free World and Communism and the basis for the famous "domino theory" by which the fall of Indochina would lead to the deterioration of American security around the globe. President Kennedy publicly reaffirmed the falling domino concept. His primary concern, however, was for his "reputation for action" after the Bay of Pigs fiasco, the Vienna meeting with Khrushchev, and the Laos crisis, and in meeting the challenge of "wars of national liberation" by counter-insurgency warfare. Under President Johnson, the code word rationales became Munich, credibility, commitments and the U.S. word, a watershed test of wills with Communism, raising the costs of aggression, and the principle that armed aggression shall not be allowed to succeed. There is every reason to assume that our leaders actually believed what they said, given both the cold war context in which they were all reared and the lack of contradictory evidence.

With very few exceptions, then, our leaders since World War II saw Vietnam as a vital factor in alliance politics, U.S-Soviet-Chinese relations, and deterrence. This was as true in 1950 and 1954 as it was in 1961 and 1965. The record of United States military and economic assistance to fight Communism in Indochina tells this story quite clearly. From 1945 to 1951, U.S. aid to France totaled over $3.5 billion. Without this, the French position in Indochina would have been untenable. By 1951, the U.S. was paying about 40 percent of the costs of the Indochina war and our share was going up. In 1954, it is estimated, U.S. economic and technical assistance amounted to $703 million and military aid totaled almost $2 billion. This added up to almost 80 percent of the total French costs. From 1955 to 1961, U.S. military aid averaged about $200 million per year. This made South Vietnam the second largest recipient of such aid, topped only by Korea. By 1963, South Vietnam ranked first among recipients of military assistance. In economic assistance, it followed only India and Pakistan.

The *domestic* repercussions of "losing" Vietnam probably were equally important in Presidential minds. Letting Vietnam "go Communist" was undoubtedly seen as:

opening the floodgates to domestic criticism and attack for being "soft on Communism" or just plain soft;

dissipating Presidential influence by having to answer these charges;

alienating conservative leadership in the Congress and thereby endan-
gering the President's legislative program;
    jeopardizing election prospects for the President and his party;
    undercutting domestic support for a "responsible" U.S. world role; and
    enlarging the prospects for a right-wing reaction—the nightmare of a
McCarthyite garrison state.

U.S. domestic politics required our leaders to maintain both a peaceful
world and one in which Communist expansion was stopped. In order to
have the public support necessary to use force against Communism, our
leaders had to employ strong generalized, ideological rhetoric. The price
of this rhetoric was consistency. How could our leaders shed American
blood in Korea and keep large numbers of American troops in Europe at
great expense unless they were also willing to stop Communism in Vietnam?

Bureaucratic judgments and stakes were also involved in defining U.S.
interests in Vietnam. Most bureaucrats probably prompted or shared the
belief of their leaders about the serious repercussions of losing Vietnam.
Once direct bureaucratic presence was established after the French departure, this belief was reinforced and extended. The military had to prove
that American arms and advice could succeed where the French could not.
The Foreign Service had to prove that it could bring about political stability in Saigon and "build a nation." The CIA had to prove that pacification would work. AID had to prove that millions of dollars in assistance and
advice could bring political returns.

The U.S. commitment was rationalized as early as 1950. It was set
in 1955 when we replaced the French. Its logic was further fulfilled by
President Kennedy. After 1965, when the U.S. took over the war, it was
immeasurably hardened.

There was little conditional character to the U.S. commitment—except
for avoiding "the big war." Every President talked about the ultimate responsibility resting with the Vietnamese (and the French before them).
This "condition" seems to have been meant much more as a warning to
our friends than a real limitation. In every crunch, it was swept aside. The
only real limit applied to Russia and China. Our leaders were not prepared
to run the risks of nuclear war or even the risks of a direct conventional
military confrontation with the Soviet Union and China. These were separate decisions. The line between them and everything else done in Vietnam
always held firm. With this exception, the commitment was always defined
in terms of the objective to deny the Communists control over all Vietnam.
This was further defined to preclude coalition governments with the
Communists.

The importance of the objective was evaluated in terms of cost, and
the perceived costs of disengagement outweighed the cost of further engagement. Some allies might urge disengagement, but then condemn
the U.S. for doing so. The domestic groups which were expected to criticize growing involvement always were believed to be outnumbered by

those who would have attacked "cutting and running." The question of whether our leaders would have started down the road if they knew this would mean over half a million men in Vietnam, over 40,000 U.S. deaths, and the expenditure of well over $100 billion is historically irrelevant. Only Presidents Kennedy and Johnson had to confront the possibility of these large costs. The point is that each administration was prepared to pay the costs it could forsee for itself. No one seemed to have a better solution. Each could at least pass the baton on to the next.

Presidents could not treat Vietnam as if it were "vital" without creating high stakes internationally, domestically, and within their own bureaucracies. But the rhetoric conveyed different messages:

To the Communists, it was a signal that their actions would be met by counteractions.

To the American people, it set the belief that the President would ensure that the threatened nation did not fall into Communist hands—although without the anticipation of sacrificing American lives.

To the Congress, it marked the President's responsibility to ensure that Vietnam did not go Communist and maximized incentives for legislators to support him or at least remain silent.

To the U.S. professional military, it was a promise that U.S. forces would be used, if necessary and to the degree necessary, to defend Vietnam.

To the professional U.S. diplomat, it meant letting our allies know that the U.S. cared about their fate.

To the President, it laid the groundwork for the present action and showed that he was prepared to take the next step to keep Vietnam non-Communist.

Words were making Vietnam into a showcase—an Asian Berlin. In the process, Vietnam grew into a test case of U.S. credibility—to opponents, to allies, but perhaps most importantly, to ourselves. Public opinion polls seemed to confirm the political dangers. Already established bureaucratic judgments about the importance of Vietnam matured into cherished convictions and organizational interests. The war dragged on.

Each successive President, initially caught by his own belief, was further ensnarled by his own rhetoric, and the basis for the belief went unchallenged. Debates revolved around how to do things better, and whether they could be done, not whether they were worth doing. Prior to 1961, an occasional senator or Southeast Asian specialist would raise a lonely and weak voice in doubt. Some press criticism began thereafter. And later still, wandering American minstrels returned from the field to tell their tales of woe in private. General Ridgway as Chief of Staff of the Army in 1954 questioned the value of Vietnam as against its potential costs and dangers, and succeeded in blunting a proposed U.S. military initiative, although not for the reasons he advanced. Under Secretary of State George Ball raised the issue of international priorities in the summer of 1965 and lost. Clark Clifford as Secretary of Defense openly challenged the winnability of the war, as well as Vietnam's strategic significance, and argued for domestic priorities. But no systematic or serious examination of Vietnam's importance to the United States was ever undertaken within the government. Endless assertions passed for analysis. Presidents neither encouraged nor permitted serious questioning, for to do so would be to foster the idea that their resolve was something less than complete. The objective of a non-Communist Vietnam, and after 1954 a non-Communist South Vietnam, drove U.S. involvement ever more deeply each step of the way.

II. Means: "Take the Minimal Necessary Steps"

None of our Presidents was seeking total victory over the Vietnamese Communists. War critics who wanted victory always knew this. Those who wanted the U.S. to get out never believed it. Each President was essentially doing what he thought was minimally necessary to prevent a Communist victory during his tenure in office. Each, of course, sought to strengthen the anti-Communist Vietnamese forces, but with the aim of a negotiated settlement. Part of the tragedy of Vietnam was that the compromises our Presidents were prepared to offer could never lead to an end of the war. These preferred compromises only served to reinforce the conviction of both Communist and anti-Communist Vietnamese that they had to fight to the finish in their civil war. And so, more minimal steps were always necessary.

Our Presidents were pressured on all sides. The pressures for victory came mainly from the inside and were reflected on the outside. From inside the administrations, three forces almost invariably pushed hard. *First*, the military establishment generally initiated requests for broadening and intensifying U.S. military action. Our professional military placed great weight on the strategic significance of Vietnam; they were given a job to do; their prestige was involved; and of crucial importance (in the 1960's)—the lives of many American servicemen were being lost. The Joint Chiefs of Staff, the MAAG (Military Assistance Advisory Group) Chiefs and later the Commander of U.S. forces in Vietnam were the focal points for these pressures. *Second*, our Ambassadors in Saigon, supported by the State Department, at times pressed for and often supported big steps forward. Their reasons were similar to those of the military. *Thirdly*, an ever-present group of "fixers" was making urgent demands to strengthen and broaden the Saigon government in order to achieve political victory. Every executive agency had its fixers. They were usually able men whose entire preoccupation was to make things better in Vietnam. From outside the administration, there were hawks who insisted on winning and hawks who wanted to "win or get out." Capitol Hill hawks, the conservative press, and, for many years, Catholic organizations were in the forefront.

The pressures for disengagement and for de-escalation derived mostly from the outside with occasional and often unknown allies from within. Small for most of the Vietnam years, these forces grew steadily in strength from 1965 onward. Isolated congressmen and senators led the fight. First they did so on anticolonialist grounds. Later their objections developed moral aspects (interfering in a civil war) and extended to non-winnability, domestic priorities, and the senselessness of the war. Peace organizations and student groups in particular came to dominate headlines and air time. Journalists played a critical role—especially through television reports. From within each administration, opposition could be found: (1) among isolated military men who did not want the U.S. in an Asian land war; (2) among some State Department intelligence and area specialists who knew Vietnam and believed the U.S. objective was unattainable at any reasonable price; and (3) within the civilian agencies of the Defense Department and isolated individuals at State and CIA, particularly after 1966, whose efforts were trained on finding a politically feasible way out.

Our Presidents reacted to the pressures as brakemen, pulling the switch against both the advocates of "decisive escalation" and the advocates of disengagement. The politics of the Presidency largely dictated this role, but the personalities of the Presidents were also important. None were as ideological as many persons around them. All were basically centrist politicians.

Their immediate aim was always to prevent a Communist takeover. The actions they approved were usually only what was minimally necessary to that aim. Each President determined the "minimal necessity" by trial and error and his own judgment. They might have done more and done it more rapidly if they were convinced that: (1) the threat of a Communist takeover were more immediate, (2) U.S. domestic politics would have been more permissive, (3) the government of South Vietnam had the requisite political stability and military potential for effective use and (4) the job really would have gotten done. After 1965, however, the minimal necessity became the maximum they could get given the same domestic and international constraints.

The tactic of the minimally necessary decision makes optimum sense for the politics of the Presidency. Even our strongest Presidents have tended to shy away from decisive action. It has been too uncertain, too risky. They derive their strength from movement (the image of a lot of activity) and building and neutralizing opponents. Too seldom has there been forceful moral leadership; it may even be undemocratic. The small step that maintains the momentum gives the President the chance to gather more political support. It gives the appearance of minimizing possible mistakes. It allows time to gauge reactions. It serves as a pressure-relieving valve against those who want to do more. It can be doled out. Above all, it gives the President something to do next time.

The tactic makes consummate sense when it is believed that nothing will fully work or that the costs of a "winning" move would be too high. This was the case with Vietnam. This decision-making tactic explains why the U.S. involvement in Vietnam was gradual and step by step.

While the immediate aim was to prevent a Communist victory and improve the position of the anti-Communists, the longer term goal was a political settlement. As late as February 1947, Secretary of State Marshall expressed the hope that "a pacific basis of adjustment of the difficulties" between France and the Vietminh could be found.[1] After that, Truman's policy hardened, but there is no evidence to suggest that until 1950 he was urging the French not to settle with the Vietnamese Communists. Eisenhower, it should be remembered, was the President who tacitly agreed (by not intervening in 1954) to the creation of a Communist state in North Vietnam. President Kennedy had all he could do to prevent complete political collapse in South Vietnam. He had, therefore, little basis on which to compromise. President Johnson inherited this political instability, and to add to his woes, he faced in 1965 what seemed to be the prospect of a Communist military victory. Yet, by his standing offer for free and internationally supervised elections, he apparently was prepared to accept Communist participation in the political life of the South.

By traditional diplomatic standards of negotiations between sovereign states, these were not fatuous compromises. One compromise was, in effect, to guarantee that the Communists could remain in secure control of North Vietnam. The U.S. would not seek to overthrow this regime. The other compromise was to allow the Communists in South Vietnam to seek power along the lines of Communist parties in France and Italy, i.e. to give them a "permanent minority position."

But the real struggle in Vietnam was not between sovereign states. It was among Vietnamese. It was a civil war and a war for national independence.

Herein lies the paradox and the tragedy of Vietnam. Most of our leaders and their critics did see that Vietnam was a quagmire, but did not see that the real stakes—who shall govern Vietnam—were not negotiable. Free elections, local sharing of power, international supervision, ceasefires—none of these could serve as a basis for settlement. What were legitimate compromises from Washington's point of view were matters of life and death to the Vietnamese. For American leaders, the stakes were "keeping their word" and saving their political necks. For the Vietnamese, the stakes were their lives and their lifelong political aspirations. Free elections meant bodily exposure to the Communist guerrillas and likely defeat to the anti-Communists. The risk was too great. There was no trust, no confidence.

The Vietnam war could no more be settled by traditional diplomatic compromises than any other civil war. President Lincoln could not settle

[1] *New York Times,* February 8, 1947.

with the South. The Spanish Republicans and General Franco's Loy-
alists could not have conceivably mended their fences by elections. None
of the post-World War II insurgencies—Greece, Malaya, and the Philippines—ended with a negotiated peace. In each of these cases, the civil
differences were put to rest—if at all—only by the logic of war.

It is commonly acknowledged that Vietnam would have fallen to the
Communists in 1945–46, in 1954, and in 1965 had it not been for the in-
tervention of first the French and then the Americans. The Vietnamese
Communists, who were also by history the Vietnamese nationalists,
would not accept only part of a prize for which they had paid so heavily.
The anti-Communist Vietnamese, protected by the French and the
Americans, would not put themselves at the Communists' mercy.

It may be that our Presidents understood this better than their critics.
The critics, especially on the political left, fought for "better compromises," not realizing that even the best could not be good enough, and
fought for broad nationalist governments, not realizing there was no
middle force in Vietnam. Our Presidents, it seems, recognized that
there was no middle ground and that "better compromises" would
frighten our Saigon allies without bringing about a compromise peace.
And they believed that a neutralization formula would compromise
South Vietnam away to the Communists. So the longer-term aim of peace
repeatedly gave way to the immediate needs of the war and the next
necessary step.

III. Expectations: "We Must Persevere"

Each new step was taken not because of wishful thinking or optimism
about its leading to a victory in South Vietnam. Few of our leaders
thought that they could win the war in a conventional sense or that the
Communists would be decimated to a point that they would simply fade
away. Even as new and further steps were taken, coupled with expressions of optimism, many of our leaders realized that more—and still
more—would have to be done. Few of these men felt confident about
how it would all end or when. After 1965, however, they allowed the
impression of "winnability" to grow in order to justify their already heavy
investment and domestic support for the war.

The strategy always was to persevere. Perseverance, it seemed, was
the only way to avoid or postpone having to pay the domestic political
costs of failure. Finally, perseverance, it was hoped, would convince the
Communists that our will to continue was firm. Perhaps, then, with domestic support for perseverance, with bombing North Vietnam, and with
inflicting heavy casualties in the South, the Communists would relent.
Perhaps, then, a compromise could be negotiated to save the Communists' face without giving them South Vietnam.

Optimism was a part of the "gamesmanship" of Vietnam. It had a purpose. Personal-organizational optimism was the product of a number of motivations and calculations:

Career services tacitly and sometimes explicitly pressured their professionals to impart good news.

Good news was seen as a job well done; bad news as personal failure.

The reporting system was set up so that assessments were made by the implementors.

Optimism bred optimism so that it was difficult to be pessimistic this time if you were optimistic the last time.

People told their superiors what they thought they wanted to hear.

The American ethic is to get the job done.

Policy optimism also sprang from several rational needs:

To maintain domestic support for the war.

To keep up the morale of our Vietnamese allies and build some confidence and trust between us and them.

To stimulate military and bureaucratic morale to work hard.

There were, however, genuine optimists and grounds for genuine optimism. Some periods looked promising: the year preceding the French downfall at Dienbienphu; the years of the second Eisenhower Presidency when most attention was riveted on Laos and before the insurgency was stepped up in South Vietnam; 1962 and early 1963 before the strategic hamlet pacification program collapsed; and the last six months of 1967 before the 1968 Tet offensive.

Many additional periods by comparison with previous years yielded a sense of real improvement. By most conventional standards—the size and firepower of friendly Vietnamese forces, the number of hamlets pacified, the number of "free elections" being held, the number of Communists killed, and so forth—reasonable men could and did think in cautiously optimistic terms.

But comparison with years past is an illusory measure when it is not coupled with judgments about how far there still is to go and how likely it is that the goal can ever be reached. It was all too easy to confuse short-term breathing spells with long-term trends and to confuse "things getting better" with "winning." Many of those who had genuine hope suffered from either a lack of knowledge about Vietnam or a lack of sensitivity toward politics or both.

The basis for pessimism and the warning signals were always present. Public portrayals of success glowed more brightly than the full range of classified reporting. Readily available informal and personal accounts were less optimistic still. The political instability of our Vietnamese allies —from Bao Dai through Diem to President Thieu have always been apparent. The weaknesses of the armed forces of our Vietnamese allies were common knowledge. Few years went by when the fighting did not gain in intensity. Our leaders did not have to know much about Vietnam to see all this.

Most of our leaders saw the Vietnam quagmire for what it was. Optimism was, by and large, put in perspective. This means that many knew that each step would be followed by another. Most seemed to have understood that more assistance would be required either to improve the relative position of our Vietnamese allies or simply to prevent a deterioration of their position. Almost each year and often several times a year, key decisions had to be made to prevent deterioration or collapse. These decisions were made with hard bargaining, but rapidly enough for us now to perceive a preconceived consensus to go on. Sometimes several new steps were decided at once, but announced and implemented piece-meal. The whole pattern conveyed the feeling of more to come.

With a tragic sense of "no exit," our leaders stayed their course. They seemed to hope more than expect that something would "give." The hope was to convince the Vietnamese Communists through perseverance that the U.S. would stay in South Vietnam until they abandoned their struggle. The hope, in a sense, was the product of disbelief. How could a tiny, backward Asian country *not* have a breaking point when opposed by the might of the United States? How could they not relent and negotiate with the U.S.?

And yet, few could answer two questions with any confidence: Why should the Communists abandon tomorrow the goals they had been paying so dear a price to obtain yesterday? What was there really to negotiate? No one seemed to be able to develop a persuasive scenario on how the war could end by peaceful means.

Our Presidents, given their politics and thinking, had nothing to do but persevere. But the Communists' strategy was also to persevere, to make the U.S. go home. It was and is a civil war for national independence. It was and is a Greek tragedy.

IV. After Twenty-Five Years

A quick review of history supports these interpretations. To the Roosevelt Administration during World War II, Indochina was not perceived as a "vital" area. The United States defeated Japan without Southeast Asia, and Indochina was not occupied by the allies until *after* Japan's defeat. FDR spoke informally to friends and newsmen of placing Indochina under United Nations trusteeship after the war, but—aware of French, British and U.S. bureaucratic hostility to this—made no detailed plans and asked for no staff work prior to his death. For all practical purposes, Truman inherited *no* Southeast Asia policy.

In 1946 and 1947, the U.S. acquiesced in the re-establishment of French sovereignty. Our policy was a passive one of hoping for a negotiated settlement of the "difficulties" between Paris and the Vietminh independence movement of Ho Chi Minh. To the south, in Indonesia, we had started to pressure the Dutch to grant independence and withdraw, and a residue of anticolonialism remained in our first inchoate approaches to an Indochina policy as well.

But events in Europe and China changed the context from mid-1947 on. Two important priorities were to rearm and strengthen France as the cornerstone of European defense and recovery in the face of Russian pressure, and to prevent a further expansion of victorious Chinese Communism. The Truman Doctrine depicted a world full of dominoes. In May 1950, before Korea, Secretary of State Acheson announced that the U.S. would provide military and economic assistance to the French and their Indochinese allies for the direct purpose of combating Communist expansion.[2] After years of hesitating, Truman finally decided that anti-Communism was more important than anticolonialism in Indochina.

Acheson admits that U.S. policy was a "muddled hodgepodge":

> The criticism, however, fails to recognize the limits on the extent to which one may successfully coerce an ally. . . . Furthermore, the result of withholding help to France would, at most, have removed the colonial power. It could not have made the resulting situation a beneficial one either for Indochina or for Southeast Asia, or in the more important effort of furthering the stability and defense of Europe. So while we may have tried to muddle through and were certainly not successful, I could not think then or later of a better course. One can suggest, perhaps, doing nothing. That might have had merit, but as an attitude for the leader of a great alliance toward an important ally, indeed one essential to a critical endeavor, it had its demerits, too.[3]

Several months after the Korean War began, Acheson recalled the warning of an "able colleague": "Not only was there real danger that our efforts would fail in their immediate purpose and waste valuable resources in the process, but we were moving into a position in Indochina in which 'our responsibilities tend to supplant rather than complement those of the French'." Acheson then remembers: "I decided however, that having put our hand to the plow, we would not look back."[4] He decided this despite the fact that he "recognized as no longer valid an earlier French intention to so weaken the enemy before reducing French forces in Indochina that indigenous forces could handle the situation."[5]

V. The Eisenhower Administration

President Eisenhower inherited the problem. Although, with Vietminh successes, the situation took on graver overtones, he, too, pursued a policy of "minimum action" to prevent the total "loss" of Vietnam to Com-

[2]*Department of State Bulletin*, May 1950, p. 821.
[3]Dean Acheson, *Present at the Creation*, (New York: W. W. Norton, 1969), p. 673.
[4]*Ibid.*, p. 674.
[5]*Ibid.*, p. 676–7.

munism. Sherman Adams, Eisenhower's assistant, explains how the problem was seen in the mid-1950's:

> If the Communists had pushed on with an aggressive offensive after the fall of Dienbienphu, instead of stopping and agreeing to stay out of Southern Vietnam, Laos and Cambodia, there was a strong possibility that the United States would have moved against them. A complete Communist conquest of Indochina would have had far graver consequence for the West than a Red victory in Korea.[6]

Apparently the President felt he could live with Communist control in the restricted area of North Vietnam, away from the rest of Southeast Asia.

Eisenhower did not take the minimal necessary step to save *all* of Indochina, but he did take the necessary steps to prevent the loss of most of Indochina. He paid almost all the French war cost, increased the U.S. military advisory mission, supplied forty B-26's to the French, and continued the threat of U.S. intervention, first by "united action" and then by forming SEATO. In taking these actions, Eisenhower was deciding against Vice-President Nixon and Admiral Radford, Chairman of the Joint Chiefs of Staff, who favored U.S. intervention in force, and against General Ridgway, Chief of the Army Staff, who opposed any action that could lead to an Asian land war. He was treading the well-worn middle path of doing just enough to balance off contradictory domestic, bureaucratic, and international pressures. The Vietnamese Communists agreed to the compromise, believing that winning the full prize was only a matter of time.

In public statements and later in his memoirs, President Eisenhower gave glimpses of his reasoning. At the time of Dienbienphu, he noted, "... we ought to look at this thing with some optimism and some determination ... long faces and defeatism don't win battles."[7] Later he wrote, "I am convinced that the French could not win the war because the internal political situation in Vietnam, weak and confused, badly weakened their military position."[8] But he persevered nevertheless, believing that "the decision to give this aid was almost compulsory. The United States had no real alternative unless we were to abandon Southeast Asia."[9]

The Geneva Conference of 1954 was followed by eighteen bleak and pessimistic months as official Washington wondered whether the pieces could be put back together. Despite or perhaps because of the pessimism, U.S. aid was increased. Then, in the fall of 1956, Dulles could say: "We have a clean base there now, without a taint of colonialism.

---

[6]Sherman Adams, *Firsthand Report* (New York: Harper & Row, 1961), p. 120.

[7]Public Papers of the Presidents, Eisenhower, 1954, p. 471. This remark was made on May 12, 1954.

[8]Dwight D. Eisenhower, *Mandate for Change,* (New York: Doubleday, 1963), p. 372.

[9]*Ibid.,* p. 373.

Dienbienphu was a blessing in disguise."[10] The years of "cautious optimism" had begun.

President Eisenhower kept the U.S. out of war because he allowed a territorial compromise with the Communists. More critically, he decided to replace the French and maintain a direct U.S. presence in Indochina. With strong rhetoric, military training programs, support for Ngo Dinh Diem in his refusal to hold the elections prescribed by the Geneva accords, and continuing military and economic assistance, he made the new state or "zone" of South Vietnam an American responsibility. Several years of military quiet in South Vietnam did not hide the smoldering political turmoil in that country nor did it obscure the newspaper headlines which regularly proclaimed that the war in Indochina had shifted to Laos.

VI. The Kennedy Administration

The Administration of John F. Kennedy began in an aura of domestic sacrifice and international confrontation. The inauguration speech set the tone of U.S. responsibilities in "hazardous and dangerous" times.

Vietnam had a special and immediate importance which derived from the general international situation. Kennedy's predictions about dangerous times came true quickly—and stayed true—and he wanted to show strength to the Communists. But it was also the precarious situation in Laos and the "neutralist" compromise which Kennedy was preparing for Laos that were driving the President deeper into Vietnam. In Sorensen's words, Kennedy was "skeptical of the extent of our involvement [in Vietnam] but unwilling to abandon his predecessor's pledge or permit a Communist conquest. . . ."[11]

Kennedy had to face three basic general decisions. First, was top priority to go to political reform or fighting the war? On this issue the fixers, who wanted to give priority to political reform, were arrayed against the military. Second, should the line of involvement be drawn at combat units? On this issue the fixers were more quiet than in opposition. The military and the Country Team pushed hard—even urging the President to threaten Hanoi with U.S. bombing. Some counterweight came from State and the White House staff. Third, should the President make a clear, irrevocable and open-ended commitment to prevent a Communist victory? Would this strengthen or weaken the U.S. hand in Saigon? Would it frighten away the Communists? What would be the domestic political consequences?

Kennedy's tactics and decisions—like Eisenhower's—followed the pattern of doing what was minimally necessary. On the political versus

[10]Emmet John Hughes, *The Ordeal of Power,* (New York: Dell, 1962), p. 182. Eisenhower himself wrote that in 1954 "The strongest reason of all for United States refusal to respond by itself to French pleas was our tradition of anti-colonialism." (in *Mandate for Change,* p. 373).

[11]Theodore Sorensen, *Kennedy,* (New York: Harper & Row, 1965), p. 639.

military priority issue, Kennedy did not make increasing military assistance definitively contingent on political reform, but he pointed to the absence of reform as the main reason for limiting the U.S. military role. On the combat unit issue, according to biographer Sorensen, "Kennedy never made a final negative decision on troops. In typical Kennedy fashion, he made it difficult for any of the pro-intervention advocates to charge him privately with weakness."[12] On the third issue, he avoided an open-ended commitment, but escalated his rhetoric about the importance of Vietnam. While he did authorize an increase of U.S. military personnel from 685 to 16,000, he did so slowly, and not in two or three big decisions. He continually doled out the increases. He gave encouragement to bureaucratic planning and studying as a safety valve—a valve he thought he could control. He kept a very tight rein on information to the public about the war. In Salinger's words, he "was not anxious to admit the existence of a real war . . ."[13] By minimizing U.S. involvement, Kennedy was trying to avoid public pressures either to do more or to do less.

The President would make it "their" war until he had no choice but to look at it in a different light. He would not look at it in another light until Diem, who looked like a losing horse, was replaced. He would not gamble on long odds. But it is not clear what he expected to get as a replacement for Diem.

With the exception of much of 1962, which even the North Vietnamese have called "Diem's year," the principal Kennedy decisions were made in an atmosphere of deterioration, not progress, in Vietnam. This feeling of deterioration explains why Kennedy dispatched so many high-level missions to Vietnam. As Kennedy's biographers have written, the President was not really being told he was winning, but how much more he would have to do.

Writing in 1965, Theodore Sorensen summed up the White House view of events following the Diem coup in November 1963:

> The President, while eager to make clear that our aim was to get out of Vietnam, had always been doubtful about the optimistic reports constantly filed by the military on the progress of the war. . . . The struggle could well be, he thought, this nation's severest test of endurance and patience. . . . He was simply going to weather it out, a nasty, untidy mess to which there was no other acceptable solution. Talk of abandoning so unstable an ally and so costly a commitment 'only makes it easy for the Communists,' said the President. 'I think we should stay.'[14]

VII. The Johnson Administration

Lyndon Johnson assumed office with a reputation as a pragmatic politician and not a cold war ideologue. His history on Southeast Asia indi-

[12]*Ibid.*, p. 654.
[13]Pierre Salinger, *With Kennedy,* (New York: Doubleday, 1966), pp. 319–329.
[14]Sorensen, *op. cit.*, p. 661.

cated caution and comparative restraint. And yet it was this same man who as President presided over and led the U.S. into massive involvement.

Three facts conspired to make it easier for Johnson to take the plunge on the assumed importance of Vietnam than his predecessors. First, the world was a safer place to live in and Vietnam was the only continuing crisis. Europe was secure. The Sino-Soviet split had deepened. Mutual nuclear deterrence existed between the two superpowers. Second, the situation in Vietnam was more desperate than it ever had been. If the U.S. had not intervened in 1965, South Vietnam would have been conquered by the Communists. Third, after years of effort, the U.S. conventional military forces were big enough and ready enough to intervene. Unlike his predecessors, Johnson had the military capability to back up his words.

In sum, Vietnam became relatively more important, it was in greater danger, and the U.S. was in a position to do something about it.

At Johns Hopkins in April 1965, the President told the American people what he would do: "We will do everything necessary to reach that objective [of no external interference in South Vietnam], and we will do only what is absolutely necessary." But in order to prevent defeat and in order to keep the faith with his most loyal supporters, the minimum necessary became the functional equivalent of gradual escalation. The Air Force and the Commander in Chief, Pacific (CINCPAC) pressed hard for full systems bombing—the authority to destroy 94 key North Vietnamese targets in 16 days. Johnson, backed and pressured in the other direction by Secretary McNamara, doled out approval for new targets over three years in a painstaking and piecemeal fashion. Johnson accommodated dovish pressure and the advice of the many pragmatists who surrounded him by making peace overtures. But these overtures were either accompanied with or followed by escalation. Johnson moved toward those who wanted three-quarters of a million U.S. fighting men in Vietnam, but he never got there. Guided by judgments of domestic repercussion and influenced again by McNamara, the President made at least eight separate decisions on U.S. force levels in Vietnam over a four-year period.[15] For the "fixers" who felt that U.S. conduct of the war missed its political essence and for the doves who wanted to see something besides destruction, Johnson placed new emphasis on "the other war"—pacification, nation-building, and political development— in February 1966. Johnson referred to this whole complex of actions and the air war in particular as his attempt to "seduce not rape" the North Vietnamese.

The objective of the Johnson Administration was to maintain an independent non-Communist South Vietnam. In the later years, this was rephrased: "allowing the South Vietnamese to determine their own fu-

[15]See the Chronology in U.S. Senate Foreign Relations Committee, *Background Information Relating to Southeast Asia and Vietnam*, March 1969.

ture without external interference." As the President crossed the old barriers in pursuit of this objective, he established new ones. While he ordered the bombing of North Vietnam, he would not approve the bombing of targets which ran the risk of confrontation with China and Russia. While he permitted the U.S. force level in Vietnam to go over one-half million men, he would not agree to call up the Reserves. While he was willing to spend $25 billion in one year on the war, he would not put the U.S. economy on a wartime mobilization footing. But the most important Johnson barrier was raised against invading Cambodia, Laos, and North Vietnam. This limitation was also a cornerstone in the President's hopes for a compromise settlement. He would agree to the permanent existence of North Vietnam—even help that country economically—if North Vietnam would extend that same right to South Vietnam.

In order to sustain public and bureaucratic support for his policy, Johnson's method was to browbeat and isolate his opponents. To the American people, he painted the alternatives to what he was doing as irresponsible or reckless. In either case, the result would be a greater risk of future general war. The bureaucracy used this same technique of creating the bug-out or bomb-out extremes in order to maintain as many of its own members in "the middle road." The price of consensus—within the bureaucracy and in the public at large—was invariably a middle road of contradictions and no priorities for action.

President Johnson was the master of consensus. On Vietnam this required melding the proponents of negotiations with the proponents of military victory. The technique for maintaining this Vietnam consensus was gradual escalation punctuated by dramatic peace overtures. As the war was escalated without an end in sight, the numbers of people Johnson could hold together diminished. The pressures for disengagement or for "decisive military action" became enormous, but with the "hawks" always outnumbering and more strategically placed than the "doves."

Johnson knew he had inherited a deteriorating situation in Vietnam. Vietcong military successes and constant change in the Saigon government from 1964 to 1966 were not secrets to anyone. Throughout the critical year of 1965, he struck the themes of endurance and more-to-come. In his May 4, 1965 requests for Vietnam Supplemental Appropriations he warned: "I see no choice but to continue the course we are on, filled as it is with peril and uncertainty." In his July 28, 1965 press conference he announced a new 125,000 troop ceiling and went on to say: "Additional forces will be needed later, and they will be sent as requested."

Talk about "turning corners" and winning a military victory reached a crescendo in 1967. At the same time a new counterpoint emerged—"stalemate."[16] The message of the stalemate proponents was that the U.S. was strong enough to prevent defeat, but that the situation defied victory.

[16]R. W. Apple, "Vietnam: The Signs of Stalemate," New York Times, August 7, 1967.

Hanoi would continue to match the U.S. force build-up and would not "cry uncle" over the bombing. The Saigon government and army had basic political and structural problems which they were unlikely to be able to overcome. Stalemate, it was urged, should be used as a basis for getting a compromise settlement with Hanoi.

These arguments were not lost on the President. At Guam in March 1967, while others around him were waxing eloquent about progress, the President was guardedly optimistic, speaking of "a favorable turning point, militarily and politically." But after one of the meetings he was reported to have said: "We have a difficult, a serious, long-drawn-out, agonizing problem that we do not have an answer for."[17] Nor did the President overlook the effects of the 1968 Tet offensive, coming as it did after many months of virtually unqualified optimism by him and by others. He stopped the bombing partially, increased troop strength slightly, he made a peace overture, and announced his retirement.

In November 1963, Johnson is quoted as saying: "I am not going to be the President who saw Southeast Asia go the way China went."[18] In the spring of 1965, Lady Bird Johnson quoted him as saying: "I can't get out. I can't finish it with what I have got. So what the Hell can I do?"[19] President Johnson, like his predecessors, persevered and handed the war on to his successor.

VIII. Where Do We Go From Here?

If Vietnam were a story of how the system failed, that is, if our leaders did not do what they wanted to do or if they did not realize what they were doing or what was happening, it would be easy to package a large and assorted box of policy-making panaceas. For example: Fix the method of reporting from the field. Fix the way progress is measured in a guerrilla war. Make sure the President sees all the real alternatives. But these are all third-order issues, because the U.S. political-bureaucratic system did not fail; it worked.

Our leaders felt they had to prevent the loss of Vietnam to Communism, and they have succeeded so far in doing just that. Most of those who made Vietnam policy still believe that they did the right thing and lament only the domestic repercussions of their actions. It is because the price of attaining this goal has been so dear in lives, trust, dollars, and priorities, and the benefits so intangible, remote, and often implausible, that these leaders and we ourselves are forced to seek new answers and new policies.

Paradoxically, the way to get these new answers is not by asking why did the system fail, but why did it work so tragically well. There is, then,

[17]Quoted in Henry Brandon, *Anatomy of Error*, (Boston: Gambit, 1969), p. 102.

[18]Tom Wicker, *JFK and LBJ*, (New York: Penguin Books, 1968), p. 208.

[19]Lady Bird Johnson, *A White House Diary*, (New York: Holt, Rinehart and Winston, 1970), p. 248.

only one first-order issue—how and why does our political-bureaucratic system decide what is vital and what is not? By whom, in what manner, and for what reasons was it decided t᾽?at all Vietnam must not fall into Communist hands?

Almost all of our leaders since 1949 shared this conviction. Only a few voices in the wilderness were raised in opposition. Even as late as mid-1967, most critics were arguing that the U.S. could not afford to lose or be "driven from the field," that the real problem was our bombing of North Vietnam, and that this had to be stopped in order to bring about a negotiated settlement. Fewer still were urging that such a settlement should involve a coalition government with the Communists. Hardly any-one was saying that the outcome in Vietnam did not matter.

There is little evidence of much critical thinking about the relation of Vietnam to U.S. security. Scholars, journalists, politicians, and bureau-crats all seem to have assumed either that Vietnam was "vital" to U.S. na-tional security or that the American people would not stand for the loss of "another" country to Communism.

Anti-Communism has been and still is a potent force in American pol-itics, and most people who were dealing with the Vietnam problem sim-ply believed that the Congress and the public would "punish" those who were "soft on Communism." Our leaders not only anticipated this kind of public reaction, but believed that there were valid reasons for not per-mitting the Communists to take all of Vietnam by force. In other words, they believed in what they were doing on the national security "merits." The domino theory, which was at the heart of the matter, rested on the widely shared attitude that security was indivisible, that weakness in one place would only invite aggression in others.

What can be done?

The President can do more than Presidents have in the past to call his national security bureaucracy to task. He can show the bureaucracy that he expects it to be more rigorous in determining what is vital or impor-tant or unimportant. Specifically, he can reject reasoning which simply asserts that security is indivisible, and he can foster the belief that while the world is an interconnected whole, actions can be taken in certain parts of the world to compensate for actions which are not taken elsewhere. For example, if the real concern about Vietnam were the effect of its loss on Japan, the Middle East and Berlin, could we not take actions in each of these places to mitigate the "Vietnam fallout"?

None of these efforts with the bureaucracy can succeed, however, un-less there is a change in general political attitudes as well. If anti-Com-munism persists as an overriding domestic political issue it will also be the main bureaucratic issue. Altering public attitudes will take time, education, and political courage—and it will create a real dilemma for the President. If the President goes "too far" in re-educating public and congressional opinions about Communism, he may find that he will have little support for threatening or using military force when he believes that our security really is at stake. In the end, it will still be the President who is held responsible for U.S. security. Yet, if our Vietnam experience has taught us anything, it is that the President must begin the process of re-education despite the risks.

Philip E. Slater
HALF SLAVE, HALF FREE

Americans in the fifties candidly viewed themselves as more materialistic than some of their predecessors, a circumstance which inevitably invited rebels against the prevailing conformity. "The Beat Generation" rejected ranch homes and tail-finned cars in favor of new life-styles and modes of expression. If the "beatniks" did not create a new mass culture, it was not necessarily because most Americans resisted the temptation to imitate them. The beatniks tended towards bohemian elitism, quartering themselves in colonies from New York's Greenwich Village to San Francisco's North Beach, seeking new literary modes like Jack Kerouac's "On the Road," and celebrating the anti-bourgeois life. They were lampooned by most Americans as eccentrics, and the beatniks soon became shop-worn curiosities and faded from popular interest.

The "Hip Generation" of the sixties, on the other hand, found a society that was much more receptive to anti-bourgeois innovations. The "hippies" were not concerned with literary or philosophical elitism. Through a mass communications media they appealed to youth's passion for innovative music, clothing, and language. Without meaning to, they proselytized millions of Americans, including the young and the would-be young. While ostensibly rejecting the "straight" nature of American commercialism, hippies encouraged imitation. Commerce-wise people created vast businesses based upon the outlandish appeal of the hippies, who unintentionally made the anti-bourgeois lifestyle bourgeois.

The hippies did not produce an intelligentsia, and their colonies were not centered in any particular cities. They were so broad-based in appeal and so widely imitated that it soon became difficult for many critics to distinguish the rebels from the targets of their rebellion. A new culture arose with the assent of the old, and its significance is explained here by Philip Slater.

We shall be able to rid ourselves of many of the pseudomoral principles which have hag-ridden us for two hundred years, by which we have exalted some of the most distasteful of human qualities into the position of the highest virtues.

KEYNES

Consider the lilies of the field, how they grow; they toil not, neither do they spin: and yet I say unto you, that even Solomon in all his glory was not arrayed like one of these.

MATTHEW 6:28–29

Don't you know that it's a fool
Who plays it cool
By making his world a little colder.

LENNON AND MC CARTNEY

And what's the point of revolution
Without general copulation.

WEISS

In the new there is always an admixture of the old, and this is true of the protean counterculture now burgeoning in the United States. This makes it very difficult, as we saw in the last chapter, to tell what is a true counterculture and what is simply a recruiting outpost for the old culture. But the mere fact that the old culture tries to gobble up something new does not invalidate the potential revolutionary impact of this novelty. At some point a devourer always overreaches himself, like the witch or giant in folk tales who tries to drink up the sea and bursts, or like the vacuum monster in *Yellow Submarine* who ultimately devours himself and disappears. This seems to me the most probable future for the old culture in America.

When I talk of two separate cultures in America I do not mean rich and poor, or black and white (or science and humanism), but rather the opposition between the old scarcity-oriented technological culture that still predominates and the somewhat amorphous counterculture that is growing up to challenge it. At times this distinction may seem synonymous with old-versus-young, or radical-versus-conservative, but the overlap is only approximate. There are many young people who are dedicated to the old culture and a few old people attracted to the new; while as to politics, nothing could be more old-culture than a traditional Marxist.

I speak of two cultures, first because each is in fact a total system with an internal logic and consistency: each is built upon a set of assumptions which hangs together and is viable under some conditions. Second, I wish to emphasize a fact which has escaped the liberal-centrist group that plays so dominant a role in America: that they are no longer being wooed so fervently by those to the left and right of them. The seduction of the center is a phenomenon that occurs only in societies fundamentally united. This has in the past been true of the United States and most parliamentary democracies, but it is true no longer. I speak of two cultures because we no longer have one. Mixing the two that exist does not add up to the American way of life. They cannot be mixed. From two opposing systems—each tightly defined—can only come a collision and a confusion. No meaningful compromise can be found if the culture as a whole is not articulated in a coherent way. American centrists— liberal university presidents are the best example—are still operating under the illusion that all Americans are playing by the same rules, an assumption which puts the centrists into the advantageous position of mediators. But this is not the case. Indeed, the moderates are increasingly despised by both radicals and conservatives as hypocritical, amoral, and opportunistic—people who will take no stand and are only interested in their own careers.

What we see instead are two growing absolutistic groups with a shrinking liberal one in between, a condition that will probably obtain until some new cultural structure emerges which is more widely shared. The left attacks the middle most vigorously, since its equivocating stances and lack of conviction make it morally the most vulnerable. Times of change are times when the center is crushed in this way—when it is regarded as the least rather than the most valid, when it is an object of contempt rather than a court of appeal. As the new culture settles in, a new center will grow in strength—become dominant and sure, acquire moral conviction.

So long as our society had a common point of moral reference there was a tendency for conflicts to be resolved by compromise, and this compromise had a moral as well as practical basis. Today this moral unity is gone, and the *only* basis for compromise is a practical one. Whenever moral sentiments are aroused, the opposing groups are pulled in opposite directions, and mere expedience is usually too weak a consideration to counteract this divergence.

For the older generation, the ultimate moral reference group is the far right—authoritarian, puritanical, punitive, fundamentalist. Such views are of course considered extreme, impractical, and "moralistic," but they are accorded an implicit and unquestioned *moral* validity. The liberal majority generally feel uncomfortable and awkward defining issues in moral terms, but when it becomes inescapable it is this brand of morality that they tend to fall back upon. They are practical and "realistic" as long as possible, but when accused of moral flabbiness or being too compromising they feel called upon to pay homage to a kind of Bible Belt morality. They tend to view their position as one of sensible men mediating between hypermoralistic conservatives and amoral radicals, bending the rigid rules of the former to accommodate and indulge the latter.

For middle-class college students the ultimate moral reference group tends increasingly to be the New Left, with its emphasis on equalitarianism, radical democracy, social justice, and social commitment. Once again the moderate majority among the young tend to view the proponents of their moral code as extreme, moralistic, and fanatic. They regard the militant activists as pursuing a course which is too pure and demanding to be realistic. Allowances must be made for human frailty—the narcissistic needs of those in power, resistance to change, and so on. They, too, see themselves as mediating, but this time between hypermoralistic radicals and amoral conservatives.

So long as the two sides do not feel that a significant moral issue is at stake they can reach a compromise, and the illusion of a unitary culture can be maintained. But sooner or later a moral issue *is* at stake, and negotiations then break down. This is because each side feels it has to justify itself to its moral reference group—to prove that it is not merely giving in out of weakness and cowardice—to prove that it is willing to stand up for some principle. But instead of being common principles, shared by the vast central majority of the society, with each side attempting to show that they are closer to this central morality, the principles are at opposite poles, pulling the sides apart. Today expedience is the *only* unifying force in campus confrontations; no morally based unity is possible.

This may have something to do with the peculiar obtuseness that seems to afflict college presidents, who appear to learn nothing from each other's mistakes or even their own. They are unwilling to face the absence of an even minimal value consensus and keep trying to manufacture one ("the preservation of the university," "the maintenance of free expression and rational discourse," etc.). They talk of "outside agitators" and "a small disruptive minority" and, acting on their own rhetoric, soon find themselves confronted with a hostile majority. They shrink from facing the fact that an ever increasing number of students (for despite the deliberate attempts of admissions officers to prevent it, each entering class is more radical than the last) reject the legitimacy of the established order. The legal monopoly of violence is being challenged by students—they see the crimes of "legitimate" order as demanding extra-legal countermeasures: "An opposition which is directed . . . against a given social system as a whole, cannot remain legal and lawful because it is the established legality and the established law which it opposes." Since the crimes of the society are defended and protected by legal techniques they can only be attacked by extra-legal means. Since the forces of law and order fail to comply with their own standards their "betrayed promises are, as it were, 'taken over' by the opposition, and with them the claim for legitimacy."[1]

What all this means is that the university is no longer one society with shared norms of proper behavior, fair play, tolerance and so on, as university administrators try to pretend. Students are not simply challeng-

[1] Herbert Marcuse, *An Essay of Liberation* (Boston: Beacon Press. 1969), pp. 66, 73, 77–78.

ing an authority they fundamentally accept. Campus confrontations are warfare, with neither side accepting the validity of occupation and control by the other. Students who take over a building hold the same view of this act as police do of wiretapping: the enemy is too dangerous to give them the benefit of the doubt; their crimes require emergency measures.

The Old Culture and the New

There are an almost infinite number of polarities by means of which one can differentiate between the two cultures. The old culture, when forced to choose, tends to give preference to property rights over personal rights, technological requirements over human needs, competition over cooperation, violence over sexuality, concentration over distribution, the producer over the consumer, means over ends, secrecy over openness, social forms over personal expression, striving over gratification, Oedipal love over communal love, and so on. The new counterculture tends to reverse all of these priorities.

Now it is important to recognize that these differences cannot be resolved by some sort of compromise or "golden mean" position. Every cultural system is a dynamic whole, resting on processes that must be accelerative to be self-sustaining. Change must therefore affect the motivational roots of a society or it is not change at all. An attempt to introduce some isolated element into such a system produces cultural redefinition and absorption of the novel element if the culture is strong, and deculturation if it is susceptible. As Margaret Mead points out, to introduce cloth garments into a grass- or bark-clad population, without simultaneously introducing closets, soap, sewing, and furniture, merely transforms a neat and attractive tribe into a dirty and slovenly one. Cloth is part of a complex cultural pattern that includes storing, cleaning, mending, and protecting—just as the automobile is part of a system that includes fueling, maintenance, and repair. A fish with the lungs of a land mammal still will not survive out of water.

Imagine, for example, that we are cooperation purists attempting to remove the invidious element from a foot race. We decide, first of all, that we will award no prize to the winner, or else prizes to everyone. This, we discover, brings no reduction in competitiveness. Spectators and participants alike are still preoccupied with who won and how fast he ran relative to someone else now or in the past. We then decide to eliminate even *announcing* the winner. To our dismay we discover that our efforts have generated some new cultural forms: the runners have taken to wearing more conspicuous identifying clothing—bright-colored trunks or shirts, or names emblazoned in iridescent letters—and underground printed programs have appeared with names, physical descriptions, and other information facilitating this identification. In despair we decide to have the runners run one at a time and we keep no time records. But now we find that the sale of stopwatches has become a booming enterprise, that the underground printed programs have expanded to include voluminous statistics on past time records of participants, and that private "timing services," comparable to the rating services of the television industry, have grown up to provide definitive and instantaneous results for spectators willing to pay a nominal sum (thus does artificial deprivation facilitate enterprise).

At this point we are obliged to eliminate the start and finish lines— an innovation which arouses angry protest from both spectators and participants, who have evinced only mild grumbling over our previous efforts. "What kind of a race can it be if people begin and end wherever they like? Who will be interested in it?" To mollify their complaints and combat dwindling attendance, we reintroduce the practice of having everyone run at the same time. Before long we observe that the runners have evolved the practice of all starting to run at about the same time (although we disallow beginning at the same place), and that all of the races are being run on the circular track. The races get longer and longer, and the underground printed programs now record statistics on how many laps were run by a given runner in a given race. All races have now become longevity contests, and one goes to them equipped with a picnic basket. The newer fields, in fact, do not have bleachers, but only tables at which drinks are served, with scattered observation windows through which the curious look from time to time and report to their tables the latest news on which runners are still going. Time passes, and we are increasingly subjected to newspaper attacks concerning the corrupt state into which our efforts have fallen. With great trepidation, and in the face of enormous opposition from the ideologically apathetic masses, we inaugurate a cultural revolution and make further drastic alterations in racing rules. Runners begin and end at a signal, but there is no track, merely an open field. A runner must change direction every thirty seconds, and if he runs parallel with another runner for more than fifteen seconds he is disqualified. At first attendance falls off badly, but after a time spectators become interested in how many runners can survive a thirty-minute race without being eliminated for a breach of these rules. Soon specific groups become so skilled at not running parallel that none of them are ever disqualified. In the meantime they begin to run a little more slowly and to elaborate intricate patterns of synchronizing their direction changes. The more gifted groups become virtuosi at moving parallel until the last split second and then diverging. The thirty-second rule becomes unnecessary as direction changes are voluntarily frequent, but the fifteen-second rule becomes a five-second one. The motions of the runners become more and more elegant, and a vast outpouring of books and articles descends from and upon the university (ever a dirty bird) to establish definitive distinctions between the race and the dance.

The first half of this parable is a reasonably accurate representation of what most liberal reform amounts to: opportunities for the existing system to flex its muscles and exercise its self-maintaining capabilities. Poverty programs put very little money into the hands of the poor because middle-class hands are so much more gifted at grasping money—they know better where it is, how to apply for it, how to divert it, how to concentrate it. That is what being middle class means, just as a race means competition. No matter how much we try to change things it somehow ends as merely a more complex, intricate, bizarre, and interesting version of what existed before. A heavily graduated income tax somehow ends by making the rich richer and the poor poorer. "Highway beautification" somehow turns into rural blight, and so on.

But there is a limit to the amount of change a system can absorb, and the second half of the parable suggests that if we persist in our efforts and finally attack the system at its motivational roots we may indeed be successful. In any case there is no such thing as "compromise": we are either strong enough to lever the train onto a new track or it stays on the old one or it is derailed.

Thus it becomes important to discern the core motivational logic behind the old and the new cultures. Knowing this would make rational change possible—would unlock the door that leads most directly from the old to the new.* For a prolonged, unplanned collision will nullify both cultures, like bright pigments combining into gray. The transition must be as deft as possible if we are to minimize the destructive chaos that inevitably accompanies significant cultural transformations.

The core of the old culture is scarcity. Everything in it rests upon the assumption that the world does not contain the wherewithal to satisfy the needs of its human inhabitants. From this it follows that people must compete with one another for these scarce resources—lie, swindle, steal, and kill, if necessary. These basic assumptions create the danger of a "war of all against all" and must be buttressed by a series of counternorms which attempt to qualify and restrain the intensity of the struggle. Those who can take the largest share of the scarce resources are said to be "successful," and if they can do it without violating the counternorms they are said to have character and moral fibre.

The key flaw in the old culture is, of course, the fact that the scarcity is spurious—man-made in the case of bodily gratifications and man-allowed or man-maintained in the case of material goods. It now exists only for the purpose of maintaining the system that depends upon it, and its artificiality becomes more palpable each day. Americans continually find themselves in the position of having killed someone to avoid sharing a meal which turns out to be too large to eat alone.

The new culture is based on the assumption that important human needs are easily satisfied and that the resources for doing so are plenti-

*This of course makes the assumption that some kind of drastic change is either desirable or inevitable. I do not believe our society can long continue on its old premises without destroying itself and everything else. Nor do I believe it can contain or resist the gathering forces of change without committing suicide in the process.

ful. Competition is unnecessary and the only danger to humans is human aggression. There is no reason outside of human perversity for peace not to reign and for life not to be spent in the cultivation of joy and beauty. Those who can do this in the face of the old culture's ubiquity are considered "beautiful."

The flaw in the new culture is the fact that the old culture has succeeded in hiding the cornucopia of satisfactions that the new assumes— that a certain amount of work is required to release the bounty that exists from the restraints under which it is now placed. Whereas the flaw in the old culture has caused it to begin to decompose, the flaw in the new culture has produced a profound schism in its ranks—a schism between activist and dropout approaches to the culture as it now exists. We will return to this problem a little later.

It is important to recognize the internal logic of the old culture, however absurd its premise. If one assumes scarcity, then the knowledge that others want the same things that we have leads with some logic to preparations for defense, and, ultimately (since the best defense is offense), for attack. The same assumption leads to a high value being placed on the ability to postpone gratification (since there is not enough to go around). The expression of feelings is a luxury, since it might alert the scarce resources to the fact that the hunter is near.

The high value placed on restraint and coldness (which, as the Beatles observe in the epigraph for this chapter, creates even greater scarcity) generates in turn another norm: that of "good taste." One can best understand the meaning of such a norm by examining what is common to those acts considered to be in violation of it, and on this basis the meaning of "good taste" is very clear. "Good taste" means tasteless in the literal sense. Any act or product which contains too much stimulus value is considered to be "in bad taste" by old-culture adherents. Since gratification is viewed as a scarce commodity, arousal is dangerous. Clothes must be drab and inconspicuous, colors of low intensity, smells nonexistent ("if it weren't for bad taste there wouldn't be no taste at all"). Sounds should be quiet, words should lack affect. Four-letter words are always in bad taste because they have high stimulus value. Satire is in bad taste if it arouses political passions or creates images that are too vivid or exciting. All direct references to sexuality are in bad taste until proven innocent, since sexual arousal is the most feared result of all. The lines in old-culture homes, furnishings, and public buildings are hard and utilitarian. Since auditory overstimulation is more familiarly painful than its visual counterpart, brilliant, intense, vibrant colors are called "loud," and the preferred colors for old-culture homes are dull and listless. Stimulation in any form leaves old-culture Americans with a "bad taste" in their mouths. This taste is the taste of desire—a reminder that life in the here-and-now contains many pleasures to distract them from the carrot dangling beyond their reach. Too much stimulation makes the carrot hard to see. Good taste is a taste for carrots.

In the past decade, however, this pattern has undergone a merciless assault from the new culture. For if we assume that gratification is easy and resources plentiful, stimulation is no longer to be feared. Psychedelic colors, amplified sound, erotic books and films, bright and elaborate clothing, spicy food, "intense" (i.e., Anglo-Saxon) words, angry and irreverent satire—all go counter to the old pattern of understimulation. Long hair and beards provide a more "tactile" appearance than the bland, shaven-and-shorn, geometric lines of the fifties. Even Edward Hall's accusation that America is a land of "olfactory blandness" (a statement any traveler will confirm) must now be qualified a little, as the smells of coffee shops, foreign cooking, and incense combine to breathe a modicum of sensation even into the olfactory sphere. (Hall is right, however, in the sense that when America is filled with intense color, music, and ornament, deodorants will be the old culture's last-ditch holdouts. It is no accident that hostility to hippies so often focuses on their olfactory humanity). The old culture turned the volume down on emotional experience in order to concentrate on its dreams of glory, but the new culture has turned it up again.

New-culture adherents, in fact, often display symptoms of *under*sensitivity to stimuli. They saw "Wow!" in response to almost everything, but in voices utterly devoid of either tension or affect. They seem in general to be more certain that desire can be gratified than that it can be aroused.

This phenomenon probably owes much to early child-rearing conditions. Under ordinary circumstances a mother responds to her child's needs when they are expressed powerfully enough to distract her from other cares and activities. Mothers who overrespond to the Spockian challenge, however, often try to anticipate the child's needs. Before arousal has proceeded very far they hover about and try several possible satisfactions. Since we tend to use these early parental responses as models for the way we treat our own impulses in adulthood, some new-culture adherents find themselves moving toward gratification before need arousal is clear or compelling. Like their mothers they are not altogether clear which need they are feeling. To make matters worse they are caught in the dilemma that spontaneity automatically evaporates the moment it becomes an ideology. It is a paradox of the modern condition that only those who oppose complete libidinal freedom are capable of ever achieving it.

Another logical consequence of scarcity assumptions is structured inequality. If there is not enough to go around then those who have more will find ways to prolong their advantage, and even legitimate it through various devices. The law itself, although philosophically committed to equality, is fundamentally a social device for maintaining structured systems of inequality (defining as crimes, for example, only those forms of theft and violence in which lower class persons engage). One of the major thrusts of the new culture, on the other hand, is equality: since the good things of life are plentiful, everyone should share them: rich and poor, black and white, female and male.

It is a central characteristic of the old culture that means habitually become ends, and ends means. Instead of people working in order to obtain goods in order to be happy, for example, we find that people should be made happy in order to work better in order to obtain more goods, and so on. Inequality, originally a consequence of scarcity, is now a means of creating artificial scarcities. For in the old culture, as we have seen, the manufacture of scarcity is the principal activity. Hostile comments of old-culture adherents toward new-culture forms ("people won't want to work if they can get things for nothing," "people won't want to get married if they can get it free") often reveal this preoccupation. Scarcity, the presumably undesired but unavoidable foundation for the whole old-culture edifice, has now become its most treasured and sacred value, and to maintain this value in the midst of plenty it has been necessary to establish invidiousness as the foremost criterion of worth. Old-culture Americans are peculiarly drawn to anything that seems to be the exclusive possession of some group or other, and find it difficult to enjoy anything they themselves have unless they can be sure that there are people to whom this pleasure is denied. For those in power even life itself derives its value invidiously: amid the emptiness and anesthesia of a power-oriented career many officials derive reassurance of their vitality from their proximity to the possibility of blowing up the world.

The centrality of invidiousness offers a strong barrier to the diffusion of social justice and equality. But it provides a *raison d'être* for the advertising industry, whose primary function is to manufacture illusions of scarcity. In a society engorged to the point of strangulation with useless and joyless products, advertisements show people calamitously running out of their food or beer, avidly hoarding potato chips, stealing each other's cigarettes, guiltily borrowing each other's deodorants, and so on. In a land of plenty there is little to fight over, but in the world of advertising images men and women will fight before changing their brand, in a kind of parody of the Vietnam war.

The fact that property takes precedence over human life in the old culture also follows logically from scarcity assumptions. If possessions are scarce relative to people they come to have more value than people. This is especially true of people with few possessions, who come to be considered so worthless as to be subhuman and hence eligible for extermination. Many possessions, on the other hand, entitle the owner to a status somewhat more than human. But as a society becomes more affluent these priorities begin to change—human life increases in value and property decreases. New-culture adherents challenge the high relative value placed on property, although the old priority still permeates the society's normative structure. It is still considered permissible, for example, to kill someone who is stealing your property under certain con-

HALF SLAVE, HALF FREE 349

ditions. This is especially true if that person is without property himself
—a wealthy kleptomaniac (in contrast to a poor black looter) would
probably be worth a murder trial if killed while stealing.*

A recent sign of the shift in values was the *Pueblo* courtmartial. While
the Navy, standing firmly behind old-culture priorities, argued that the
Commander of the spy ship should have sacrificed the lives of ninety
men to prevent the loss of "expensive equipment" to the enemy, the public at large supported his having put human life first. Much of the intense legal upheaval visible today—expressed most noticeably in the
glare of publicity that now attaches to the activities of the U.S. Supreme Court—derives from the attempt to adapt an old-culture legal
system to the changing priorities that render it obsolete.

It would not be difficult to show how the other characteristics of the
old culture are based on the same scarcity assumptions, or to trace out in
detail the derivation of the new culture from the premise that life's satisfactions exist in abundance and sufficiency for all. Let us instead look
more closely at the relationship that the new culture bears to the old—
the continuities and discontinuities that it offers—and explore some of
the contradictions it holds within itself.

First of all it should be stressed that affluence and economic security
are not in themselves responsible for the new culture. The rich, like
the poor, have always been with us to some degree, but the new culture
has not. What is significant in the new culture is not a celebration of
economic affluence but a rejection of its foundation. The new culture is
concerned with rejecting the artificial scarcities upon which material
abundance is based. It argues that instead of throwing away one's body
so that one can accumulate material artifacts, one should throw away
the artifacts and enjoy one's body. The new culture is not merely
blindly reactive, however, but embodies a sociological consciousness. In
this consciousness lies the key insight that possessions actually generate
scarcity. The more emotion one invests in them the more chances for
significant gratification are lost—the more committed to them one becomes the more deprived one feels, like a thirsty man drinking salt water. To accumulate possessions is to deliver pieces of oneself to dead
things. Possessions can absorb an emotional cathexis, but unlike personal
relationships they feed nothing back. Americans have combined the proliferation of possessions with the disruption, circumscription, and trivialization
of most personal relationships. An alcoholic becomes malnourished because
drinking obliterates his hunger. Americans become unhappy and vicious
because their preoccupation with amassing possessions obliterates their
loneliness. This is why production in America seems to be on such an endless upward spiral: every time we buy something we deepen our emotional

*A more trivial example can be found in the old culture's handling of noise control.
Police are called to prevent distraction by the joyous noises of laughter and song, but not
to stop the harsh and abrasive roar of power saws, air hammers, power mowers, snow
blowers, and other baneful machines.

deprivation and hence our need to buy something. This is good for business, of course, but those who profit most from this process are just as trapped in the general deprivation as everyone else. The new-culture adherents are thus not merely affluent—they are trying to substitute an adequate emotional diet for a crippling addiction.

The new culture is nevertheless a product of the old, not merely a rejection of it. It picks up themes latent or dormant or subordinate in the old and magnifies them. The hippie movement, for example, is brimming with nostalgia—a nostalgia peculiarly American and shared by old-culture adherents. This nostalgia embraces the Old West, Amerindian culture, the wilderness, the simple life, the utopian community—all venerable American traditions. But for the old culture they represent a subordinate, ancillary aspect of the culture, appropriate for recreational occasions or fantasy representation—a kind of pastoral relief from everyday striving—whereas for the new culture they are dominant themes. The new culture's passion for memorabilia, paradoxically, causes uneasiness in old-culture adherents, whose future-oriented invidiousness leads to a desire to sever themselves from the past. Yet for the most part it is a question of the new culture making the old culture's secondary themes primary, rather than simply seeking to discard the old culture's primary theme. Even the notion of "dropping out" is an important American tradition—neither the United States itself nor its populous suburbs would exist were this not so.

Americans have always been deeply ambivalent about the issue of social involvement. On the one hand they are suspicious of it and share deep romantic fantasies of withdrawal to a simple pastoral or even sylvan life. On the other hand they are much given to acting out grandiose fantasies of taking society by storm, through the achievement of wealth, power, or fame. This ambivalence has led to many strange institutions— the suburb and the automobile being the most obvious. But note that both fantasies express the viewpoint of an outsider. Americans have a profound tendency to feel like outsiders—they wonder where the action is and wander about in search of it (this puts an enormous burden on celebrities, who are supposed to know, but in fact feel just as doubtful as everyone else). Americans have created a society in which they are automatically nobodies, since no one has any stable place or enduring connection. The village idiot of earlier times was less a "nobody" in this sense than the mobile junior executive or academic. An American has to "make a place for himself" because he does not have one.

Since the society rests on scarcity assumptions, involvement in it has always meant competitive involvement, and, curiously enough, the theme of bucolic withdrawal has often associated itself with that of cooperative, communal life. So consistently, in fact, have intentional communities established themselves in the wilderness that one can only infer that society as we know it makes cooperative life impossible.

Be that as it may, it is important to remember that the New England colonies grew out of utopian communes, so that the dropout tradition is not only old but extremely important to our history. Like so many of the more successful nineteenth-century utopian communities (Oneida and Amana, for example) the puritans became corrupted by involvement in successful economic enterprise and the communal aspect was eroded away—another example of a system being destroyed by what it attempts to ignore. The new culture is thus a kind of reform movement, attempting to revive a decayed tradition once important to our civilization.

In stressing these continuities between the new culture and the American past, I do not mean to imply a process unique to our society. One of the most basic characteristics of all successful social systems—indeed, perhaps all living matter as well—is that they include devices that serve to keep alive alternatives that are antithetical to their dominant emphases, as a kind of hedge against change. These latent alternatives usually persist in some encapsulated and imprisoned form ("break glass in case of fire"), such as myths, festivals, or specialized roles. Fanatics continually try to expunge these circumscribed contradictions, but when they succeed it is often fatal to the society. For, as Lewis Mumford once pointed out, it is the "laxity, corruption, and disorder" in a system that makes it viable, considering the contradictory needs that all social systems must satisfy.[2] Such latent alternatives are priceless treasures and must be carefully guarded against loss. For a new cultural pattern does not emerge out of nothing—the seed must already be there, like the magic tricks of wizards and witches in folklore, who can make an ocean out of a drop of water, a palace out of a stone, a forest out of a blade of grass, but nothing out of nothing. Many peoples keep alive a tradition of a golden age, in which a totally different social structure existed. The Judeo-Christian God, patriarchal and omnipotent, has served in matrifocal cultures to keep alive the concept of a strong and protective paternal figure in the absence of real-life examples. Jesters kept alive a wide variety of behavior patterns amid the stilted and restrictive formality of royal courts. The specialized effeminate roles that one finds in many warrior cultures are not merely a refuge for those who fail to succeed in the dominant pattern—they are also a living reminder that the rigid "protest masculinity" that prevails is not the only conceivable kind of behavior for a male. And conversely, the warrior ethos is maintained in a peaceful society or era by means of a military cadre or reserve system.

These phenomena are equivalent to (and in literate cultures tend increasingly to be replaced by) written records of social practices. They are like a box of seldom-used tools, or a trunk of old costumes awaiting the proper period-play. Suddenly the environment changes, the tolerated eccentric becomes a prophet, the clown a dancing-master, the doll an idol, the idol a doll. The elements have not changed, only the arrangement and the emphases have changed. Every revolution is in part a revival.

Sometimes societal ambivalence is so marked that the latent pattern

[2]Lewis Mumford, "The Fallacy of Systems," *Saturday Review of Literature*, XXXII, October 1949; Gideon Sjoberg, "Contradictory Functional Requirements of Social Systems," *Journal of Conflict Resolution*, IV, 1960, pp. 198–208.

is retained in a form almost as elaborated as the dominant one. Our society, for example, is one of the most mobile (geographically, at least) ever known; yet, unlike other nomadic cultures it makes little allowance for this fact in its patterns of material accumulation. Our homes are furnished as if we intended to spend the rest of our lives in them, instead of moving every few years. This perhaps represents merely a kind of technological neurosis—a yearning for stability expressed in a technological failure to adapt. Should Americans ever settle down, however, they will find little to do in the way of readjusting their household furnishing habits.

Ultimately it seems inevitable that Americans must either abandon their nomadic habits (which seems unlikely) or moderate their tendency to invest their libido exclusively in material possessions (an addiction upon which the economy relies rather heavily). The new culture is of course pushing hard to realize the second alternative, and if it is successful one might anticipate a trend toward more simply furnished dwellings in which all but the most portable and decorative items are permanent installations. In such a case we might like or dislike a sofa or bed or dresser, but would have no more personal involvement with it than we now do with a stove, furnace, or garage. We would possess, cathect, feel as a part of us, only a few truly personal and portable items.

This tendency of human societies to keep alternative patterns alive has many biological analogues. One of these is *neoteny*—the evolutionary process in which foetal or juvenile characteristics are retained in the adult animal. Body characteristics that have long had only transitional relevance are exploited in response to altered environmental circumstances (thus many human features resemble foetal traits of apes). I have not chosen this example at random, for much of the new culture is implicitly and explicitly "neotenous" in a cultural sense: behavior, values, and life-styles formerly seen as appropriate only to childhood are being retained into adulthood as a counterforce to the old culture.

I pointed out earlier, for example, that children are taught a set of values in earliest childhood—cooperation, sharing, equalitarianism— which they begin to unlearn as they enter school, wherein competition, invidiousness, status differentiation, and ethnocentrism prevail. By the time they enter adult life children are expected to have largely abandoned the value assumptions with which their social lives began. But for affluent, protected, middle-class children this process is slowed down, while intellectual development is speeded up, so that the earlier childhood values can become integrated into a conscious, adult value system centered around social justice. The same is true of other characteristics of childhood: spontaneity, hedonism, candor, playfulness, use of the senses for pleasure rather than utility, and so on. The protective, child-oriented, middle-class family allows the child to preserve some of these qualities longer than is possible under more austere conditions, and his intellectual precocity makes it possible for him to integrate them into an ideological system with which he can confront the corrosive, life-abusing tendencies of the old culture.

When these neotenous characteristics become manifest to old-culture adherents the effect is painfully disturbing, for they vibrate feelings and attitudes that are very old and very deep, although long and harshly stifled. Old-culture adherents have learned to reject all this, but since the learning antedated intellectual maturity they have no coherent ideological framework within which such a rejection can be consciously understood and thoughtfully endorsed. They are deeply attracted and acutely revolted at the same time. They can neither resist their fascination nor control their antipathy. This is exemplified by the extravagant curiosity that hippie communes attract, and by the harassment that so often extinguishes them.[3] It is usually necessary in such situations for the rote-learned abhorrence to discharge itself in persecutory activity before the more positive responses can be released. This was true in the case of the early Christians in Rome, with whom contemporary hippies are often compared (both were communal, utopian, mystical, dropouts, unwashed; both were viewed as dangerous, masochistic, ostentatious, the cause of their own troubles; both existed in societies in which the exclusive pursuit of material advantages had reached some kind of dead end), and seems equally true today. The absorption of this persecution is part of the process through which the latent values that the oppressed group protects and nurtures are expropriated by the majority and released into the mainstream of the culture.

Up to this point we have (rather awkwardly) discussed the new culture as if it were an integrated, monolithic pattern, which is certainly very far from the case. There are many varied and contradictory streams feeding the new culture, and some of these deserve particular attention, since they provide the raw material for future axes of conflict.

The most glaring split in the new culture is that which separates militant activism from the traits we generally associate with the hippie movement. The first strand stresses political confrontation, revolutionary action, radical commitment to the process of changing the basic structure of modern industrial society. The second involves a renunciation of that society in favor of the cultivation of inner experience and pleasing internal feeling-states. Heightening of sensory receptivity, commitment to the immediate present, and tranquil acceptance of the physical environment are sought in contradistinction to old-culture ways, in which the larger part of one's immediate experience is overlooked or grayed out by the preoccupation with utility, future goals, and external mastery. Since, in the old culture, experience is classified before it is felt, conceptualization tends here to be forsworn altogether. There is also much emphasis on aesthetic expression and an overarching belief in the power of love.

[3]See, for example, Robert Houriet, "Life and Death of a Commune Called Oz," *New York Times Magazine*, February 16, 1969.

This division is a crude one, and there are, of course, many areas of overlap. Both value systems share an antipathy to the old culture, both share beliefs in sexual freedom and personal autonomy. Some groups (the Yippies, in particular) have tried with some success to bridge the gap in a variety of interesting ways. But there is nonetheless an inherent contradiction between them. Militant activism is task-oriented, and hence partakes of certain old-culture traits such as postponement of gratification, preoccupation with power, and so on. To be a competent revolutionary one must possess a certain tolerance for the "Protestant Ethic" virtues, and the activists' moral code is a stern one indeed. The hippie ethic, on the other hand, is a "salvation now" approach. It is thus more radical, since it remains relatively uncontaminated with old-culture values. It is also far less realistic, since it ignores the fact that the existing culture provides a totally antagonistic milieu in which the hippie movement must try to survive in a state of highly vulnerable parasitic dependence. The activists can reasonably say that the flower people are absurd to pretend that the revolution has already occurred, for such pretense leads only to severe victimization by the old culture. The flower people can reasonably retort that a revolution based to so great a degree on old-culture premises is lost before it is begun, for even if the militants are victorious they will have been corrupted by the process of winning.

The dilemma is a very real one and arises whenever radical change is sought. For every social system attempts to exercise the most rigid control over the mechanisms by which it can be altered—defining some as legitimate and others as criminal or disloyal. When we examine the characteristics of legitimate and nonlegitimate techniques, however, we find that the "legitimate" ones involve a course of action requiring a sustained commitment to the core assumptions of the culture. In other words, if the individual follows the "legitimate" pathway there is a very good chance that his initial radical intent will be eroded in the process. If he feels that some fundamental change in the system is required, then, he has a choice between following a path that subverts his goal or one that leads him to be jailed as a criminal or traitor.

This process is not a Machiavellian invention of American capitalists, but rather a mechanism which all viable social systems must evolve spontaneously in order to protect themselves from instability. When the system as it stands is no longer viable, however, the mechanism must be exposed for the swindle that it is; otherwise the needed radical changes will be rendered ineffectual.

The key to the mechanism is the powerful human reluctance to admit that an achieved goal was not worth the unpleasant experience required to achieve it.[4] This is the basic principle underlying initiation rituals: "if I had to suffer so much pain and humiliation to get into this club it must be a wonderful organization." The evidence of thousands of years

[4]Leon Festinger, *A Theory of Cognitive Dissonance* (Stanford, Calif.: Stanford University Press, 1965).

is that the mechanism works extremely well. Up to some point, for example, war leaders can count on high casualties to increase popular commitment to military adventures.

Thus when a political leader says to a militant, "why don't you run for political office (get a haircut, dress conservatively, make deals, do the dirty work for your elders) and try to change the system in that way"—or the teacher says to the student, "wait until you have your Ph.D. (M.D., LL.B.) and then you can criticize our program," or the white man says to the black man, "when you begin to act like us you'll receive the same opportunities we do"—there is a serious subterfuge involved (however unconscious it may be) in that the protester, if he accepts the condition, will in most cases be automatically converted by it to his opponent's point of view.

The dilemma of the radical, then, is that he is likely to be corrupted if he fights the *status quo* on its own terms, but is not permitted to fight it in any other way. The real significance of the New Left is that it has discovered, in the politics of confrontation, as near a solution to this dilemma as can be found: it is always a bit problematic whether the acts of the new militants are "within the system" or not, and substantial headway can be made in the resulting confusion.

Yet even here the problem remains: if an activist devotes his life to altering the power structure, will he not become like old-culture adherents—utilitarian, invidious, scarcity-oriented, future-centered, and so on? Having made the world safe for flower people will he be likely to relinquish it to them? "You tell me it's the institution," object the Beatles, "you'd better free your mind instead." But what if all the freed minds are in jail?

The dilemma is particularly clear for blacks. Some blacks are much absorbed in rediscovering and celebrating those characteristics which seem most distinctively black and in sharpest contrast to white Western culture: black expressiveness, creativity, sensuality, and spontaneity being opposed to white constrictedness, rigidity, frigidity, bustle, and hypocrisy. For these blacks, to make too great a commitment to the power game is to forsake one's blackness. Power is a white hangup. Yet the absence of power places rather severe limits on the ability of blacks to realize their blackness or anything else.

There is no way to resolve this dilemma, and indeed, it is probably better left unresolved. In a revolutionary situation one needs discipline and unity of purpose, which, however, leads to all kinds of abuses when the goal is won. Discipline and unity become ends in themselves (after the old-culture pattern) and the victory becomes an empty one. It is therefore of great importance to have the envisioned revolutionary goals embodied in a group culture of some kind, with which the acts of those in power can be compared. In the meantime the old culture is subject to a two-pronged attack: a direct assault from activists—unmasking its life-destroying proclivities, its corruption, its futility and pointlessness, its failure to achieve any of its objectives—and an indirect assault by the expansion of expressive countercultures beyond a tolerable (i.e., freak) size.

Closely related to the activist-hippie division is the conflict over the proper role of aggression in the new culture. Violence is a major theme in the old culture and most new-culture adherents view human aggression with deep suspicion. Nonviolence has been the dominant trend in both the activist and hippie segments of the new culture until recently. But more and more activists have become impatient with the capacity of the old culture to strike the second cheek with even more enthusiasm than the first, and have endorsed violence under certain conditions as a necessary evil.

For the activists the issue has been practical rather than ideological: most serious and thoughtful activists have only a tactical commitment to violence. For the dropout ideologues, however, aggression poses a difficult problem: if they seek to minimize the artificial constriction of emotional expression, how can they be consistently loving and pacific? This logical dilemma is usually resolved by ignoring it: the love cult typically represses aggressive feelings ruthlessly—the body is paramount only so long as it is a loving body.

At the moment the old culture is so fanatically absorbed in violence that it does the work for everyone. If the new culture should prevail, however, the problem of human aggression would probably be its principal bone of contention. Faced with the persistence of aggressiveness (even in the absence of the old culture's exaggerated violence-inducing institutions), the love cult will be forced to re-examine its premises, and opt for some combination of expression and restraint that will restore human aggression to its rightful place as a natural, though secondary, human emotion.

A third split in the new culture is the conflict between individualism and collectivism. On this question the new culture talks out of both sides of its mouth, one moment pitting ideals of cooperation and community against old-culture competitiveness, the next moment espousing the old culture in its most extreme form with exhortations to "do your own thing." I am not arguing that individualism need be totally extirpated in order to make community possible, but new-culture enterprises often collapse because of a dogmatic unwillingness to subordinate the whim of the individual to the needs of the group. This problem is rarely faced honestly by new-culture adherents, who seem unaware of the conservatism involved in their attachment to individualistic principles.

It is always disastrous to attempt to eliminate any structural principle altogether; but if the balance between individualistic and collective emphases in America is not altered, everything in the new culture will be perverted and caricatured into simply another bizarre old-culture product. There must be continuities between the old and the new, but these cannot extend to the relative weights assigned to core motivational principles. The new culture seeks to create a tolerable society within the context of persistent American strivings—utopianism, the pursuit of happiness. But nothing will change until individualism is assigned a subordinate place in the American value system—for individualism lies at the core of the old culture, and a prepotent individualism is not a viable foundation for any society in a nuclear age.

George S. McGovern
NEW PERSPECTIVES ON AMERICAN SOCIETY

In recent years it has become a conventional wisdom bordering on a cliché to say that the United States must reorder its priorities: that the country must choose from among its domestic needs and national objectives those goals it will seek to accomplish first. A nation conscious of its abundance must recognize that not everything is possible in the immediate future. There is, after all, a limited quantity of money available for public spending. Health, housing, and education must vie for the federal dollar with defense and space, the latter two sectors having held the upper hand for most of the cold war while the former went begging. Obvious waste in the defense establishment and success in landing men on the moon have sharpened our doubts about continued federal spending in those programs, while it becomes increasingly evident that state and local governments are unequal to the task of fulfilling our welfare needs.

In August, 1963, during the euphoria of the Test Ban Treaty debate and before the escalation of American military involvement in Vietnam, Senator George S. McGovern of South Dakota preached a reassessment of national goals; his Senate speech contained assumptions which had been heard rarely before in Congress but were repeated widely during the next decade. He urged the Senate to cease rubber-stamping defense appropriation requests and weigh them against other national requirements. The demand for a reappraisal of priorities, however, remained merely a counterpoint to administration arms requests. A trained historian with a doctorate from Northwestern University, the 1972 Democratic nominee for President thoughtfully brought much of his training to bear upon one of the most profound issues of the cold war. In essence, he asks how secure a nation can be when it depletes its society by mas-

sive expenditures for overkill weapons. Does defense spending strengthen a whole nation or merely its military arm? The experience of the sixties would seem to suggest that a sense of well-being is not derived from military security.

New Perspectives on American Security

Mr. McGovern. Mr. President, 18 years ago, as the pilot of an American B-24 bomber, I completed the last of 35 missions in the European theater of World War II. A few days after the completion of that tour of duty the war in Europe ended.

Our crew climbed into a battle-scarred bomber to return to the United States with the grim knowledge that we had used the most devastating weapons in the long history of warfare. Our four-engine bomber had day after day dumped 5 tons of TNT on its targets below.

But we had scarcely reached home before news stories told of a fantastic new bomb that had incinerated 100,000 Japanese men, women, and children in a single searing flash. Suddenly, our 5-ton monster lost its significance in the shadow of that 20,000 ton destroyer of Hiroshima.

Although the new dimensions of death were beyond comprehension, book titles in the afterglow of Hiroshima—"One World or None," "Modern Man Is Obsolete," "Five Minutes to Midnight"—attempted to assess the meaning of the nuclear age.

Recognizing that humanity stood in deadly peril, we drew comfort only in the conviction that the new techniques of destruction were so terrifying that man surely would never use them—would he?

Five years later, the A-bomb of Hiroshima passed into obsolescence, not because it was too fearful to use, but because it had been replaced by the H-bomb—a thousand times more powerful than the bomb that had devastated Hiroshima.

Meanwhile, the Soviet Union became a nuclear power, and in 1957, Sputnik I ushered in the space age. Today, the two great powers, America and Russia, have piled up nuclear weapons with an explosive power of 60 billion tons of TNT—enough to put a 20-ton bomb at the head of every human being on the planet.

A single warhead from the American or Russian stockpile if exploded over a great city would instantly transform it into a raging fireball 3 miles in diameter with a direct heat and blast capable of burning human flesh and collapsing buildings 25 miles from its center. Above a smoking crater a mile wide and several blocks deep, a gigantic, poisonous radioactive cloud would rise 20 or 25 miles to rain down tortuous death on

Reprinted from the *Congressional Record,* August 2, 1963.

millions of human beings not fortunate enough to be incinerated quickly in the initial firestorm.

In spite of this grim prospect, the accumulation of more and more devastating weapons continues. The great powers are spending over $100 billion yearly on arms—each side justifying its investment in the name of defense. Yet, modern science supports the ancient Biblical wisdom, "there is no place to hide."

Speaking to the United Nations assembly in 1961, President Kennedy said:

> Today, every inhabitant of this planet must contemplate the day when it may no longer be habitable. Every man, woman, and child lives under a nuclear sword of Damocles, hanging by the slenderest of threads, capable of being cut at any moment by accident, miscalculation, or madness. The weapons of war must be abolished before they abolish us . . . . The risks inherent in disarmament pale in comparison to the risks inherent in an unlimited arms race.

We accept the logic of Mr. Kennedy's words, just as we accepted the earlier warning of former President Eisenhower "There is no longer any alternative to peace." Why, then, does the arms race with its mounting military budgets continue?

Doubtless, a major factor is the uncertain quest for security through superior military strength. The Congress and the Nation have willingly responded to the architects of our military security and have granted them unprecedented sums to insure the defense of our shores. Americans have felt that the growing technical complexity of the military art has required leaving the main judgments about security to our military officers.

As a freshman Congressman in 1957, I was tempted to raise some questions about what seemed to me to be a staggering military appropriations bill. But I lapsed into silence when one of the most respected Congressmen took the floor to say:

> If our military leaders are wrong and we listen to their advice, it will cost us some money. But if these experts are right, and we do not heed their requests, it may cost us our country.

Given that grim choice, it is a reckless man indeed who would challenge the demand for more military spending. Every patriotic citizen desires that his country be prepared to defend itself against attack. Even the most ardent economizers—men who vote with zeal to cut funds for education, conservation and health—are quick to shout "Aye" for more billions for arms.

I share the conviction that America ought to have a defense force which is second to none, and fully adequate to meet any need.

But, Mr. President, has the time not come to question the assumption that we are adding to defense and security by adding more and more to the nuclear stockpile? I suggest that we need to examine carefully the assumptions on which our military budget rests. We need a thoroughly honest discussion and debate, not so much about competing weapons systems, but rather about the basic postulates of our defense strategy.

Have we remembered that the defense of a great nation depends not only upon the quality of its arms, important as that is, but also on the quality of its economic, political, and moral fabric?

Have we considered the impact upon these other sources of strength of our vast military investment?

Is there a point of diminishing returns in the race for security through arms?

Have we made the wisest possible allocation of our material and human resources to insure maximum security?

Are we building national strength by creating a higher pile of nuclear bombs and adding to our overkill capacity while failing to match our millions of idle, untrained youth with the Nation's needs for constructive economic growth?

Is our national security jeopardized by an outflow of gold that weakens the international value of the dollar?

Is the size of our military budget the chief criterion of effective international leadership and national strength in today's world?

What is the mounting arms race doing to our freedom and the quality of our lives?

And most important of all, are we following a blueprint for peace or racing toward annihilation?

For this fiscal year, we are asked to approve a Department of Defense budget of $53.6 billion, plus additional billions for the Atomic Energy Commission and the space program. That is well over half of our entire Federal budget. It represents more than the combined cost of all the social and economic programs of the New Deal period from 1933 through 1940.

Soon, we will be called upon to vote on the appropriation of funds for this enormous arms budget. This is a tremendously important vote for all of us, not only because it represents a great deal of money, but because it can give us an opportunity to examine some of the basic assumptions that now guide our national life. A Federal budget is, after all, a careful listing of the public priorities and goals of the Nation. When we devote more than half of that entire budget to one purpose, we certainly need to be reasonably sure of our ground.

My limited effort to prepare myself for this forthcoming vote as a Senator whose chief concern is the security of our country and the peace of the world has led me to certain tentative conclusions. I set them forth now, not as final judgments, but simply as one person's convictions about a most complex problem. It is my hope that these suggestions may stimulate in some way the larger debate which needs to be waged by those Senators and Representatives having greater experience and knowledge than mine. Perhaps the insights of others may lead me to abandon or modify some of my present judgments.

In that spirit, I suggest the following propositions:

First. The United States now has a stockpile of nuclear weapons in excess of any conceivable need.

Second. Bringing the arms race under control involves risks less dangerous than the proliferation of nuclear warheads and the acceleration of the arms race.

Third. Present levels of military spending and military foreign aid are distorting our economy, wasting our human resources, and restricting our leadership in the world.

Fourth. Diverting some of our present and proposed military spending to constructive investments both at home and abroad will produce a stronger and more effective America, a more secure America, and will improve the quality of our lives and strengthen the foundations of peace.

Current Defense Assumptions

To place these convictions in better perspective, I would like to sketch some of the considerations which seem pertinent to our defense policy decisions.

Those who advocate surrender or passive submission to the forces of international communism will find little or no support in the United States. Most of us are willing to risk death rather than give the world over to a tyranny that is alien to all that we hold of value.

Likewise, few, if any, Americans would support the concept of an all-out military onslaught initiated by ourselves to wipe out the inhabitants of the Communist world. This, in another equally fundamental sense, would be a surrender of our values and traditions.

As a nation we have rejected both the concept of aggressive war and passive surrender. We have operated from the premise that the Communist threat is checked only because of our awesome military machine. This is the theory of deterrence which has guided our thinking for most of the period since World War II. When one looks for a more specific answer as to how that policy would be applied in the form of military strategy, he encounters some rather confusing and conflicting assumptions.

It has generally been believed that the deterrent or retaliatory power of America's strategic airpower was targeted on the great cities of Russia to be used in the event of a major Soviet attack.

On June 16, 1962, however, Defense Secretary McNamara, one of the ablest and most courageous men to come into Government in modern times, made an important speech at Ann Arbor, Mich. In this address Mr. McNamara spelled out the "controlled counterforce" or "no cities" doctrine. The Ann Arbor speech set forth the theory that instead of seeking first the mass destruction of the Russian populace, we would aim our missiles and bombers at Soviet nuclear weapons in an effort to cripple their capacity to hit the United States. Only if the Soviets attacked our cities would we strike at theirs.

This speech touched off a wide-ranging controversy, partly because its success would seem to depend upon the United States launching a first strike against the Soviet Union.

If the United States were aiming at the effective destruction of Russia's nuclear forces, how could we apply such a strategy unless we knocked out the Soviet missiles before they were launched from their silos? What military objective could we achieve by knocking out empty missile launchers after their rockets had hit American targets?

Secretary McNamara flatly denied that the United States has any intention of launching a first strike, but the "no cities" or "controlled counterforce" theory seems a most unlikely and impractical strategy.

In lengthy testimony before the House Armed Services Committee early this year, Mr. McNamara said:

> What we are proposing is a capability to strike back after absorbing a first blow. This means we have to build and maintain a second strike force. Such a force should have sufficient flexibility to permit a choice of strategies, particularly an ability to: (1) strike back decisively at the entire Soviet target system simultaneously; or (2) strike back first at the Soviet bomber bases, missile sites, and other military installations associated with their long-range nuclear forces to reduce the power of any follow-on attack—and then, if necesary, strike back at the Soviet urban and industrial complex in a controlled and deliberate way.

The Secretary's own testimony, then, seems to make the above strategy highly unlikely. Mr. McNamara pointed out that the Soviets have always insisted that their nuclear power is aimed at the great urban, industrial, and government centers of America. He then stressed the virtual impossibility of either side destroying the other's hardened ICBM weapons or Polaris-type submarine missiles. And then the Secretary added a third point which would seem to remove any real feasibility of concentrating our nuclear power on Soviet missile sites rather than cities. In his words:

> Furthermore, in a second strike situation we would be attacking, for the most part, empty sites from which the missiles had already been fired.

It might be reassuring to draw the conclusion from the "no cities" strategy that it is possible to fight a nuclear war centered on destroying missiles rather than people—if only we could build enough missiles to destroy the enemy's nuclear capacity. But anyone who is laboring under the impression that our Defense Department believes this to be feasible should read the congressional testimony of Secretary McNamara of last February. The following brief excerpts from that important 163-page statement should be pondered carefully, especially by the Members of

Congress who are responsible with the President for the defense policies of our Nation.

Secretary McNamara said:

> Even if we were to double and triple our forces we would not be able to destroy quickly all or almost all of the hardened (Russian) ICBM sites. And even if we could do that, we know no way to destroy the enemy's missile-launching submarines at the same time. We do not anticipate that either the United States or the Soviet Union will acquire that capability in the foreseeable future. . . . We could not preclude casualities counted in the tens of millions.

Secretary McNamara said further:

> The expanding arsenals of nuclear weapons on both sides of the Iron Curtain have created an extremely dangerous situation not only for their possessors but also for the world. As the arms race continues and the weapons multiply and become more swift and deadly, the possibility of a global catastrophe, either by miscalculation or design, becomes more real.

One final quotation from the Secretary of Defense is as follows:

> More armaments, whether offensive or defensive, cannot solve this dilemma. We are approaching an era when it will become increasingly improbable that either side could destroy a sufficiently large portion of the other's strategic nuclear force, either by surprise or otherwise, to preclude a devastating blow. This may result in mutual deterrence but it is still a grim prospect. It underscores the need for a renewed effort to find some way, if not to eliminate these deadly weapons completely, then at least to slow down or halt their further accumulation, and to create institutional arrangements which would reduce the need for either side to resort to their immediate use in moments of acute international tension.

Realities of Soviet-American Overkill

I think it is imperative that every American fully understand what our Secretary of Defense has told us. If nuclear war comes—no matter who strikes first—both sides will count their losses in tens of millions of human lives. There is no such condition as true nuclear superiority in the sense that either the United States or Russia could escape mass destruction should it attack the other. Hardened ICBM sites and nuclear-armed submarines have made the so-called counterforce and no cities doctrines obsolete before they were fully expressed.

Even before Mr. McNamara spelled out the Ann Arbor doctrine of a nuclear strike confined to military installations, the distinguished chairman of the Senate Armed Services Committee warned that this notion was an empty hope. Said Senator Russell on April 11, 1962:

> There have been some estimates and some so-called mathematical computations of the casualties that would result from a nuclear war under vari-

ous assumptions, including a positive attempt by the adversaries to limit
targeting to military installations and facilities. I have no hesitancy in saying,
however, that to me these extrapolations, or projections, or hypotheses are
exceedingly unrealistic.

The highly respected Senator from Georgia concluded:

> In my opinion, if nuclear war begins, it will be a war of extermination.

The unprecedented condition of today's strategic military power is
this: neither the United States nor the U.S.S.R. can prevent the other
from wielding a society-destroying blow, regardless of who attacks first.
Offensive military power has been made so varied and strong that all
conceivable defensive systems can be overwhelmed or bypassed by the
power of offensive nuclear weapons.

Under these conditions, the classic military task of defending the shores
of our country can no longer be performed. The present array of military doctrines gives a design for emerging from a nuclear exchange with
more missiles than the opponent. But this sort of win would be paralleled
by the loss of our society.

The Russians do not have a nuclear capacity equal to ours, but our
superiority is largely a meaningless concept in view of their relative
parity. In the days when warfare was limited to rifles and cannons and
tanks and conventional aircraft, the side with the most weapons and
soldiers had a great military advantage. But in today's age, when a nuclear exchange of a few minutes' duration means instant death and in-
describable devastation to both sides, what consolation is there to the
dazed survivors to know that there remains under the poisoned skies
somewhere in the rubble some unused overkill capacity?

When asked at the congressional hearings what the military situation
would be after a nuclear exchange between Russia and the United
States, Secretary McNamara replied:

> This is a question we have considered, and I can't answer it. I think prob-
> ably the fatalities in Western Europe would approach 90 million, the fatali-
> ties in the United States would approach 100 million, and the fatalities in
> the Soviet Union would approach 100 million.
>
> Now when you consider on the order of 300 million people dead in those
> areas, it is very difficult to conceive of what kind of military weapons . . .
> would continue to exist. We have nonetheless faced that issue, and we have
> systems provided that we believe would survive.
>
> But it exceeds the extent of my imagination to conceive of how those
> forces might be used and of what benefit they would be to our Nation at
> that point.

It might be argued by some that our excessive nuclear spending
serves an indirect purpose in that it forces the Soviets to strain their less
affluent economy to match our effort. But the Russians, from all indica-

tions, seem to be avoiding construction of highly sophisticated weapons beyond what they regard as enough to destroy the United States in the event of war.

During the late 1950's when the Soviets could have built hundreds of the latest types of long-range bombers they constructed less than 200 as against our more than 1,600. There is no indication that they intend to try to narrow this gap. At the present time, while we have a capability of a thousand ICBM's—perhaps considerably more—and are building many more, the Russians have built only a minor fraction of that number. Indications are that they will improve and replace rather than greatly increase the number of their missiles.

The question is whether the United States can afford the vast "overkill" capacity which seems to underlie much of our military budget.

I want to make it clear I am not underestimating the enormous nuclear power of the Soviet Union. Certainly they have an overkill capacity.

My own conviction is that we cannot afford this policy of adding to overkill capacity economically, politically, or morally and that if we persist in following it we will weaken our Nation both at home and abroad.

The United States has used its great power in the period since World War II with a sense of responsibility and restraint. We have done a remarkable job of providing a defense shield to war-torn Europe and assisting the rebuilding of that continent, whose welfare is so important to our own. We have shared our human and material resources with the developing countries around the world. We have strengthened the peace-keeping functions of the United Nations. There is no parallel in world history for the generous, farsighted manner in which the United States has provided world leadership and assistance since 1945.

But if our leadership is to remain effective, we must make certain that we do not fall into a rigid pattern that ignores new conditions and new challenges in the world. I submit that the continuing quest for an ever larger measure of nuclear overkill capacity makes no sense in the perspective of today.

No informed person doubts that we have the power to destroy Soviet society several times over, or that they have the capacity to destroy us. One recent study concluded that we could now erase the bulk of the Russian populace more than a thousand times. Even if that estimate is 100 times too high, we would be able to destroy the Soviet Union with only a partial use of our existing weapons.

Before the substantial increases in our military power of the past 2 years, Secretary McNamara testified that "there is no question but that today, our Strategic Retaliatory Forces are fully capable of destroying the Soviet target system, even after absorbing an initial surprise attack."

We have been building missiles, bombs, and other weapons steadily since then so that our capacity to destroy is much greater today than when the Secretary made that statement early in 1962.

Speaking of our present capability, Mr. McNamara said, on February 6 of this year:

> Allowing for losses from an initial enemy attack and attrition en route to target, we calculate that our forces today could still destroy the Soviet Union without any help from the deployed tactical air units or carrier task forces or Thor or Jupiter IRBM's.

Now, Mr. President, I ask what possible advantage there can be to the United States in appropriating additional billions of dollars to build more missiles and bombs when we already have excess capacity to destroy the potential enemy? How many times is it necesary to kill a man or kill a nation?

If the Secretary is correct—and I think his estimates are conservative—that one quick nuclear exchange would now leave 100 million Americans dead, an equal number of Russians, and nearly as many West Europeans, is that not enough to deter anyone other than a madman from setting off such a catastrophe?

And if either side yields to madness or miscalculation, can any number of arms save us?

A Proposed Arms Budget Adjustment

I think we need to take another careful look at our enormous arms budget, asking ourselves: What part of this budget represents additions to an already surplus overkill capacity? What alternative uses can be made of surplus military funds for strengthening the economic and political foundations of our society?

Our highly able Secretary of Defense has effected many needed economies and efficiencies in operation of the Defense Department. For that he should have the gratitude and praise of all. Congress can encourage him to make much larger savings by limiting the further pileup of overkill capacity.

I have pored over the complicated tables and charts of the defense budget for hours. I certainly do not pretend to understand all of the implications. Indeed, the data as made available to Congress in the Defense budget does not enable one to perceive the full functional pattern proposed.

But I am fully convinced that there is enough talent and brainpower among our military and civilian arms experts to eliminate $5 billion of proposed spending that goes beyond our real defense needs.

A front-page story in the Sunday New York Times of June 30 reports:

> The administration is giving serious consideration to ordering the first substantial cutback in the production of atomic weapons since the United States began building up its nuclear arsenal after World War II. Behind the current study is a belief that the United States with an arsenal of tens of

thousands of atomic weapons has a sufficient and perhaps an excessive number of nuclear arms to meet its military needs.

The same article reports:

Rising concern is felt in high administration circles over the multiplying number of warheads that have been assigned to the military forces in the last 5 years. The major fear is that continuing profusion would only increase the chances of accidental explosion or unauthorized use of the weapons

The Times reported a growing fear of the members of the Joint Committee on Atomic Energy that the production of atomic weapons is "coming to be based more on the capabilities of the Atomic Energy Commission to manufacture them than on the actual requirements of the military."

The Atomic Energy Commission now has an annual budget of $1.8 billion to produce new warheads to add to our already enormous stockpile. The Times asserts that at a recent Pentagon press briefing "a highly placed Defense Department official" estimated that it might be desirable to make a $1 billion cut in this expenditure. Another policymaking official said:

We have tens or hundreds of times more weapons than we would ever drop even in an all-out war, and we have had more than we needed for at least 2 years.

None of the sections in this important news article have been challenged by any administration spokesman so I think it is safe to assume that they are well-grounded.

I believe that, in addition to a cut of $1 billion in the Atomic Energy Commission's weapons procurement program, we could wisely cut an additional $4 billion from the proposed budgets of the Air Force, Navy, and Army without reducing the security of the Nation. Indeed, such reductions could enable us to strengthen our overall national security. Any such substantial cut should, of course, be applied and administered with the expertise of the Secretary of Defense. I will listen thoughtfully to the presentation of our Appropriations Committee and others. I intend to follow the coming debate and discussion with a frank willingness to change my views if there is compelling contrary evidence.

It may be argued that the economy of many of our communities has become so intertwined with military spending that an arms cut of several billion dollars which I have proposed would result in a painful economic dislocation.

It is true that many American communities have come to lean heavily on the economic stimulus of arms production and military installations. We need to accelerate and expand our efforts on the Federal, State, and local level to prepare these communities for a conversion to a more permanent economy appropriate to the conditions of peace.

Competence for converting from a military to a civilian economy is a basic requirement for the economic and political security of the United States.

Planning the Conversion to a Peace Economy

Capability for economic conversion must be developed at all establishments—manufacturing, research, and others—engaged in fulfilling contracts or otherwise working for the Department of Defense or the Atomic Energy Commission.

In order to minimize dislocation; facilitate industrial expansion; reduce regional dependence on single markets; reduce regional dependence on single government markets; and plan for growth in employment, I recommend the following procedure:

First, all establishments that fulfill Defense Department or Atomic Energy Commission work for at least 1 calendar year and whose personnel are 25 percent or more so engaged, should henceforth be required—as a condition of contract fulfillment and acceptable administration—to establish in their managements an operating conversion committee. This committee should actively engage in planning for conversion of the facility from military to civilian work as required in the event of termination, cutbacks, stretchout, or other curtailment of Defense or AEC requirements.

Second, in order to estimate the support that may be required to complement local and regional conversion, an Economic Conversion Commission should be established by the President under the direction of the Secretary of Commerce and including experts from other concerned Government departments. Our Arms Control and Disarmament Agency already has a small but able group of people giving thought to this matter.

The Economic Conversion Commission shall have responsibility for blueprinting appropriate action by departments and agencies of the Federal Government that are required to facilitate conversion from a military to a civilian economy.

In addition to such activities as it should deem necessary, the Commission would prepare schedules of possible private and public investment patterns and the employment and income effects to be expected therefrom. The information would be reported to the President and to the Congress in preliminary form within 6 months after the enactment of authorizing legislation and in final form within 12 months.

The Commission would take counsel with the Governors of all States to encourage appropriate and timely studies and conferences by the States in support of conversion from a military to a civilian economy.

Third, the Commission would, within 12 months of establishment, convene a National Conference on Economic Conversion and Growth to focus nationwide attention on the problems of conversion and economic growth and to encourage appropriate study and organization in all relevant parts of the Nation's economy. This conference should include invited representatives of trade associations, trade unions, professional societies, representatives of appropriate agencies of the Federal and State Governments, and selected individuals with specialized knowledge.

Through intelligent planning we can make a satisfactory transition to an economy less dependent upon arms spending.

Weaknesses in an Arms Economy

A closer look at our present level of arms spending will show that it is not an unmixed blessing now as a stimulus to our economy.

First of all, we have distorted our economy in allocating such a high percentage of our highly trained manpower, research, and technology to weapons production at the expense of our other industry. Japan and our West European Allies have all modernized their civilian industrial plants at a much higher rate than the United States, largely because of our concentration on arms production. This has added to our civilian production costs, decreased our efficiency, undercut our competitive position in international trade, and aggravated the balance-of-payments problem.

American machine tool production was once the envy of the world, but today we have slipped to fourth or fifth rank among the nations. Our best scientific and technical competence is going into arms, not to the modernization of our civilian plant.

Building weapons is a seriously limited device for building the economy—partly because it cannot be counted upon as a permanent system and partly because a military item leads to no further production; it is an end in itself. Disarmament chief William C. Foster said recently that "defense spending of the type we now have has no intrinsic merit in terms of its ability to create production and income as compared to other forms of demand."

Many U.S. industries are losing their capacity to compete not only in world trade but also in the United States. The concentration of capital and technical skill in arms production is a basic cause of our declining competitive ability.

As matters now stand, the U.S. Government is financing 65 percent of all research and development, and most of that is for military purposes. In Germany, by contrast, 85 percent of research is privately financed, and nearly all of it is being used to modernize civilian industries which compete with ours. Those who view military spending as an unmixed blessing to our economy should take a look at the gleaming up-to-date civilian plants in Germany, Belgium, Holland, Italy, and Japan—plants that are surpassing our own neglected civilian production in both quality and low-cost operation. Where will this kind of imbalance leave us in the toughening competition of international trade?

The U.S. economy is jeopardized further by the flow of our gold overseas and the undermining of the dollar as a unit of international exchange. Today, we have a favorable trade balance, but because of our military investments overseas and the flight of investment capital we are suffering an unfavorable balance of payments. Heavy arms spending has aggravated a U.S. fiscal situation that has led many American investors to seek more attractive oversea outlets for their capital.

Our traditionally strong currency has been a powerful instrument in American economic and political leadership in the world. But the strain imposed on our gold reserves as a result of heavy military commitments abroad and excessive arms spending at home is a threat to our international position. The loss of American gold can be halted by reducing some of the burden we have been carrying for the defense of now prosperous allies and by encouraging the conversion of foreign claims on our gold into investments to modernize our industrial system.

While retaining our massive military power, the overriding present need of American security is prompt reinforcement of the economic and political aspects of security at home and abroad.

The Military-Industrial Complex and American Life

It is admittedly difficult to calculate the impact of the arms budget on our civilian economy. It is even more difficult to measure the impact of what former President Eisenhower called "the military-industrial complex" on our moral strength and the climate of freedom. Americans have always feared that any trend toward militarism was a threat to the quality of our democracy. I believe that this is still a legitimate concern. Mr. Eisenhower, whose life has been devoted to military matters, was so concerned about the growing impact of the military-industrial combination on American institutions that he devoted his farewell address to this danger. "We must never let the weight of this combination endanger our liberties or democratic processes," he warned.

Democracy is based on a fundamental respect for the dignity and worth of human life. Its great strength is that it opens the way for the full flowering of man's intellectual, moral, and cultural development.

When a major percentage of the public resources of our society is devoted to the accumulation of devastating weapons of war, the spirit of democracy suffers. When our laboratories and our universities and our scientists and our youth are caught up in war preparations, the spirit of freeman is hampered.

America must, of course, maintain a fully adequate military defense. But we have a rich heritage and a glorious future that are too precious to risk in an arms race that goes beyond any reasonable criteria of need.

We need to remind ourselves that we have sources of strength, of prestige, and international leadership based on other than nuclear bombs.

Conversely, we need to remember that the greatest Communist victories, including the Chinese Communist takeover, came at the moment of our greatest nuclear superiority.

The global contest raging before our eyes today will doubtless continue for as long as we can see into the future, but it need not, indeed cannot, be settled by nuclear warfare.

The United States must be prepared to lead that contest into areas that draw on our true sources of greatness—politics, economics, and morality. There is a growing indication that the course we follow may play a major part in determining the course which our adversaries take for good or ill.

The self-defeating nature of the arms race is that each side reacts to the other's moves in a constantly rising scale of armaments. In his congressional testimony earlier this year, Secretary McNamara explained how the United States tries to evaluate expected Soviet arms moves so that we can plan to counter their efforts by moves of our own. "We are, in effect," said the Secretary, "attempting to anticipate production and deployment decisions which our opponents themselves may not yet have made."

Is it not reasonable to assume that, just as we attempt to counter arms moves by the Soviets, so do they try to gear their efforts to counter ours? Could we not then well afford to make a serious effort to put the arms race in reverse by carefully calculated moves designed to shift the competition with Russia away from arms spending into more peaceful pursuits.

Our Unmet Public Needs: An Alternative to Overkill

We have millions of idle youth who could be employed in existing job vacancies if only they had sufficient training and education. A sizable proportion of these are Negroes and their idleness is at the base of the explosive civil rights crisis now convulsing the Nation. What better use could we make of some of our excess military spending than to divert it to an expanded program of vocational and technical training?

Our civil rights problems require for their solution a major expansion of employment opportunity. The economically depressed regions of the country require fresh capital and technical talent. Both these basic problems of economic development require sizable productive investment.

We have an urgent need for more classrooms, laboratories, libraries, and capable teachers.

We have millions of citizens, particularly among our older people, who need more adequate hospital and nursing home care.

Some of our present defense installations might in the future be converted into vocational schools, community colleges, or health centers.

We have rivers and streams to be saved from pollution and waste—a task calling for considerable engineering and technical manpower.

We have a growing number of farm youth who can no longer make an adequate living on the farm, whose lives would be enriched by an expanded rural area development effort.

And for years to come there will be hungry, afflicted people abroad who look to us for help. As the former director of our Nation's food for peace program, I came to a keen realization that most of the people of the world are undernourished rural families who are trying to scratch an existence from the soil by incredibly primitive methods.

We have an opportunity with our amazing agricultural know-how to use an increased volume of farm products and agricultural assistance as development tools abroad. The recent World Food Congress held in Washington underscored the fact that mankind now has the scientific capacity to eliminate hunger from the world.

I think that we should seriously consider diverting $5 billion of our arms budget into the kind of worthwhile programs at home and abroad which I have just sketched. Perhaps some of the military reductions should be expressed in tax reduction. This move would not only result in a stronger and better America, but it might invite a constructive response from the Soviet Union. The Soviets have more to gain than we from a reduction of military spending. They have deprived themselves of the appliances, automobiles, attractive clothing, and personal comforts which we take for granted.

The cold war is now showing some signs of a possible limited thaw. In his inspired address to the Nation last Friday evening, President Kennedy described in cautious but hopeful terms the larger meaning of the proposed nuclear test ban as a first important step to peace. I trust that after careful consideration the Senate will lend its support to this initiative for peace.

As we weigh the proposed test-ban agreement, we can usefully take into account three factors that I have discussed today.

First, when both sides already possess overkill capacity, that lessens the temptation for either side to break the test ban.

Second, some Americans may wonder if the next steps, after a test-ban agreement, might not mean declining military spending and a sag in our economy. I am confident that practical steps which I have outlined for preparing and supporting economic conversion will reassure our people on this count.

Third, the test-ban agreement can lead to savings of many millions of dollars from the funds hitherto used for large-scale testing.

There are hopeful signs other than the proposed test ban. The myth of a solidly united, monolithic Communist bloc was long ago thrown in doubt by Tito. But how much more significant is the mounting evidence of a major convulsion of the Sino-Soviet bloc. We should watch these new developments with caution, knowing well that while Communist powers may differ with each other, they continue to follow a tyrannical system that is alien to American democracy.

But we must also keep free from a rigid diplomacy or excessive reliance on arms that might jeopardize our capacity to exploit for peace these fast-developing changes in the international climate.

Thirteen years ago, the late Senator Brien McMahon, chairman of the Joint Committee on Atomic Energy, made two memorable addresses from the floor of the Senate. The Connecticut Senator warned that a continuance of the arms race would lead sooner or later to catastrophe, and in any event would induce a climate of fear and a Government-controlled allocation of resources that would dry up the wellsprings of

American freedom and dignity. The Senator concluded, on March 1, 1950, with this warning:

> Mr. President, the clock is ticking, ticking, and with each swing of the pendulum the time to save civilization grows shorter. When shall we get about this business? Now, or when Russia and the United States glower at one another from atop competing stacks of hydrogen bombs?

We have arrived at the point in history where we indeed "glower at one another from atop competing stacks of hydrogen bombs." And if the present trend continues, in a few short years, a half dozen, and then a dozen, new powers will climb atop their hydrogen stockpiles to glower at their frightened neighbors.

The clock which Senator McMahon heard ticking 13 years ago is still ticking, but our ears have become so accustomed to the sound that we scarcely hear it. Yet, scientists of our day flatly assert that if we do not reverse the arms race, a major nuclear accident will occur before this decade ends even without the intent of the nuclear powers. And how can we rest secure knowing that any one of three, six or a dozen national defense ministries or subordinate military officers could set off a nuclear holocaust through miscalculation, impulsive madness, or simply human wickedness.

There are powerful options of peace as well as options of war. Still alive in the world is a faith that can move mountains if we will only seize upon it. From our own heritage the philosophy of Jefferson and Lincoln speaks with a voice that is more effectively heard in Asia, Africa, and Latin America than any number of nuclear explosions or moon shots. A conscientious effort on our part to eliminate excessive nuclear stockpiling will give that voice of peace and reason an even clearer tone.

I pray that our country will in every possible way use its unique power and influence on the side of peace. I know that is what President Kennedy and his administration seek. I am sure that is the sense of the Congress and the American people. I even dare to believe that is what Mr. Khrushchev and his people have come to accept as the only condition of their survival.

Both Americans and Russians must make a choice between the quick and the dead. Negotiators of the test-ban proposal have cast their lot on the side of hope and life. The further steps to peace will be tortuous and hard, but they lead, however slowly, away from catastrophe toward salvation.

If we hold fast to that course, taking into account the new conditions of American security, generations to come will call us blessed, and, as peacemakers, we shall know the Scriptural promise:

> The Lord will give strength unto his people; the Lord will bless his people with peace.